TRADITION:
A HISTORY
OF THE PRESIDENCY
OF CLEMSON UNIVERSITY

TRADITION:
A HISTORY
OF THE PRESIDENCY
OF CLEMSON UNIVERSITY

Edited and with a Foreword by
DONALD M. McKALE
Illustrated by
KATE SALLEY PALMER

ISBN 0-86554-296-1

Tradition:
A History of the Presidency
of Clemson University
Copyright © 1988
Mercer University Press, Macon, Georgia 31207
All rights reserved
Printed in the United States of America

The paper used in this publication meets the minimum requirements
of American National Standard for Information Sciences
Permanence of Paper for Printed Library Materials, ANSI Z39.48-1984

Library of Congress Cataloging-in-Publication Data
Tradition: a history of the presidency of Clemson University
   Includes bibliographical references and index.
   1. Clemson University—Presidents. 2. Clemson
University—Administration—History.
I. McKale, Donald M., 1943– .
LD1061.C3T73   1987   378.757'21   87-31382
ISBN 0-86554-296-1 (alk. paper)

CONTENTS

Illustrations ix
Contributors x
Foreword xi

1 The Founder
  Thomas Green Clemson, 1807-1888
  Ernest McPherson Lander, Jr. 3
  - A Scientist with Interest in the Arts • • 4
  - Clemson and the Calhouns • • 5
  - Plantation Owner, Diplomat, and Agriculturalist • • 8
  - The War: "The North is no place for a Confederate" • • 11
  - A Frustrated Reformer Returns to Fort Hill • • 14
  - Final Lonely Years and Desire for a College • • 17

2 The Builder of a College
  Henry Aubrey Strode, 1890-1893
  Robert S. Lambert 21
  - A Virginian with South Carolina Ties • • 21
  - The Trustees and Financing the School • • 24
  - First Buildings, Faculty, and Curricula • • 26
  - The Mystery of Strode's Resignation • • 30

3 The Controversial Humanities Professor
  Edwin Boone Craighead, 1893-1897
  John L. Idol, Jr. 35
  - The Farmboy and Classicist • • 35
  - The First Session • • 37
  - From Marching Orders to Trouble • • 40
  - The Conflict over Clemson's Mission • • 45
  - Craighead Leaves Clemson • • 49

4 A Youthful Administrator
  Henry Simms Hartzog, 1897-1902
  Michael F. Kohl 53
  - A Native Son and Preacher • • 54
  - Growing Pains • • 56
  - "The most popular game is football" • • 62
  - The Walkout: "Tottering on the Brink" • • 64

5 The Trusted Substitute
  Mark Bernard Hardin, 1897, 1899, 1902
  Donald M. McKale 69
    From Model Military Man to Chemist • • 69
    1902: President for a Month • • 73

6 A Scholar's Turmoil
  Patrick Hues Mell, 1902-1910
  Robert P. Green, Jr. 79
    The Making of a Geologist • • 80
    The "Big Game" of 1902 • • 81
    Defending the Clemson Education • • 84
    The Military and Conflict with the Trustees • • 87
    Mell's Contributions • • 95

7 The Master Executive
  Walter Merritt Riggs, 1910-1924
  C. Alan Grubb 99
    Early Career and Acting Presidency • • 100
    "Clemson has a President at last" • • 107
    The Impact of the European War • • 117
    The Walkout of 1920 and Aftermath • • 120

8 The Conservative Caretaker
  Samuel Broadus Earle,
  1919 and 1924-1925
  Susan Duffy 127
    The Road to Clemson • • 127
    1919: Following Carefully Prescribed Instructions • • 129
    1924-1925: Administering Unrest • • 132

9 The Plowboy Scholar
  Enoch Walter Sikes, 1925-1940
  Bruce Yandle 141
    Early Years • • 142
    Clemson: The College and Town in 1925 • • 144
    Economic Changes and the New Trend in Education • • 146
    Finances and the Great Depression • • 150
    Episodes in the Sikes Administration and Retirement • • 155

10 The Gentleman Manager
    Robert Franklin Poole, 1940-1958
    James C. Hite 161
        From Graduate to President of Clemson • • 162
        Leading a Sleepy Country College • • 166
        The War Weakens the Military Tradition • • 169
        Toward a Civilian and Coeducational School • • 176
        The Trustees Seek Poole's Retirement • • 180

11 A Take-Charge Businessman
    Robert Cook Edwards, 1958-1979
    Stephen H. Wainscott 187
        From Textile Executive to Clemson Vice-President • • 188
        Protecting Clemson from Disaster: The Hartwell Project • • 190
        The New President and New Era • • 194
        Integration without Violence: A Conspiracy for Peace? • • 196
        The University and Limited Enrollment • • 202
        Trouble in Tigertown • • 206
        The President and His Legacy • • 210

12 The Outsider
    Bill Lee Atchley, 1979-1985
    William F. Steirer, Jr. 215
        Background, Personality, and Philosophy • • 216
        Great Expectations, Broken Commitments, and Failure • • 220
        The Conflict with the Trustees over Athletics • • 229

13 A Good Sport
    Walter Thompson Cox, 1985-1986
    John R. Wunder 241
        The Young Walter Cox • • 242
        Athletic Careers • • 243
        Dean of Students • • 246
        Cox and the Atchley Presidency • • 251
        The Cox Presidency • • 256

    Afterword
        Max Lennon, President of Clemson Univeristy 261

    Appendix
        The Will of Thomas Green Clemson 265

    Index 273

ILLUSTRATIONS

1 Founder Thomas Green Clemson, 1807–1888 2
  Clemson Caricature 12
2 President Henry Aubrey Strode, 1890–1893 20
  Strode Caricature 27
3 President Edwin Boone Craighead, 1893–1897 34
  Craighead Caricature 43
4 President Henry Simms Hartzog, 1897–1902 52
  Hartzog Caricature 61
5 President Mark Bernard Hardin, 1897, 1899, 1902 68
  Hardin Caricature 74
6 President Patrick Hues Mell, 1902–1910 78
  Mell Caricature 89
7 President Walter Merritt Riggs, 1910–1924 98
  Riggs Caricature 113
8 President Samuel Broadus Earle, 1919, 1924–1925 126
  Earle Caricature 133
9 President Enoch Walter Sikes, 1925–1940 140
  Sikes Caricature 151
10 President Robert Franklin Poole, 1940–1958 160
   Poole Caricature 174
11 President Robert Cook Edwards, 1958–1979 186
   Edwards Caricature 200
12 President Bill Lee Atchley, 1979–1985 214
   Atchley Caricature 229
13 President Walter Thompson Cox, 1985–1986 240
   Cox Caricature 252
14 President Max Lennon, 1986– 260
   Lennon Caricature 263

CONTRIBUTORS

Susan Duffy
  Associate Professor of Speech
Robert P. Green, Jr.
  Associate Professor of Education
C. Alan Grubb
  Assistant Professor of History
James C. Hite
  Alumni Professor of Agricultural Economics and Rural Sociology
John L. Idol, Jr.
  Professor of English
Michael F. Kohl
  Head of Special Collections, R. M. Cooper Library
Robert S. Lambert
  Head and Professor Emeritus of History
Ernest McPherson Lander, Jr.
  Alumni Professor Emeritus of History
Max Lennon
  President of Clemson University and Professor of Animal Science
Donald M. McKale
  Professor of History
Kate Salley Palmer
  Illustrator
William F. Steirer, Jr.
  Associate Professor of History
Stephen H. Wainscott
  Associate Professor of Political Science
John R. Wunder
  Head and Professor of History
Bruce Yandle
  Alumni Professor of Economics

FOREWORD

Since Clemson University was founded a century ago as an agricultural college and South Carolina's land-grant school, it has had eleven presidents and two temporary or acting chief executives.[1] The presidential biographies in this volume show that each of these leaders contributed in his own unique way to the development of the school, which became a university in 1964. The essays also reveal that the collective background these men brought to the Clemson presidency and the service they gave to it have established a clearly identifiable tradition for the office.

The formation of that tradition began with the origin of Clemson Agricultural College in 1889. That year the general assembly (legislature) of South Carolina, amid a bitter conflict in the state over the issue, accepted Thomas Green Clemson's bequest of his Fort Hill property near Pendleton to the state to establish such a school. With his gift, Clemson joined a distinguished long line of land-grant benefactors in America, such as Ezra Cornell of New York and Benjamin Thompson of New Hampshire, who provided some of the necessary funds and a farm for a site for a college. Clemson, in seeking to found an agricultural school, had declared in his will of 1886 that in South Carolina, which remained overwhelmingly rural as well as desolate and impoverished twenty years after the Civil War, there could be "no permanent improvement in agriculture without a knowledge of those sciences which pertain particularly thereto."[2]

However, he clearly intended for the new college to be based on the culture and ideals of the Old South. He stipulated that the school's gov-

---

[1] The acting presidents were Mark B. Hardin and Samuel B. Earle. Walter T. Cox was originally appointed "Interim President," but the university's board of trustees later granted him the title of "President Emeritus." Before becoming president, W. M. Riggs and R. C. Edwards held the title of "Acting President."

[2] A copy of the will is in the appendix below. Regarding the conflict surrounding the origin of Clemson College, see Ernest McPherson Lander, Jr., *A History of South Carolina, 1865-1960*, 2nd ed. (Columbia SC: University of South Carolina Press, 1970) 32, 138-40; and Alester G. Holmes and George R. Sherrill, *Thomas Green Clemson: His Life and Work* (Richmond: Garrett and Massie, 1937) ch. 8. For a brief discussion of the other land-grant benefactors, note Edward Danforth Eddy, Jr., *Colleges for Our Land and Time: The Land-Grant Idea in American Education* (New York: Harper & Brothers, 1957) 15.

erning body, the board of trustees, be comprised of a self-perpetuating majority of his friends and business associates and the remainder chosen by the general assembly. Because of the dominance of the "life" trustees and because few boards organized like Clemson's existed in American higher education by the end of the nineteenth century, popular opinion viewed the Clemson board as conservative by nature and anachronistic.[3] Yet despite the composition of the board, it did not differ significantly from the governing bodies of the other new land-grant and state universities emerging in America in 1900. Such bodies were often appointed by governors or selected by legislators and alumni association members. Many were dominated by businessmen and alumni; what was more, the average age of nearly half of the boards was over sixty and their political and economic beliefs were generally laissez faire, conservative, and Victorian.[4]

In comparison, farmers and lawyers have occupied the largest number of places on the Clemson board since its inception, with businessmen holding third place. Nearly forty percent of the board members have graduated from Clemson, and fifty-seven percent reached or surpassed the age of sixty by the time they left the body. Virtually all the trustees have been Protestant.[5] In addition, their ranks have included such powerful figures in the state as Benjamin R. Tillman, Richard W. Simpson, Alan Johnstone, Richard I. Man-

---

[3] According to the professor of textiles at Clemson, Gaston Gage, in his address, "The Past Presidents of Clemson College," presented to the Forum Club of Clemson, 25 May 1948, Gage papers, folder 28, Special Collections, R. M. Cooper Library/Clemson University (hereafter cited as RMCL/CU): "The press and especially the politicians made much of the fact that the seven life members of the board of trustees could, if they wished, control the destiny of the college, free from any legislative interference because the six members elected by the legislature were always in the minority." A more recent assessment, however, emphasizes that "provisions in the legislature's Act of Acceptance guaranteed that the life trustees would be unable to run roughshod over elected trustees" and that the "continuity of membership provided by life trustees . . . has proved a stabilizing influence"; see Wright Bryan, *Clemson: An Informal History of the University, 1889-1979* (Columbia SC: R. L. Bryan, 1979) 25-26.

[4] A good discussion is in John S. Brubacher and Willis Rudy, *Higher Education in Transition: A History of American Colleges and Universities, 1636-1976*, 3rd ed. (New York: Harper & Row, 1976) 354-55, 363-65.

[5] These conclusions are drawn from a study of 72 of the trustees, based on biographical material in the Clemson University (hereafter cited as CU) Trustees file, RMCL/CU: 31 (43%) were farmers; 19 (26%) were lawyers; 14 (19%) were in business; 28 (39%) graduated from Clemson; and 41 (57%) were over 60 when they left the board. Sixty-seven of the trustees studied were Protestant; information was lacking for the other five. The editor wishes to thank Bryan McKown, history graduate assistant, for help in compiling the data.

ning, Christie Benet, Jr., Edgar A. Brown, James F. Byrnes, Robert M. Cooper, Charles E. Daniel, and James M. Waddell, Jr.[6]

Already in 1890 the Clemson board indicated its agreement with Thomas Green Clemson's philosophy by attempting to appoint as the college's first president a former Confederate general, Stephen D. Lee, who headed the Mississippi Agricultural and Mechanical College (now Mississippi State University). When Lee refused the board's offer, it hired Henry A. Strode (who served as Clemson's president during 1890-1892), a Virginia educator and veteran of the Confederate army. Furthermore, another Confederate soldier, Colonel Mark B. Hardin, served brief terms as the college's acting president and president *pro tempore* (1897, 1899, and 1902).

The Clemson presidency has remained the preserve of Southerners. Each chief executive, including the newest, Max Lennon (1986–   ), was born, reared, and educated in the South; three of the presidents—Robert F. Poole (1940–1958), Robert C. Edwards (1958–1979), and Walter T. Cox (1985–1986)—received their undergraduate degrees at Clemson. This regionalism in choosing presidents is not unusual in the South, although some Southern colleges and universities have avoided it. Moreover, Clemson's appointment of only one clergyman as president, Henry S. Hartzog (1897–1902), coincided with a nationwide trend in higher education at the end of the nineteenth century. The expansion of American industry and science by 1900 and the increase of enrollments and endowments hastened the shift in schools of higher learning away from clergymen presidents to men who had risen through the faculty and the avenue of scholarship.[7]

---

[6]A list of the trustees is in Bryan, 264-65.

[7]Regarding the change away from the clergymen, see Brubacher and Rudy, 365-66. According to Earle D. Ross, *Democracy's College: The Land-Grant Movement in the Formative Stage* (Ames IA: Iowa State College Press, 1942) 104-105, 208n89, colleges and universities in the midwestern and southern United States were more likely than their counterparts in other regions to continue hiring clerical presidents. The University of South Carolina (USC) was more receptive to the nonclerical president. While some of the early chief executives of USC were born and reared in the South, they were often educated outside the region; note Daniel Walker Hollis, *University of South Carolina*, 2 vols. (Columbia SC: University of South Carolina Press, 1951, 1956) 1:33, 77, 126-27, 143, 148-49, 162-63, 195, 207; 2:22, 107, 166, 178, 198, 242, 264, 266-67, 296. The same was true for the presidents of the University of Georgia until the 20th century; it elected a clergyman to the presidency in 1811, however, and maintained that tradition for the next one hundred years. See Thomas G. Dyer, *The University of Georgia: A Bicentennial History, 1785-1985* (Athens GA: University of Georgia Press, 1985) 10, 12-13, 22-23, 25-26, 36, 99-100, 124, 133-44, 153-54. For examples of Southern schools that recruited their leaders almost

The essays in this book also show that the majority of Clemson presidents upheld at the school the values that had dominated the region's history. Until the 1950s and 1960s, when social and cultural pressures across the United States forced the presidents and board of trustees to change, they rigorously defended the school as a land-grant and military institution, all male and all white. Clemson was one of the last land-grant schools to admit women and abandon the military emphasis.[8] However, much to the credit of the seventh and eighth presidents, Poole and Edwards, the dramatic changes during their administrations to coeducation, racial integration, and university status occurred peacefully and with dignity.

From Clemson's beginning, its presidents developed a strong tradition of involving themselves with the faculty and students in the issues affecting the everyday operation of the school. Such matters included the admission and discipline of students, the hiring and removal of personnel, and the conduct of instruction. However, ultimate control in such affairs, again as in most other American colleges and universities, never resided in the presidents or faculty, but in the board of trustees. During the early years of Clemson Agricultural College, the board established its own committees for curriculum and campus construction and appointed the faculty committee on student discipline.

The faculty noted the board's close supervision of the presidents and their work.[9] The earliest public instance in which the board overruled the president and faculty occurred in 1902 during the first large student walkout. Seven years later, Clemson's fourth president, Patrick Hues Mell (1902-1910), resigned because of anger at the board, publicly accused it of interfering in the internal functioning of the college, and urged it to give his successor "sympathetic support and allow him proper control of

---

exclusively from the South, see Harrison Hale, *University of Arkansas, 1871-1948* (Fayetteville AR: University of Arkansas Alumni Association, 1948) 256-57; and M. L. Brittain, *The Story of Georgia Tech* (Chapel Hill: University of North Carolina Press, 1948) 20, 33, 46, 93, 311.

[8]Compare, for example, Clemson's experience to the other land-grant schools discussed in Eddy, 61-62, 94.

[9]For instance, according to one of the college's first mathematics professors, Samuel M. Martin, in "A Personal Sketch of Dr. Henry Hartzog," undated, CU President's papers, Hartzog, RMCL/CU; "In the early days of the College the Board of Trustees made frequent visits to the college and exercised the closest supervision over the selection of the faculty and the courses of study and naturally there would be conflicts between the early presidents and the Trustees." Gage, "The Past Presidents of Clemson College," later observed, "In the early years the trustees were very active in the actual administration of the college, the first presidents having very little real authority."

the affairs of his office."[10] How much Mell's attack on the board contributed to the stronger hand held against it by the next president, Walter Merritt Riggs (1910-1924), is uncertain. Riggs made many decisions that had previously been the province of the board, its committees, and other officers of the college. He strengthened the Clemson presidency significantly, giving it an authority and dignity it had not possessed before, either on the campus or among the public.

The years following the world wars saw the rapid growth of American higher education, and particularly of Clemson, whose new students included servicemen returning home from Europe and elsewhere. From an enrollment of 648 in 1909, the college expanded steadily toward 800 cadets by 1920 and 1,012 three years later.[11] Growing enrollments, larger budgets, and demands for new curricula necessitated the expansion of Clemson's administration which, instead of heightening the president's power, diluted it. After 1925 much of his authority in financial affairs passed to the college's newly created office of business manager.

The Great Depression resulted in severe financial difficulties at the school and nearly destroyed its academic accreditation, which it received during the administration of Enoch Walter Sikes (1925-1940), with the Southern Association of Colleges. By the 1950s and the end of the Poole administration, the influence of the board of trustees had reemerged, as some members eagerly sought to adapt Clemson's management to the rapid economic and social changes beginning to transform the South. However, the board deferred significantly to Poole's successor, Edwards, who developed a friendly and more harmonious association with not only the trustees, but with the leading public figures in South Carolina. Not since Riggs had a Clemson president dominated the board so effectively.

Despite the long-term administrative issues and controversies that characterized the relationship of the Clemson presidents to the board of trustees, faculty, and students, each president has displayed an unwavering dedication to the academic principles on which the school was founded. Five of the presidents were formally trained in math or science, three in engineering, two in agriculture, two in the social sciences, and one in the

---

[10]See P. H. Mell, "Annual Report of the President of the College," 1909, in *Forty-First Annual Report of the State Superintendent of Education of the State of South Carolina, 1909* (Columbia SC: Gonzales and Bryan, State Printers, 1910) 284.

[11]The figures are from ibid., 268; W. M. Riggs, "Report of the President of the College," 15 Dec. 1923, in *Fifty-Fifth Annual Report of the State Superintendent of Education of the State of South Carolina, 1923* (Columbia SC: Gonzales and Bryan, State Printers, 1924) 6; and Bryan, 97.

humanities. Only six have held the doctorate degree, with Mell the first to do so.

That less than half of the Clemson presidents have held the most advanced research degree may explain in part why only Mell among them arrived at the school with a national reputation for scholarship in his academic fields (geology and botany). Except for Mell, Bill L. Atchley (1979-1985), and now Max Lennon, the other Clemson presidents have placed little emphasis on faculty research and related scholarly activities. Clemson's lack of focus on research until recently has probably reflected two things. First, the school has only recently begun maturing into a major university. Second, it appears finally to have overcome the mistrust of and hostility toward higher education and the scholar's role that dominated America, and especially the South and some of Clemson's supporters, when the school was founded at the end of the nineteenth century.[12]

Another feature of the Clemson presidents is that their heavily scientific and technical backgrounds have not precluded them from encouraging Clemson to join the leading schools among the land-grant institutions and state universities that have applied the original broad land-grant interpretation to their educational mission.[13] Although at times Clemson has seemed limited by its land-grant origins to providing an agricultural and mechanical training for its students, the school's founder, Thomas Green Clemson, possessed wider educational and cultural interests. He had also requested in his will of 1886 that the school offer "thorough theoretic and practical instruction in those sciences *and arts* which bear directly upon agriculture."[14]

---

[12]For example, the supporters of South Carolina College (now the University) feared that the Clemson trustee and gubernatorial candidate in 1890, Benjamin Tillman, would abolish their school; see Lander, 139-40. According to Lawrence R. Veysey, *The Emergence of the American University*, 3rd ed. (Chicago and London: University of Chicago Press, 1974) 15: "It was in such an unfriendly climate as this that the American university initially had to make its way." Regarding this general problem, note Richard Hofstadter, *Anti-Intellectualism in American Life* (New York: Knopf, 1963).

[13]The sources are unclear regarding the role of the broader curriculum and liberal arts in the early land-grant schools. According to Ross, 116-17, for example, "the traditional, both in subject matter and instruction, lingered." A different view, however, is in Brubacher and Rudy, 117; Veysey, 68-71, 79; and Frederick Rudolph, *The American College and University: A History* (New York: Knopf, 1968). Eddy, 214, observes: "In many instances liberal studies were an accepted part of the [land-grant] college scheme from the very start. In others, the emphasis was so heavily on agriculture that it was not until modern times that liberal education came into its own. As a result, not a few institutions were identified popularly as 'cow colleges,' perhaps justifiably so until recent decades."

[14]See the appendix below. The emphasis is the editor's.

The controversy surrounding the origins of the college added fuel to the questions about the school's mission. Some state leaders and others disliked Clemson's competition with the state university in Columbia and the South Carolina Military Academy (now The Citadel). Strode, the first Clemson president, resigned in 1892 in part because the trustees disliked the preponderance of "literary" professors in the higher ranks of the faculty, whom Strode—a mathematician—had hired. His successor, Edwin Boone Craighead (1893–1897), a professor of Greek, and the only man from the humanities to lead Clemson, also resigned over such issues.

Despite the fate of Strode and Craighead, later Clemson presidents urged the school to broaden its curriculum, thereby not only teaching students a specific profession or technique for making a living, but how to live a successful life. Mell, for example, studied science because of his belief in its importance for humanity.[15] Moreover, one of Clemson's acting presidents and later the dean of engineering, the venerable Samuel B. Earle (1920, 1924–1925), urged that engineering students learn not only their particular technology, but that they study the humanities. Shortly after Clemson became a university during the Edwards administration, the latter established a college of liberal arts.[16]

Another characteristic of the Clemson presidency that emerges in the essays below has been its long standing and steady promotion of athletics. This tradition stands in sharp contrast to the impression left by the controversy during 1982–1985, which focused on the Clemson football and track programs and resulted in the resignations of both the Clemson president, Atchley, and the athletic director, H. C. ("Bill") McLellan. The incident became popularly portrayed as a conflict between "academics" and "athletics" and between Atchley and McLellan. Consequently, not only Atchley but the office he represented, Clemson's highest, its presidency, appeared to the public as hostile to athletics.

The history of the office, however, reveals that from Clemson's earliest years, its chief executives encouraged intercollegiate sports. Nearly all of Clemson's presidents would have shared Atchley's philosophy about the role of athletics at the school. "Athletics," he declared in 1979, "can

---

[15]Mell, shortly before he resigned in 1909, received strong evidence from a survey of Clemson's graduates that they appreciated the breadth of the school's education. Samples from the survey were presented to the board of trustees in Mell, "Annual Report of the President of the College," 270-75. For instance, one graduate observed: "In my opinion boys do not go to college to learn how to farm; they go to get an education." Another declared: "The general training at Clemson, no matter the course chosen, is so broadening that a graduate is capable of holding most any position. . . ."

[16]Bryan, 255.

set a spotlight on an institution like Clemson, so that the president of the school can stand in the spotlight and tell about the fine students and faculty of the university."[17] Clemson's third president, Hartzog, saw football in 1899 as a means for Clemson to excel among its fellow institutions and to enliven the support for it among students and alumni. He differed little in this regard from many of his colleagues at other colleges and universities at the turn of the century who sought the same for their institutions.[18] Hartzog's administration witnessed the college's first major intercollegiate football successes led by John Heisman, one of the sport's future legends. Other Clemson presidents—Riggs, Poole, and Cox—had either played or coached football at the school; Sikes had starred during his undergraduate days on the team at Wake Forest College; and Atchley had played semi-professional baseball. Edwards, however, probably supported Clemson athletics more than the others; during his presidency, he missed only one of the football team's 242 games.

The history of the Clemson presidency over the past century, therefore, reveals a tradition that has strongly reflected the Southern culture and society in which the school and its presidents have developed. Yet the Clemson presidency has also had much in common with its counterpart in colleges and universities throughout America. A final important likeness of the Clemson office with the others is especially worthy of mention. Today its occupant is no longer merely a "first among equals" and a leader of the faculty as were the first Clemson chief executives. The president is now the representative of the university and its governing board and a significant power in his own right.

Donald M. McKale

---

[17] Note the *Greenville News*, 25 Feb 1979.
[18] See Brubacher and Rudy, 131-36; Rudolph, ch. 18; and Veysey, 275-76.

TRADITION:
A HISTORY
OF THE PRESIDENCY
OF CLEMSON UNIVERSITY

• *Founder Thomas Green Clemson, 1807–1888* •

• 1 •
THE FOUNDER THOMAS GREEN CLEMSON, 1807–1888

Ernest McPherson Lander, Jr.

On 6 November 1886 Thomas Green Clemson signed the final draft of a document willing the bulk of his estate at Fort Hill near Pendleton to the state of South Carolina. He wished, the will declared, to establish "an agricultural college" that would provide both "instruction in agriculture" and "in those sciences and arts which bear directly upon agriculture."[1] Since returning to Fort Hill following his career as a diplomat, agricultural scientist, plantation owner in South Carolina and Maryland, and member of the Confederacy in the Civil War, he had attempted repeatedly and without success to gather support for such a school. Although Clemson's dream of a college resulted from his lifelong interest in education, the Fort Hill property had come to him through his marriage to Anna Maria Calhoun, the daughter of John Caldwell and Floride Colhoun Calhoun.

Clemson, a tall striking man ten years her senior, had married the twenty-one-year-old Anna on the evening of 13 November 1838. The ceremony was performed at Calhoun's Fort Hill home by the rector of St. Paul's Episcopal Church in Pendleton. A reception followed immediately, a gala affair attended by friends and relatives, far and near.

During the reception Anna's brother Andrew aptly noted that their father was "not as affable as usual" for he was "losing his favorite, his pride, his *confident.*" As for Clemson, his fortunes, for good or ill, would be inex-

---

[1] A copy of the will appears in the appendix below.

tricably entwined with those of his Calhoun in-laws for almost four decades.²

A Scientist with Interest in the Arts

Thomas Green Clemson, born on 1 July 1807, was the son of Thomas Green Clemson, Sr., a wealthy Philadelphia Quaker merchant, and Elizabeth Baker Clemson. The senior Clemson died in 1813, leaving a widow and six children, all under fourteen. The widow and children were well fixed financially, for Clemson's estate was estimated to be worth $100,000.

Little is known of young Clemson's boyhood. Apparently his relationship with his guardian was cordial, and his inheritance permitted a good education. From 1822 to 1824 he was a cadet at Captain Alden Partridge's Norwich Academy, forerunner of Norwich University. While at Norwich Clemson developed a special interest in chemistry and other sciences, and in 1826 he sailed for Europe to study under renowned scientists at the Royal School of Mines in Paris.³

Clemson enrolled as a free auditor, receiving no diploma from the school, although he studied in Paris more than three years. However, after an examination by the Royal Mint in Paris, he was awarded a diploma as assayer in June 1831. While in Paris he enjoyed the delights of the city and even participated in the revolution of 1830 that overthrew the monarchy. By late summer the next year he was back in the United States.⁴

The young scientist's activities from late 1831 through 1837 are obscure. There are no family letters, but a sketchy journal he kept reveals that he spent some time in Europe. There is other evidence that he visited Cuba as a mining engineer and acquired property there. He worked as a mining engineer elsewhere, and by the time he met Anna Maria Calhoun he had acquired a favorable reputation in his profession.⁵

---

²Charles M. Wiltse, *John C. Calhoun: Nullifier, 1829-1839* (Indianapolis and New York: Bobbs-Merrill, 1949) 318; and Mary Bates to Anna Clemson, 29 Apr. 1850, Calhoun papers, Special Collections, R. M. Cooper Library/Clemson University (hereafter cited as RMCL/CU). For fuller details of Clemson's life and his relations with the Calhouns, see Ernest M. Lander, Jr., *The Calhoun Family and Thomas Green Clemson: The Decline of a Southern Patriarchy* (Columbia SC: University of South Carolina Press, 1983).

³Alester G. Holmes and George R. Sherrill, *Thomas Green Clemson: His Life and Work* (Richmond: Garrett and Massie, 1937) 2-5; and J. B. Gest, Jr., to Clemson, 3 Jan. 1884, Clemson papers RMCL/CU.

⁴Holmes and Sherill, 5-10; Lefte Neal to Clemson, 17 July 1831; and Kate Neilson to A. G. Holmes, 14 July 1826, Clemson papers, RMCL/CU.

⁵Thomas Green Clemson's Record Book, 1832-1837, Clemson papers, RMCL/CU. For Clemson's scientific interests, see Holmes and Sherrill, 11, 47-69, 92-122.

Clemson's interests were varied. Not only did he master several sciences, he also became fluent in French and German and possibly Spanish. As hobbies, he painted and collected art—some for W. W. Corcoran in Washington; he played the violin and composed music; he collected guns and fine furniture; and he loved horses, dogs, and hunting.

Unfortunately for those closely associated with Clemson, he was an inveterate worrier, especially over money matters; he envisioned his last days in a poor house. He was a person of mercurial temperament, despondent moods and ofttimes tactlessness in personal relations. Some of his despondency was due to bouts of ill health, more frequent as he grew older. In his anxiety for financial ease and security, Clemson several times rushed too hastily into business arrangements that seemed to offer a quick profit. And some of these arrangements were with Calhoun in-laws. On one occasion in later years Clemson complained to his lawyer that he had been robbed "very largely by my wife's connections." All in all, this well-read and highly intelligent scientist never seemed to find a satisfactory niche for his gifted talents.[6]

Clemson and the Calhouns

When and under what circumstances Clemson met Anna are not known, but it was probably in early summer 1838 in Washington, where she was visiting and he was on a business trip. Whatever the circumstances, the confirmed bachelor was soon deeply in love. In July the attractive girl from South Carolina agreed to marry him. But before their wedding day the couple was separated, and for several weeks the lovesick Clemson did not hear from his "blessed idol." The absence of a letter tormented him to "craziness," he said. He could not even sleep at night. Then the dark cloud lifted. A letter arrived and soon the couple were together again to be wed.[7]

The early years of the Clemsons' married life were beset with numerous domestic difficulties. After their first child was born in August 1839, both mother and baby contracted fevers. The infant died within weeks and Anna suffered intermittent relapses for months. More than a year later she became utterly discouraged and almost resigned herself to be an invalid for life.

---

[6]Clemson to [Armistead Burt], 16 Dec. 1868, Clemson papers, RMCL/CU.

[7]Clemson to Anna Calhoun, 22 July, 5, 19 Aug. 1838; Clemson to Patrick Calhoun, 16 Aug. 1838; and Anna Calhoun to Maria Simkins, 21 June 1838, Calhoun papers, South Caroliniana Library/University of South Carolina, Columbia SC (hereafter cited as SCL/USC).

After the birth of Calhoun Clemson, 17 July 1841, Anna developed a serious, painful infection in one breast which took five months to heal completely. Following the birth of Floride Clemson, 29 December 1842, Anna developed such a high fever and rapid pulse beat that her family momentarily feared for her life.[8]

While Anna was struggling with pregnancies, babies, and ill health, Clemson was trying to get some permanent occupation. He was a partner in a mining venture in Missouri when he married, but the company faltered, and he never received a cent for his work in it. In 1840 he was persuaded to try his hand at managing one of James Edward Calhoun's plantations in Abbeville District. (James Edward was Mrs. John C. Calhoun's brother—he changed the spelling of his name.)

Clemson found James Edward's plantation badly run down and soon regarded its owner as too impractical and too stubborn to try new methods. He got off civilly—even loaned James Edward money, and returned to Fort Hill, where in the winter and spring of 1840-1841 he managed his father-in-law's plantation while the latter was in Washington.

Calhoun did not need his son-in-law's services when Congress was not in session, though he was highly pleased with Clemson's management. After a few months of idleness Clemson journeyed to Havana in November 1841 to superintend a mining operation until the following spring. The pay was lucrative enough, but the climate was injurious to his health. Upon his return to the United States in May 1842, Clemson was importuned by Calhoun to hurry to Dahlonega, Georgia, to manage his gold mining properties. A new strike had just been reported.[9]

For a few weeks Clemson did all right at Dahlonega, but the rich vein soon petered out. Moreover, Clemson became dissatisfied living in a crude shack with his family on a rough frontier that teemed with gamblers and lawless persons. However, while at Dahlonega he made the mistake of entering a partnership to renovate a rundown ironworks at Clarksville, Georgia. It never profited. A partner's son who was in charge of operations turned out to be a crook.

---

[8]Anna Clemson to Maria Calhoun, 19 Sept. 1838, 16 Sept., 13 Dec. 1841; to Patrick Calhoun, 19 Feb., 8 Mar. 1843, Calhoun papers, SCL/USC; John C. Calhoun to James E. Calhoun, 1 Nov. 1841; to Clemson, 25 July 1841; and Clemson to John C. Calhoun, 15 Jan., 17 Feb. 1843, Calhoun papers, RMCL/CU.

[9]Anna Clemson to Patrick Calhoun, 4 Oct. 1840; to Maria Calhoun, 1, 14 June 1842, Calhoun papers, SCL/USC; John C. Calhoun to Clemson, 13 Dec. 1840, 29 Nov., 31 Dec. 1841, 28 May 1842; to James E. Calhoun, 1 Nov. 1841; Clemson to John C. Calhoun, 22, 27 Dec. 1840, 10 Jan. 1841, Calhoun papers, RMCL/CU; and *Camden Journal*, 22 June 1842.

In the fall of 1842 Clemson left Dahlonega determined to buy a cotton plantation and become a gentleman planter. With the aid of his father-in-law and Colonel Francis W. Pickens, a Calhoun kinsman, Clemson purchased the 1,050-acre Cane Brake plantation in Edgefield District (near present-day Saluda). A number of problems delayed his moving onto the plantation until early 1844. Meanwhile, he and his family remained at Fort Hill.[10]

Investing in the Clarksville ironworks and buying a plantation and slaves placed Clemson in a financial bind. Worse still, it provoked a bitter feud between him and his brother-in-law, Andrew Calhoun. Within months of his marriage Clemson had loaned $17,000 to Andrew to invest in an Alabama cotton plantation—the money had been difficult to raise. The elder Calhoun added another $3,000 to the venture. As ill luck would have it, cotton prices dropped in 1839 and remained low for a decade. Clemson and Andrew soon had a misunderstanding over the arrangement, and when Andrew was remiss in reporting on operations or paying interest on Clemson's money, the latter became increasingly disturbed.

Time and again Clemson, meticulous about finances, complained to Calhoun about Andrew's lackadaisical business habits. Finally, he completely lost his temper. For four years he had received no interest on his money, he said. Thus, Andrew's name had become "odious" to him, and he wished never to see nor hear of him again. He threatened to sue.

Calhoun, ever patient and tactful and indulgent of his children, tried his best to mediate the dispute, offering to pay the debt himself—he too lacked the capability. Meanwhile, he borrowed money to help Clemson meet his obligations, and the storm subsided. But Andrew Calhoun and Thomas Clemson remained estranged for the rest of their lives.[11] In later years Clemson maintained that he never recovered his Alabama investment.

This was not to be Clemson's only unfortunate business arrangement with Calhoun in-laws. He had a falling out with James Edward Calhoun over the latter's delay in repaying a $1,000 loan. Again he threatened a suit. Later, in the 1850s, he entrusted his brother-in-law, James Calhoun,

---

[10]Clemson to John C. Calhoun, 9 July, 14 Aug., 6 Sept., 13 Dec. 1842; John C. Calhoun to Clemson, 3 Aug., 12 Nov. 1842, Calhoun papers, RMCL/CU; Anna Clemson to Maria Calhoun, 14 Aug. 1842; to Patrick Calhoun, 22 Aug., 3 Dec. 1842, Calhoun papers, SCL/USC; Clemson to John C. Calhoun, 20 Aug. 1842; and Anna Clemson to John C. Calhoun, 20 Aug. 1842, Clemson papers, RMCL/CU.

[11]John C. Calhoun to Clemson, 17 June 1840, 26 Dec. 1842, 8 Jan. 1843; Clemson to John C. Calhoun, 30 December 1841, 15 Jan. 1843, Calhoun papers, RMCL/CU; and Edgefield County deeds, CCC, 395-97.

with some $13,000 to invest in high-interest mortgages on San Francisco real estate. James squandered the money on a Mexican surveying venture instead. Again, Clemson lost all.[12]

Plantation Owner, Diplomat, and Agriculturalist

Clemson moved his family into a drafty and uncomfortable house on Cane Brake plantation in January 1844. But hardly had they settled down when events in Washington brought John C. Calhoun into President John Tyler's cabinet as secretary of state. Anxious for a chance to return to Europe, Clemson seized upon the opportunity to get Calhoun to procure a diplomatic mission for him. The post of chargé d' affaires to Belgium was the best available at the moment.[13]

From late 1844 to early 1851 Clemson served as chargé in Brussels. His diligent work and dependability commended him to official Washington. This was clearly indicated by the unusual fact that three presidents and three secretaries of state kept him at his post as long as they did. While in Brussels Clemson was frustrated over the low pay of a chargé and sought unsuccessfully to have the post upgraded to that of minister, and he frequently complained about the incompetence of some other American diplomats, their drunkenness and inability to speak a foreign language. When he requested home leave in the summer of 1850, following a recent change of Washington administrations, he was recalled, to be effective the following spring. In the meantime, his mentor John C. Calhoun had died in March 1850.[14]

During his years in Brussels, Clemson's greatest worry was not over the low pay of a chargé but over operations at Cane Brake plantation, where he suffered a succession of ill or mediocre overseers and no profits. Becoming increasingly concerned about his investment, Clemson requested

---

[12]Clemson to James E. Calhoun, 8 Jan., 19 Feb., 25 Mar. 1843; to James Calhoun, 1 Feb. 1855, 1 June 1860; to J. Mora Moss, 1 June 1860; James Calhoun to Clemson, 15 Mar. 1855, 5 June, 4 Nov. 1857; and Moss to Clemson, 28 June 1860, Clemson papers, RMCL/CU.

[13]John C. Calhoun to Clemson, 16 Mar. 1844; and to Anna Clemson, 10 May 1844, Calhoun papers, RMCL/CU.

[14]Clemson to John C. Calhoun, 28 Nov. 1845, Calhoun papers, RMCL/CU. For details of Clemson's diplomatic career, see Holmes and Sherrill, 70-91; and John W. Rooney, Jr., *Belgian-American Diplomatic and Consular Relations, 1830-1850* . . . (Louvain: Publications Universitaires de Louvain, 1969) 184-224.

Francis Pickens to seek a buyer. (Pickens and Calhoun visited the plantation and directed operations as often as possible.)[15]

Clemson was elated in late 1849 when Pickens wrote that he had a prospective buyer for the plantation and the slaves. His high hopes, however, were dashed shortly thereafter when the sale fell through. Clemson bitterly wrote his father-in-law: "If ever there was a person that should be sick of a country I am the person that should be sick of the South, and if it please the Almighty to grant me a safe deliverance I promise never again to place my foot on its soil." Later, before Clemson returned to America, Pickens managed to sell his property for $38,000, or $3,000 more than his asking price.[16]

Once back in America the Clemson family, after visiting Fort Hill and attending to business, moved north. The South no longer charmed Thomas Green Clemson. He hoped to secure another mission but failed for lack of political influence. Nevertheless, he wished to remain in a region where his growing children could be assured of good schooling and where there might be greater opportunity to use his scientific talents. After drifting for almost two years, Clemson in June 1853 bought a 100-acre farm on the outskirts, of Bladensburg, Maryland.[17] He named the place "The Home," and there he lived with his family until the Civil War. It was there that their last child Cornelia ("Nina") was born 3 October 1855, and died 20 December 1858.

During the Bladensburg years Clemson performed his most significant work in scientific study and publication. He attended scientific meetings, addressed the Smithsonian Institution, wrote articles for leading scientific and agricultural journals, and carried on agricultural experiments on his farm. His studies attracted attention and comment from other scholars. His biographers note that Clemson was one of about half a dozen reputable agricultural chemists in the United States at that time.[18]

Clemson was also greatly interested in scientific education. He played an active role in the organization of Maryland Agricultural College, now

---

[15]Clemson to John C. Calhoun, 27 Mar., 29 May, 15, 19 July, 28 Aug. 1846; and John C. Calhoun to Clemson, 25 Apr., 29 June, 20 Sept., 6 Nov., 9 Dec. 1846, 22 Mar., 10 June, 8 July, 15 Aug., 6 Sept., 7, 24 Oct., 10 Dec. 1847, Calhoun papers, RMCL/CU.

[16]Clemson to John C. Calhoun, 24 Sept. 1849, Calhoun papers, RMCL/CU; Floride Calhoun to Anna Clemson, 15 Dec. 1850; Francis Pickens to Clemson, 14 May 1856, Clemson papers, RMCL/CU; and Edgefield County deeds, GGG, 170-74.

[17]Clemson to R. K. Crallé, 15, 30 Jan., 27 Feb., 8 Mar., 10 July 1853; Crallé to Clemson, 17 Feb., 13 Apr., 1 July 1853; and agreement between N. G. Stephens and Clemson, 8 June 1853, Clemson papers, RMCL/CU.

[18]Holmes and Sherrill, 103, 121.

the University of Maryland. He presented his views on the subject in "The Necessity and Value of Scientific Instruction," published in *The American Farmer* in 1859. Among his comments Clemson wrote: "No one more than myself appreciates the blessings of our civilization, which are greatly due to the influence of the classics and I believe they will continue to have a most happy effect for all time, in their sphere—but at the same time it appears no less clear, that the sciences are destined to increase the amount of knowledge in the world, far beyond what imagination conceives." He was thus convinced that "the course pursued in our institutions of learning, falls short of the requirements of our age."[19]

Clemson's active participation in scientific organizations in the Washington area and his personal acquaintance with Jacob Thompson, secretary of the interior, led to his appointment on 3 February 1860, as the first Superintendent of Agricultural Affairs, a bureau in the Patent Office. The position was a forerunner of the Department of Agriculture.[20]

The new office was an exhilarating challenge for Clemson. His health and spirits both improved. He took his work seriously, spruced up his farm, and made an official visit to Europe the following summer.

Anna was elated over her husband's change, for there had been some unpleasant family scenes during the 1850s. Devoted and loyal, Anna was generally able to cope with her husband's varying moods. Once, in 1850, she confided to her brother Patrick: "I always said from the first, that his ill health arose in a great degree from his habit of giving way to low spirits, and I commenced by never worrying him myself, and trying to prevent his having any real cause to fret, and then, when he got low spirited, I amused him, and joked with him, and tho I *took him too old,* and can never make him a gay or amiable man it is really wonderful how much he has improved."[21]

But the two oldest children, upon becoming teenagers, often irritated their father and received the brunt of his wrath. On these occasions Anna often had difficulty restoring calm in the household. Then, when precious little Nina died in December 1858, both parents were greatly distraught. Clemson's despondency lingered so long that his family feared for his sanity, feared he would commit suicide.

Clemson had hardly recovered from that blow when, in October 1859, his New York friend and investment broker, Charles M. Leupp, in finan-

---

[19]Quoted in ibid., 129-30.

[20]Ibid., 132-33; and Anna Clemson to Floride Clemson, 8 Jan. 1860, Clemson papers, RMCL/CU.

[21]Anna Clemson to Patrick Calhoun, 2 Apr. 1850, Calhoun papers, SCL/USC.

cial trouble with Jay Gould, took his own life. Clemson had always enjoyed visits to New York, where he and Leupp would gad about with friends and discuss art and other things. He now not only suffered personal loss with Leupp's death, but $17,000 of his investment funds were tied up for years with Leupp's estate.[22]

But, as noted, Clemson's new position as Superintendent of Agricultural Affairs improved his spirits, and upon his return from Europe in October 1860, Anna was pleased to find him in "a wonderfully good humour." For this she credited a doctor who had advised her husband to remain calm. She confided to daughter Floride that if the doctor effected a cure, "I think we should erect a monument to him."[23]

The War:
"The North is no place for a Confederate"

Soon the family had greater worries. South Carolina seceded on 20 December, and within a few weeks six other states followed suit. With the advent of the Lincoln administration Clemson tendered his resignation, 9 March 1861, as Superintendent of Agricultural Affairs. Before doing so, however, he submitted a lengthy and valuable report on the "Advocacy of Agricultural Education" to the Patent Office.

A few days after his resignation Clemson and Anna made a hurried trip south to attend business and visit Anna's mother in Pendleton. The old lady was as excited as anyone about the impending Confederate attack on Fort Sumter. Just as the crisis reached its climax the Clemsons hurried back to Bladensburg where they had left Floride and Calhoun.[24]

The outbreak of the Civil War placed Thomas Green Clemson in a quandary. This Pennsylvania-born scientist, who had earlier declared his intention never again to live in the South, now found himself sympathetic to the Confederate cause. On the other hand, much of his property and investments were in the North. Matters became more serious when General Winfield Scott, on 27 April, suspended the writ of habeas corpus

---

[22]C. M. Leupp to Clemson, 22 Dec. 1858; Floride Calhoun to Clemson, 27 Dec. 1858; to Anna Clemson, 29 Sept., 15 Oct., 23 Dec. 1858, 4, 23, Jan. 1859; and Laura Leupp to Clemson, 6 Oct. 1859, Clemson papers, RMCL/CU. An account of Leupp's suicide appeared in *New York Times,* 7 Oct. 1859.

[23]Anna Clemson to Floride Clemson, 21 Oct., 4, 11 Nov. 1860, Clemson papers, RMCL/CU.

[24]Anna Clemson to Floride Clemson, 24 Mar. 1861; and Floride Calhoun to Anna Clemson, ? Apr., 17 May 1861, Clemson papers, RMCL/CU. For Clemson's report to the Patent Office, see Holmes and Sherrill, 137-39.

Thomas Green Clemson 1807-1888   Kate Salley Palmer

in parts of Maryland. Soon persons suspected of Southern loyalties were questioned and a few arrested.

Believing himself to be under suspicion, Clemson with his son Calhoun quietly departed south on 9 June, leaving Anna and Floride at Bladensburg surrounded by Yankee soldiers. Clemson had been assured by New York friends and Pennsylvania relatives that they would intercede in behalf of his wife and daughter, if need be. On occasion they did.[25]

Details of Clemson's wartime activities are scarcely known as hardly any of his wartime correspondence has been preserved. Apparently he resided most of the time at Mi Casa, Mrs. Calhoun's Pendleton home, until he joined the Confederacy in May 1863. Afterwards he was sent as a civilian to the Trans-Mississippi Department to take charge of the Nitre and

---

[25]D. W. Lee to Clemson, 25 Apr., 6 May 1861; and note by Clemson on back of letter from James H. Rion, 19 Aug. 1883, Clemson papers, RMCL/CU. The Clemson family wartime activities are largely followed after 1 Jan. 1863 in the diary of Floride Clemson. See Charles M. McGee, Jr., and Ernest M. Lander, Jr., eds., *A Rebel Came Home . . .* (Columbia SC: University of South Carolina Press, 1961).

Mining Bureau. In that or related service Clemson continued until the war ended. Meanwhile, he kept in touch with his wife by way of Nassau.

Calhoun Clemson enlisted in the Confederate army in 1861 and was captured in Mississippi in September 1863 while in charge of a small squad escorting a Confederate payroll to the Trans-Mississippi Department. He sat out the remainder of the conflict in a federal prison at Johnson's Island in Lake Erie.[26]

Anna remained close to The Home at Bladensburg, whereas Floride visited friends and relatives throughout the Northeast during the war. The two moved to Beltsville, Maryland, in June 1864, leaving The Home in the care of a relative. From Beltsville Anna, after ceaseless efforts, managed to secure passes for Floride and herself to return south. They arrived at Mi Casa on 31 December to find Mrs. Calhoun in ill health and straitened circumstances.

The two weary travelers arrived in South Carolina just in time to witness the collapse of the Confederacy. Sherman's army wreaked havoc across South Carolina in February; Lee surrendered in April; and Yankee raiders visited Pendleton in May.

Calhoun Clemson returned to Pendleton in June and Clemson arrived 1 July. Of her father Floride wrote in her diary: "He looks pretty well, but is iron grey now, . . . is nicer and more pleasant than I ever saw him." She noted that he had given up smoking and was "wonderfully improved" in playing the violin. During the war Clemson apparently suffered nothing worse than a broken arm, and his loyalty to the Confederacy did not seriously affect his finances. He invested little in Confederate securities. But his Confederate service killed any slight chance that he might again secure a federal office.[27]

In mid-fall 1865, as Clemson surveyed the wreckage of war, he wrote: "This country is in a wretched condition, no money and nothing to sell. . . . The negroes are utterly demoralized. Murders and robberies common occurrences. . . . Everyone is ruined, and those who can are leaving." At the same time Clemson began efforts to regain control of his property in the North. Correspondents advised him of the necessity of his personal

---

[26]McGee and Lander, 27-34, 41-43, 49; and H. Gourdin to Clemson, 8 Jan. 1862, 12 Mar. 1863, Clemson papers, RMCL/CU. For Calhoun Clemson's capture, see "Civil War Record of William O. Dundas," typescript in William O. Dundas papers, Georgetown University Library, Washington DC

[27]D. W. Lee to Anna Clemson, 22 Dec. 1864, Clemson papers, RMCL/CU; and McGee and Lander, 68-71, 88-91. All during the war, D. W. Lee, brother-in-law of the late Charles Leupp, frequently visited and aided Anna and Floride.

attention; hence, in May 1866 he journeyed to Washington, secured a pardon, and reclaimed The Home. (He had to wait until the mid-1870s to recover his investments entangled with the Leupp estate.) During his Northern visit he found some of his old friends cool to him; whereupon, on his return to South Carolina he remarked: "The North is no place for a Confederate."[28]

A Frustrated Reformer Returns to Fort Hill

In the years immediately following the war, Clemson devoted time to the promotion of the Blue Ridge Railroad, European immigration, and scientific education. He joined the Pendleton Farmers' Society, became its president in 1868, and enlisted its support for an agricultural and mechanical college. He sought Northern philanthropy and persuaded James Edward Calhoun to offer 1,000 acres of Pickens (now Oconee) land for the proposed school. His letters, speeches, and circulars bore no fruit. His timing was poor, and he lacked the forum that "New South" editors Henry W. Grady and Francis W. Dawson later enjoyed.

Suffice it to note that by 1870 Clemson was utterly discouraged. He dropped out of the Pendleton Farmers' Society and never again attended a meeting. In his frustration he severely criticized the South: "Look at the late war, conceived in arrogance, matured in ignorance, and delivered in imbecility," he wrote James Edward. "They the hapiest [sic] people on the face of the earth, where are they? Had they counted the cost and prepared measures things would have ended differently." He said he had explained publicly the economic course for the South to follow, but "the people are too ignorant or too apathetic to understand and too shortsighted to venture a dollar to make thousands."[29]

With the advent of the depression in 1873 Clemson had even gloomier forebodings. No one had any cash. Worse still, he wrote his friend Armistead Burt, was the "fall" of the University of South Carolina. As bad as its curriculum was, Clemson regarded the institution as the state's last hope. "To see the rising generation neglected for education since 1861,"

---

[28]McGee and Lander, 94-96; Clemson to Tazewell Taylor, 18 Oct. 1865; to James E. Calhoun, 29 May, 22, 24 June 1866; to W. M. Evarts, 23 Feb. 1870; D. W. Lee to Clemson, 18 Oct. 1866; and C. M. Leupp and Company to Clemson, 24 Oct. 1867, 2 Apr. 1868, Clemson papers, RMCL/CU.

[29]Clemson to James E. Calhoun, 29 May, 10 July 1866, 14 Mar. 1867, 24 June, 13 Sept. 1870; D. W. Lee to Clemson, 29 Jan. 1867, Clemson papers, RMCL/CU; minutes of the Pendleton Farmers' Society, RMCL/CU; and Anna Clemson to James E. Calhoun, 2 Feb. 1867, Calhoun papers, SCL/USC. See also, Holmes and Sherrill, chap. 7.

he asked, "what is the future of So. Ca. & the South. We are rapidly going back to the dark ages." The next year, with Anna's support, he renewed his efforts to obtain Northern aid for an educational institution.[30]

By that time the Clemsons had suffered great personal tragedy. Floride, who married Gideon Lee, of Carmel, New York, in 1869, died in July 1871, probably of tuberculosis, leaving an infant daughter, Floride Isabella. Calhoun Clemson, unmarried, died seventeen days later in a train collision near Seneca. Bereft of the last of their four children, the Clemsons were devastated and bitter, for they felt that Calhoun's and Floride's deaths were due to others' neglect.[31] Thus their immediate family was gone when they took possession of Fort Hill in early 1872.

Both Clemson and Anna were in poor health. She was overweight and suffered from a heart condition while he was often bedridden with bouts of rheumatism. They lived a quiet and rather secluded life until Anna, the last of the Calhoun children, died of a heart attack in September 1875. In describing his feeling upon the sad occasion, the shocked and grief-stricken old man poured out his heart to his friend Burt: "I am crushed, sick in mind, sick in body. Job's example is scarcely worse than my own. . . . How disconsolate and wretched I feel it is impossible for any one to imagine."[32]

With Anna's death her husband inherited the bulk of the Fort Hill estate. Mrs. Calhoun had inherited the property in 1850 and sold it and fifty slaves to her son Andrew in 1854 for $49,000, for which she took a mortgage. In 1863 Andrew sold his Alabama plantation (that Clemson helped finance) for $100,000 in Confederate bonds, but his mother would not accept Confederate securities to satisfy the mortgage on Fort Hill. Andrew suddenly succumbed to a heart attack in March 1865, never having paid off his debt to his mother.

When Mrs. John C. Calhoun died in July 1866, after a painful battle with cancer, she willed three-fourths of the mortgage to Anna and one-fourth to granddaughter Floride. Andrew's family contested the will in a long court battle that was not finally settled until January 1872. Anna and Floride's heir were awarded the property. Anna and Gideon Lee, guardian

---

[30]Gideon Lee to Clemson, 9 July 1874; Mrs. Henry Wigfall to Clemson, 21 Apr. 1874; Joseph Henry to Clemson, 10 Sept. 1874, Clemson papers, RMCL/CU; and Clemson to Burt, 16 Nov. 1873, Armistead Burt papers, Perkins Library, Duke University, Durham NC (hereafter cited as PL/DU).

[31]*Charleston News and Courier*, 14 Aug. 1871; McGee and Lander, 118; Anna Clemson to Louisa Washington, 7 Mar. 1873; and Clemson to J. D. Smith, 3[?] Apr. 1884, Clemson papers, RMCL/CU.

[32]Clemson to Gourdin, 11 Oct. 1875, Burt papers, PL/DU.

for Floride Isabella, agreed on a division of the Fort Hill estate: 288 acres for Floride Isabella and 814 acres, including the Fort Hill house, for Anna.[33]

After Anna's death, Clemson, with rare exception, remained close to Fort Hill. He secured a housekeeper and lived much to himself. Shortly he became restless and dissatisfied with his quiet rural life and no society. In 1878 he unburdened himself to his friend Armistead Burt: "I have become intolerant and utterly disheartened with the people of So. Carolina," he said. "I am now anxious, (and have been for some time) to quit the state and once more become a wanderer." He then revealed that certain parties had approached him about purchasing Fort Hill, which he was willing to sell for $25,000. He asked lawyer Burt to make the arrangements, yet somehow the proposed deal was never worked out.[34]

Within a couple of years Clemson gave up ideas of moving away. He settled down to running his farm, occasionally feuding with neighbors and his distant brother John Baker Clemson, and seeking a biographer of John C. Calhoun, for whom he always had the utmost respect. After a false start, in 1883 he secured the services of William Pinkney Starke, an elderly bachelor and literary man. Starke spent considerable time as Clemson's guest at Fort Hill.

Starke got along well with Clemson, who accorded him kindness and every comfort, but he worried about his host. He privately noted that the old man was "without exception the most desolate and miserable man I ever knew. He has quarreled with all his family, with all his wife's family and with all his neighbors. His age, debility and temper render him unlovable to the world in general but he is greatly to be commiserated. He has had great afflictions and the prospect of death to one who has scoffed at religion all his life is not alluring."[35] Starke overstated his case, for Clemson had always been on friendly terms with some of his in-laws and family. And in his late years he apparently began to reexamine his agnostic views about religion.

---

[33]Clemson to James E. Calhoun, 10 July 1866; Anna Clemson to James E. Calhoun, 2 Feb. 1867; and E. Noble to Clemson, 6 Sept., 28 Oct. 1867, Clemson papers, RMCL/CU. For a detailed account of Mrs. Calhoun's will and the court battle over her estate, see Holmes and Sherrill, 172-76. In his old age Clemson became confused about how he acquired the Fort Hill estate. Rion, the lawyer, furnished him a detailed account. Rion to Clemson, 7, 16 July 1886, Clemson papers, RMCL/CU.

[34]Clemson to Burt, 10 Nov. 1876, 21 June, 17 Oct. 1878, 26 Jan. 1879, 30 Aug., 11 Sept. 1880, Burt papers, PL/DU; and Clemson to Burt, 14 Dec. 1878, Clemson papers, RMCL/CU.

[35]W. P. Starke to Margaret Calhoun, 6 Mar. 1885, Calhoun papers, SCL/USC.

Clemson was never to see the biography of his father-in-law come to fruition. Starke died unexpectedly in October 1886 after a brief illness. Clemson was further shocked two months later when Colonel James H. Rion, his lawyer and financial adviser, died of a heart attack. With his own physical and mental vigor in serious decline, Clemson now turned primarily to his neighbor, Colonel Richard W. Simpson, for counsel thereafter.

Rion's widow Mary, in advising Simpson how to deal with Clemson, wrote: "You will have to have address and skill and a world of patience with the poor old gentleman. He has no faith in anybody and regards everybody in the world as robbers, not excluding you and I." Mrs. Rion believed that Clemson was friendly to her "but to his money more."[36]

Final Lonely Years and Desire for a College

Clemson's most enduring ambition in his last years was to establish an agricultural and mechanical college. Earlier efforts had borne no fruit and, as noted, for a time Clemson considered leaving South Carolina. But sometime between 1880 and 1882 he confided to Richard Simpson about a plan to donate the Fort Hill tract to the state for such an institution. The idea was also presented to James Rion, who drafted a new will for that purpose, executed 14 August 1883, giving the name "Fort Hill Scientific Institute" to the proposed college.

Changes were later made in the will by Simpson after consultation with Clemson, Benjamin R. Tillman, and D. K. Norris. The final document, dated 6 November 1886, changed the name to "Clemson Agricultural College of South Carolina." A codicil of 26 March 1887 added a few minor changes.[37]

In the spring of 1887 Clemson, nearing eighty years of age and becoming increasingly infirm, grew anxious to see his sixteen-year-old granddaughter in faraway Carmel, New York. It had been more than ten years since they last met, and Floride Isabella was likewise anxious to see her grandfather. Clemson implored her father to bring her to Fort Hill, to live, if they would, or at least pay a visit. Gideon Lee, past sixty and in poor health himself, kept finding excuses to postpone a visit.

By late February 1888 the old man was confined to his bed with bronchitis and not expected to live much longer. His housekeeper's daughter sent Floride Isabella a touching letter about his critical condition. She said:

---

[36]Kate Campbell to Clemson, 14 Oct. 1886; Clemson to R. W. Simpson, 14 Dec. 1886; and Mary Rion to R. W. Simpson, 9 Aug. 1887, Clemson papers, RMCL/CU.

[37]For details, see Holmes and Sherrill, 152-62; and the appendix below.

"The dear old man said the other day that he had almost given up all hope of seeing you in this life—in the dead hours of night he often cries out Oh! Lord is it possible I will have to die without ever again seeing my only grandchild; he had prayed to be spared to see you."

Simpson added his plea for Lee to hasten on to Fort Hill with Floride Isabella, but Lee did not come, and Thomas Green Clemson's dying wish to gaze once more on the face of his only grandchild remained unfulfilled. On 6 April 1888, the old gentleman died. He was buried in St. Paul's churchyard beside his beloved Anna.[38]

After Clemson's death his estate was appraised at $106,179.61 plus thirty-nine oil paintings, nine family portraits, and numerous books and maps that the assessors did not attempt to value. Clemson willed $15,000 and some personal items to Floride Isabella and most of the remainder to the state—Fort Hill's 814 acres and about $80,000 in securities and cash.

Gideon Lee contested the will but lost after a lengthy court battle. The South Carolina legislature fiercely debated whether or not to accept Clemson's bequest. Many objected to such a school, while others objected to the terms of Clemson's will. The opposition was narrowly defeated. Today Clemson University is located on the Fort Hill grounds, and the Calhoun home, with many of the Calhoun and Clemson furnishings, is preserved in the middle of the campus.[39]

It was only by good fortune that the Calhoun estate was preserved, fell into Thomas Green Clemson's hands, and was not sold, nor willed to Floride Isabella, nor refused by the South Carolina legislature.

---

[38]Clemson to Floride Lee, 26 Apr. 1887; Hester Prince to Floride Lee, 25 Feb. 1888, Clemson papers, RMCL/CU; Gideon Lee to Clemson, 12, 28 Dec. 1887; and to R. W. Simpson, 28 Mar. 1888, Simpson papers, RMCL/CU.

[39]*Appraisal Bill of the Property of the Estate of Thomas Green Clemson* (24 Nov. 1888), a printed brochure in Clemson papers, RMCL/CU. For the court battle over Clemson's will and the establishment of the college, see Holmes and Sherrill, chap. 8; and Wright Bryan, *Clemson: An Informal History of the University, 1889-1979* (Columbia SC: R. L. Bryan, 1979) 12-31.

• *President Henry Aubrey Strode, 1890–1893* •

• 2 •

THE BUILDER OF A COLLEGE HENRY AUBREY STRODE 1890–1893

Robert S. Lambert

On 19 July 1890 H. A. Strode accepted the offer of the board of trustees, a body created by Thomas Green Clemson's will to govern the new Clemson Agricultural College, to become the school's first president.[1] Although Strode began the construction of the college's campus, faculty, and curricula, not a single student attended the school during his presidency. Financial and other problems delayed its opening and, only two and a half years after his appointment, Strode resigned suddenly, apparently the result of his relationship with the trustees and of the difficult economic and political atmosphere in South Carolina.

A Virginian with South Carolina Ties

Strode, a native of Fredericksburg, Virginia, had enlisted in the Confederate army at seventeen and served throughout the Civil War. He taught school after the war, then enrolled at the University of Virginia where he

---

The author is grateful to the following persons for help in the research for this essay: Strode descendants J. Wilson Newman, Charlottesville VA, and Mrs. St. George T. Lee, Richmond VA; Mrs. John D. Lane, Clemson SC; Dewey W. Grantham, Vanderbilt University; the staffs of the manuscripts department, Alderman Library/University of Virginia (hereafter cited as AL/UVA), the John Davis Williams Library, University of Mississippi, and Special Collections, R. M. Cooper Library/Clemson University (hereafter cited as RMCL/CU); and Robert Krick, chief historian, Fredericksburg and Spotsylvania National Military Park.

[1]Strode to Richard W. Simpson, 19 Aug. 1890, Simpson papers, RMCL/CU.

earned the bachelor of arts degree and the medal in mathematics and, after filling several brief appointments in preparatory schools, returned to Charlottesville to earn the master of arts degree, with special study in chemistry. In 1872 he purchased property in Amherst county on which he established, and for the next seventeen years was principal of the Kenmore University High School, a preparatory school for the University of Virginia. There he met and married Mildred Ellis, a granddaughter of the man from whom he had purchased Kenmore, and they settled in her ancestral home.

One of his pupils described Kenmore as being "almost without rules; that it had two ends in view, health and scholarship," which each student was free to pursue as he saw fit, but "must always be a gentleman." At his school "the atmosphere was scientific not classical," and Strode's teaching "methods were unique, absolutely original, and perfectly suited to the needs of his students." In 1889 Strode closed Kenmore to become head of the department of mathematics at the University of Mississippi. He resigned this appointment in 1890 to accept the presidency at Clemson.[2]

Clemson's trustees had sought but failed to employ General Stephen D. Lee, president of Mississippi Agricultural and Mechanical College (now Mississippi State University), as Clemson's first president. Strode was their second choice. He had been highly recommended by faculty members of the University of Virginia and several of his fellow graduates who knew of the high standards he had maintained at Kenmore. Further, among his students at Kenmore were boys from such distinguished South Carolina families as the Hamptons, Mannings, Boykins, Memmingers, Adgers, and Rions.[3]

---

[2]Compiled service record, National Archives and Records Administration, Washington DC, microcopy 324, roll 331; Krick to Jan Gambrell, 11 Sept. 1986, RMCL/CU; *Catalogue of the University of Virginia, 1867-1868* (Wytheville VA: D.A. St. Clair, 1868) 16; *Students of the University of Virginia: A Semi-Centennial Catalogue* (Baltimore: Charles Harvey & Co., [1878]); *Amherst New Era-Progress*, 31 Dec. 1959. For Kenmore, see these sources in the AL/UVA: Records of Pupils at Kenmore University High School, Amherst, Virginia, 1871-1899; Kenmore University High School: Commencement Exercises, June 1887; and Strode to B. Johnson Barbour, 11 Apr., 19 May 1888, Barbour papers. The description of Strode's methods at Kenmore is by a former pupil who later served as professor of medicine and founder of the hospital, University of Virginia, and president of Virginia Polytechnic Institute, in *The Natural Bent: The Memoirs of Dr. Paul B. Barringer* (Chapel Hill: University of North Carolina Press, 1949) 179-81, 257-74. Enrollment at Kenmore fluctuated during the 1880s, and only 20 boys attended in the year before Strode went to Mississippi. See also *Historical Catalogue of the University of Mississippi, 1849-1909* (Nashville TN: Marshall and Bruce Co., 1910).

[3]The secretary of the trustees discarded the "testimonials" for Strode but later recalled

After moving his family to Virginia for the summer, Strode came to Fort Hill to be interviewed in July 1890. He knew that a bitter political battle was being fought in South Carolina that year between supporters and opponents of gubernatorial candidate and Clemson trustee, Benjamin Tillman. The conflict between the two sides had gained momentum during 1888 and 1889, when the debate raged throughout South Carolina over whether the general assembly should accept Thomas Green Clemson's bequest. Opposition had risen from many sides. Friends of South Carolina College (which would soon become the University again) and the South Carolina Military Academy (now The Citadel), for example, believed that those institutions provided the state with sufficient agricultural and military training. Supporters of South Carolina College especially disliked Tillman's violent public slurs against the school and feared that, if elected governor, he would abolish it. Tillman, in addition to his antagonism toward aristocrats in general and Charlestonians in particular, believed that lawyers and merchants had seized control of the general assembly to the detriment of farmers' interests. He led the Farmers' Association, which maintained that adequate education and research for farmers could only be achieved through a separate agricultural college. His forces finally prevailed, not only triumphing when the general assembly accepted the Clemson gift, but using the issue to thrust Tillman into the governorship of the state in 1890 and later into the United States Senate (1895-1918).

During 1890, however, J. L. Orr, another trustee and a friend of Strode, had been suggested as a possible candidate to run against Tillman in the election. Although Orr chose not to enter the race, he was identified with the opposition to Tillman. Strode, therefore, seeking protection for himself against potential factionalism in the board, had stipulated that he would accept the presidency only if offered it by a "nearly unanimous" vote of the trustees. He was offered the position on that basis, but at a lower salary than the board would have paid Stephen Lee. Strode accepted promptly by telegram; he indicated in a following letter that "the fame of being the founder President of a College, which, I am sure is going to be a great success," had overcome his disappointment at being offered the

---

that he had been "strongly recommended" for the Clemson position by Charles Scott Venable of the University of Virginia. Several other Virginians, J. L. Orr, a Clemson trustee, and president J. M. McBryde of the University of South Carolina, also wrote in Strode's behalf. It is interesting to note, moreover, that Richard W. Simpson, the first president of the trustees, had family ties in Amherst county, Virginia. See Transcription, "Minutes of the Board of Trustees" (1888-1908), 20 May, 16 July 1890, 10-13, 14-15, RMCL/CU; Alan Johnstone to Simpson, n.d. [1891], Simpson papers; and Records of Pupils at Kenmore, AL/UVA.

lower salary. Because of his large family (the Strodes had eight children), however, he asked for the use of a pasture for his livestock and free firewood for himself and other faculty members, an amenity he had enjoyed at Mississippi. Strode's appointment was as president of the college and director of the experiment station at $3,500 and included $1,500 from federal funds for the latter position. Pending the construction of a president's house, the Strodes were to live in the John C. Calhoun home.[4]

The Trustees and Financing the School

Thomas Green Clemson had willed three-fourths of the Fort Hill estate and his other assets to the state of South Carolina to establish "an agricultural college" whose model should be the "Agricultural College of Mississippi." Such an institution should, in Clemson's words, "afford thorough instruction in agriculture and the natural sciences connected therewith"; "combine, if practicable, physical and intellectual education, and should be a high seminary of learning" where graduates of "the common schools can commence, pursue, and finish the course of studies terminating in thorough theoretic and practical instruction in those sciences and arts which bear directly upon agriculture." To bind the state to the purposes of the bequest, Clemson stipulated that the school would be governed by a thirteen-member board of trustees; that seven men whom he named should form a self-perpetuating majority of the board, empowered to fill future vacancies among their number (the so-called "life" trustees); and that the remaining six should be chosen by the South Carolina general assembly. Trustees were given authority to establish and change the curriculum in order to provide students with the best preparation for the "agricultural and mechanical industries."[5]

The general assembly followed its acceptance of the Clemson gift in 1889 by passing a statute to "provide for the building and maintenance" of the college. The project was to be financed from several sources: annual income from two federal programs originally vested in the University of South Carolina—one-half of the land scrip fund to support agricultural

---

[4]Strode to Simpson, 1, 19 July, 1 Aug. 1890, Simpson papers. The politics of the election campaign in 1890 should be remembered as background to Strode's resignation in 1892; Johnstone to Simpson, 24 May, and Orr to Simpson, 26 May 1890, in ibid. Details on the battle over whether the general assembly would accept Clemson's gift are in Alester G. Holmes and George R. Sherrill, *Thomas Green Clemson: His Life and Work* (Richmond: Garrett and Massie, Inc., 1937) ch. 8; and Wright Bryan, *Clemson: An Informal History of the University, 1889-1979* (Columbia: R. L. Bryan, 1979) 12-28.

[5]The will appears in the appendix below.

education under the Morrill Act of 1862, which yielded about $5,750, and $15,000 under the Hatch Act of 1887 to support agricultural experiment stations—were transferred to Clemson's "legislative" trustees; a yearly grant of $15,000 under a third federal program, the Morrill Act of 1890, supporting land-grant education; a one-time appropriation of $15,000 by the general assembly for "building and maintenance;" and annual appropriations derived from the net proceeds of the state "privilege tax on fertilizers," about $25,000 for 1889 and 1890. The act also authorized the state penitentiary to furnish the labor of fifty convicts, later increased by 100, for construction and preparation of buildings and grounds. The Clemson bequest, valued at just over $73,000 in 1891, was converted into state stock which yielded six percent annually, the smallest item of income available to the college.[6]

It is well to remember the political and economic circumstances under which preparations were made to plan and build Clemson Agricultural College. Although Benjamin Tillman was elected governor in 1890 and his partisans controlled the legislature, resentment from the long and bitter campaign still lingered in the state. Further, economic conditions in South Carolina, never really prosperous after the Civil War, had by the early 1890s entered a period of severe economic depression accompanied by declining state revenues.

By the time President Strode reported for duty in August 1890, certain steps had already been taken to carry out the commitment the general assembly had assumed in accepting Thomas Clemson's gift. When the trustees organized for business in the previous January, they created an executive committee and a committee on curriculum. The executive committee was charged with constructing the campus. That meant advertising for bids to provide brick, arranging for cutting timber on the property, receiving proposals from architects, and choosing sites for some buildings and a railroad station. Strode's principal tasks in his new position would be threefold: to plan and supervise construction of a campus, to hire a faculty, and to draw up the curriculum and regulations for the special kind of college envisioned by Thomas Green Clemson and enthusiastically sought by the adherents of Tillman. In all of these, Strode was expected to work in close conjunction with the executive committee of the trustees to whom he reported every two weeks.[7]

---

[6]*Journal of the House of Representatives of the State of South Carolina. . . , 1891* (Columbia, 1891) 44; and Clemson Bequest Ledger, 1890, Records of the State Treasurer, South Carolina Department of Archives and History, Columbia SC.

[7]"Minutes of the Board," 20 Jan. 17, 18 Apr., 20 May, 16 July 1890, 2-15.

First Buildings, Faculty, and Curricula

Priority in planning and constructing the campus was given to the facilities needed to carry on the existing state programs to be transferred to Clemson from Spartanburg, Darlington, and Columbia—particularly the buildings and farms for the experiment station and the laboratory for fertilizer analysis—so that these services could continue and the college would become eligible for the federal and state funds supporting them. The farms could produce much of the food for the convict labor force and feed for the dairy cattle. Classroom buildings, shops, and residential and support facilities for the faculty and an entering class estimated at 300 students were to be built concurrently as funds permitted.[8]

At first it was hoped that sufficient facilities would be ready so that instruction for agricultural students might begin in the fall of 1891. Almost immediately, however, obstacles appeared to hinder progress toward that goal. The brick contractor "abandoned" his contract, and the trustees had to buy his facilities in order to meet their production goals for the work planned for 1891. Then shortly after assuming his duties, Strode notified the board that by law no Morrill funds could be used for buildings or their maintenance.[9]

Even more upsetting to plans for an early opening was the great interest shown in the school, for by the end of 1890 over 600 boys had applied for admission, and the number continued to grow. The trustees decided to enlarge the plant to meet this demand and to move the date for the opening of the school to February 1892. Although more convicts were brought in to perform the necessary labor, the funds that had been sufficient to carry out the original plans could not match the new demands. The trustees tried to meet this problem by committing over $27,000 of their personal notes toward continuing progress on the building program.

By the fall of 1891 the chemical laboratory, mechanical hall, experiment station, some residences and support facilities, and some of the farms and the access roads from Calhoun and Pendleton were virtually complete; the cornerstone of the main or classroom building was laid in July, and construction was begun on it, an attached chapel, a dormitory, kitchens, boiler room, an infirmary, and other residences. The trustees then

---

[8]"Minutes of the Executive Committee of the Board of Trustees of Clemson Ag[ricultura]l College," 2-15, RMCL/CU; and H. A. Strode, "The Aims of Clemson College . . . ," *Transactions of the State Agricultural and Mechanical Society of South Carolina, Nov. 13, 1890–Aug. 7, 1890* (Columbia: Berg, 1891) 78-90.

[9]"Minutes of the Board," 1 Oct. 1890, 17; and Strode to Simpson, 23 Nov. 1890, Simpson papers.

Henry Aubrey Strode 1890–1893

sought a special appropriation of $65,000 from the general assembly to meet their revised goal; in his annual message Governor Tillman pointed out that without the requested funds the admission of students must be delayed for a year. The general assembly did not find the money, and the trustees were forced to adopt stringent economy measures, stretch out the work, and notify applicants that the school would not be ready to open as planned.[10]

Despite the shortage of funds, by the end of 1892 a few carpenters and a reduced convict labor force had finished all but the last details of the principal buildings and the grounds as well as a number of brick and frame residences, the "cowhouses," stables, silos, and a canning factory. During that year the farm had produced substantial quantities of a wide variety of vegetables, and over 1400 fruit trees had been planted. President Strode's role in this phase of his work was essentially that of a construction super-

---

[10]"Minutes of the Board," 18 Nov., 29 Dec. 1891, 50, 53-55; and "For the Year Ending October 31, 1891," Littlejohn papers, folder 53, RMCL/CU. See, moreover, *Journal of the House of Representatives*, 25 Nov. 1891, 43-45.

intendent carrying out the orders of the executive committee—contracting for materials, arranging for the convict labor and its maintenance, choosing the sites for some buildings and farms, and a variety of related tasks (as he wrote once, "to see that mules are properly treated").[11]

In March 1891, the trustees, apparently on Strode's recommendation, established a number of "chairs," faculty positions that might form the basis for later "departments," to carry out the academic program of the institution. The two principal areas of instruction, agriculture with four chairs and mechanical with one and several shop foremen, were to be supported by five chairs in English and literature, mathematics, physics, history and political economy, and chemistry. It is not clear how extensive a search was conducted to fill these positions, but most of the first sixteen appointments announced by the trustees that summer were South Carolinians. The salaries of professors Charles M. Furman in English and William S. Morrison in history were set at $2,000; M. B. Hardin of Virginia Military Institute was appointed professor of chemistry and director of the fertilizer laboratory at $2,500; J. S. Newman of Alabama Agricultural and Mechanical College (now Auburn University) was named professor of agriculture and vice-director of the experiment station at $3,000; a naval officer was appointed as professor of mechanical and civil engineering and drawing; and Strode was to be professor of mathematics.

Several appointments were also made at the associate and assistant professor ranks. The shortage of funds and the several postponements in opening the College forced the original plan to be modified: "chairs" in horticulture and botany were abolished and the positions placed under agriculture and biology, respectively, then filled at lower rank and salary; the engineering chair was changed to applied mechanics, with civil engineering placed under mathematics and drawing given to someone at lower rank. When the college opened in 1893, several of the planned chairs and other positions had not been filled. The appointees were told that their salaries would begin when their "services were called for" and that they

---

[11]*Third Annual Report of the Board of Trustees of Clemson Agricultural College . . . , 1892* in *Reports and Resolutions of the General Assembly of the State of South Carolina, 1892* (Columbia: Charles A. Calvo, Jr., 1893) 2:511-33. The details of Strode's role in this phase of his duties can be followed in his letters to Simpson during 1891 and the first half of 1892, Simpson papers; and in "Minutes of the Executive Committee," 3 Feb., 3, 31 Mar., 14 Apr., 12 May, 9 June, 15 Sept., 13 Oct., 15 Dec., 1891, 29 Mar. 1892, 30, 32-33, 34, 36-38, 42, 43-54, 56, 60, 64, 68-69. These show that Strode rarely proceeded on his own authority, but sought permission from or notified Simpson and the committee.

might be asked to teach in fields other than those to which they were appointed.[12]

Strode served as chairman of the trustee committee on curriculum whose report was adopted by the board in March 1891. He expressed his views on curriculum in an interview shortly after his arrival: the course of study would "vary from two years to four or five years, according to the needs and ambitions of the students," who were to receive "a very thorough education in all but purely literary lines." Except for courses that "bear upon a thorough English education and upon the opening of foreign scientific literature to our students," duplication with "the State University at Columbia" would be avoided.[13]

Unless one recalls Strode's reference to the "needs" of students, the course of study that appeared in the first Clemson catalog appears to belie his statement about avoiding "purely literary" subjects, for English and history or economics appear in each year of both the agriculture and engineering curricula. From his long experience in Virginia preparatory schools, Strode recognized almost immediately that because "the College is intended primarily for the benefit of the farming classes and the public schools in the country are not of a high grade generally, the College will have its own preparatory classes to bridge the gap between the country public schools and the regular College classes." On another occasion he pointed out that "a better grade of public schools in the country is a crying want," but until this condition was remedied "the College itself must provide a way to bring its students up to a college basis." Strode was clearly prepared to accept the necessity of remedial courses, at least temporarily, and a preparatory department or "fitting school" was created after the college opened.[14]

Strode participated in drawing up the first student regulations. Boys could be admitted to the college at fifteen, they were to be under military discipline and required to purchase dress and fatigue uniforms. Because the

---

[12]*The State* (Columbia SC), 31 July 1891; and *Prospectus of Clemson Agricultural College . . . To be Opened July 6, 1893 at Fort Hill, S.C.* (Fort Hill: Board of Trustees, 1893) 1. The navy department was short of engineering officers and refused to detail lieutenant A. V. Zane to Clemson; acting secretary to Simpson, 29 Aug. 1891, Simpson papers.

[13]*Charleston News and Courier,* 8 Oct. 1890; and "Minutes of the Board," 4 Mar. 1891.

[14]*Prospectus of Clemson Agricultural College,* 4-8; and Strode, "Aims of Clemson College," 85. That Strode, a former preparatory school headmaster, should defend this type of sub-college program demonstrated his commitment to the kind of technological education to be introduced at Clemson. See Charles Foster Smith, *Southern Colleges and Schools* (Nashville TN: University Press Printers, 1891) 34 (reprinted from *Atlantic Monthly,* Oct. 1884, Dec. 1885).

farms would provide much of the food and fuel consumed on the campus, costs were kept low; a "poor boy" need pay only $104 annually for room and board, uniforms, laundry, and medical expenses and could earn a small wage for the daily two hours of work required of all students "in field and shop." Boys "of means" were required to pay $40.00 for tuition.[15]

The Mystery of Strode's Resignation

There is little evidence to indicate how capably Strode fulfilled the duties expected of him, but the few contemporary references are generally favorable. Shortly after he was appointed, he was saluted by the first president of the trustees, Richard Simpson, as one who, "while possessed of very fine literary attainments, . . . has shown himself to be eminently a practical man, and one thoroughly in sympathy . . . with affording technological education to the youth of our country." Trustee J. E. Wannamaker later praised Strode publicly for being so "busily engaged from early morning until the late hours of the night" in carrying out Clemson's building program.[16]

Yet in November 1892 the trustees suddenly accepted Strode's resignation as president, effective immediately, and as director of the experiment station, effective at the end of January 1893. Surviving documentary evidence is scanty, but it suggests that his resignation was not voluntary. When the trustees accepted it, they voted to "expunge" certain references to Strode in their proceedings of the previous 3 June; however, the minutes of that date reveal that the board passed Governor Tillman's motion that President Strode "be notified that he must release the board of expenses as to his salary after July 1st until the College opens, or until he be called into service again, or that he be given notice that after Feby. 1st 1893 his services be dispensed with." A substitute motion offered by J. L. Orr that "on account of the uncertainty of the time of opening the College, Mr. Strode be notified that after 1st of October next we will not be able to continue his salary until the College is opened," was defeated. Strode continued to perform his duties as president, presumably without pay, until his resignation six months later, but was paid as director of the experiment station.[17]

---

[15]*Charleston News and Courier*, 8 Oct. 1890; and "Minutes of the Board," 4 Mar. 1891, 32-33.

[16]*Charleston News and Courier*, 8 Oct. 1890; and Strode, 88-89.

[17]In Sept. the trustees had voted to defer action "to a fuller meeting" on certain "letters from President Strode;" see "Minutes of the Board," 3 June, 15 Sept., 30 Nov., 1892, 63, 65, 69; and Account book, Experiment Station [1891-1906], Clemson College financial

Did Strode or his policies create divisions among the trustees, or was he caught between existing factions in that body? That the latter explanation may have been the case is suggested by the fact that Tillman had urged the chairman to call the June meeting of the board and that Orr was indignant when he suspected that the request had come from the governor. Then in October Strode wrote to Tillman and offered his services as "a happy medium of reconciliation between two such ardent friends of the College" as Orr and the governor, and he pledged that, should "this reconciliation not meet your approval," the matter should be kept confidential. No documentary evidence survived that might explain what led at least a majority of the board to support Tillman's motion. Did they consider Strode to be responsible for the delays in opening the school or for the preponderance of "literary" professors in the higher ranks of the faculty, a position taken by an investigating committee of the board several years later? Did they feel that he lacked the leadership qualities they wanted, or had he grown restive under the constant and close scrutiny of the executive committee? Did Strode decide that only by his resignation a measure of harmony might be restored within the board? Or was his health so poor that he was unable to carry out his duties? Without more concrete evidence, these must remain speculations.[18]

The Clemson College that opened in 1893 naturally reflected the ideas of its trustees in carrying out the wishes of the founder. For the first president they sought someone with academic credentials to contribute in areas outside their expertise, and Strode must have influenced the choice of the first faculty and the design of the curriculum. But most of his time was spent in the day-to-day problems of building a campus under the watchful eyes of the executive committee during very hard times, conditions that hardly offered him many opportunities to exert leadership.

Strode remained at Clemson as professor of mathematics and occasionally presided at faculty meetings in the absence of his successor as president, E. B. Craighead. But at the beginning of 1896 a trustee committee investigating the management of the college called for a number of changes

---

records, RMCL/CU. The general assembly, which had refused to grant Clemson a special appropriation in 1891, responded favorably to the trustees' request in 1892 for $50,000 to finish the buildings and to purchase the equipment needed to open school in the following year; *Third Annual Report*, 515.

[18]Strode to Benjamin R. Tillman, 11 Oct. 1892, Tillman papers, RMCL/CU. An undated draft of a biographical sketch of Strode in the Littlejohn papers states that Strode resigned because of poor health, but presents no evidence for the statement. Bryan, 41, gives the same reason for Strode's resignation without providing a source for the information.

in the faculty; among their recommendations was that since instruction in mathematics was "greatly impeded because of the inefficiency of Prof. Strode," he be asked to resign. The board adopted the proposal and Strode promptly complied. That his "inefficiency" was caused by declining health is suggested by the committee's statement that it could not "permit our sympathy for any individual to outweigh" its concern for the preparation of students and by the fact that Strode had not received his salary after 1 July 1895.[19]

Strode moved his family back to Amherst, and there he died and was buried in 1898. His eldest son reopened the Kenmore school until after his father's death, but retained the property while engaged in a career in law and business. H. A. Strode's connection with Clemson was continued, however, through the marriage of his daughter, Grace, to Charles Carter Newman, an early Clemson graduate who served there for many years as professor of horticulture.[20]

---

[19]See *Prospectus of Clemson Agricultural College*; and the following records in RMCL/CU: Register of H. A. Strode, 1893-1894, Clemson University (hereafter cited as CU), President's papers, Strode; "Minutes of the Board," 22 Jan. 1896, 153-56; and Account book [Nov. 1894-Dec. 1896], financial records.

[20]Note *Amherst New Era Progress*, 31 Dec. 1959; and Records of Pupils at Kenmore, AL/UVA. The only official recognition of Strode's services to Clemson are a portrait commissioned by the trustees in 1896 and, upon receiving news of his death, a resolution of the faculty which noted the "high character, . . . and scholarly attainments of our late associate." See these sources in RMCL/CU: "Minutes of the Board," 22 Jan. 1896; Committee on Resolutions of the Faculty, 13 Sept. 1898, CU President's office official correspondence, Sept. 12, 1898-Jan. 12, 1899.

• *President Edwin Boone Craighead, 1893–1897* •

• 3 •
THE CONTROVERSIAL HUMANITIES PROFESSOR EDWIN BOONE CRAIGHEAD, 1893–1897

John L. Idol, Jr.

Praised and denounced at practically every college or university he led, E. B. Craighead, Clemson's second president and successor to H. A. Strode, found himself in the middle of controversy throughout his career. During his presidency, Clemson greeted its first students and held its initial graduation ceremonies. The new president, the only person trained in the humanities ever to hold that position at the school, was a man of courage and charm. However, although tolerant of opposing opinions, he was uncompromising in his own, and even when failure was inevitable he stubbornly refused to yield. While he gave vitality and broader ideals to Clemson, he soon became a casualty of the conflict among South Carolina's leaders over the college's high academic standards and what role the liberal arts were to play in its mission.

The Farm Boy and Classicist

Administrative responsibility had come early to Craighead. Born in Missouri in 1861 to Scotch-Irish parents, his father had died at an early age, leaving the boy to help his mother operate the family farm. He eventually entered Central College, a small Missouri school supported by the Methodist church,[1] where he excelled in Greek, Latin, and English. Fol-

---

[1]See "Edwin Boone Craighead," *Dictionary of American Biography*, ed. Allen Johnson and Dumas Malone, 10 vols. (New York: Charles Scribner's Sons, 1958) 2:496-97. I grate-

lowing his graduation from Central College and a first taste of teaching at Neosha Collegiate Institute, he sought to improve his skills as a professor by enrolling for a year at Vanderbilt University, where he pursued his studies in classical languages and English. Craighead left Vanderbilt to study in Germany with a leading Shakespearean scholar, but his disgust at the famed teacher's three straight lectures on bibliography led him to move on to Paris for advanced work in the French language and literature.[2]

Returning to America, he taught languages at Emory and Henry College in Virginia and then received an appointment in 1891 at Wofford College to teach Greek and French. Wofford advertised him as a "wonderful find" and took pride in his gifts as a public speaker.[3] Craighead's performance at the Spartanburg school and his promise as one of the brightest young educators in the South stood him in good stead when he found himself one of three candidates to replace H. A. Strode as president of Clemson Agricultural College.

The board of trustees invited Craighead to visit the campus on 8 June 1893 and, although the board's minutes reflect nothing of its discussions with him, its members surely liked his agricultural background and how he had worked tirelessly to keep his family's farm operating while acquiring an excellent education. At an institution where practical farm and mechanical work would be expected of every student, such a man seemed ideal to greet Clemson's first class. On 21 June the trustees elected the thirty-three-year-old Greek professor president of the college and director of its experiment station.[4] The decision resulted in part from Craighead's attitude toward student labor, which he expressed in his report to the board in 1894:

> Labor, labor of the hand as well as of the head, labor in the shops as well as in the fields, is expected and demanded of all who enter here. The dig-

---

fully acknowledge the help of librarians and archivists at Central Missouri State University, Tulane University, the University of Montana, the North Dakota State Library, the State Historical Society of Wisconsin, and Clemson University. I had the eager and painstaking assistance of Sharon Sifford, a Clemson graduate student in English. My debt to her is great.

[2]Cassius J. Keyser, *Mole Philosophy and Other Essays* (New York: E. P. Dutton & Company, 1927) 74.

[3]David Duncan Wallace, *History of Wofford College, 1854-1949* (Nashville: Vanderbilt University Press, 1951) 113.

[4]Transcription, "Minutes of the Board of Trustees" (1888-1908), 8 June 1893, 93, in Special Collections, R. M. Cooper Library/Clemson University (hereafter cited as RMCL/CU).

nity of manual labor is the foundation stone upon which our educational edifice is raised, and must be maintained or the whole structure tumbles to the ground. To put young men in the way of maintaining themselves in honest independence, to send out real providers, men who earn the bread they eat and the clothing wherewith they are clothed, this is the mission of our State College. . . . Of these youths who leave these halls let it be asked in the language of Ruskin: "Can they plow? Can they sow? Can they plant at the right time, or build with a steady hand? Is the effort of their lives to be chaste, knightly, faithful, holy in thought, lovely in word and deed?" I trust that in the coming years we may be able to reply: "Indeed it is with some, nay, with many, and the strength of South Carolina is in them."[5]

Since students enrolled at Clemson as beneficiaries of the state, Craighead believed that "the idle, the vicious swellheads, who know more than the Board and the Faculty, dudes, adventurers, seeking now this school, now that, namby-pamby, irresolute boys, will find the atmosphere of Fort Hill extremely uncongenial. I have, I am sure, the support of the Board in my efforts to turn elsewhither all such."[6] This outburst from Craighead in his second report to the board reflected not only his style as a public speaker but, more significantly, his educational philosophy, one much in accord with the founders of Clemson and their goal of combining practice and theory.

Whatever he said to the board, it thought Craighead "the right man in the right place," words mocked several months later, if some reports can be trusted, when dissatisfied students demanded his ouster and charged that he was "the wrong man in the wrong place."[7] His tasks in opening Clemson's doors kept him from teaching, but the board, anticipating that he might find time to do so, offered him the chair in Greek.[8]

The First Session

Craighead had hardly settled into his office before students arrived for the first session on 6 July 1893. Together with Governor Benjamin Till-

---

[5]E. B. Craighead, "Report of the President," 31 Oct. 1894, *Fifth Annual Report of the Board of Trustees, President, and Officers of Clemson Agricultural College, 1894* (Columbia SC: Charles A. Calvo, Jr., State Printer, 1894) 19.

[6]Ibid., 16.

[7]*The State* (Columbia SC), 23 June 1893. The editor of *The State*, N. G. Gonzales, was a political adversary of Benjamin Tillman and kept a watchful, sometimes antipathetic, eye on Clemson in its infancy.

[8]*The State*, 23 June 1893.

man and other members of the trustees, he welcomed over 300 students and introduced them to members of his faculty and staff, including Professor James Stanley Newman, appointed chairman of the faculty after the resignation of Strode at the end of January, and Lieutenant T. Q. Donaldson, Jr., commandant of cadets and one of the heroes of the massacre at Wounded Knee. But Newman now openly disliked his position as assistant director of the experiment station and was asked on 30 November to tender his resignation. While faculty chairman, he had differences with the board, even extending to insubordination when he built a standpipe instead of a reservoir for Clemson's water supply. When Craighead became president, Newman continued as a source of friction, complaining that the new chief executive spent "most of his time in his office smoking cigars."[9] The board accepted Newman's resignation on 10 January 1894.

With this troublesome matter behind him, Craighead and his colleagues observed the students arriving at Clemson and decided that many lacked the background to do college-level work. For the two basic courses of study, one in chemistry and agriculture and the other in agriculture and mechanics, students needed more preparation than most had received in South Carolina high schools. According to Clemson's first catalogue, *Circular of Information, No. 1,* "thorough proficiency in Arithmetic, Elementary Algebra, English Grammar, Geography, and History of the United States is required for admission into the Freshman Class." With roughly half of the students falling short of the requirements, Craighead and the faculty proposed the establishment of a fitting school and a six-year program, approved by the trustees in 1894, to serve as a college preparatory course for those who needed it. Located on the third floor of the main building (now Tillman Hall), the fitting school had a staff of three headed by W. S. Morrison, a professor of history. Craighead informed the trustees: "No department of the College is more important than the 'fitting school,' which, until our public schools furnish thorough preparatory training, must always be full."[10]

Wherever he served as a college president, he sought better public schools, a stance that later brought him prominence as an educational leader in Missouri, Louisiana, and Montana. However, his support of a

---

[9]"The Past Presidents of Clemson College," 7, read by Gaston G. Gage before the Forum Club of Clemson, 25 May 1948, in Gage papers, folder 28, RMCL/CU; "Minutes of the Board," 1 Feb., 30 Nov. 1893, 74, 107; and *The State,* 7 July 1893.

[10]E. B. Craighead, "Report of the President," 31 Oct. 1895, *Sixth Annual Report of the Board of Trustees, President, and Officers of Clemson Agricultural College . . . ,* 1895 (Columbia SC: Charles A. Calvo, Jr., State Printer, 1895) 16.

fitting school for Clemson and conviction that the college's standards should not be lowered to accommodate students from South Carolina's secondary schools created a stir in the state. Not only was his insistence on higher standards of preparation and attainment for entering cadets greater than usual in the South of that day, but many state residents defined Clemson's role as a vocational institute for training farmers and engineers. Debate on the issue would soon spill into the popular press, with George Tillman, the governor's brother and a prominent state legislator, becoming the most energetic spokesman for the vocational faction in the state.[11]

Meanwhile, Craighead worked on support facilities for students, faculty, and staff. A laundry began operating; a mess hall, dependent on produce from the college farms, offered board for $7 per month; and two literary societies, "The Calhoun" and "The Palmetto," attracted many members wishing to hone their skills in oratory, declamation, and debate. (A third society, "The Columbian," was founded the next year.)[12] A reading room with newspapers and periodicals enabled students to keep abreast of contemporary events and issues. An infirmary, headed by Dr. Alexander Redfern, opened to attend, according to Craighead, to the "mumps, colds, and other slight ailments" of students.[13]

For everyone's benefit, the president spent $250, half of it donated by the faculty, to purchase periodical literature for the library, located in the main building and established from several hundred books acquired with $1,000 set aside by the trustees. Realizing that Clemson's future depended heavily on the strength of its library holdings, he told the trustees: "I trust that the Board may continue to make liberal appropriation for the purchase of new books so much needed by our students. . . . Without a good library, no college is complete."[14]

---

[11]G. Tillman believed that the liberal arts should be left to private colleges and South Carolina College (now University).

[12]E. B. Craighead, "President's Report," 1 Nov. 1893, *Fourth Annual Report of the Board of Trustees of Clemson Agricultural College to the General Assembly of South Carolina, 1893* (Columbia SC: Charles A. Calvo, Jr., State Printer, 1893) 13; and Craighead, "Report of the President," 31 Oct. 1895, 21.

[13]According to the president's report, however, one student, H. A. Powers, of Georgetown, died of pneumonia during Clemson's first session. On a happier note, Craighead announced that the cadets injured when a gangway fell beneath them as they ran to escape a pouring rain had fully recovered. See Craighead, "President's Report," 1 Nov. 1893, 13.

[14]Ibid.

From Marching Orders to Trouble

Although unable during the initial months of the college's operation to achieve his top priority, the renovation of the mechanical hall,[15] Craighead felt good about the first session as it concluded at the end of 1893. He had received his marching orders from the trustees and, although physical facilities remained limited, Clemson was stepping forth energetically. In his annual report to the board, he proudly announced that 444 students had enrolled during the session and that he intended "to make [Clemson] above all things a great agricultural school. . . . The work of the session now drawing to a close has given me unshaken faith in our final success."[16]

Events during the next year, however, tested that faith and produced tension in the relationship between the president and trustees. Following remarks he made at a graduation address at the South Carolina Medical College in Charleston in March 1894, where he reportedly offended some in the audience by criticizing the Catholic church and slurring Jews, an editorial in *The State* questioned his "common sense" and concluded: "He seems to talk too much and to talk, sometimes, rather wildly."[17] The minutes of the trustees reflected no unhappiness of the board regarding the event. In April Craighead was granted a leave of absence from the campus to attend a church conference.[18]

Shortly after his return, problems increased when a fire destroyed the main building. Beginning in the museum (on the third floor) during the night of 22 May, the blaze spread rapidly. Despite courageous efforts by students, faculty members, and firemen, the building could not be saved. Lost in the fire were classrooms, offices, the library, and museum exhibits. The estimated damage was $60,000, but insurance covered only a third of the loss.[19] Although reconstruction of the main building began immediately, a number of cadets left the campus following the fire, unhappy with makeshift classrooms and interrupted instruction. Besides tents, a tem-

---

[15]Ibid., 14. The inadequacy of this building and failings of the instructors in the mechanical arts probably contributed to the student unrest during the summer of 1894 (see herein).

[16]Craighead, "President's Report," 1 Nov. 1893, 12, 14; 165 students had matriculated in the mechanical department; 87 in the agricultural department; and 202 in the preparatory department.

[17]*The State*, 18 Mar. 1894.

[18]"Minutes of the Board," 20 April 1894, 118.

[19]*The State*, 23 May 1894; and Wright Bryan, *Clemson: An Informal History of the University, 1889-1979* (Columbia SC: R. L. Bryan, 1979) 44-45.

porary classroom building, later to be used as a hotel, accommodated most of the students.[20]

Complaints from the students, however, soon gathered momentum, particularly against the president and the educational failings of the infant college. Rumors of "trouble at Clemson" had reached the press on 23 July. *The State*, basing its reports on information from a Clemson student on his way home through Columbia, described a meeting of 125 students in the chapel that had accused Craighead of "not doing his duty." Further press reports indicated that the president had appeared before the cadets on 21 July, asking them what he had done to displease them and inviting those wanting him to remain in office to rise. Nearly a third, mostly students above the ranks of the fitting school, remained in their seats, refused to discuss their grievances, and then marched out. Once Craighead had left the meeting, his opponents returned but failed to agree on a resolution asking the trustees to investigate "the condition of affairs around the college, with particular reference to the president."[21] No further meetings apparently occurred.

The board of trustees, to halt rumors and silence charges in the press that it ignored the "row" at Clemson, investigated the unrest. On his return to Columbia from Clemson, Benjamin Tillman announced that the board had examined "the alleged trouble between President Craighead and the students" and that "there appeared to be practically nothing in it." He added that only "the president's refusal to permit some boys to go home for a summer vacation, when their parents had requested it," had caused a problem. The college's advisory body, the board of visitors, which now arrived on the campus, encountered "no trouble, nor cause for any," and praised the "pluck displayed by the president, faculty and students in rising above" the recent fire and loss of books, classrooms, laboratories, and equipment. But the board of visitors, possibly reflecting the discontent reported by Governor Tillman, recommended that the trustees "give the students to understand that discipline of the college is fully vested in the president."[22]

---

[20]The attitude of the unhappy cadets contrasted with the resolve of Craighead, the trustees, the faculty, and the other students to rebuild. For example, Governor Benjamin Tillman, when informed in Rock Hill of Clemson's loss of the building, declared: "The school will run on if we have to carry a lot of army tents or get tents like the evangelists use for use as recitation rooms." See *The State*, 24, 27 May, 1 June 1894. Craighead, to solve some of the problems of space created by the loss of the main building, sent the corps to a military encampment in Spartanburg for ten days of duty beginning 1 July; *The State*, 28 May 1894.

[21]*The State*, 26, 30 July 1894.

[22]*The State*, 4, 11 Aug. 1894.

Craighead's "pluck" appeared in many forms. He asked the trustees to enlarge the mechanical hall, purchase new equipment, and expand laboratory space for Professor M. B. Hardin in the chemistry department. Arguing that "no man can keep abreast of the progress in . . . any department of science, who is unable to read German and French periodicals," he requested that both European languages be made optional in the junior and senior years. He stressed the urgent need of replacing books lost in the fire, requesting $5,000 for their purchase. Moreover, by increasing the amount of student labor, which paid 8 cents an hour for heavy work and 4 cents for light labor, he managed to reduce students' expenses for ten months of school to $100.40, of which $70 could be earned by a boy if he worked the maximum hours available to him at the higher wage. His annual report to the trustees in October 1894 emphasized the success of the fitting school, dairy, cannery, and chemical services provided by the college to the state's farmers. The experiment station also made available to farmers agricultural periodicals and bulletins on fertilizers and dairying. Confident that he was moving the college ahead, the president ended the report on a proud note: "The whole machinery of the institution is running so smoothly as to lead some people to believe that the President has nothing to do but sit in his office, puff his cigars and watch it move."[23]

The new session in 1895, however, revealed a few squeaky wheels that needed oiling. For a sharper delineation of duties, Craighead and the faculty organized the college into five departments: agricultural (agriculture, horticulture, dairying, veterinary science, botany, entomology, and experiment station); mechanical (engineering, drawing, mechanical designing, blacksmithing, foundry work, and wood and iron work); chemical or scientific (chemistry, analytical work for the state, mineralogy, geology, and metallurgy); academic (history, mathematics, English, French, and German); and military (military science and tactics, management of the barracks, mess hall and kitchen, and discipline of the cadets).[24] In addition, provisions were made for a Young Men's Christian Association to meet Saturday nights in memorial hall to nurture the religious and social life of the cadets; once a month a faculty member spoke to the group.

But of special concern to Craighead was the financial plight of Clemson's students, the result of a mild national recession. Clemson's budget became so tight during 1895 that the college almost completely abandoned student work programs in favor of a labor force of convicts assigned by the state to the school. This bothered Craighead, who believed in the

---

[23]Craighead, "Report of the President," 31 Oct. 1894, 10-24, 49-50.
[24]Craighead, "Report of the President," 31 Oct. 1895, 16.

Edwin Boone Craighead 1893-1897   Kate Salley Palmer

nobility of work and value of a student appreciating his education by investing his own money and sweat in acquiring it. Although he had little immediate success, the president urged the trustees to find funds enabling him to hire more student help, promising that he and his faculty would weed out the "idlers and adventurers" among the boys.[25] One of the squeaky wheels he oiled, presumably the one that caused "the trouble at Clemson" the year before, involved his granting a brief (ten to fourteen days) midsummer vacation for the cadets. The decision proved popular with students, parents, and faculty.[26]

But far more difficult to grease were the rumbling wheels of the college's two major academic programs, the mechanical and agricultural. Following a meeting of the board of trustees on 14 August 1895, infor-

[25]Ibid., 23-24. Craighead also reported to the board that a $15 gift from "a noble Boston woman, herself a distinguished teacher and artist," had been sent to him to make loans to needy students. He had had such frequent use of the gift, lending it and receiving repayment, that he yearned for "a loan fund of a few thousand dollars [for the benefit of] poor boys who came to Clemson."

[26]Craighead, "Report of the President," 31 Oct. 1895, 22.

mation reached the press that Benjamin Tillman, now a senator in the United States Congress, had "declared certain departments" at Clemson "a humbug and a farce." A young reporter, Fritz McMaster, covered the meeting for *The State* and declared that to "the casual observer, matters at Clemson are running smoothly enough." However, he had found disharmony and dissent among students and faculty as well as clashes among the trustees. Although he described Craighead as "pleasing in his address and courteous in his manners," McMaster quoted unnamed students and professors at Clemson as alleging that Craighead was "not at all qualified for the presidency of an agricultural and mechanical college." One of his sources particularly criticized the mechanical department, claiming that "there was not a student in the highest class who could cut threads for a screw, and it was doubtful whether any of them knew the difference between a bolt and a nut." Still another source maintained that agricultural studies had declined since Professor Newman's resignation.

Not only did McMaster conclude that Clemson suffered from bad management, but an editorial in *The State* demanded that the trustees either "vindicate President Craighead or let him slide."[27] Despite remarks by Richard W. Simpson, chairman of the board, supportive of Craighead, and a request by a half dozen cadets to *The State*'s editor that McMaster "give the names" of his sources or "stand branded by faculty and students as a liar and slanderer," the reporter refused. The press, in questioning the trustees, learned that the board had investigated the incident and that the members conducting the inquiry held different opinions regarding Clemson's progress. While Simpson publicly declared that no serious problem existed at the school, M. L. Donaldson agreed with Senator Tillman and expressed discontent with the mechanical and agricultural programs.[28]

Officially, however, the board placed a different face on the matter. President Craighead, acting on a directive from the trustees, issued a letter to the press on 6 September. Quoting Simpson and Tillman, it noted that "after a most rigorous and searching investigation, no facts had been found which would warrant the charges of maladministration and incompetence made by *The State* reporter, and that President Craighead had come out of the ordeal unscathed." The letter added, however, that the trustees would soon consider "certain changes which they think will prove highly beneficial to the success of the College."[29] Behind the scenes, McMaster's

---

[27]*The State*, 16 Aug. 1895.
[28]*The State*, 24, 29 Aug. 1895.
[29]See the undated clipping from the *Charleston News-Courier*, in Klugh scrapbook, 42, RMCL/CU.

unacknowledged source appeared to be Clough W. Sims, an assistant chemist, whom Simpson interviewed on the board's instructions "as to his work and loyalty."[30]

Whether Williams Welch, an instructor in drawing whose resignation Simpson announced at the end of September, had also complained to the press, is unclear. Welch, however, had denounced Craighead to Tillman, asking the senator to write Craighead "a note requesting him to quit trying to hinder my work." The instructor maintained that the Clemson president "has proved himself utterly unfit for the place; he has very little honor; we can not rely on what he says; and, when he takes a personal dislike to a professor, he does all he can to damage his department." Welch accused his colleague in history, Morrison, of reporting the former's hostility to Craighead and, suspecting that the president had told Tillman about him, Welch informed the senator that "I know you are not a man to be deceived by him or anyone else."[31]

Amid the charges of poor management and the board's investigation, Craighead and Clemson's cadets and faculty continued with classes and even played host to hundreds of visitors from nearby Greenville. Smartly dressed cadets showed them around the campus, and afternoon activities featured a baseball game (between members of the college band and cadet corps), a regimental review, and presentation of a sword to Lieutenant Donaldson, back on campus during a furlough. Craighead, in giving the sword to the former Clemson commandant, appealed to the patriotism of the audience. "May you never have to unsheath it in war," he told the officer, "but I am certain that should you have to, it will always be in the cause of humanity—of God."[32]

The Conflict over Clemson's Mission

As the press stories about Clemson's problems gradually faded during the next few months, Craighead and the trustees moved to strengthen the faculty of the agricultural and mechanical departments and to purchase

---

[30]"Minutes of the Board," 25 Sept. 1895, 152.

[31]See Welch to Tillman, 13 Feb. 1895, Tillman papers, RMCL/CU. In noting Welch's resignation, Simpson remarked: "Oh, there has doubtless been more or less indiscreet talk, but not more than perhaps can be found in all college communities." Note *The State*, 27 Sept. 1895.

[32]*The State*, 31 Aug. 1895.

needed equipment.³³ The most serious question as the session of 1895 wound to its end, however, involved enrollment, which stood at roughly half the figure of the first year the college had opened its doors. It appeared unlikely that the previous months of turmoil had affected enrollment. A partial explanation for the decline lay in the economic recession still afflicting the state. Yet another cause was the rigorous standards for admission upheld by Craighead and the faculty. In November George Tillman assailed such standards and Clemson's mission, even challenging his brother in the chambers of the South Carolina general assembly to defend the program Clemson offered its students and the services it provided the farmers of the state. According to Tillman, the liberal arts and theoretical courses had gained far too strong a foothold at the college.³⁴

Despite the criticism, the new year brought with it a new session and, at least for a few months, relative quiet for President Craighead and the college. The agricultural and mechanical programs received larger appropriations.³⁵ The experiment station reached farther to serve the state's farmers, holding institutes in Orangeburg, Walhalla, Laurens, Fairview, Anderson, Manning, and Darlington, which Craighead attended along with professors Hardin, William L. McGee, and others. Craighead, moreover, explored with Senator Tillman and the president of Winthrop College the possibility of publishing "a paper suited to the farm and fireside," a journal useful for farmers, wives, and families.³⁶ The Clemson president sought to assure Tillman that the college was "doing far better work than ever before" and that "peace and harmony" existed "in our ranks." Although Craighead suggested firing Professor Sims, "whose enfeebled intellect has for a long time been under the domination of Raffanel and Welch," he lamented the loss of Professor McGee who, while teaching a class at the college barn in October, fell into a corn shredding machine and died.³⁷

---

³³Speaking of the mechanical department in his yearly report to the trustees, Craighead argued that "if Clemson is to compete with the technological institutions at the North, this department must not only have expert teachers, but must be equipped for thorough instruction in civil, electrical, and mechanical engineering." Note Craighead, "Report of the President," 31 Oct. 1895, 11-19.

³⁴*The State,* 16 Nov. 1895.

³⁵Craighead, "Report of the President," 31 Oct. 1895, 6.

³⁶Craighead to Tillman, 25 Mar. 1896, Tillman papers.

³⁷McGee, said Craighead, "was a man of stainless character, an able and conscientious teacher, a loyal and devoted friend." See Craighead, "Report of the President," 31 Oct. 1895; and Craighead to Tillman, 3 Mar. 1896, Tillman papers. Raffanel is unidentified.

The session in 1896 also produced Clemson's first graduates, fourteen who received degrees in agriculture (which included the senator's son, B. R. Tillman, Jr., whom Craighead had tutored in English) and eighteen in mechanics.[38] At commencement on 16 December 1896, Craighead chose to read from Oliver Wendell Holmes's *The Autocrat of the Breakfast Table*. The words were appropriate because they told the allegorical story of "high-bred three-year-olds" brought up for the start of the derby. The race did not last for just one day, but for a lifetime, and unexpected events helped determine how the race went, ten, twenty, thirty, forty, fifty years down the track.[39]

Two other events during the session not only made it memorable, but affected the subsequent history of Clemson. The first was the opening gridiron clash with the University of South Carolina, played on a Thursday, 12 November 1896, as one of the attractions of the state fair. The Clemson team, however, decked out in garnet and navy blue uniforms, lost the inaugural match, 12-6.[40] The second involved the visit of George Tillman to the campus. Tillman believed that the school emphasized liberal arts too much. His appointment to the college's board of visitors had probably resulted from attempts by his brother to show him what Clemson was and hoped to become. Although chosen the board's chairman, he remained unimpressed with what he saw and wrote a series of articles in *The State* alleging Clemson's failure as a farmers' college.

Tillman argued that Clemson should have at least three additional experiment stations and, basing his reasoning on the view that one military school (The Citadel) was enough for the state, that the college should drop

---

[38]For the graduating class, see Craighead, "Report of the President," 1896, *Seventh Annual Report of the Board of Trustees, President, and Officers of Clemson Agricultural College . . . , 1896* (Columbia SC: Charles A. Calvo, Jr., State Printer, 1897) 21; and Bryan, 49-51. Craighead observed in his letter to Tillman about the latter's son, 3 Mar. 1896, Tillman papers: "B. R. is helping me with my correspondence. After this year, you will not be able to make reasonable complaints about his English, though I fear neither Ben nor I will be able to please you altogether in the matter of style."

[39]A member of that first class, James Breazeale, vividly remembered the passage fifty years after Craighead had shared it with the young men who carried away Clemson's first sheepskins; see Breazeale to J. E. Hunter, quoted in *Anderson Independent and Daily Mail*, 30 Nov. 1943. Note, too, Oliver Wendell Holmes, *The Autocrat of the Breakfast Table* (Boston: Houghton, Mifflin and Company, 1892) 95-96.

[40]A few years later, a Clemson publication declared about the game: "It was the first defeat we ever received in foot ball, and will probably be the last that we will ever receive at the hands of our Carolina rivals." See The Foot Ball Aid Society, *Clemson's Football: An Historical Sketch of Foot Ball at Clemson College* (Charlotte: Queen City Printing, 1900) 16. The Clemson team had been organized in Sept. 1896.

its military corps.⁴¹ He also protested that Clemson unfairly received all federal funds supporting education because the school had been declared a land-grant institution. He complained, furthermore, that Clemson paid Craighead a salary of $2,700 a year while the president of "the South Carolina College [now university] must content himself with $2,500," the same amount, Tillman declared, that a professor of chemistry received at Clemson.⁴² In his final article, he called on the Clemson trustees and Craighead to stop proclaiming the college "a first-class institution for imparting a general education" and to reorganize it as an industrial and vocational school "where books shall be studied only one-half the time and manual labor performed the other half." Suggesting that Clemson and its leaders had dreams beyond the means of the state, Tillman added that "South Carolina is too poor to carry out the wishes of a majority of the board of trustees and perhaps the faculty, too, to erect Clemson into a second Ranessalaer [sic] polytechnic institute." He concluded that Clemson had been a "mammoth failure" in serving the state's farm families.⁴³

Neither the trustees nor Craighead attempted publicly to counter George Tillman's position. Although the latter's influence surfaced much later when Clemson established additional experiment stations in the midland and coastal regions of South Carolina, it is unclear whether his attack changed plans at the college to follow a polytechnic program blended with the liberal arts. However, just as the subject divided the Tillman brothers, the issue of how the arts could serve or become a partner with Clemson's technical mission remains even today one of the chief debates in the school's history.

Scarcely had George Tillman's finger-pointing ceased when Governor John Gary Evans, in his "state of the state" address in January 1897, declared that the fitting school at Clemson was a needless expense and that the state's secondary schools were adequately preparing students for college. If South Carolina students failed to meet Clemson's standards, said Evans, the school should lower them to accommodate the people it was to serve. In a slap at Craighead and the trustees, the governor added that Clemson "has been the idol of the Reform movement and the people have dealt with it with a lavish hand, and if there is any failure to fulfill the expectations of the people, the blame must rest where it belongs—upon

---

⁴¹*The State*, 16, 21 Aug. 1896.

⁴²According to ibid., 21 Aug. 1896, a chemistry professor at South Carolina College had to settle for $1,900.

⁴³Ibid., 23 Aug. 1896. Another article on 22 Aug. addressed the question of how many affirmative votes should be cast to hire or remove a professor or to allocate money.

the shoulders of those charged with its management." With an annual budget totalling almost $95,000, Evans maintained, Clemson seemed unfairly supported considering the needs of other state institutions and the fact that Clemson's students paid no tuition.[44]

Ben Tillman leaped immediately to Clemson's defense, insisting that the school was putting all funds to good use. He explained that the liberal arts, especially training in English, played a vital role at the college: "It was never the intention of the State to send forth boys from Clemson that could not speak and write English correctly and be able to enter into discussion with the ordinary college graduate on terms of equality."[45] He would be pleased, he added, to see the secondary school system improved enough to allow Clemson to close its fitting school. These sentiments lay near to the heart of Craighead who, following his resignation from Clemson in mid-1897, attempted to strengthen elementary and secondary programs in Missouri, Louisiana, and Montana so that high school graduates there would be spared further preparatory work once they reached college.

Craighead Leaves Clemson

Ironically, the few months before Craighead left Clemson were the quietest of his presidency. Attention regarding the college shifted to Columbia, where debate developed over Clemson's sole control over and use of the state's fertilizer tax. This "privilege tax," as it was called, yielded a high percentage of Clemson's budget. Combining the tax with federal funds and earnings from the Clemson endowment, the school paid its own way, requesting no state appropriations. But various politicians and educational leaders now questioned the college's right to receive the entire tax, an issue that became even more pressing when, by 1 May 1897, income from the tax had climbed to $60,000 for the year.

An obvious way to make such income promote Clemson's image and carry out its mission was to increase the number of farmers' institutes the college held around the state. By 31 March the college announced that institutes had been scheduled for Greer and Fairview in Greenville county and for Newberry and Chester county. Craighead explained that every county had the right to at least one institute, and he invited interested persons to write him soon regarding the subject.[46]

Most signs pointed during the spring of 1897 to a period of peaceful progress for Craighead and Clemson, following so many swirls of contro-

---

[44]Ibid., 13 Jan. 1897.
[45]Ibid., 15 Jan. 1897.
[46]Ibid., 2 Apr. 1897.

versy since he had received his marching orders four years earlier. However, he suddenly resigned in June to accept an invitation to become the president at his alma mater, Central College in Missouri. Evidence indicated that the previous turmoil centering on Clemson's mission and Craighead's role in it affected his decision. He explained to *The State* that, despite his "pleasant" relationship with the faculty and students and his hope never "to live among a more generous people than the Carolinians," he felt himself "better suited for the work of a literary than an agricultural college." Summarizing his feelings, he declared: "A call so hearty and unanimous from my alma mater and the growing desire on the part of so many of our people to see a real agriculturist at the head of Clemson are my reasons for resigning."[47]

His career in Missouri brought him greater esteem and honors. While he was at his alma mater, the University of Missouri conferred a doctor of laws degree on him. He left Central College in 1901 to assume the presidency of Missouri State Normal (now Central Missouri State University in Warrensburg) until he became the president of Tulane University in 1904. He was so well respected at the Warrensburg school that its supporters hastened to find the means to match any salary Tulane might offer.[48] Besides working for the benefit of education in Missouri, he now received an appointment to the Carnegie Foundation for the Advancement of Teaching, a post he held until 1915.

Tulane's board of trustees considered Craighead one of the South's most brilliant and able educators. Although he quickly became a controversial figure in New Orleans and Baton Rouge when he pressed the state legislature to vote public funds for Tulane, he increased its private endowment and contributed significantly to the expansion of the university's enrollment and reputation, even leading its medical faculty to international prominence. However, flaws in his personal character began creating ugly impressions of him. Piled upon his natural truculence and impatience was a drinking problem. Although not a chronic drinker, he nevertheless had difficulty holding even moderate amounts well, and when he was drunk he tended to be unbearably quarrelsome.[49]

---

[47]Ibid., 13 June 1897.

[48]Said the editor of the *Warrensburg Star:* "Where shall we look for a man of such ability as Craighead? He is honored throughout the State and he has made the State normal the best institution of its particular kind in the West. . . . " See *New Orleans Times-Democrat*, 20 Sept. 1904.

[49]John P. Dyer, *Tulane: The Biography of a University, 1834-1965* (New York: Harper & Row, 1966) ch. 8.

He left Tulane in 1912 for the presidency of the University of Montana, where he soon found himself embroiled in a political struggle involving Montana's governor and mining interests. They opposed Craighead's wish to place the state's four institutions of higher learning under one governing body, despite the president's argument that such a group would better channel Montana's limited resources towards achieving excellence within each academic program by avoiding costly duplication and bickering among supporters of the colleges. His opponents, also charging that he was drunk on the job, which Craighead stoutly denied, forced his resignation in June 1915.[50]

After two years as commissioner of education in North Dakota, he returned to Montana to join his sons in editing a newspaper, *The New Northwest*, which Craighead boldly proclaimed stood "for the rights of man." He continued his fight for better schools at every level and denounced his enemies who, in his words, exercised a "tyranny of depraved politics" over the state.[51] So appealing were his style and ideas that he was able to found two other newspapers. However, his new career, perhaps the one his temperament was best suited for, did not last long. He died of apoplexy on 22 October 1920. The manner of his death could not have been more fitting. Never a man of much patience, he died at the height of his rhetorical powers and amid conflict with his philosophic foes.

---

[50]Jules A. Karlin, "Conflict and Crisis in University Politics: The Firing of President E. B. Craighead, 1915," *Montana: The Magazine of Western History*, 36 (1986): 48-61.

[51]Keyser, *Mole Philosophy*, 72. The following idealistic credo appeared each week on the editorial page of the *New Northwest*: "To put hope in the hearts of aspiring youth; to strive to lighten the loads of all who toil; to champion the cause of woman in her fight for equality under the law; to fight for the fatherless and friendless, for the outcast, and for those who have none to help them; to encourage the upbuilding of schools and colleges; to help make Montana a great and rich state, an empire in itself, and her people the finest and noblest."

• *President Henry Simms Hartzog, 1897–1902* •

• 4 •
A YOUTHFUL ADMINISTRATOR HENRY SIMMS HARTZOG, 1897–1902

Michael F. Kohl

"Literally, greatness was thrust upon me," wrote H. S. Hartzog in describing his appointment in the autumn of 1897 as the third president of the Clemson Agricultural College. At 31, the youngest man to accept the presidency, Hartzog's personality and academic background differed sharply from those of his predecessor. Having impressed several trustees during interviews and unlikely to challenge the board's actions, he brought to Clemson extensive experience as an administrator and clergyman. Despite his youth, a contemporary described him as "a man of brilliant mind and unbounded energy and gifted with many talents."[1]

Although Hartzog instituted numerous changes and brought a greater organizational rigor to the faculty and students, relative quiet characterized most of his presidency. Clemson's enrollment climbed steadily and, under his guidance, the school reorganized its fitting or college preparatory program. It also established a textile department and witnessed the first major intercollegiate football successes led by one of the sport's future legends, John Heisman. However, the Hartzog years ended abruptly in 1902 after a major student walkout. Hartzog accepted the position of pres-

---

[1]See Samuel M. Martin, "A Personal Sketch of Dr. Henry Hartzog," undated, 1, in Clemson University (hereafter cited as CU) President's papers, Hartzog; and microfilm, Henry Simms Hartzog scrapbook, 1818-1971, 130. Both sources are in Special Collections, R. M. Cooper Library/CU (hereafter cited as RMCL/CU).

ident of the University of Arkansas, and Clemson administrators were left facing a cadet corps that would walk out again several times during the next three decades.

A Native Son and Preacher

Henry Hartzog was born in 1866 into a family of prosperous planters at Georges Creek near Olar in Bamberg county, South Carolina. The family had emigrated from Switzerland during the eighteenth century, and by the time of the Civil War Hartzog's father owned a 900-acre plantation and about thirty slaves. However, the devastation and aftermath of the war, which disrupted agriculture throughout the South, changed the fortunes of the Hartzogs. Of the eighteen members of the family who served in the Confederate army, only half survived the war. Henry's father managed to retain a portion of his wealth and moved into Bamberg by 1871. There he opened a general merchandise store and acquired a large house that had served as General William Tecumseh Sherman's headquarters when the Union army marched through the county.[2]

During his childhood Henry Hartzog developed an appreciation for enterprise and hard work. He attended a private school in Bamberg, helped in his father's store, and even involved himself in politics. When barely ten years old, he wore a red shirt and carried a pair of brass-knuckles in support of the Confederate war hero, General Wade Hampton, during the latter's disputed (but successful) gubernatorial contest with Governor Daniel H. Chamberlain.[3] It appears that only by chance Hartzog entered college six years later. His brothers-in-law, William Gilmore Simms and L. C. Rice, convinced him to take the scholarship examination for the South Carolina Military Academy (renamed The Citadel in 1910) when the institution, closed at the end of the Civil War, reopened in 1882. Hartzog, much to his surprise, won one of the two awards from his county and immediately enrolled in the academy. "The winning of this scholarship," he later recounted in his memoirs, "was the turning point in my life." He studied mathematics and engineering and proudly noted that "four years of gruelling labor were necessary to win a diploma" at the academy.[4]

Upon his graduation in 1886, Hartzog returned home and spent the next few years teaching and administering local schools. He served three years as superintendent of public schools in neighboring Allendale county,

---

[2]Hartzog scrapbook, 4-6, 87.

[3]See the clipping from the *Bamberg Herald*, 25 June 1936, in ibid., unnumbered page between 88 and 89.

[4]Hartzog scrapbook, 94-97.

then taught briefly in a log house at Hunter's chapel school, and in 1891 became superintendent of the graded school in Bamberg.[5] However, Hartzog also found time during these busy years to receive a divinity degree from the Southern Baptist Theological Seminary in Louisville, Kentucky. What prompted his decision is unclear, although a tradition in the Hartzog family claimed that it resulted from his romance with Cornelia Harley of Allendale, who wished to marry a preacher. Hartzog acquired his degree in 1889 and married Harley two years later. At one point following his marriage, he worked as Bamberg school superintendent, served as the first editor of the local newspaper, the *Bamberg Herald,* preached on Sunday mornings, did contract printing, and taught business courses in the evenings.[6]

Hartzog also actively promoted education and toured neighboring towns and counties encouraging students to enroll at Bamberg. Such dedication and industry attracted the attention of the trustees at Johnston Institute, a combined high school and boarding school in Edgefield county, which hired him as its superintendent in 1895.[7] The institute, because of its new administrator's recruitment efforts, grew rapidly in enrollment. It was hardly surprising that this success and Hartzog's background soon drew the interest of others, including South Carolina's most powerful politician and trustee of the new Clemson Agricultural College, Senator Benjamin Tillman, who lived in Trenton, only five miles from Johnston. Hartzog, in response to an invitation from the senator, visited Tillman's farm one Sunday in the spring of 1897, bicycling there with his young son on the handlebars. The educator later recalled that he did not think much about why Tillman had asked to meet with him or about why another Clemson trustee, M. L. Donaldson, had visited him at the Johnston Institute later in the spring. During the summer Hartzog had studied public speaking in Tennessee, and only on his return did he learn of Clemson's search for a new president and of the college's interest in him.[8]

His appointment by the school's board of trustees on 15 September 1897 to succeed E. B. Craighead was not without opposition. Some observers had hoped that another candidate, J. M. McBryde, the former

---

[5]Ibid., 103-11.

[6]Ibid., 111-16; and Michael Arrington, *Ouachita Baptist University: The First 100 Years* (Little Rock: August House Publishers, 1985) 45.

[7]Hartzog scrapbook, 124-28.

[8]Ibid., 130. Apparently Tillman also interviewed one of Hartzog's subordinates at the Johnston Institute "on Mr. Hartzog's qualities and administrative abilities." See Martin, "A Personal Sketch," 1, CU President's papers, Hartzog.

president of South Carolina College (now the University of South Carolina), would become the new Clemson head, while others viewed Hartzog as too young for the position. However, he received key support from Tillman and one of the members of the trustees' search committee, Donaldson, who had liked Hartzog's record. Not only was he a native son and proven administrator, but his background in mathematics and engineering would help silence those who had alleged that Hartzog's predecessor, Craighead, a humanist, had not possessed the academic training necessary to lead the infant agricultural and mechanical college. The trustees were also impressed with Hartzog's divinity degree and training at a military school.[9] He appeared an ideal choice to follow the trustees' lead and to enhance Clemson's image.

Growing Pains

The most immediate problem that awaited the young president was the drastic need to improve the college's poor sanitation and health systems which, during June 1897, had produced an outbreak of typhoid and malaria fever among the students and faculty.[10] The dairy in particular required alterations, and efforts were begun to stop drinking water used by cadets from being contaminated by the barnyard animals. Hartzog, determined to ensure health safety, personally inspected milk cans and, with the approval of the trustees, switched the primary vacation period for the cadets from winter to summer to avoid the worst time of the year for epidemics. During the summer of 1898, the buildings were disinfected and a system of ventilating pipes placed in the barracks. This led Hartzog to assure the trustees in his annual report at the end of the year that from "a sanitary point of view, Clemson College is one of the safest places in the

---

[9]Note, for example, the brief reference to Hartzog's selection in transcription, "Minutes of the Board of Trustees" (1888-1908), 15 Sept. 1897, 187, RMCL/CU; and Donaldson's role on the search committee, "Minutes of the Board," 4 Aug. 1897, 184. Other sources in RMCL/CU include Martin, "A Personal Sketch," 1, in CU President's papers, Hartzog; and "The Past Presidents of Clemson College," 1, read by Gaston G. Gage before the Forum Club of Clemson, 25 May 1948, in Gage papers, folder 28.

[10]According to the college surgeon, many cadets left the school; 35 were in bed with fever, eight of whom were "quite sick" and two or three "dangerously sick." See "Minutes of the Faculty," 18 June 1897, RMCL/CU. Hartzog later described the incident as "an unfortunate epidemic," but he did not indicate publicly how widespread the fever was; see H. S. Hartzog, "Report of President H. S. Hartzog to Board of Trustees," 1897, in *Twenty-Ninth Annual Report of the State Superintendent of Education of the State of South Carolina, 1897* (Columbia SC: The State Co. for State Printer, 1898) 210. In the same volume, 207, trustee president R. W. Simpson referred only to "the outbreak of sickness last June."

State."[11] Nevertheless, nagging problems persisted. When a cadet contracted scarlet fever in 1900, Hartzog took decisive action. He suspended classes temporarily, hoping to keep the college clear of a major epidemic.[12]

Such difficulties resulted in part because the development of sanitation facilities had not kept pace with the steady growth of the college. Reflecting Clemson's popularity among South Carolinians, enrollment increased from 337 students at the beginning of 1897 to 476 two and a half years later, making the school the largest agricultural and mechanical college in the South. Furthermore, numbers of applications for admission rose. "In anticipation of an overflow of students," Hartzog informed the trustees in December 1899, "we filed and dated the applications as received. Before College opened there were 200 more applicants than we could provide rooms for."[13]

The increases occurred despite continued poor economic times in the state. Hartzog identified several reasons for what he called "the wonderful popularity of Clemson College," including the return of larger numbers of upper classmen to the school. The cost of attending Clemson remained low. Students who demonstrated that their families were too poor to send them to school could receive scholarships from their county and tuition waivers. Although some opportunities existed for cadets to work on campus, Hartzog frequently discouraged applicants who hoped to find jobs at the school. Moreover, the college appeared to attract a better qualified student, as reflected in Hartzog's reorganization during 1897 and 1898 of the fitting school, a remedial program originally designed to prepare the many students admitted to Clemson lacking adequate preparation in high school.

---

[11]H. S. Hartzog, "Report of President," 20 Dec. 1898, *Ninth Annual Report of the Board of Trustees of Clemson Agricultural College . . . , 1898* (Columbia SC: The Bryan Co., State Printers, 1899) 13. See, moreover, the following sources in RMCL/CU: "Minutes of the Board," 4 Aug. 1897, 6 June 1898, 183-4, 195-8; Gage, "The Past Presidents of Clemson College," 25 May 1948, 9, Gage papers; and Hartzog to J. W. Hart, 12 Sept. 1898, Letterpress Book C, 5, CU President's office official correspondence. Only two years earlier the college faculty, against the opposition of some professors, had "decided that no hogs should be kept on the college grounds." Note "Minutes of the Faculty," 7 Feb. 1895.

[12]See "Circular Letter to Patrons of Clemson," 5 Dec. 1900, CU President's papers, Hartzog.

[13]Quoted from H. S. Hartzog, "Annual Report of President Henry S. Hartzog," 20 Dec. 1899, *Tenth Annual Report of the Board of Trustees of Clemson Agricultural College, 1899* (Columbia SC: Bryan Company, State Printers, 1900) 14. Note, too, Hartzog, "Report of President," 1897, 210.

Hartzog estimated in 1897 that only one in twenty students entering Clemson was prepared to do college-level work. This situation resulted from the lack of high schools to serve the overwhelmingly rural population of South Carolina. However, Clemson was in no position to deny access to the sons of its strongest supporters: the farmers. Hartzog's reform abolished the lower rank of the fitting school, changed the latter's name to "sub-freshman class," and introduced elementary agricultural and mechanical studies into its curriculum. Hartzog saw immediate results. "As a rule," he announced in December 1898, "the students going through our sub-freshman class do better in the higher classes than the others."[14]

Clemson's popularity also resulted, Hartzog maintained, from the success of the college's first two graduating classes. He did not mention that the vast majority of cadets never graduated and that the largest and smallest classes, respectively, were the subfreshman and senior. Instead, the president emphasized that many of Clemson's 62 graduates had acquired "technical positions" in agriculture and business or jobs in teaching. Obviously aware of the recent controversies over Clemson's mission to the state, Hartzog asserted to the trustees that a college "is read in the lives of its graduates. Clemson is willing to be judged by this test." The institution, he concluded with a note of pride, "is giving an education adapted to the spirit and genius of American life."[15] He succeeded to some degree in lessening the ratio between the subfreshman and senior classes and in increasing the number of graduates.

The creation of a textile department at the school appeared to confirm Hartzog's claim about the utility of a Clemson education. Some trustees, particularly D. K. Norris of Anderson county, had eagerly supported the new department. By 1897 cotton manufacturing had increased significantly in South Carolina, generating a considerable market for skilled workmen in the various areas of the business. Responding to the demand, Clemson added the textile department believing, as R. W. Simpson, president of the trustees, declared a year later, "that the best interest of

---

[14]The reform is discussed in Hartzog, "Report of President," 20 Dec. 1898, 13. For Hartzog's views on the preparatory class, see his scrapbook, 133; between 133-34 of the scrapbook is found Henry Hartzog, *The Mission of Clemson: An Address Delivered to the Students of Clemson Agricultural and Mechanical College at the Beginning of the Seventh Session, September 14, 1898* (Columbia SC: State Printers, 1898) 1-19.

[15]Of the 62 graduates, he reported, 28 were "holding profitable and responsible positions in scientific and technical pursuits, fifteen are teaching, and nine are pursuing post graduate courses." See Hartzog, "Report of President," 20 Dec. 1898, 19-20; and the booklet, "List of Graduates of Clemson College, S.C. and Occupations Presented, 1896-1901," in Mell papers, RMCL/CU.

the State would be served by placing skilled South Carolinians among the increasing number of mill operatives."[16]

Planning for the department began soon after Hartzog assumed the presidency.[17] The textile building, now Godfrey Hall, was completed in two stages. One of the speakers at the ceremony marking the laying of the cornerstone for the tower and first wing, D. A. Tompkins, a manufacturer of cotton mill machinery, praised the importance of technical colleges in modern society by citing their role in Germany's recent industrialization: "The South is in somewhat the same condition that Germany was after the Napoleonic wars. The anti-bellum [sic] wealth has been destroyed and dissipated as a result of the war. . . . Our people must learn to get more out of our natural resources than the simple products of the soil. . . ."[18]

The development of the textile department was a turning point in Clemson's history. It broadened the base of support for the college by forming ties with one of the most dynamic industries in the state and increased even more the school's applications for admission. The trustees first responded by declaring that the college's capacity to house students was strained to its limits and that the board preferred to turn away applicants rather than expand the amount of dormitory space.[19] By the spring of 1901, however, pressure intensified to handle a burgeoning student population that had swelled to 483 (of which 470 lived in the state). Admission applications that poured in compounded the problem. "For lack of room," Hartzog reported to the trustees, "we reluctantly rejected three hundred applicants. . . . A conservative estimate shows that had we had adequate dormitory accommodations and other laboratory facilities, Clemson would have opened with one thousand students this session."[20] The board reacted by raising the admission age to sixteen years and granting the president permission to admit applicants at fifteen only under spe-

---

[16]See his report for the trustees in *Ninth Annual Report*, 4; Hartzog scrapbook, 132-33; and Hartzog, *Mission of Clemson*, 20-24.

[17]"Minutes of the Board," 1 Mar. 1898, 189.

[18]"Remarks of Mr. D. A. Tompkins on Laying Corner Stone of Textile Building," CU Clippings file, Buildings-Godfrey Hall, RMCL/CU.

[19]*Ninth Annual Report*, 4.

[20]See H. S. Hartzog, "Annual Report of the President of the College," 24 Nov. 1900, *Eleventh Annual Report of the Board of Trustees of Clemson Agricultural College, 1900* (Columbia SC: The State Company, State Printers, 1901) 11-12. The enrollment figures are from H. S. Hartzog, "Annual Report of the President of the College," 24 Nov. 1901, *Twelfth Annual Report of the Board of Trustees of Clemson Agricultural College, 1901* (Columbia SC: The State Co., State Printers, 1902) 7.

cial circumstances. It also agreed to build a new dormitory, although not without the objection of some trustees.[21]

In addition to the textile department, Hartzog guided other major administrative projects during his presidency, including doubling the size of the chemistry building (now Hardin Hall), enlarging the mechanical engineering building, and constructing more farm buildings. Merely negotiating with contractors and suppliers and doing routine purchasing kept the president busy.[22] Still other duties demanded his time. For example, when he arrived at Clemson, the president's office had no secretarial staff, forcing Hartzog to answer letters by hand and make his own copies with a letterpress. Eventually he reduced the paperwork by using Samuel Martin, an assistant professor of mathematics and former subordinate of Hartzog's at the Johnston Institute, as a part-time secretary.[23]

Hartzog, presumably because of his belief in organization and his serving under the scrutiny of the trustees, also involved himself in daily matters affecting the students and faculty. For the record, however, he insisted in carefully administering Clemson because it was a new institution and many procedures had not yet been established. Not only did he register and place new students in their proper class but, according to Martin, he "believed in exercising the closest supervision over every department in the College and he would frequently 'turn-up' at the most unexpected times and places. . . . This close supervision of affairs of both faculty and students was not calculated to increase his popularity."[24] Although he declared to the trustees in 1898 that he enjoyed "co-operation and harmony in the Faculty," he admitted that because "of the unusually large attendance [of students], some of the professors are overworked." Faculty spent $28\frac{1}{2}$ hours per week in class (those who taught the smaller classes in the mechanical divisions spent more) and earned an average annual salary of $1,208. Some professors also lectured at the farmers' institutes sponsored by the college throughout the state. Furthermore, the entire faculty, in addition to spending time in two and three faculty meetings each week

---

[21]"Minutes of the Board," 2 Apr. 1901, 242; and the trustees' report in *Eleventh Annual Report*, 5-6.

[22]See, for instance, Hartzog's correspondence with J. E. Barton and Barr hardware company, June-Aug. 1901, CU President's papers, Hartzog.

[23]Martin, "A Personal Sketch," 1, in ibid.

[24]Ibid., 1-2.

Henry Simms Hartzog 1897-1902   Kate Salley Palmer

adjudicating breaches of the rules by the cadet corps, heard appeals from students regarding the classes in which the president had placed them.[25]

Such demands left little time for the faculty to do research. An example was a noted inventor and scientist who had received a doctorate from the University of Munich, Alexander P. Anderson, hired by Hartzog as botany professor and entomologist. Anderson attempted to continue his research into the effect of heat upon starch in grains, but because of his classes and other duties, he could not pursue such work and moved in 1901 to Columbia University. There he continued his study at the New York Botanical Gardens and patented the process for making puffed grains, which he eventually licensed to the Quaker Oats company. While at Clemson, moreover, Anderson apparently became the subject of much

---

[25]Hartzog, "Annual Report of President," 20 Dec. 1899, 16; and Hartzog, "Report of President," 20 Dec. 1898, 13. During 1900 Clemson held eleven institutes that attracted a total of 5,000 persons; the following year the school organized twelve institutes, plus a week-long one held on the campus that attracted 530 farmers from the state. See Hartzog, "Annual Report of the President," 24 Nov. 1900, 13; and Hartzog, "Annual Report of the President," 24 Nov. 1901, 10.

gossip when he romanced a maid (whom he later married) of another professor.[26] Both Anderson and the servant were of Swedish descent, which doubtless played a role in their meeting and their subsequent isolation from others on the campus. The distinguished Anderson represented one of the missed opportunities of the college, which possessed neither the financial resources to support research nor the ability to accept different social values.

Managing the college's finances also consumed much of Hartzog's attention. What concerned him and the trustees was that Clemson relied heavily on the state's fertilizer tax, which provided well over half of the institution's operating budget. The problem was that considerable fluctuations existed in the net receipts of the tax, ranging from a low of $52,453 in 1898-1899 to a peak of $88,105 in 1902-1903. The percentage of the school's net total receipts which the tax represented also varied widely, from 75.7 percent in 1898 to 58 percent in 1901. The resulting uncertainties in budgetary planning added to the trustees' close supervision of such matters and, on at least one occasion, the board instructed Hartzog to consult with its executive committee before incurring even emergency expenses. Despite such difficulties, the building program during Hartzog's administration was financed completely from the operating budget.[27]

"The most popular game is football"

Hartzog's reports to the trustees revealed that he not only believed in the value of athletics for education and human development, but that such activities contributed to the "wonderful popularity" of Clemson among the students and others in the state. "Manly sports are encouraged at the college," he first informed the board in 1899, "so long as they do not interfere with studies and other duties. The most popular game is football. . . . Such exercises promote temperance and help to build up an esprit de corps, so long as they are kept in moderate limits and gentlemanly bounds." In requesting funds in 1900 for a gymnasium and "a competent instructor to conduct it," he argued that "education which neglects the training of the body is defective" and that sports promoted "discipline . . . , because such exercises provide a natural outlet for surplus animal spirits."[28]

---

[26]See the clippings and correspondence in CU Faculty files, A. P. Anderson, RMCL/CU. Further information on Anderson is in Wright Bryan, *Clemson: An Informal History of the University, 1899-1979* (Columbia SC: R. L. Bryan, 1979) 201-202.

[27]"Minutes of the Board," 2 Mar. 1898, 191.

[28]See Hartzog, "Annual Report of President," 24 Nov. 1900, 16; and Hartzog, "Annual Report of President," 20 Dec. 1899, 25. Compare the space devoted in the president's report of 1900 to athletics with that of the small paragraph, 15, given to requesting more funds for the library.

Although intercollegiate sports had begun at Clemson and other Southern colleges before Hartzog's arrival, it was during his presidency that the school's football team began defeating archrivals such as South Carolina College. Playing its home games on Bowman field, named for an assistant coach and instructor in forge and foundry (R.T.V. Bowman, who died in April 1899), the team won four and lost two in 1899, which its boosters proclaimed "the most brilliant football season in the history of athletics at Clemson College."[29] But amid such success, Hartzog emphasized to the trustees that students "with unsatisfactory class records are not allowed to play in intercollegiate contests."

Prominence in the sport, however, first arrived when teams coached by John Heisman posted the best winning records. Most of the credit for bringing Heisman to Clemson went to Walter Merritt Riggs, a professor of mechanical engineering who coached the team in 1896 and again in 1899. Under Riggs's leadership, funds were acquired to hire Heisman (he received $1,800 per year, roughly a third more than the average salary of Clemson faculty), who was then coaching at the Alabama Agricultural and Mechanical College (now Auburn University). Heisman's 1900 team went undefeated and untied, beating Davidson, Wofford, South Carolina College, Georgia, Virginia Polytechnic Institute, and Alabama.[30]

The effort by Hartzog to promote athletics did not always meet with success or substantiate his claim that they encouraged an "esprit de corps" and "discipline" among the students. During the fall of 1898, for example, he attempted to organize the students for a trip by train to the Clemson-Carolina game at the state fairgrounds in Columbia. Although thousands saw the contest, which Clemson won 24-0, not enough cadets were willing to pay for the trip, so it was cancelled.[31] A few weeks after the game, moreover, the president was confronted with an unfortunate incident

---

[29]Quoted from The Foot Ball Aid Society, *Clemson's Football: An Historical Sketch of Foot Ball at Clemson College* (Charlotte: Queen City Printing, 1900) 52, which also observed: "The enrollment of students had been unusually large, thus affording a large number from which to select the team." See, too, John D. McCallum, *Southeastern Conference Football* (New York: Scribner's, 1980) 16: "By 1895, nine colleges from what is today the Southeastern conference had football teams."

[30]See Joe Sherman, *Clemson Tigers: A History of Clemson Football* (Columbia SC: R. L. Bryan, 1976) 5, 15; the Riggs papers (athletics) in RMCL/CU; and Hartzog, "Annual Report of the President," 24 Nov. 1900, 16. The Clemson football aid society, moreover, was organized in Dec. 1899 mainly to raise money for hiring "the best [coach] that could be obtained." Note Foot Ball Aid Society, 52.

[31]Hartzog to R. W. Simpson, 7 Nov. 1898; and Hartzog to Thomas W. Holloway, 8 Nov. 1898, Letterpress book C, 358-59, CU President's office official correspondence.

arising from a complaint that the Clemson team had stolen silverware while staying at a hotel in Augusta. Although Hartzog apologized for the team's behavior and managed to have some of the silverware returned, he—and, curiously, not the college—paid for the balance of what remained missing.[32]

The Walkout:
"Tottering on the Brink"

The large student walkout of 1902, the event that precipitated Hartzog's resignation, resulted from problems caused by the college's rigid military discipline and by the overcrowded conditions in the cadet barracks. How much Clemson's growth, such as larger classes and more demands on faculty, helped to trigger the uprising, is unclear. However, as the crisis unfolded, it became obvious that the students held bitter animosity towards some of their professors.[33] Controversy arose at the beginning of January when a senior, James Lynah, stole a turkey from the yard of W. S. Morrison, a professor of history, and the senior class petitioned the faculty to permit Lynah to graduate. Opinion among the faculty was divided regarding the case, because the cadet had been charged with insubordination in one of Morrison's classes during the previous semester, but had been exonerated upon appeal to the trustees.[34]

The faculty, whose meetings on such matters were secret, could not muster the three-fourths vote to expel Lynah, but suspended him indefinitely. When the cadet corps learned the results within a day, revealing a breach of confidence by someone on the faculty and sympathy with the students, Hartzog called a special meeting of the professors. According to the minutes of the meeting, he denounced the "eavesdroppers or traitors in the Faculty" and described "the condition of affairs" as "annoying, serious, and disgraceful." The professors quickly voted "that the roll be called and each member of the Faculty be called upon to state what he has said in regard to last night's proceedings since adjournment."[35]

---

[32]Hartzog to William Neill (Planters' Hotel, Augusta), 4 Dec. 1898, 11 Jan. 1899, Letterpress book C, 463, 484, CU President's office official correspondence. According to Hartzog's recollections, he paid for the silverware. His letter to Neill, however, indicated only that a check was sent.

[33]See *The State* (Columbia SC), 1 May 1902; and Simpson to Tillman, 4 May 1902, Tillman papers, incoming series, folder 27, RMCL/CU.

[34]Note "Minutes of the Faculty," 5 Nov. 1901; and "Minutes of the Board," 6 Nov. 1901, 247-48. See, moreover, Bryan, 177.

[35]"Minutes of the Faculty," 22-23 Jan. 1902. Lynah eventually graduated and became one of Clemson's most successful and loyal alumni; Bryan, 177-78, 267, 275.

But the difficulties mounted. By the spring pilferage on campus had reached such proportions that the trustees hired a detective to ferret out the culprits. Inasmuch as the sleuth spent most of his time spying on one of the professors, whom he suspected of being a ringleader, his efforts produced little. At their meeting in March the trustees urged the faculty to do all in its power to raise the moral level of the cadet corps and operate the college under more rigid discipline.[36]

The immediate cause of the 21 April student walkout occurred when the young assistant professor, R. N. Brackett, discovered a cadet, E. Allison Thornwell, taking test tubes from the chemistry laboratory supply cabinet. The professor reported the student to the faculty. The facts of the case were undisputed: Thornwell had taken the tubes from the supply cabinet to his work station and, although he had not attempted to leave the class with them, he had not asked Brackett's permission to take the tubes. The faculty met two days later to adjudicate this and a number of other disciplinary cases. The cadet admitted to taking the tubes, but denied that he had done anything wrong. The faculty, after giving the punishment of serving extra guard duty to a cadet who had been absent without leave and another who disobeyed an order that might have destroyed an expensive motor, voted fifteen to thirteen to suspend Thornwell for the remainder of the semester. Brackett and his fellow chemistry professor, M. L. Hardin, voted against the motion.[37]

On 28 April the faculty met again to consider petitions, signed by a vast majority of the sophomore class, to reinstate the cadet. The petitions stated that the punishment failed to fit the crime, that similar cases had not been dealt with as severely by the faculty, and that Thornwell's action had been a common practice for years. After refusing to reinstate the student, the faculty adjourned without permitting the sophomores to present other statements. The situation quickly deteriorated. The next day, sixty-nine of the seventy-four members of the sophomore class packed their bags and left Clemson by train. The senior class immediately supported the sophomores' action, and the junior and freshman classes prepared to leave on 30 April. Trustee chairman Simpson pleaded with the cadets to reconsider their joining the sophomores and promised that the board would hear the sophomores' grievances. The crisis spilled into the newspapers, which quoted the chairman as saying that "Clemson College was tottering

---

[36]"Minutes of the Faculty," 9 Mar. 1902; and Hartzog scrapbook, 137.
[37]"Minutes of the Faculty," 23 Apr. 1902; *The State*, 3 May 1902; and Bryan, 64.

on the brink" and that if the majority of the cadet corps left the school, irreparable harm would result.[38]

The trustees and the public, believing that discipline must be maintained or education would end, rallied to the side of Hartzog and the faculty. Questions soon arose, however, that diminished this support. The father of the suspended cadet, the Reverend J. H. Thornwell, protested his son's treatment and demanded that the trustees hear the case. The major complaint involved the issue of due process. Apparently, a delegation of the sophomore class had approached President Hartzog on the evening of 28 April and asked permission to leave the college to present its grievances to Simpson in nearby Pendleton. Hartzog, however, had refused the request and declared that he would present the students' petitions to the board chairman. The sophomores had not trusted the president to present their case fairly and they departed the campus.[39]

With the walkout continuing, the trustees met on 8-9 May 1902 to rule on the dispute. It soon became evident that the faculty, and the president in particular, were on trial more than the suspended student and his colleagues. This resulted in part because Hartzog submitted his resignation amid the demands for it by the sophomores. Further questions arose when the trustees rejected the official minutes of faculty meetings as unreliable evidence because a number of statements had been added to the original versions. As a consequence of the hearings, which were held in the chapel in the presence of the faculty and cadet corps, the board overruled the faculty by reinstating Thornwell and the entire sophomore class on the condition that they make up the classes they had missed.[40]

On the other hand, the trustees did not accept Hartzog's resignation, much to the dismay of many cadets. The situation remained confused into the summer, with both the faculty and students demoralized by the unpleasant affair. Brackett resigned as secretary of the faculty, and widespread drinking was reported at the June commencement. Clemson was the subject of several articles in the Columbia newspaper, *The State*, attacking the college and Senator Tillman.[41] Undeniably, the walkout and aftermath had produced problems for Hartzog, and possibly even between him and the trustees. He resigned in June 1902 for a second time and accepted the presidency of the University of Arkansas.

---

[38]*The State*, 30 Apr. 1902; "Minutes of the Faculty," 28 Apr. 1902; and Bryan, 64.

[39]*The State*, 1, 3, 10 May 1902.

[40]Ibid., 11 May 1902; Bryan, 66; and the faculty document signed by Brackett and Hardin, "The Walk-out of 1902," 22 Apr. 1902, Littlejohn papers, folder 79, RMCL/CU.

[41]*The State*, 13, 16 May, 6, 9, 17 June 1902.

While only in his mid-thirties, Hartzog revitalized the Arkansas school. During his presidency, its enrollment increased, numerous building projects were initiated, and Hartzog won the strong support of the faculty and students. This did not protect him, however, from being fired by Jeff Davis, the governor of Arkansas, who wished to appoint his own candidate to head the university. Hartzog then served as president of Ouachita Baptist College (now University), during which term its enrollment grew.[42] After leaving the college he sold textbooks and published a series of grade school workbooks, whose royalties permitted him and his family to live comfortably in St. Louis until his death on 15 December 1953.

---

[42] Arrington, 49-52; Hartzog scrapbook, 179-89; and Harrison Hale, *University of Arkansas, 1871-1948* (Fayetteville AR: University of Arkansas Alumni Association, 1948) 80-87.

• *President Mark Bernard Hardin, 1897, 1899, 1902* •

• 5 •
THE TRUSTED SUBSTITUTE MARK BERNARD HARDIN, 1897, 1899, 1902

Donald M. McKale

In the aftermath of the bitter student walkout of 1902, as the Clemson College board of trustees searched for a new president to replace H. S. Hartzog, the board appointed the school's first temporary chief executive. Its choice, M. B. Hardin, the senior member of the Clemson faculty, had previously served as acting president for five weeks in 1897, received the title of president "pro tem" from the board in August 1899, and occasionally led faculty meetings in Hartzog's absence from campus. Little of significance occurred during the brief terms that Hardin served in the presidency. However, the chemist and former Civil War veteran, who was distinguished by his long beard and thin face, continued to serve as second-in-command to Hartzog's successor, P. H. Mell. Shortly before Hardin's retirement in 1910 because of ill health, he refused another offer from the board to act as temporary president. Because of his conservative views, trustworthiness, and dedication to the school and its trustees, the board, upon receiving his resignation, praised him with "tributes of respect and appreciation" and later named the college's first chemistry building Hardin Hall.[1]

From Model Military Man to Chemist

Born on 14 August 1838 and reared in Alexandria, Virginia, Hardin proudly traced his ancestry on his father's side back to French Huguenots,

---

[1] See Wright Bryan, *Clemson: An Informal History of the University, 1899-1979* (Columbia SC: R. L. Bryan, 1979) 35; and microfilm, "Minutes of Board of Trustees," reel 2 (July 1908-June 1940), 1-2 Mar. 1910, in Special Collections, R. M. Cooper Library/Clemson University (hereafter cited as RMCL/CU).

who had emigrated during the seventeenth century from France to Canada and eventually to Virginia. His mother's family descended from Rice Howe, an Englishman who migrated to Virginia in 1620. Both families in colonial America numbered among their members prominent burgesses, magistrates, and judges. The young Mark Hardin enjoyed literature, art, reading, drawing, and painting. When only seven years old, however, he suffered deeply from the death of his mother. Consequently, his father, Lauriston B. Hardin, a longtime registrar of the United States navy department, influenced him significantly. The elder Hardin's integrity, impartiality, and precision in discharging his duties and in keeping records gave his son a bias in favor of the exact methods and measurements of the analytical chemist.[2]

The son, however, appeared in his early years destined for a military career. In September 1854 he entered the Virginia Military Institute (hereafter cited as VMI) in Lexington, Virginia, studying a course in science and graduating four years later at the head of his class of nineteen. He remained at the college, achieving the ranks of major and assistant commandant of cadets and the position of adjunct professor of chemistry, minerology, and geology.[3] A warm friendship developed between him and another instructor at the school, Thomas J. Jackson, who later became known as "Stonewall" as a Confederate leader in the Civil War. During the war, Hardin served in the Confederate army, first as major of artillery in the volunteer forces of Virginia, then as major of artillery in the provisional army of the Confederacy, and after 1862 as commander of the Eighteenth Virginia battalion. Wounded on two occasions and captured in 1864, Union forces sent him to the Old Capitol Prison in Washington, D. C. The evening he arrived there President Abraham Lincoln died from an assassin's bullet, which created such intense feelings that, for safety, Hardin, together with the other Confederate officers, were transferred to Johnson's Island in Lake Erie until the war's end.[4]

Upon his release on 3 July 1865, Hardin worked as an analytical chemist in New York city. He returned to VMI as a colonel and full professor of chemistry, positions he held until 1890. His reputation as a

---

[2]Note "Mark Bernard Hardin," an undated summary of his career, in Hardin papers, RMCL/CU.

[3]William Couper (an executive officer at VMI) to Mrs. J. W. Gantt (Hardin's daughter), 23 June 1953, in ibid.

[4]An extensive discussion of Hardin's war record is in Clement A. Evans, ed., *Confederate Military History: A Library of Confederate States History,* 12 vols. (Atlanta: Confederate Publishing Co., 1899) 5:629-30; and "Mark Bernard Hardin."

chemist developed quickly; the American Chemical Society, upon its organization in 1876, elected him to its ranks. He received membership in 1886 in the Lyceum of Natural History of New York, which later became the New York Academy of Sciences. While residing in Lexington, Hardin lived near to and developed a friendship with the former Confederate leader, General Robert E. Lee, then president of Washington College (now Washington and Lee University).

It is unclear why Hardin moved four years later to the newly established land-grant school in South Carolina, Clemson Agricultural College. Possibly the latter's attractive salary offer of $2,500 and provision for a house on the campus lured him and his wife, Mary M. Payne Hardin, and their eight children. Clemson was also a military school, which matched his background. Hardin's decision, moreover, probably resulted from the opportunity he found at Clemson to advance his career. The college, because it received much of its financial support from the state's privilege tax on fertilizers, assumed responsibility for fertilizer inspection in the state. For this important work the board of trustees chose Hardin in October 1890 as chief chemist at the college's experiment station and, three months later, provided him with a clerk and four fertilizer inspectors to work around the state. He took charge of the state's laboratory in Columbia, which analyzed fertilizers offered for sale in the state, and arranged for the laboratory's eventual removal to Clemson. Under Hardin's supervision the fertilizer department's work expanded rapidly; by 1909 it had nearly tripled its annual number of inspections of fertilizers, water, rocks, and minerals.[5]

Hardin also received the positions of professor and chairman of the department of chemistry at the college, which enabled him to play a significant role in the initial stages of the college's organization. The trustees appointed him head of a faculty committee, which included C. W. Welch (professor of physics) and C. M. Furman (professor of English), that prepared "a list of books" on "History, Biography, Poetry, Fiction, and mis-

---

[5]See Hardin's chart, "Yearly Averages of Analysis from 1891 to 1909, Inclusive," as part of his annual report to Mell, 23 Sept. 1909, in *Forty-First Annual Report of the State Superintendent of Education of the State of South Carolina, 1909* (Columbia SC: Gonzales and Bryan, State Printers, 1910) 305; "Hardin, M. B. Chemist," undated, in Clemson University (hereafter cited as CU) Faculty files, Hardin, RMCL/CU; Bryan, 35; transcription, "Minutes of the Board of Trustees" (1888-1908), 21 Oct. 1890, 19, RMCL/CU; and Alester G. Holmes and George R. Sherrill, *Thomas Green Clemson: His Life and Work* (Richmond: Garrett and Massie, 1937) 189. Information regarding the friendship of Lee and Hardin, and especially that of their wives, is from the author's interview with Hardin's granddaughter, Mary Hardin Keitt Hinton of Clemson, 12 July 1987.

cellany in general literature with reference books" that served as "the foundation of the College library." In addition, shortly after Clemson's first president, H. A. Strode, resigned at the end of 1892, which preceded the arrival of the first students at the college, the trustees showed further interest in Hardin's abilities by selecting him director of the experiment station "till," said the board's resolution, "a president is elected." Hardin, however, for unknown reasons, "respectfully declined" the offer.

But Hardin contributed in other ways to the college's development. The board continued the work begun by Strode in building the school by instructing the faculty to choose a chairman "who shall preside over their deliberations and act as the head of the college" and who, "together with two other professors also selected by the faculty," would "map out the details of the organization of the college." The faculty elected its senior professor of agriculture, J. S. Newman, as chairman, and Hardin and Welch to assist him. By March 1893 they had produced a comprehensive structure for the college that provided for the courses of study, daily exercises (reveille, drill, study hours, and taps), section marches, mass hall, post office, fire department, infirmary, laundry, dairy, janitors, equipment and furniture for buildings, and meeting of boys at the nearby railroad station.[6] The curriculum for the four-year program in chemistry drafted by Hardin included courses in general, industrial, agricultural, and analytical chemistry.[7]

Hardin's prominence with the board and faculty continued to grow following the arrival during the summer of the new president, E. B. Craighead. Those outranking Hardin on the faculty soon left. Conflicts arose between Craighead and Newman, resulting in the latter's resignation in January 1894, and the former president, Strode, retired as professor of mathematics in March 1895. A month later Hardin presided for the first time at a faculty meeting, substituting for the absent Craighead. He chaired such gatherings on five other occasions during the remainder of the year.[8]

Although no evidence exists that the trustees granted him official authority to substitute for the president, the minutes of faculty meetings first referred to Hardin as "Acting President" on 3 June 1896. In the following meetings which he chaired, furthermore, the faculty considered more sig-

---

[6]"Minutes of the Board," 1 Feb., 15 Mar. 1893, 74-75, 83-87; and "Minutes of the Faculty," 1 Feb. 1893, RMCL/CU.

[7]"Minutes of the Faculty," 1 Feb. 1893. This course of study remained essentially unchanged while Hardin headed the chemistry department; see, for instance, Clemson College of South Carolina, *Catalogue 1898-99* (Atlanta: Foote and Davies Co., 1899) 38.

[8]Note "Minutes of the Faculty," 10 Apr., 5 June, 9, 30 Oct., 6, 13 Nov. 1895.

nificant issues than when he had previously presided over it.⁹ Less than a month after Craighead resigned, Hardin's influence appeared to increase. The board, while searching for a new president, moved to provide Clemson with an element of leadership and someone who could function as the board's representative to the faculty. At their meeting on 4 August 1897, the trustees authorized Hardin to "act as President from [the] date of Pres[ident] Craighead's departure." In the eight faculty meetings over which he subsequently presided prior to the arrival in mid-September of the new president, Hartzog, he obediently implemented the board's agenda, which included securing the faculty's approval for and creation of "a two year [curriculum] in Agriculture and in Mechanics" and a course on metallurgy. When issues involving the requests of students for permission to enroll in "irregular" courses not prescribed in the major curriculums, Hardin also sought the ruling of the board.¹⁰

1902: President for a Month

Neither the faculty nor board minutes suggest why the trustees decided two years later, amid the Hartzog administration, to enhance Hardin's position even more by presenting him with an official title and empowering him to serve as the president's temporary replacement. However, Hartzog offered a clue in his annual report to the trustees in 1899 by observing that Hardin had substituted for him during the summer while the president had been ill. The board appointed Hardin on 8 August 1899 "Pres[ident] pro tem" and authorized him "to perform all duties of the Pres[ident] in his absence or disability."¹¹ Hardin's immediate situation remained unaltered; he merely continued his usual duty of chairing faculty meetings when the president was unable to attend. He owned the best attendance at such meetings during his two decades at Clemson, almost never missing them except during the illness and death of his wife in September 1901.¹²

But his position soon changed with the disruptive student-faculty conflict in 1902, which led to a major walkout of the cadets in the spring and

---

⁹Particularly involving decisions to punish cadets who had disobeyed college rules; ibid., 3, 10 June, 12, 17 Dec. 1896.

¹⁰Ibid., 1, 6, 8, 15, 16, 22, 23, 29 Sept. 1897. See, furthermore, "Minutes of the Board," 4 Aug. 1897, 185; the board elected Hartzog president at its meeting on 15-16 Sept. 1897.

¹¹"Minutes of the Board," 8 Aug. 1899, 213; and H. S. Hartzog, "Annual Report of President Henry S. Hartzog," 20 Dec. 1899, in *Tenth Annual Report of the Board of Trustees of Clemson Agricultural College, 1899* (Columbia SC: Bryan Co., State Printers, 1900) 27.

¹²Her death is noted in the undated handwritten note by Hinton, in Hardin papers. See, too, "Minutes of the Faculty," Sept.-Oct. 1901.

Mark Bernard Hardin (acting + Pro Tem) - 1897, 1899, 1902

Kate Salley Palmer

to Hartzog's eventual resignation. During the controversy, Hardin repeatedly opposed the majority of the faculty that voted to suspend or dismiss disobedient cadets. In the notorious incident that prompted nearly seventy sophomores to leave the campus, the faculty suspended a cadet, E. A. Thornwell, until the end of the term. The action had resulted from a bitter disciplinary hearing in which the student was charged with the unauthorized taking of test tubes from a chemistry laboratory cabinet to his desk. In the close vote that saw the professors deeply divided on the case, Hardin and his assistant (and later successor) in the chemistry department, R. N. Brackett, opposed the punishment, and Hardin was the only faculty member that rejected the faculty's decision to send a report on the affair to the board.

More than his colleagues, Hardin appeared to grasp the weaknesses in the faculty's position. Possibly sensing that the records of its hearings were incomplete, he declared that he "could not vote for any paper" being dispatched to the trustees "which did not consist entirely of evidence."[13] The

---

[13]"Minutes of the Faculty," 23 Apr., 1, 8 May 1902; and details of the incident in Bryan, 64-66.

trustees, eager to end the unrest among the students and criticism of the college in the state's newspapers, overruled the faculty and reinstated Thornwell. When Hartzog resigned because of the affair, the board selected Hardin "Chairman of the Faculty" and empowered him to act as "President Pro Tem of the College" until a permanent chief executive could be found.

Except for receiving the board's directive to repair a few of the buildings on campus and for presiding at a faculty meeting on 3 September, which considered only routine business such as student appeals regarding coursework and living quarters, Hardin did little during his month as Clemson's president. Two days later, the new permanent president, P. H. Mell, arrived on campus.[14] Hardin served Mell as loyally as he had the previous presidents, substituting for him at faculty meetings and providing a steadying influence on the faculty's most important committee, chosen by the board, that handled the disciplining of the students.

Despite the carefully monitored military regimen at Clemson, the cadets during the early years were rough and rugged individuals who often settled differences by brawling, dueling, and even shooting into an antagonist's room. Disciplining such behavior consumed much of the faculty's time. Hardin, from the time of his arrival at Clemson, helped establish policies regarding punishments and opposed demerits in the military department counting as part of a cadet's academic standing. Caution, consistency, and a sense of fairness characterized his votes on disciplinary cases decided by the faculty.

For example, Hardin rarely hesitated approving dismissal from school those cadets who repeatedly violated regulations, such as leaving the barracks or college grounds without permission, making false statements, or accumulating 100 demerits. Moreover, while he agreed with the expulsion in October 1897 of a cadet, W. A. Reckling, for stabbing another student during a fight, Hardin also called the faculty's attention "to the necessity, under the regulations of punishing" the injured cadet "for fighting."[15] When the evidence against a student was unclear or revealed that a professor had provoked the cadet's misbehavior, Hardin defended the boy.[16] In another instance, he was only one of two professors on the fac-

---

[14]"Minutes of the Faculty," 3 Sept. 1902; and "Minutes of the Board," 5-6 Aug. 1902, 261.

[15]See "Minutes of the Faculty," 27 June, 4 July 1893; 14 July 1896; 2, 6 Oct. 1897.

[16]As, for example, when he opposed in 1901 the faculty's suspension for a month of James Lynah for allegedly "behaving in a refractory and grossly disrespectful manner" in a class taught by W. S. Morrison, professor of history. An investigation of the incident had

ulty who voted not to dismiss two cadets for writing and posting a poem in the barracks "disrespectful to the Faculty and Trustees and calculated to produce disorder in the Barracks."[17]

Hardin, possibly because of his flexibility in judging disciplinary matters, earned the respect and friendship of the students. He often invited cadets to his home, always insisting, however, that they arrive promptly. His penchant for order and regimentation, moreover, occasionally extended to his family. Each Sunday, for instance, he marched his children across the campus to the Episcopalian church.[18] Regarding issues other than discipline, however, Hardin frequently resisted change; he opposed the beginning of classes an hour earlier each day and the dividing of school terms into four equal parts for making up class grades and reports to parents.

He chaired his last faculty meeting on 23 April 1908. By then he was nearing seventy years of age and his health had begun failing him. Consequently, when Mell resigned during the following year and the board unanimously elected Hardin to act as president, he declined the offer and then supported the board's appointment of W. M. Riggs, the head of the engineering department, as acting and, eventually, permanent chief administrator.[19] Even Hardin's usually meticulous supervision of the chemistry department appeared to slacken; in February 1910, for example, Riggs informed him "that certain of your instructors are in the habit of having rifle target practice behind your building." The president urged Hardin to investigate the matter immediately, because "it jeopardizes the safety of the employees in the [nearby] Laundry, and they are a little nervous about it."[20]

The board accepted Hardin's retirement in July 1910 with reluctance and voted him the title of "Professor Emeritus of Chemistry." There fol-

---

shown that Morrison had taunted Lynah by criticizing his "homeraising." See "Minutes of the Faculty," 5 Nov. 1901. Two months later, the faculty dismissed Lynah permanently for stealing a turkey from Morrison's yard. He eventually graduated from the college, however, and became one of its most dedicated and successful alumni; Bryan, 177-78.

[17]The vote to dismiss the students was 16-2; eventually, however, President Hartzog asked that the faculty reconsider the case, and the students were allowed to return on probation. See "Minutes of the Faculty," 16 Dec. 1898, 25 Jan. 1899.

[18]Hinton/McKale interview, 12 July 1987.

[19]His action is recorded in "Minutes of Board of Trustees," 2-3 Dec. 1909.

[20]See Riggs to Hardin, 24 Feb. 1910, CU President's papers, Riggs, RMCL/CU. Hardin replied on 2 Mar. 1910: "I have questioned each one of the gentleman employed in the Department, and also the janitor, and all say that there has been no shooting by anyone connected with the Department."

lowed an affectionate exchange of letters between Hardin and Riggs in which the latter asked Hardin to remain on the faculty discipline committee and to allow the president "to consult freely with you in regard to all matters where your long experience and more conservative judgment will be of the greatest service to me." Hardin, flattered by such requests, expressed happiness at being "of further service to the Institution in which I feel so deeply interested."[21] Upon his death on 26 April 1916,[22] Clemson buried him with military honors in the churchyard of the Old Stone Church.

---

[21]Note Hardin to Riggs, 15, 20 July 1910; and Riggs to Hardin, 3 Mar., 14, 18 July 1910; CU President's papers, Riggs.

[22]See Clemson headquarters corps of cadets, "General Order No. 81," 27 Apr. 1916, CU President's papers, Riggs; and the undated handwritten note by Hinton, Hardin papers.

• *President Patrick Hues Mell, 1902–1910* •

• 6 •
A SCHOLAR'S TURMOIL PATRICK HUES MELL, 1902–1910

Robert P. Green, Jr.

Before becoming in 1902 Clemson's fourth president, P. H. Mell had earned a national reputation for himself as a scientist and scholar. He had studied science because of his belief in its importance for humanity. In the view of a contemporary, Mell "was not a mere specialist; he was a scientist with broad sympathies and an attractive personality. . . . To him human life was the great thing, and even his beloved science got its value and its charm for him from the light that it threw on life and on the world we live in."[1]

Although Mell's presidency lasted until 1910, the longest yet in Clemson's brief history, it was marked from beginning to end by controversy and tumult. In his first weeks in office, unfortunate events surrounding the Clemson–South Carolina College (now University) football game resulted in the suspension of the contest for seven years. Moreover, the public criticism of Clemson that had characterized the administrations of Mell's predecessors continued during his. Although a strong defender of the concept of the agricultural and mechanical colleges, Mell nevertheless disagreed with Clemson's governing body, the board of trustees, over issues involving military training, discipline for the cadets, and the relationship of the commandant to the president. The conflict resulted not only in Mell's resignation, but in his public denunciation of the board.

---

[1]Quoted from Fred H. H. Calhoun, "Memorial of Patrick Hues Mell," *Bulletin of the Geological Society of America*, 30 (31 Mar. 1919): 45-46. A brief sketch of Mell's career is also in *Dictionary of American Biography* (hereafter cited as *DAB*), ed. Allen Johnson and Dumas Malone, 10 vols. (New York: Charles Scribner's Sons, 1958) 6:515.

The Making of a Geologist

Mell was born in Penfield, Georgia, on 24 May 1850, the son of Patrick Hues and Lurene Howard (Cooper) Mell. His father was a Baptist minister and for many years a professor at Mercer University. Late in his life Mell's father accepted the chancellorship of the University of Georgia, where Mell enrolled in 1866, receiving his bachelor's degree in 1871 and degrees in both chemical and mining engineering in 1872 and 1873, respectively.[2]

Although raised in a college atmosphere, it was in the outdoors that Mell found his great love, the natural sciences. As a youth he took long excursions in the woods, becoming familiar with the great variety of southern plants and minerals. His first job after graduation in 1873 allowed him to remain in the outdoors as a consulting mining engineer. With the establishment of the Georgia State Agricultural Department in 1874, however, Mell was called to the laboratory as a state chemist. In that capacity he analyzed soils and commercial fertilizers which, at the time, were first being manufactured. Yet chemical work disagreed with Mell, and in 1877 his health broke down, forcing him to return to the outdoors.

Again serving as a mining engineer, he traveled on foot and horseback throughout the South, collecting geological specimens in the process. During this period he was invited by the editors of the *Engineering and Mining Journal* to write a series of articles on the clays, gold, and corundum of the region. One result of his studies was the display of a collection of Alabama minerals at the 1878 industrial convention in that state. The president of the Alabama Agricultural and Mechanical College (after 1899 the Alabama Polytechnical Institute and since 1960 Auburn University) was so impressed by the exhibit that he offered Mell the chair of natural history at his school. Although later in life he would argue that his eighteen months surveying Alabama's minerals had been the happiest of his life and, on occasion, regret that he had not dedicated himself entirely to applied geology, he returned to academics in the fall of 1878. Shortly after his arrival at the Alabama Agricultural and Mechanical College, Mell completed work on and received his doctor of philosophy degree from the University of Georgia.

Despite his return to the classroom, he spent his vacations in the mountains or at Claiborne, Alabama, where he collected the fossils that provided the basis for a natural history museum at Alabama Agricultural

---

[2]Unless otherwise noted, the material in this section is drawn from Calhoun, "Memorial of Patrick Hues Mell," 43-47.

and Mechanical College. Arranging a system for the exchange of specimens, and thus acquiring many valuable exhibits, Mell established a collection that became nationally recognized and considered by many the finest in the South. Unfortunately, the building holding the collection burned down in 1887, completely destroying the collection.

The breadth of his scientific interest was reflected in his work with the weather service and Alabama experiment station. The state weather service was initiated in 1884, and Mell was asked, in addition to his college duties, to take charge of the meteorological work in Alabama, Georgia, and Florida. Later, when state bureaus were formed, he continued in the directorship of that in Alabama, developing the system of weather signals that is still in use today. Mell retained this position until 1893, in the interim turning down a number of requests from Washington, D.C., that he take the job of chief of the national weather bureau. From 1898 until 1902 Mell was connected with the Alabama experiment station. His experiments in cotton breeding, most notably crossing American and foreign varieties in an attempt to improve the length and strength of the fiber,[3] developed such a reputation for him in that arena that he was asked to arrange the cotton exhibit of the southern states for the Paris exposition in 1900.

During his tenure at the agricultural and mechanical college in Auburn, he was offered the presidency of Mercer University in 1893 and North Georgia Agricultural College in 1897, turning both down, however, to remain in Alabama. When offered the presidency of Clemson in August 1902, he accepted, although it is unclear why. Nominated for the position by Senator Benjamin Tillman, Mell won the job over four other candidates, including K. G. Matheson, for many years president of Georgia Tech.[4] Not only was the South Carolina school's new president a nationally known scholar, but he was a dedicated teacher and major proponent of the concept of the agricultural and mechanical colleges.

The "Big Game" of 1902

Mell had barely assumed his new duties when he found himself embroiled in the controversies that had plagued the administrations of his

---

[3]*The Birmingham News*, 10 Sept. 1902.

[4]The transcription, "Minutes of the Board of Trustees" (1888-1908), 30 Aug. 1902, 262, in Special Collections, R. M. Cooper Library/Clemson University (hereafter cited as RMCL/CU), noted only "that the ballot for P. H. Mell for President of the College and Director of the Station was unanimous." Regarding those nominated for president of the college at the trustees' meeting the previous day, see the minutes for 29 Aug. 1902, 262; and Wright Bryan, *Clemson: An Informal History of the University, 1889-1979* (Columbia SC: R. L. Bryan, 1979) 67.

predecessors, E. B. Craighead and H. S. Hartzog, regarding Clemson's educational mission and control over its students. The issue this time, however, was football which, in the autumn of 1902, was very much in the air. The "big game" between Clemson and South Carolina College was scheduled for 30 October at the fairgrounds in Columbia and, as usual, the state was abuzz with anticipation. Newspaper articles covered both teams and provided interviews with the coaches and managers and position-by-position analyses of the squads.

Interest in the game that year was, if possible, even greater than in the past. Clemson had a new president, but the school had also retained the services of the indomitable football coach, John W. Heisman, already on his way toward legendary stature. Both Clemson and Carolina were undefeated, and the latter was fielding what many considered to be their best team in years. "The friends of both institutions and those interested in football in general are shaking their heads in doubt as to the result," declared the Columbia paper, *The State*. A Clemson fan argued that "Carolina realizes that never before have her chances for defeating the Tigers been so bright and she is bending every effort to the task. But Clemson realizes that fact also and is working tooth and nail to roll back the tide of defeat staring them in the face."[5]

Although the prose was melodramatic, the sentiments were those which many of today's fans could appreciate. Perhaps these early games, and this one in particular, set the tone for the continued rivalry. In any case, *The State*, with misguided prescience, closed its pregame treatment by predicting: "No matter how fierce and intense the struggle, good feeling is sure to characterize it as always and that, after all, is the finest part of these Clemson–Carolina games."[6] But *The State* was wrong. The events surrounding the game led to its suspension for seven years and, more immediately, the first of many defenses of Clemson by its new president.

The game itself was well played, by all accounts, and Carolina won, 12-6. "Carolina simply outplayed us," Heisman was quoted in the press. "She has a right to feel proud of her magnificent team and the great game they put up yesterday. The Clemson tigers were simply up against a proposition they could not solve."[7] However, after the game, when several Carolina students displayed a banner "representing the Clemson tiger with

---

[5]Note the undated clipping, "When The Tigers Have Come To Town," *The State* (Columbia SC), in Mell papers, RMCL/CU.

[6]Ibid.

[7]*The State*, 1 Nov. 1902. A brief summary of the game is in Joe Sherman, *Clemson Tigers: A History of Clemson Football* (Columbia SC: R. L. Bryan, 1976) 16.

a twist in his tail and a game cock crowing from his perch on top of the tiger," an overenthusiastic group of Clemson cadets tore it down, and in the process at least one cadet and a number of Carolina students were roughed up. Warned that the same fate would await them should the banner appear in the next day's parade, South Carolina students felt they had no recourse but to reconstruct the display and do just that. Consequently, immediately after Friday's parade, the cadets converged en masse upon a much smaller group of Carolina students outside the gates of the college, demanding the destruction of the banner. A potentially disastrous situation was avoided, however, when Christie Benet, Jr., a recent graduate of Carolina who had helped coach the Gamecock football team (and who later, ironically, would be elected a life trustee of Clemson), offered to stand for Carolina against any individual Clemson might put forward. Seeing no takers, Benet negotiated a compromise with the cadets, and the banner—understood to include the symbols of both schools—was burned.[8]

The press had a heyday with the event. *The State*, in an editorial on 3 November, decried the cadets' "raid" and called for the dismissal of Clemson's commandant of cadets, Lieutenant E. A. Sirmyer. According to Benet's account, Sirmyer had warned the parade committee that he would not be responsible for the actions of the cadets should the offending banner appear in Friday's parade. "There is no evidence anywhere," *The State* argued concerning Sirmyer, "that he gave orders which if obeyed would have restrained the cadets from their march upon the South Carolina college. They openly announced their intention to make this march as soon as they returned to their headquarters after the parade—and at that moment Lieut. Sirmyer disappeared from the public view." The paper called on the Clemson trustees to take action and suggested that the South Carolina general assembly should follow developments closely.[9]

Nothing was done to Sirmyer, and on 6 November *The State* published President Mell's analysis of the affair. "Unwilling to remain silent while [his] boys [were] under fire," Mell explained the admittedly overenthusiastic reaction of the cadets and attempted to exonerate Sirmyer.[10] Although the defense itself was hardly notable, the circumstances surrounding it presaged a number of concerns that Mell would face during his presidency at Clemson. First, the claim that Clemson failed to maintain adequate discipline among its students occurred only a few months after the mass cadet walkout that had forced the resignation of Hartzog, Mell's pre-

---

[8]See Christie Benet, Jr., to the editor, *The State*, 2 Nov. 1907; and Bryan, 76-77.
[9]*The State*, 3 Nov. 1902.
[10]See Mell's letter to the paper in *The State*, 6 Nov. 1902.

decessor. Moreover, discipline was an issue with which Mell had to contend a number of times. On most occasions, it would arise in the context of the military training of the cadets, thus providing a second major area of controversy, the question of the nature of military training at Clemson and, more specifically, the relationship of the commandant to the president.

Finally, *The State*'s rebuttal to Mell's letter of 6 November pointed out that in the past the paper had been "sincerely desirous to find in the college the fullest justification for its existence and for the very liberal support given it by the State of South Carolina."[11] Implicit in this statement was a recognition that many South Carolinians still doubted that either Clemson's existence or its "very liberal support" were justified. Mell, therefore, was forced to expend much effort during his presidency attempting to defend the notion of agricultural and mechanical education in South Carolina and protect Clemson's source of state funding. In this regard, however, it is difficult to imagine that the institution could have found a more able advocate.

Defending the Clemson Education

Mell was, above all, one who valued education. But while he rigorously supported agricultural and mechanical schooling, he did not limit himself to that domain. During his presidency at Clemson he argued for the importance of higher education in general and supported the expansion of secondary schools. A letter in 1907 to R. H. Edmonds, the editor of the journal *Manufacturers' Record*, reflected his concern:

> Sometimes I fear that the country is running wild over the building of factories and the extension of railroads and the vast income from the crops that they forget the importance of the moral and intellectual side of life. They become so much engrossed in the chase after the almighty dollar they lose sight of the importance of developing the moral and intellectual side of their nature. . . . I believe if the South will take advantage of her increase in wealth and use a generous portion of this money in equipping schools and colleges it would do much toward helping the condition of the country.[12]

Yet Mell's view of education was not totally liberal in nature. An element of utilitarianism, tinged with regional pride, also manifested itself.

---

[11]Ibid.

[12]Mell to Edmonds, 18 Feb. 1907, in Clemson University (hereafter cited as CU) President's papers, Mell, RMCL/CU.

"The Southern youths," he wrote in the same letter, "must be trained to take charge of our factories and railroads and must be equipped to develop our industrial resources and in order to do this, they must be well prepared in college." On a previous occasion he had maintained to the journal that the South was "forging rapidly to the front in all industrial and intellectual activities, and will soon take its position in the United States in industrial lines which it occupied many years ago as a section of great wealth and refinement."[13]

At the beginning of 1907 the general assembly passed legislation appropriating funds for the establishment of a high school in each county in the state. Mell enthusiastically supported the move, even to the extent of recommending the abolition of the preparatory class at Clemson. "I am urging the Board of Trustees," he wrote to C. C. Thach, president of the Alabama Polytechnic Institute, "to abolish the Preparatory class as soon as practicable, and gradually to raise the standard of entrance in order to help sustain the high schools which are now being established in the counties of South Carolina."[14]

Mell nevertheless recognized the problems inherent in raising admission standards too high. "I think, however," he continued in his letter to Thach, "that it would be an unwise thing for the Agricultural and Mechanical Colleges to raise their standards above the conditions of the schools of their respective States."[15] He involved himself in a lively debate on the issue with Craighead, who had become the president of Tulane and a major advocate of the adoption of the Carnegie unit, a standard of measurement for high school credits accepted by American colleges and universities. Noting that Clemson depended "largely" on financial support from state funds, Mell told Craighead that "if I was in favor of your policy and should endeavor to raise the standard of the institution above the condition of the schools, I would bring such condemnation upon myself and upon the college as to practically cut off our income."[16]

---

[13]See in ibid., Mell to Edmonds, 18 Feb. 1907; and Mell to *Manufacturer's Record*, 18 Oct. 1906.

[14]Mell to Thach, 13 May 1907, in CU President's papers, Mell.

[15]Ibid.

[16]Mell to Craighead, 27 Mar. 1907, in ibid. Although the Carnegie Foundation did not invent the unit for measuring high school credits, it so popularized it that it became known as the "Carnegie unit." A writer in 1911 parodied the unit thus: 45 minutes make an hour; 5 hours make a week; 36 hours make a unit; 15 units make a matriculant; 5 matriculant hours (for one year) make a point or count; 60 points make a degree. See John S. Brubacher and Willis Rudy, *Higher Education in Transition: A History of American Colleges and Universities, 1636-1976*, 3rd ed. (New York: Harper & Row, 1976) 249, 475 n. 45.

Conscious of the public attacks on Clemson before he had arrived at the college, Mell was careful to do nothing that would produce a public outcry against the school. There were still many South Carolinians at the turn of the century who questioned their state's need for Clemson. Some felt that it was not achieving the objective for which it had been founded, and even more opposed the means by which it was funded and the way its trustees were selected.

The college, for example, was criticized for failing to produce a large number of agriculturalists. "Clemson was founded primarily as an agricultural college," observed the Anderson paper, the *Daily Mail*, in June 1903, "and yet, judging from the list of graduates and the courses of study they have pursued, it would seem that the science of agriculture has a very small place in the curriculum."[17] Although there were only eight graduates in agriculture that year (there were many more by the end of Mell's presidency), it was not difficult for Mell to respond to such charges. "Every boy that applies for entrance in Clemson," he informed the paper, "is required to take a year's course in agriculture at least, even though he may enter for the purpose of becoming a civil or electrical engineer." He also reminded the paper that Thomas Green Clemson's will specifically prescribed an agricultural *and* mechanical institution, as did the Morrill Act, a source of federal support for the school. Emphasizing the inherent value of learning regardless of the major, the Clemson president concluded that "it makes no difference what course of education the farmer's son takes [because] he goes home a better citizen and far more able to cope with the serious problems of life than he was before he completed his education."[18]

Another target of critics was the method used by the state to fund the college. By statute, Clemson scientists were responsible for testing and certifying the quality of the commercial fertilizer sold in the state. The fertilizer manufacturers paid a "tag tax" to cover the cost of the service and, one can assume, passed the cost along to the farmers. All the funds generated from the service went to the college. This produced a hefty, and controversial, annual sum. The question of the college's purpose often led opponents to attack the funding. Clemson's "income is far beyond its needs," declared the *Columbia Record*, "but because it was the 'farmer's college' legislators did not have the backbone to divert some of the income to purposes where it would do some good in relieving the strain of

---

[17]See the undated clipping, "Few Farmer Graduates," from *Anderson Daily Mail*, in Mell papers.

[18]Mell to *Anderson Daily Mail*, 20 June 1903, in ibid.

taxation about which there is so much just complaint."[19] Repeatedly Mell had to explain that the funds generated by the fertilizer tax were consumed by the services the college provided to farmers: farmers' institutes, the experiment station (including its free bulletins), veterinary inspection, entomological inspection, and, not least of all, quality-controlled fertilizer. Subtracting these costs from the total figure left a much more modest per-pupil expenditure than most realized.

Yet the attack on the funding of Clemson was often merely a preface to a greater concern. "The State of South Carolina," John J. McMahan, a candidate for governor, maintained in a speech in August 1906, "has no authority in the government of Clemson college." He added that "a majority of the board of trustees . . . [has] the power to perpetuate themselves and thus rule forever this institution upon which the State of South Carolina should lavish her wealth. No State institution should be beyond state control."[20] McMahan, however, addressed an even touchier subject for Clemson proponents. "It has long been felt," he proclaimed, "that Clemson college is a closed corporation, largely officered by the kinsmen and other favorites of these life trustees, who will control even beyond the period of their natural lives, because they choose their successors. Nepotism, the bane of efficiency and fairness, honeycombs the institution."[21] This last was a charge that Mell was never able to counter and, ultimately, one with which he agreed. In fact, tension between Mell and the trustees over such issues as nepotism and the board's involvement in the day-to-day affairs of the college finally led to his resignation. But the proximate cause of his split with the board was the issue of military discipline at Clemson.

The Military
and Conflict with the Trustees

The most vexing problem with which Mell had to contend revolved around the college's military department. It appears that South Carolina produced its share of free-spirited youth at the turn of the century, not readily susceptible to strict military discipline. Therefore, clashes between the students and the college and military authorities were not uncommon. Mell's attitude toward the students was, in most situations, understanding

---

[19]Note "The Farmers' College," *Columbia Record,* quoted in *Daily Mail,* 19 June 1903, clipping in Mell papers.
[20]See the speech by McMahan, 21 Aug. 1906, quoted in unidentified clipping in Mell papers.
[21]Ibid.

and fatherly. While he rigidly prohibited some actions (he particularly condemned hazing), others he recognized as the thoughtless pranks of "boys." Thus, although he felt that authority had to be maintained, he was not an advocate of the overbearing use of military discipline, especially when such appeared to interfere with the primary mission of the college, the schooling of the boys in their academic subjects. Unfortunately, Mell suffered a succession of commandants whose actions placed his desire for moderation in jeopardy.

Already in February 1903 his correspondence with Sirmyer reflected the president's concern over the commandant's conception of his disciplinary role. Perhaps Mell felt that Sirmyer was too much the martinet. Later, in loose handwritten notes to himself, Mell evidently attempted to draft the basis for an understanding with Sirmyer. "Demerits must not be given by Commandant so as to send boys home," he wrote. That should be left to the president and faculty discipline committee. Removal from campus needed only result because of "absences from Educational duties and for violation of moral rules." Moreover, Mell believed, the cadet should be "allowed to decorate his rooms with pictures" and not be bothered by "such petty reports as cup in place, etc."[22] At the beginning of 1904, he compared the hours of military duty at Clemson to those required at other agricultural and mechanical schools, finding that Clemson demanded substantially more.

By the spring, tension between the president and commandant had become obvious. It came to a head after the annual inspection of the college by the federal government's War Department (required under the Morrill Act), in which Sirmyer evidently unburdened himself to the inspecting officer, Captain C. L. Beckwith, whose report in June was quite negative. "Very little importance appears to be attached to the military instruction," he observed about Clemson. "The officer on duty . . . is not cordially supported by the faculty in the matter of military instruction and discipline."[23] Mell, suddenly threatened with the removal of War Department support, wrote a lengthy letter to the adjutant general in August 1904 indicating Clemson's position and making a distinction between the school and institutions like West Point and Virginia Military Institute. He maintained that Sirmyer had "failed to catch the position the president holds" at Clemson and that the commandant mistakenly believed that the

---

[22]See Mell's loose-leaf notes (1904) in CU President's papers, Mell.

[23]Beckwith's report regarding the Clemson military department, 3 June 1904, is in ibid.

college "should be governed in the same way as West Point, that the military department should be prominent."[24]

On another occasion he made his position even clearer, emphasizing to J. L. Snyder, the chairman of a committee of the Association of Agricultural Colleges and Experiment Stations studying military requirements for such schools, that he did "not intend to make soldiers of our students." Instead, Clemson sought "to reap from the Military work all that is valuable in the way of exercise, the proper training of the body, the admirable features of the drill. . . . Moreover, it becomes necessary to limit the military exercises so that the other duties of the college may be properly carried on."[25] Mell, therefore, argued that the military aspect of the school should be kept in perspective. By the 1904-1905 school year, Clemson maintained three hours a week for drill and two hours for military science, one for juniors and one for seniors. The commandant re-

---

[24]Mell to adjutant general, 4 Aug. 1904, in ibid.
[25]Mell to Snyder, 11 Nov. 1904, in ibid.

tained responsibility for the barracks and discipline. The president did not want the military work reduced any further.[26]

Evidently Clemson successfully addressed the War Department's concerns in the fall of 1904. Sirmyer was transferred, and a new commandant of cadets was appointed, Captain Charles D. Clay. The latter, according to Mell, was "a gentleman having a clear conception of what the military regulations should be in a college of this character." The president and military department also stressed to the trustees the importance of the mess hall and its steward, A. Schilletter, in improving the food for the students, and of the campus doctor, Arthur M. Redfern, "who exerted every effort to keep the boys in good health."[27] However, although Clay was successful in directing the boys during his first year at Clemson, difficulties soon arose regarding him. He had been wounded during the Spanish-American war and, as a result of the wounds' failure to respond to treatment, he began to rely on drink and/or drugs to relieve his pain. As a consequence he was extremely erratic in the application of discipline—one moment arbitrary, the next conciliatory—which played havoc with his relationship to the cadets.[28]

Problems reached a peak during the 1906-1907 academic year. On 1 April 1907, in an April Fools' Day prank, the cadets absented themselves from class and marched around Bowman field dressed as women. Chastised for their actions and evidently contrite, they deported themselves excellently the next day at the annual inspection by the War Department. Clay, however, had now lost the respect of his charges. The "shirt tail parade" during the night before commencement in June exacerbated relations. Early on the morning of 11 June, seniors relieved from their military duties marched around campus, stopping at professors' homes and serenading the inhabitants. Upon their return to barracks, Clay ordered them arrested. The seniors, feeling that his response was not merited, refused to comply. Clay was incensed and demanded that the trustees withhold the diplomas that were to be awarded the following day.

However, neither the board nor the administration supported the request. Subsequently, Clay wrote a scathing report to the adjutant general concerning the college's failure to support him as commandant and pun-

---

[26]Mell to Snyder, 7 Jan. 1905, in ibid.

[27]See P. H. Mell, "Annual Report of the President of the College," 1 Oct. 1904, *Thirty-Sixth Annual Report of the State Superintendent of Education of the State of South Carolina, 1904* (Columbia SC: Gonzales and Bryan, State Printers, 1905) 348; and Mell to R. W. Simpson, 26 Sept. 1904, in CU President's papers, Mell.

[28]Mell to adjutant general, 10 July 1907, CU President's papers, Mell.

ish insubordination and rioting.[29] Amid the crisis Clay was relieved of his duties, but the War Department hesitated to appoint a successor. A delegation composed of President Mell and a number of senior professors quickly visited Washington, D.C., and the War Department, and the issue was resolved once again to the satisfaction of the military authorities, who posted Captain J. C. Minus as commandant at the college.

Minus, too, made a good first impression. A native of the state, he had attended the South Carolina Military Academy (now The Citadel) and graduated from West Point. Mell praised the officer in the president's report to the trustees in March 1908, applauding his "strict interpretation of the regulations and rigid enforcement of the rules of the college." Although the cadets were initially "somewhat restless" and "disposed at first to pull away from his authority," Mell concluded, they realized that Minus was "working for the best interests of the college."[30] Because the recent events had been reviewed in the press and Clemson's reputation for a lack of discipline continued, Mell undoubtedly welcomed the stricter enforcement under Minus. Yet the president was again too hasty (as in the case of Clay) in attributing to the commandant control over the cadets.

On 1 April another major incident occurred. Some 300 cadets, having been warned that no disruptions like the previous year's April Fools' prank would be tolerated, decided to test Minus by absenting themselves from campus. Early in the morning they marched to Pendleton and spent the day there, lolling about the town. Furthermore, while in Pendleton, the boys endorsed a declaration that if anyone were dismissed as a result of the incident, they would all leave school. Thus was formed the famous (or infamous) "Pendleton guards."

This blatant challenge to authority, however, could neither be tolerated nor excused. Each cadet who had left the campus that day was charged with "absence without permission" and reviewed individually by the discipline committee. By 7 April 306 students had been dismissed. Mell, although aware of the anguish which the action caused many parents, seemed satisfied with the results. "Presidents of Colleges in other States," he informed J. W. Harris, a Spartanburg farmer who had supported his position, "are expressing not only commendation for this action of the

---

[29]Mell to adjutant general, 10 July 1907; and Mell to Simpson 13, 29 June 1907, both in ibid.

[30]See the president's report to the trustees, 17 Mar. 1908, in ibid. For Minus's background, note P. H. Mell, "Annual Report of the President of the College," 1907, *Thirty-Ninth Annual Report of the State Superintendent of Education of the State of South Carolina, 1907* (Columbia SC: Gonzales and Bryan, State Printers, 1908) 256.

authorities here, but state that they believe that the lesson will be of value to the colleges elsewhere, particularly where the impression exists among college boys that in large numbers they can control."[31]

Mell felt that his point had been made with the cadets. He was satisfied with the way in which those dismissed had accepted their punishment. That attitude led the college in the fall of 1908 to readmit a large number of the boys. "If the dismissed cadet showed that he is penitent," a newspaper quoted Mell as saying, "and that he is heartily sorry for his action on All-Fools' Day, the discipline committee has been disposed to readmit him."[32] Yet records do not exist that show the reaction of Captain Minus to the decision. According to Walter Merritt Riggs, director of the mechanical department and Mell's successor in 1910 as Clemson's president, Minus was a man of "irascible temper, bitter, vindictive, and disloyal to higher authority."[33] An indication of his nature was an incident concerning the athletic coach, Frank Shaughnessey, prior to the "Pendleton guards" affair. In February 1908, Shaughnessey, by his account merely blowing off steam, had complained informally to Minus about a professor's reporting one of his star baseball players on a disciplinary matter. Minus in turn had mentioned the dialogue to other professors, whereupon an official inquiry led to Shaughnessey's dismissal. The former coach was shocked, as he felt his discussion with Minus had been informal, merely a passing and private complaint, and that Minus had not seemed to interpret it at the time as insubordinate to the regulations of the college.[34]

By the beginning of 1909 Minus believed that President Mell was trespassing against the school's military regulations. The president, Minus felt, was undercutting the latter's efforts to foster discipline among the cadets. In one case, for example, a cadet had returned from Christmas vacation forty-two hours late with a note from his dentist concerning dental work that had delayed the student's return. Minus refused to accept the excuse, but Mell did. In another instance, a prospective cadet who had failed to complete his entry examinations because he had arrived at the college late on the day of the tests, was sent by Mell to the barracks for overnight accommodations. There he was hazed and, subsequently, left school. Shortly after his return home, his mother appealed to Mell for his reinstatement, which the president approved over Minus's objection.[35]

---

[31]Bryan, 68-70; and Mell to Harris, 15 Apr. 1908, CU President's papers, Mell.

[32]See Mell, unidentified clipping, Mell papers; and Mell to Harris, 15 Apr. 1908, CU President's papers, Mell.

[33]Riggs to Sirmyer, 20 Apr. 1909, CU President's papers, Mell.

[34]Shaughnessey to Riggs, 3 Mar. 1908, in ibid.

[35]See Minus's letter, unidentified clipping, Mell papers.

At the meeting of the trustees in March 1909, Minus sought to force the issue between Mell and himself, apparently expecting the board to support him and request Mell's resignation. Some board members did back Minus, including the chairman, Alan Johnstone, R. W. Simpson, and C. D. Mann. Benjamin Tillman, however, forced a vote in favor of Mell,[36] and Minus consequently resigned. "[D]ue to his inability," Riggs wrote to Sirmyer about the affair, "to concede the same sincerity of motives to other people which he arrogates to himself," Minus decided to take his case to the public. In a series of letters to newspapers in the state, he scored the Mell administration, airing some of the incidents cited above. Unfortunately for Mell, trustee C. D. Mann endorsed Minus's account and called publicly for the president's resignation.[37]

As the days passed, speculation in the press grew concerning Mell's fate. Furthermore, the controversy reopened in the press the old arguments critical of Clemson, its funding, and its board of trustees. Mell, "a man of such extreme sensitiveness to criticism," Riggs told trustee Johnstone at the end of April,[38] must have been hurt. A letter to Riggs from an unidentified member of the college community expressed concern over Mell's emotional state: "Have you seen Dr. Mell within the last twelve hours. I just had a talk with him and fear he may do something that will hurt him and the college. The Mann article seems to have had more effect on him than anything else that has happened."[39]

Most informative in tracing developments during the spring and summer of 1909 was the correspondence between Riggs and Tillman's sons, Ben Jr. and Henry. Each recognized Mell's frustration and hurt, as well as a number of problems in the operation of the college. These included nepotism and interference by certain board members, particularly Simpson, in the day-to-day affairs of the school. According to Mell, five trustees, including Simpson and Johnstone, both of whom had opposed the president in the Minus affair, had relatives employed by the college. Riggs posed a litany of rhetorical questions to Ben Jr.:

> Do you believe the board as a whole wants one-man rule at Clemson? That is what I believe in. Do they wish to demand efficiency of every man who draws a salary, regardless of who he is? Do they want economy practiced

---

[36]Riggs to Alan Johnstone, 28 Apr. 1909, CU President's papers, Mell.
[37]Riggs to Sirmyer, 20 Apr. 1909; and C. D. Mann to *The State*, 23 Apr. 1909, Mell papers.
[38]Riggs to Johnstone, 28 Apr. 1909, CU President's papers, Mell.
[39]See the unidentified and undated (but is 1909) letter to Riggs, in ibid.

in every Department of the College work, regardless of whom it might affect? Are they willing to elect the President's nominees when he comes to select the tools whereby he must succeed or fail—the members of his faculty? Are they willing to give him absolute control in their absence, and that overshadowing authority which no President has yet exercised, and make him responsible for results without dictating the ways and means by which he shall attain it? Have they arrived at that point where they are willing to trust the President; to believe that as an expert he knows more about the details of the College management than they do, and let him alone, unhampered by personal or committee interference?[40]

The answer to all of the questions, from Riggs's perspective, was "no."

Despite their sympathy for Mell, Riggs and the Tillmans were concerned that the president might act in a way injurious to Clemson. That, in their opinion, was what he did when, in July 1909, he submitted his resignation and publicized the reasons for it: interference of the trustees in the day-to-day affairs of the institution, the board's circumvention of the president in faculty and curriculum affairs, and the prevalence of nepotism at the school. In his final report to the trustees, he urged the board to give his successor "sympathetic support and allow him proper control of the affairs of his office." Responding to what Mell had done, Henry Tillman informed Riggs: "I sympathize with wronged men at Clemson and elsewhere, but when, for personal spite, any man hits at the fundamentals of Clemson he is hitting too near home for me to tolerate or excuse. Dr. Mell's action would amount to this."[41]

Many Clemson supporters, therefore, despite personal admiration and sympathy for Mell, were upset with him. Of particular concern was his testimony to the annual legislative committee, which visited the campus at the end of 1909. Mell had been asked by the trustees to stay on until a new president could be named, and he took advantage of the investigation to air his grievances again. He wrote Benjamin Tillman in December that, while he did not intend to make himself "unduly obnoxious either to the Legislative Committee or to other parties," he would "not allow an opportunity to slip through my hands to give this committee full and explicit information concerning all matters which have seriously disturbed the

---

[40]Riggs to B. R. Tillman, Jr., 3 May 1909, in ibid. For Mell's specific charges regarding the trustees and nepotism, see Bryan, 70.

[41]Henry C. Tillman to Riggs, 3 July 1909, in CU President's papers, Mell; P. H. Mell, "Annual Report of the President of the College," 1909, *Forty-First Annual Report of the State Superintendent of Education of the State of South Carolina, 1909* (Columbia SC: Gonzales and Bryan, State Printers, 1910) 284; and Bryan, 70.

welfare of the College." The committee published its results, noting "a deplorable lack of cooperation between trustees and President." Its report also showed that ten Clemson officers and professors (out of a total of fifty-two professors and thirty-six officers and employees) were related to trustee members, thus fueling the cries about nepotism.[42] Old wounds were re-opened.

Mell's Contributions

A positive result of Mell's revelations to the legislative investigating committee was the restructuring of the college bylaws, a move recommended by Mell when he resigned. The new bylaws reduced the number of board committees and focused more authority in the office of the president. However, further treatment of the ills of the college would have to await a later date—and perhaps the passing of the original life trustees.[43]

Despite the difficulties that confronted Mell throughout his presidency and that eventually contributed to his resignation, there can be no doubt that Clemson and its academic reputation grew under his leadership. *The State,* in assessing his achievements, reported that when he had arrived at the college, it was "largely a military school" with "low" entrance requirements.[44] By 1907, however, Mell felt justified in writing the head of the Carnegie Foundation that "Clemson College is the leading agricultural institution in the South."[45] The college enrollment grew roughly forty percent from 1902 to 1908 (although attendance reached its peak in 1905 with 673 students), and the value of its property increased over a quarter of a million dollars—a not unimpressive number for those days.

---

[42]The committee's report in this regard is discussed in the small booklet by W. M. Riggs, "Questions and Answers Relating to Clemson College, 1910," Clemson: Clemson College Print, 1910, 33-34, defending the college; and Bryan, 70. See, moreover, Mell to Benjamin R. Tillman, 7 Dec. 1909, CU President's papers, Mell.

[43]The remaining original life trustees, who had served on the board since 1888, were U. S. Senator B. R. Tillman (Trenton); M. L. Donaldson (Greenville); R. W. Simpson (Pendleton); and J. E. Wannamaker (St. Mathews); Bryan, 264-65. The other life trustees were Alan Johnstone (Newberry); W. W. Bradley (Abbeville); and R. I. Manning (Sumter); see Riggs, 10. Also note the published booklet, "Report of the Committee on the Revision of By-Laws of the Clemson Agricultural College, 1909," second revision, esp. 1-3, 10-17, in Mell papers.

[44]See the lengthy summary of Mell's administration in *The State,* 13 July 1909.

[45]Mell to Henry S. Pritchett, 4 May 1907, CU President's papers, Mell. Two years later, however, in the bitter aftermath of his resignation and the conflict with the trustees, he informed the board of his frustration at being unable "to build a high grade agricultural, engineering and scientific institution." See Mell, "Annual Report of the President," 1909, 283.

Mell reorganized the faculty, establishing a hierarchy of positions and salaries that eliminated much dissatisfaction and reduced the number of resignations. He was also the first Clemson president to emphasize to the trustees the role of several faculty in research and in professional organizations at the state and national levels.[46] Under his direction the agricultural experiment station was separated from the college, allowing professors to focus on their teaching duties and the administration to hire scientific specialists for the work in the field. A gymnasium, museum, and reorganized library (which, by 1909, held 35,000 volumes and, Mell reported to the trustees, "some thousands of pamphlets") were his initiatives. He was a great supporter of the daily prayer meetings of students and faculty in the chapel and of the Young Men's Christian Association (YMCA). The Clemson branch of the YMCA became one of the largest in the country by 1907.[47]

When Mell left Clemson in 1910, he retired from academic life to a home in Atlanta. His friends remembered him most because of his warm and sensitive personality and his dedication to education. "He was a very modest man," recalled George Petrie of the Alabama Polytechnic College in describing the former Clemson president, "and an extremely courteous one, but his influence was not to be resisted. In this he was a fine type of the Southern professor of the old days. . . . He loved his work and his enthusiasm was contagious. He was never too busy to help a friend, never

---

[46]Among the faculty he commended were F. H. H. Calhoun (geology), W. S. Morrison (history), and M. B. Hardin (chemistry); P. H. Mell, "Annual Report of the President of the College," *Fortieth Annual Report of the State Superintendent of Education of the State of South Carolina, 1908* (Columbia SC: Gonzales and Bryan, State Printers, 1909) 259-60. See, moreover, *The State*, 13 July 1909; and the highest enrollment figure during his administration in P. H. Mell, "Annual Report of the President of the College," 1905, *Thirty-Seventh Annual Report of the State Superintendent of Education of the State of South Carolina, 1905* (Columbia SC: Gonzales and Bryan, State Printers, 1906) 341.

[47]Mell declared in his "Annual Report of the President," 1907, 258-59 (in which he noted the college possessed the sixth largest group of students among colleges in the United States and Canada involved in YMCA Bible study [Clemson had 346 students in its group out of a total enrollment that year of 659]): "There can be no question raised by any serious thinking man that the work of these boys in their study of the Bible and their endeavor to lead better lives will produce a wonderful effect upon the entire college in all of its departments." Regarding the library, which students were permitted to use from nine in the morning to five in the afternoon, see Mell, "Annual Report of the President," 1909, 283. Note, further, *The State*, 13 July 1909.

too worried to listen to another's troubles, or too absorbed to sympathize with him. This was the personal touch which endeared him to his friends."[48] Mell remained active in community work in Atlanta, serving during the last years of his life on the Baptist Home Mission Board. He died on 12 October 1918 in Fredericksburg, Virginia, while visiting a brother-in-law.[49]

---

[48]The quote is in Calhoun, 45-46.
[49]*DAB*, VI:515.

• *President Walter Merritt Riggs, 1910–1924* •

· 7 ·

THE MASTER EXECUTIVE WALTER MERRITT RIGGS, 1910–1924

C. Alan Grubb

When the Clemson College board of trustees, seeking to settle the crisis at the school caused by the resignation of President P. H. Mell in 1909, chose W. M. Riggs as acting president, it could hardly have foreseen the impact his selection would have on the college. In March 1911 the board appointed Riggs Clemson's fifth president. The person to whom the trustees turned amid the crisis was in nearly every sense a "Clemson man," having joined the college in 1896 and risen rapidly through the ranks to professor and director of the engineering department. Although he did not seek the Clemson presidency and even believed himself ill-suited to hold the position, Riggs became the kind of chief executive he believed the college needed—a "big man," if not in scholarly or professional reputation, then in administrative skill, leadership, and loyalty to the school. He became an almost legendary figure at the college, the only Clemson president to have a building or place, Riggs Field, named after him during his presidency.

Athletic and stern in appearance, forceful and authoritarian by nature, Riggs strengthened the presidency significantly, dominating every aspect of the college, including the strong-willed board. He quickly produced order, stability, and efficiency at Clemson, intensifying the college's military discipline, expanding its technical and public service missions, and consolidating its position in the hearts of South Carolinians. These were not easy tasks. Popular opinion in the state by 1909 was hostile toward the troubled and divided school. World War I, which began in 1914, undermined Clemson's financial support and military discipline, complicating Riggs's job even more. His performance in meeting such challenges, however, prompted one contemporary to call him "the Master Executive."[1] Despite a disruptive walkout of the students in 1920, Riggs retained his firm, but benevolent, hand over the institution until his death in 1924.

Early Career and Acting Presidency

Riggs was born in Orangeburg, South Carolina, on 24 January 1873, the son of Harpin and Emma Gowan Riggs. He graduated from the Alabama Polytechnic Institute (Auburn) in 1893, where he excelled as both a student and athlete. A year later he received his engineering and master of engineering degrees at Auburn and remained there first as an instructor of English and then of physics. He arrived at Clemson in February 1896 as an assistant in mechanical and electrical engineering, the position he held until 1901, when he became professor of electrical engineering and director of the engineering department.

His first years at Clemson, Riggs later recalled, "were the happiest of my life."[2] He participated in the formative stages of the college's growth, established a close relationship with his students,[3] and organized the football team and glee club. Enthusiasm for athletics ran high at the college. Riggs, one of the best tight ends in Auburn's football history, coached Clemson's teams during 1896-1899. He was responsible for the college's hiring of the popular Auburn coach and later football legend, John Heisman, who produced winning teams and big-time football at Clemson. Riggs also brought from his alma mater several athletic traditions to the college, including it colors (purple and orange) and namesake, the "Tigers."

Riggs spent much of his time, furthermore, working with organizations to regulate intercollegiate sports. He established the South Carolina

---

[1] See J. J. Corcoran to Riggs, 3 Mar. 1920, in Clemson University (hereafter cited as CU) President's papers, Riggs, in Special Collections, R. M. Cooper Library/Clemson University (hereafter cited as RMCL/CU). Corcoran wrote: "Clemson and Dr. Riggs as the Master Executive are to my mind absolutely indissoluble, one only truly lives propped up by the other."

[2] Note "Remarks of the President W. M. Riggs in Response to Cadet G. G. Gilmer in Chapel, 24 Feb. 1921;" and Riggs's speech to the farmer's institute, 1 Sept. 1910, detailing his reasons for attending Auburn, in CU President's papers, Riggs.

[3] S. B. Earle, "In Memoriam, Walter Merritt Riggs," 16 Apr. 1926, CU Faculty files, Earle, RMCL/CU. J. C. Littlejohn, who worked for Riggs for eighteen years, primarily as registrar and then assistant to the president, made the same observation of Riggs's rapport with his students in these early years: "Riggs thought of that group more like younger brothers than students." See Littlejohn to Mrs. Richard Hall (Riggs's widow, Eula), 16 Feb. 1957, Littlejohn papers, RMCL/CU.

Intercollegiate Athletic Association in 1900, of which he was president until his death, and he served as vice president for fifteen years and then president (1912-1915) of the Southern Intercollegiate Athletic Association (SIAA). Although he loved sports, which he believed were a vital part of college life, he always insisted on "athletic purity" and on athletics playing a secondary role to academics. "I am not one of those who puts athletics above scholarship," he once wrote H. M. Snyder, the president of Wofford College. "If a boy imagined that he could come to Clemson, and without making satisfactory progress in his classes, engage in intercollegiate athletics, he would find himself sorely disappointed." Throughout his career Riggs used sports analogies and allusions in his speeches (for example, "A College is a mental gymnasium"), but he often reminded the students that they should "not allow athletics, or any other thing, to stand in the way of getting an education, for that is the primary thing."[4]

As director of the engineering department he displayed early the qualities that subsequently prompted the board of trustees' selection of him as acting president. He was hardworking, thorough, and steadfastly dedicated to the college; President Mell, for example, considered him "one of the most loyal and systematic men in the faculty." Riggs also assisted in the construction of numerous buildings and other physical facilities on the campus, including the power station, cadets' barracks, experiment station, switchboard, greenhouse, water supply, and heating and lighting systems in the agricultural hall. He received no pay for such extra time-consuming duties, explaining to Mell in 1906 that "I love to work" and "to help any interest of the College in any way. I am anxious to remain at Clemson, for I love the College, and I value most highly of all, your and the Board's appreciation of my work."[5]

Thus when Riggs was appointed by the board of trustees on the evening of 6 December 1909 to the office of acting president, he possessed an

---

[4] See his "Address to the New Men, 1921"; and Riggs to H. M. Snyder, 1 Aug. 1913, CU President's papers, Riggs. In his letters to colleagues in the SIAA, Riggs used the term "athletic purity" often. He was particularly associated with the "one-year rule," an early attempt to regulate eligibility and eliminate "ringers" from college football. He insisted on following the rules, and his frustration in enforcing them in large part—as much as the demands of the presidency of Clemson—explained his resignation as president of the SIAA in Dec. 1915. See "President's Address, 22nd Annual Convention of S.I.A.A, New Orleans, Dec. 11, 1915," in CU President's papers, Riggs. Regarding Heisman's success at Clemson, note Joe Sherman, *Clemson Tigers: A History of Clemson Football* (Columbia SC: R. L. Bryan, 1976) 5; and Wright Bryan, *Clemson: An Informal History of the University, 1889-1979* (Columbia SC: R. L. Bryan, 1979) 71-76.

[5] Riggs to Mell, 22 Mar. 1906; and Mell to Riggs, 24 Mar. 1909, CU President's papers, Mell, RMCL/CU.

intimate knowledge of Clemson, including its physical plant and academic strengths and weaknesses. He had not been the board's first choice and, moreover, he had resisted efforts after Mell's resignation to nominate him for the temporary position. His reluctance appeared to rest on his belief that he was neither an ideal nor a likely choice to lead the college. Not only was he uncertain about the support that he would receive from the board, but he realized that, despite the high regard in which he was held by students, alumni, and most of the faculty, he had enemies among his peers and other employees of the college. These would probably work against him, he thought, if he could not count fully on the board's backing.[6]

Few realized more than Riggs, however, the serious nature of Clemson's recent internal problems and turmoil, its unfavorable public image in the state, and the vulnerability of its president to the board of trustees. During the final crisis-ridden stage of Mell's presidency, even before Riggs's appointment, the latter had a clear vision of what he believed the college needed. This was illustrated in November 1909 when, at the request of the most powerful member of the board, United States Senator Benjamin R. Tillman, who had long had his eye on Riggs as Mell's successor, Riggs submitted a memorandum to the senator. He emphasized to Tillman that despite "the present conditions," he suspected that the college was "on the eve of a new order of things." Tillman's leadership, Riggs thought, would "pull the College out of the slough that it has been mired in particularly the past two years. . . . To lop off the dead branches, to make some economies and every man employed by the College show *results* and *proper economy*, this should be the great work of the Board in the next few years to come. It is a big work and will require big men."[7]

Although Riggs had not sought the appointment as acting president, he nevertheless intended to exercise authority in leading the college. Long before his selection he had declared that he believed in "one-man rule"

---

[6]In a letter to B. R. Tillman, Jr., the son of the senator and Clemson trustee, 3 May 1909, in CU President's papers, Mell, Riggs declared that his selection as president "would bring not peace, but a sword, and above all else we need peace—peace in the student body, in the faculty, and above all, in the Board meetings."

[7]Memorandum, Riggs to Tillman, 29 Nov. 1909, CU President's papers, Riggs. The report was not an attempt by Riggs to curry Tillman's favor. Riggs made it clear that while he supported "proper economy exercised in every direction," he did not agree with the senator on all points. He concluded by telling Tillman: "Agreeing with you in almost everything you advocate, I yet heartily disagree with the policy of asking the Legislature to curtail our income, or give it to some other purpose, and I hope and trust mature consideration will cause you to modify your views along this line."

by the president "at Clemson," but that he doubted the board would agree. On 8 December 1909, moreover, Riggs informed Alan Johnstone, the board's president, that "if I am to be responsible for affairs here . . . [I intend] to put everything to the test of my own judgment."[8] He did just that. From his first days in office, he took firm control of the controversial matters that had plagued Clemson during the last months of Mell's presidency. These included the dispute over the president's authority, the state general assembly's threat to investigate the college, the public charges of nepotism at the school practiced by the trustees, and the persistent attacks on the institution in the press. While Riggs continued to deny that he wanted the permanent presidency, he quickly made himself indispensable by succeeding where his predecessors had failed with the board, faculty, and public.

He succeeded in part because of his forceful personality, which soon earned him the nickname "Bull." He also profited from the college's new bylaws, which the board passed as a consequence of its conflict with Mell and which finally placed the responsibility for running the school clearly in the president's hands. This was an essential tool in Riggs's consolidating his authority. It was the means by which he asserted his control over the college's officers, faculty, and students, thereby ending their practice of communicating directly with the board and undermining the president's power. Equally important, the new bylaws enabled Riggs to keep the trustees from intervening in the daily operation of the college and sabotaging his authority. In this regard, he was able to count on the board's support, as his predecessors had not, and particularly on the backing of trustees Tillman, Johnstone, and B. H. Rawl.

Amid a board full of politicians, Riggs showed an almost instinctive grasp of board politics and of how to protect the college from hostile public opinion. Tillman's support of him was particularly critical.[9] The senator took a special interest in Riggs and considered himself the new president's mentor and strongest ally on the board. Although their views were not always identical, they shared a common belief in the value of technical education and Clemson's special mission as a land-grant institution, emphasizing learning in agriculture and mechanical arts. In words that Riggs fully endorsed, Tillman wrote the president in 1911 discussing the senator's role in founding the college: "I dreamed that there ought to be a College for boys and girls that would equip them for the battle of life;

---

[8]Riggs to Johnstone, 8 Dec. 1909, CU President's papers, Riggs; and Riggs to B. R. Tillman, Jr., 3 May 1909, CU President's papers, Mell.

[9]As he noted in his "Tillman Memorial," 10 Dec. 1919, CU President's papers, Riggs.

a College where the studies would be not only Latin and Greek and the Classics, but such as would prepare a man to make his bread and butter."[10] The two men corresponded often; sometimes daily Riggs wrote long letters to Tillman, in which the president made allusions to "our work" and outlined Riggs's position regarding the various problems confronting the college and its future direction.[11]

However, important as Tillman's support was, his declining health proved equally fortuitous for Riggs. Partial paralysis had struck the once fiery senator in 1908; his stroke at the end of January 1910, however, had almost ended his career. It enabled Riggs to establish his own authority apart from Tillman. Riggs quickly demonstrated that he was his own man in administering the college and not, as some believed, little more than the senator's creature. Riggs's handling of Tillman and the often contentious board during the early months of his acting presidency was skillful—and would remain so until the end of his career. From his first days in office Riggs kept the trustees informed of college matters, writing them detailed and informative notes that eventually evolved into a regular circular letter that he sent to the board between its meetings. Although such correspondence consumed much of his time, it reflected Riggs's industry and methodical organization. But above all, it allowed him to reduce the number of board meetings, thereby leaving him increasingly in undisputed control of the college. Thus, whereas the authority of Riggs's predecessors had been undermined by the board, his was consolidated from the outset through the trustees—first by the bylaws that protected him from the board and second by his tactful, solicitous attention to the trustees, who reciprocated by leaving him alone.

Moreover, Riggs made clear from the beginning that he, and not the board, was in charge at the college. He indicated to the trustees that while he desired their advice, he also intended to be president in fact as well as in name, his "acting" status notwithstanding. On one occasion, for example, he informed Rawl that "while I am sometimes egotistical enough to think my judgment along certain lines is better than that of the board . . . all I ask is a fair field, and no favors, and let the cause win if it is wor-

---

[10]Tillman to Riggs, 13 June 1911, in ibid. That the senator considered himself Riggs's mentor and protector is seen in Tillman's letter to Riggs of 5 Jan. 1916, in which he recalled: "I have never been able to dominate the Trustees and never wanted to, except when I had to 'cuss' them out and leave the Board in disgust because they would not elect you President pro tempore."

[11]Tillman to Riggs, 23 Sept. 1910; and particularly the senator's letter of 24 Jan. 1910, as an example of the "advice" Tillman gave Riggs, CU President's papers, Riggs.

thy." He emphasized to Tillman that "I don't want any one [on the board] to be disappointed or surprised if after taking council with my associates here, I carry out the plans according to my best judgment."[12]

Already by the board's first meeting in March 1910, Riggs had clarified the relationship between himself and the trustees. In anticipation of the meeting, he declared to Tillman: "I am convinced that the Board is willing to back someone who has plans to offer and can present their desirability, and when I am convinced of the need of any particular thing, I am going to make a fight for it, regardless of whether it is a popular or unpopular measure."[13] Riggs knew what he wanted and what he believed the college's situation demanded. Unlike his predecessor, Mell, he was a fighter and determined not only to avoid being a casualty of the board's factionalism and opposition, but to end the weakness of the Clemson president in policy making.

The acting president tackled the college's other problems with equal energy and ingenuity. Particularly pressing was the possibility of a legislative investigation of the college, which stemmed from charges made to a legislative committee during the final months of Mell's administration that nepotism, fiscal irregularity, and extravagance existed at Clemson. Most alarming was the discovery that Mell, as Riggs informed Johnstone, had "loaded the legislative committee with his grievances" and "given them a lot of written matter." Although none of the trustees appeared to fear an investigation, Riggs did. He opposed it because he thought such an inquiry would likely reveal the factionalism in the board that had contributed to Mell's demise and raise anew the public claims that the school had not always been administered effectively or in the interest of the state. "I am a believer of correcting any evils that may exist within the Board," Riggs told Tillman, "and not furnishing our enemies with clubs with which to belabor us."[14]

Nevertheless, in anticipation of a legislative inquiry, Riggs began his own internal investigation of the college's finances and of charges that board members had forced the college to hire their relatives. He also moved to counteract the recent bad publicity in the press regarding Clemson by

---

[12]Riggs to Tillman, 24 Jan. 1910; and Riggs to Rawl, 5 Mar. 1909, in CU President's papers, Riggs. Regarding Tillman's enfeeblement and its effects on his career, see Ernest McPherson Lander, Jr., *A History of South Carolina, 1865-1960*, 2nd ed. (Columbia SC: University of South Carolina, Press, 1970) 52.

[13]Riggs to Tillman, 8 Feb. 1910, in CU President's papers, Riggs.

[14]See in ibid., Riggs to Tillman, 17, 26 Jan. 1910; Riggs to M. E. Ziegler (a state legislator), 24 Jan. 1910; and Riggs to Johnstone, 11 Jan. 1910.

establishing contacts with editors of newspapers sympathetic to the college and regularly sending them reports underscoring the school's position. The most important of these efforts was the booklet he wrote entitled "Questions and Answers Relating to Clemson College 1910," subsequently called the "Clemson Catechism," which Riggs had distributed to parents, alumni, and prominent individuals. He defended the college point by point in the publication, particularly concentrating on the accusation of nepotism. He concluded—somewhat disingeniously—that there was no such problem and that of the individuals involved, "each and every one of them" had been appointed by previous presidents rather than the board.

In this regard Riggs especially blamed Mell's weakness in appointing relatives of board members to the Clemson faculty and staff. He appeared most unhappy, however, with Mell's public attack on the trustees, which Riggs interpreted as an assault on the college. As early as July 1909, amid the turmoil that produced Mell's resignation, Riggs had written Tillman's son, Henry: "I am very fond of Dr. Mell, and have done all I could to uphold his administration and defend him from foes within and without. But (like yourself) anyone who strikes at Clemson's vitals becomes a public enemy and must take what comes, in loss of sleep, prestige, friends. No friend can stand in the way of my loyalty to the College."[15]

Riggs's measures in defending the college seemed to lessen the troubled atmosphere that he inherited as acting president, although the threat of a legislative investigation of Clemson and the enactment of a law against nepotism continued into 1911. During the remainder of 1910 Riggs turned his attention to other issues, such as long-range plans that included a reorganization of many aspects of the college; the introduction of greater efficiency, particularly in the agricultural department; and increasing the college's visibility in the state. By his own admission he had little knowledge of agriculture, but he devoted his greatest attention to it, not only because it was the area of the college most often criticized, but because he saw the teaching of agriculture as the school's principal mission. In his justification of Clemson to farmers' groups and others in the state, moreover,

---

[15]Note in CU President's papers, Riggs, Riggs to H. C. Tillman, 23 July 1909; and Riggs's booklet, "Questions and Answers Relating to Clemson College 1910," specifically no. 73, in which Riggs answered the nepotism charges. Even Tillman, in his long letter to Riggs of 24 Jan. 1910, conceded nepotism on the part of trustees Richard W. Simpson, J. E. Wannamaker, and Johnstone. Riggs took a more "technical" view of the charges, however, which explains the results of his otherwise thorough investigation of the particularly damaging allegations. More information regarding the issue of nepotism is in Bryan, 70-71.

he emphasized the school's "covenant with the people," by which he meant its responsibility for public service.[16]

"Clemson has a President at last"

By the beginning of 1911 it was apparent that Clemson had found someone special to lead the college. Riggs not only possessed a vision about where he wished to direct the school, but he had the authority to dominate the trustees. He had also shown that he was a staunch, pugnacious defender of the college and its unique mission. He had already demonstrated the characteristics of a superior administrator and shown himself motivated by a fanatical loyalty to Clemson. It was not surprising, therefore, that on 7 March 1911 the trustees unanimously elected Riggs as president. Although he had continued to insist that he did not want the position, pressure from alumni, friends on the board, and others made the board's offer and his acceptance inevitable. Aside from the change of title, however, there was little alteration in his leadership, except that now he was able to pursue even more vigorously his plans to reorganize, expand, and improve Clemson.

The first years of Riggs's presidency returned stability to the college. Except for financial problems that confronted Clemson during World War I and that are discussed later in this essay, a tranquility rarely enjoyed by the young college characterized his administration. One newspaper, the *Charleston News and Courier,* remarked in June 1912: "There seems to be a kind of settled atmosphere about the place now. There is no uneasiness in the air; things are fixed. . . . No, the boys are not cowed! They have just come to realize that there is a master hand over them, and they cannot get from under it." One trustee, E. T. Hughes, wrote Riggs, in February 1914: "I have heard a number of people say that 'Clemson has a President at last.' "[17]

An incident that occurred shortly after Riggs's appointment as president illustrated how little his policies and attitudes changed. It also revealed major qualities he exhibited throughout his presidency—discipline, efficiency, and a fierce loyalty to the school. His dedication to Clemson was so strong, in fact, that it persuaded him not to seek punishment by

---

[16]Note Riggs's speech to the farmers' institute, 1 Sept. 1910, "The Relation of Clemson College to the State"; and Riggs to A. F. Lever (a member of Clemson's board of visitors and, from 1913 to 1940, a life trustee), 4 Feb. 1910, in CU President's papers, Riggs. See also Bryan, 265.

[17]Hughes to Riggs, 28 Feb. 1914, in CU President's papers, Riggs; and *Charleston News and Courier,* 11 June 1912.

law officials of a college employee found guilty of criminal activity. In the spring of 1912 Riggs discovered that August "Shorty" Schilletter, the steward of the mess hall, had stolen large amounts of money from the college. Although the cadets frequently complained about the food and other conditions in the mess hall, Schilletter had worked at the college for nineteen years and was generally popular with the students.

What prompted Riggs to suspect Schilletter's activity is unclear, but in May the president hired a private detective from Atlanta to investigate the mess hall official. Riggs paid the detective from his own pocket rather than leave a record of the payment in the college's financial records. A month later Riggs informed Tillman that Schilletter had been embezzling money for at least "the fifteen years before I took charge of affairs" and that the mess hall leader "must have knocked down between five and eight thousand dollars a year."[18]

This was serious pilfering, particularly when one considered that Riggs's salary was $3,500 annually and his campus residence was valued at $2,500. The question that Riggs faced was what he should do with Schilletter. Not only was the latter popular with students, but the revelation of his stealing would seem to confirm what Clemson's many detractors had been charging about corruption and poor management at the college. Riggs had already struggled hard to counteract such claims. In the end it was the desire to protect Clemson's public image from further damage that determined the president's actions, not his revulsion at Schilletter's dishonesty. To have dismissed or prosecuted Schilletter would have opened the scandal to the public, exposed Clemson to attacks from the press, politicians, and general assembly, and undermined Riggs's previous efforts to improve the college's public standing.

Riggs appeared unconcerned about the potential legal problems that might arise from his decision. Instead he decided to keep Schilletter at the college but to place him under close supervision—indeed under a kind of bondage. Henceforth, he informed Schilletter on 23 June, the latter would only retain control of the kitchen. A matron would supervise the dining hall and the quartermaster would issue supplies to Schilletter, whose records would be checked carefully each day. Schilletter, when confronted by Riggs, "made no protest" and "no excuse" for his behavior, telling the president that he did not want to leave the College" and that he "would be only too glad to work" under the new conditions. Riggs added to his account of the interview, which he carefully recorded and filed away, that he did not intend to relax his vigilance over Schilletter. He promised Till-

---

[18]Riggs to Tillman, 19 June 1912, CU President's papers, Riggs.

man in July 1912 to ask for Schilletter's resignation if the latter "goes back to his old tricks, or seeks to stir up dissension among the students out of revenge for my detection of his actions, and depriving him of a very lucrative business."[19]

This arrangement worked surprisingly well, although the complaints about the mess hall continued and Riggs in 1919 was able to force Schilletter to leave Clemson. The stealing stopped and the school avoided a public scandal and certain scrutiny, which Riggs had always feared. He suppressed the affair so completely, in fact, keeping it from the public, legal authorities, and college community, that many years later the school named one of its dining halls after Schilletter.

Most of Riggs's attention during the first years of his presidency, however, centered on the expansion of the college. Both enrollments and campus construction grew rapidly; whereas 653 cadets attended Clemson in January 1910, 1,012 enrolled in 1923. Moreover, despite the college's financial hardships during World War I, much of Riggs's building program was realized. The Young Men's Christian Association (YMCA) building, constructed primarily with Rockefeller funds and completed in 1916; the new athletic field; the addition of another story to the old barracks in 1911, thus making possible an increase in enrollment; and the dairy buildings were the work of his administration. However, in an article in 1914 in the college newspaper, *The Tiger*, Riggs envisioned far more construction for the campus.[20]

He also made important changes in curriculum, academic standards, and the faculty. Although Riggs sought to raise Clemson's standards, which even some graduates found too low, he did not wish to widen the gap between Clemson and the state's high schools. Referring to the problem of the "unfit" or "backward student" among the college's freshmen, he declared that Clemson nevertheless had "a responsibility to this type of student beyond sending him back home."[21] Yet he abolished the remedial or

---

[19]See in ibid., Riggs, "Epitome of Conversation with A. Schiletter [sic]. Sunday, June 23, 1912. 9:30 A.M. to 12;" and his correspondence with the Pinkerton detective agency and Tillman regarding the matter.

[20]*The Tiger*, 14 Mar. 1914. The enrollment figures for 1910 and Riggs's building plans are also in his "Report of the Acting President of the College," 21 Nov. 1910, for the board of trustees, in *Forty-Second Annual Report of the State Superintendent of Education of the State of South Carolina* (Columbia SC: Gonzales and Bryan, State Printers, 1911) 378, 379. The figures for 1923 are in Riggs, "Report of the President of the College," 15 Dec. 1923, in *Fifty-Fifth Annual Report of the State Superintendent of Education of the State of South Carolina, 1923* (Columbia SC: Gonzales and Bryan, State Printers, 1924) 6.

[21]Riggs, "Notes for a Talk," 1916, CU President's papers, Riggs.

preparatory class in 1914, whose existence had been a major barrier to his ambition to raise the esteem of Clemson among the public and other land-grant schools.

In addition, architectural studies were introduced, and the college began offering courses during the summer. The summer school stressed agricultural courses, and by 1919 it had expanded to include women in the classes. The college also increased its number of farmers' institutes and in 1912 began a one-year program in agriculture for students who possessed neither the time nor money to invest in a four-year curriculum. Simultaneously Riggs introduced a "work-boy course," where a student attended classes one week and worked a week.[22]

Related to these changes that strengthened the practical side of Clemson's curriculum were Riggs's further efforts, begun already when he was acting president, to enhance the school's public visibility and image. During 1912 he entered into an agreement with the United States Department of Agriculture to enlarge the college's extension program, which sponsored farm demonstration work, boys' clubs, girls' canning clubs, and farmers' institutes. Such activities were augmented by the United States Congress's Smith-Lever Act of 1914, which created a nationwide system of agricultural extension services and whose cosponsor was A. Frank Lever, a Clemson trustee and congressman from South Carolina. The board of trustees, however, refused to implement a proposal from the Department of Agriculture that Clemson's extension program employ several blacks as agents.[23]

Two of Riggs's most important innovations in promoting the view that Clemson served the public were his establishment of a publicity department at the college and his cultivating good relations with the editors of papers like the *Greenville News*, *Anderson Independent*, and *Charleston News*

---

[22]*The State*, 15 Jan. 1912; see, moreover, Riggs, "Report of President of the College," 15 Sept. 1912, in *Forty-Fourth Annual Report of the State Superintendent of Education of the State of South Carolina, 1912* (Columbia SC: Gonzales and Bryan, State Printers, 1913) 365, 372; and Riggs, "Report of the President of the College," 1 Sept. 1914, in *Forty Sixth-Annual Report of the State Superintendent of Education of the State of South Carolina, 1914* (Columbia SC: Gonzales and Bryan, State Printers, 1915) 335-36.

[23]Riggs informed Bradford Knapp of the Department of Agriculture, 6 Jan. 1912, that the board was "unwilling that the College should undertake it [the hiring of blacks], because of the necessity of our having negroes in our employ." The board, he added, indicating the real source of its objection, was "anxious that it shall be made plain that the proposition to co-operate came from you rather than from us at this particular time." See also Riggs, "Memo," 11 Jan. 1912. Both documents are in CU President's papers, Riggs. Regarding the Smith-Lever Act, note Edward Danforth Eddy, Jr., *Colleges for Our Land and Time: The Land-Grant Idea in American Education* (New York: Harper, 1957) 140-44.

and Courier.[24] This campaign was designed to counter the persistent criticism from political candidates, legislators, newspapers (particularly *The State*), and occasionally disgruntled parents, that Clemson failed to serve the farmers. Riggs's many speeches around the state also defended Clemson's value to the public. He once boasted to a farmer's institute, for example, that Clemson "aspires to be *great,* not only as an educator of youth, but as a helper of all the people as well." The college, he continued, was like "a city set upon a hill—it cannot, it will not, be hid."[25]

Less striking were changes during Riggs's presidency in faculty matters and student life. Although hampered by the college's poor financial situation after 1914, he nevertheless persuaded the board to increase faculty salaries. The raises lessened the number of resignations of faculty, particularly in the agricultural department, but in 1923 Riggs informed the trustees that salaries at Clemson were "on the average about 20% below that of similar institutions in the country." The president also sought to improve the quality of the faculty, particularly by taking a personal interest in its members' teaching abilities.[26] However, Riggs placed the greatest value on a professor's loyalty to the college and its officers.

He also continued his lively interest in the cadets after he became president, although it was not until 1920 that he and the board created an office of director of students. His authoritarian views notwithstanding, Riggs enlisted the students' opinions on a variety of matters (for example, the mess hall, military discipline, social life, and the faculty) through surveys that he regularly conducted among the cadets.[27] This anticipated much later policies during the 1960s and 1970s at Clemson and other schools of higher learning that provided students with a greater voice in the operation of their institutions.

---

[24]Riggs to Johnstone, 5 Sept. 1910, in CU President's papers, Riggs.

[25]Some of the publicity from Riggs and the college suggested that they remained sensitive to the continued public criticism. Data released by the college regarding the students in attendance in Nov. 1913, for example, were clearly designed to counter charges that Clemson did not serve the state's farmers. The press release concluded that the college's figures "show that Clemson College is indeed an Agricultural College in the best and truest sense, meeting fully the objects and purposes of its founders." All materials are in CU President's papers, Riggs. According to Riggs, "Report of the President of the College," 1 Sept. 1914, 321: "Of the patrons of the College, 84.5 percent are or have been farmers. . . . "

[26]Especially regarding salaries, note Riggs, "Report of the President of the College," 1 Sept. 1914, 331; and Riggs, "Report of the President of the College," 15 Dec. 1923, 19-20.

[27]See, for instance, "Riggs Surveys of Student Opinion, 1910-1922," in CU Archives files, RMCL/CU. These surveys, however, represented but a small sample of those Riggs conducted, as seen in CU President's papers, Riggs.

The president also ended what he called the "semi-military system" of his predecessors and the conflicts between the college's military commandant and the president, which had played such a significant role in Mell's resignation. Clemson's new commandant, Captain J. M. Cummins, who arrived in 1911, was similar in temperament to Riggs and, like the president, was strict but fair in his relations with the cadets. Riggs, while not a military man himself, favored a rigid military order as conducive to efficient government. "A military system seems to me a necessity *here,*" he told board member E. T. Hughes, "and I believe that if we *have* discipline we ought to have *efficient* discipline—just as we ought to have efficiency along other lines."[28] Riggs, during the first years of his presidency, consequently supported Cummins and the commandant's strict military discipline. Interestingly enough, those years produced Riggs's staunchest supporters among the cadets.

The president, moreover, insisted to the trustees that he and the college's discipline committee had the sole authority to punish students. He declared to Tillman in July 1914 that the college had "in the past suffered from participation on the part of the Board in discipline" and that it would "be a great mistake if . . . the Board overrules the action of the Committee or extends leniency." Two years later, when Hughes, a trustee and Marion attorney, protested the dismissal of a cadet, Riggs disagreed with the board member and bluntly informed him: "I have an abiding faith in your loyalty, although I believe you are less judicial-minded than any man I have ever known—and you a lawyer!" Hughes reacted angrily to Riggs's view and resigned from the board in December 1916.[29]

Surprisingly, those who often applauded Riggs's stern policy were the parents of cadets whom he dismissed or expelled. Although he was a believer in strict obedience and thus regularly removed boys for violations of the military regulations, he showed great sympathy for the parents and compassion for the students, sending them home, he said, "not in wrath but in sorrow."[30] Such was his force of character that he often heard from boys he had dismissed. "I received your letter several days ago," he wrote one, Dugan Arthur, "and I was glad indeed to hear from you. I want you

---

[28]Riggs to Hughes, 12 Jan. 1915, CU President's papers, Riggs.

[29]Hughes to Riggs, 27 June 1916; Riggs to Hughes, 18 June 1916; and Riggs to Tillman, 27 July 1914, in CU President's papers, Riggs. Regarding Hughes' service on the board and resignation, see "Hughes, Eddings Thomas, Marion, S.C.; lawyer," in CU Trustees file, Hughes, RMCL/CU.

[30]Note, for example, Riggs's letter to the brother of a dismissed cadet, 20 June 1910; and his letters to parents, 15 Oct. 1910, 3 June 1918, CU President's papers, Riggs.

Walter Merritt Riggs 1910-1924   Kate Salley Palmer

to feel always that in me you have a friend who will do whatever he can to help you to grow into upright manhood."[31]

Along with the military regimen and athletics, Riggs believed church or religious activities were vital to college life. Cadets still lined up and marched to church on Sunday; those who did not attend local churches were expected to go to Sunday services in the college chapel. Some contemporaries depicted Riggs as an ardent churchgoer, but the president described himself otherwise and joined the Fort Hill Presbyterian church only when he was offered the Clemson presidency.[32]

Riggs matched his insistence on discipline among the students with a demand for productivity and a careful, honest accounting from his sub-

---

[31] Arthur wrote Riggs numerous letters after his dismissal, each apprising the president of the boy's "rehabilitation." See, moreover, Riggs's letters, 7 June, 4 July 1910 to another student, B. F. Dick, who had been dismissed. All letters are in CU President's papers, Riggs.

[32] According to W. H. Mills, the former pastor of the church, who had joined the Clemson faculty as professor of rural sociology, "Walter Merritt Riggs. An Appreciation," *South Carolina Education*, 5 (15 Mar. 1924): 5, Riggs once said: "I have always been a successful man so far, I have not felt the need of God in my life, but I know this job is too much for me alone. I must seek the aid of God. I am going to join the church."

ordinates in the administration and faculty. These were important traits, particularly in view of the public's perception of Clemson as a poorly managed, wasteful institution, basking in luxury allegedly provided by funds from the state's fertilizer tax. However, already by 1916, even *The State*, which was one of Clemson's steadiest critics, was forced to admit, "Clemson has had several presidents, but none prior to Dr. Riggs seemed able to keep the big institution running in an economic and profitable manner."[33]

In this regard Riggs set the example. He refused a salary increase in 1914, believing that accepting one would make a poor impression on the faculty when college finances were becoming precarious. He also rejected more lucrative offers to move as president to other colleges.[34] Demonstrating his lack of concern and ambition for material rewards, he regularly dug into his own pockets to provide train fare for students he had to dismiss and send home. In 1915, furthermore, when college funds fell short in adding to the Rockefeller monies for the new YMCA building, he contributed a substantial sum himself.

Much of Riggs's demand for efficiency stemmed from his love of work. S. B. Earle, who served as acting president during Riggs's visit to Europe in 1919-20, described Riggs after the latter's death in 1924 as "a remarkable executive" whose "work was his religion." Riggs kept a demanding schedule, working long and strenuous hours; he took few vacations and was away from the college only on business. Inasmuch as he made Clemson his life, he found little time for socializing and abandoned the activities he had enjoyed before becoming president, such as singing, meeting with student groups, and attending athletic contests.[35] Riggs consequently suffered from nervous tension and high blood pressure, prompting some of his associates, including Tillman and South Carolina's governor and Clemson trustee, Richard I. Manning, to warn him (unsuccessfully) "to take care of your health."[36]

---

[33]*The State*, 3 Feb. 1916. Regarding Riggs's demand for administrative efficiency, see Riggs to B. F. Robertson, 14 July 1919; Riggs to Carter Newman, 18 Jan. 1915; and Riggs to Capt. J. W. Moore (The Citadel), 15 Sept. 1916, in CU President's papers, Riggs.

[34]See, for example, Riggs to Tillman, 3 Apr. 1915, in CU President's papers, Riggs.

[35]Mrs. Richard Hall (formerly Eula Riggs) to Littlejohn, 13 Apr. 1951, Littlejohn papers, folder 154; and Earle, "In Memoriam, Walter Merritt Riggs," 16 Apr. 1926, CU Faculty files, Earle.

[36]Manning to Riggs, 14 July 1915; and Tillman to Riggs, 15 Oct. 1915, CU President's papers, Riggs. Tillman advised him: "You are too valuable a man to die young, but unless you check up on your eating and take physical culture exercises and reduce your embonpoint, I predict that you will never live to be as old as I am, and you will be lucky to pass 63." Tillman died in 1918.

Even more than efficiency Riggs insisted on loyalty to the college from his subordinates. For example, when J. N. Harper resigned in 1917 as head of the agricultural department, Riggs concluded that it was best for the college because the department needed a stronger director. The president informed Tillman, however, that no one had "loved Clemson College more and was more zealous in its service" than Harper. Similarly, when W. W. Long, with whom Riggs worked closely on extension matters and who was one of the college's most tireless department heads, accumulated debts that Long could no longer manage, Riggs assumed personal control over the subordinate's financial affairs.[37] When college officials or faculty showed a lack of dedication to either Riggs or the school, he quickly called them to account, as he did Schilletter in 1912. Later Riggs reprimanded Mrs. Middleton, the dining hall matron, and Katherine Trescott, the librarian, whom he accused of spreading dissension and undermining authority.[38] He also reproached the always contentious professor of history, W. A. Morrison, and even the students during the walkout of 1920.

He possessed definite views on politics and race relations. Although Riggs was a Democrat in the tradition of President Woodrow Wilson, he sought to avoid involving himself and Clemson in political matters because he believed they would likely harm the college. But keeping out of politics was no easy task, inasmuch as each political campaign seemed to produce attacks on the school. Demands were made repeatedly that the general assembly investigate Clemson, and numerous members of the board of trustees were powerful political figures (for example, Tillman, Manning, Lever, Johnston, and Hughes). On only two occasions did Riggs appear to participate in politics. When Rawl, one of Riggs's staunchest supporters, was not reelected to the board in 1914, the president continued to send him board reports and worked secretly for Rawl's return to the body, which occurred two years later. Riggs also supported Manning's successful candidacy for governor in 1914, mainly because of his intense dislike for the past occupant of the executive mansion, Coleman Livingston Blease. The latter, who tried to win a United States Senate seat in 1914,

---

[37]See in CU President's papers, Riggs, the bank book for the American Bank in Greenville in Long's name, but which only Riggs could use (1916, 1917). The value Riggs placed on loyalty was illustrated in his bitter reaction to the failure of Rawl, one of Riggs's principal supporters, to be reelected to the board of trustees in 1914. Note Riggs to H. C. Tillman, 23 Jan. 1914; and herein.

[38]See Riggs's record of his talk with Middleton, 25 June 1920, in CU President's papers, Riggs.

supported Manning's opponent, John G. Richards. Riggs may also have been influenced by the feud between Blease and Tillman.[39]

The Clemson president held attitudes toward blacks that, while supportive of improved conditions for such persons, were nevertheless characteristic of his day. As a native of Orangeburg, someone keenly involved in higher education, and responsible for the state's agricultural extension service, he took a personal interest in the state's school for blacks, South Carolina State College, located in his hometown. A close friendship developed between himself and its president, R. S. Wilkinson.[40] Although Riggs would have liked blacks working as extension service agents, which the U. S. Department of Agriculture pressed the state to accept, the sentiment in the board and general assembly prevented it. Despite his progressive view in this regard, Riggs appeared to believe in the system of racial segregation that existed in the American South, stressing in a speech in July 1919 at South Carolina State that "the white and colored races can live together in peace only as they wisely recognize that they are different peoples, and that each must develop and live its social life apart from the other."

He emphasized both during and after World War I that while the war would produce significant changes in race relations, likely improving the black man's life, it would not alter his status. In his address at South Carolina State, for example, he asserted that a "great gulf of experiences yawns between the colored [American] soldiers who have lived in France and their brothers at home." He believed that the blacks who had fought in Europe would soon recognize "that race prejudice is not local or sectional, but national in scope." Only when "the colored race shall develop a society of its own with which it can be satisfied," he continued, would there "be laid a spectre that now bars the way to progress":

> Then will come in large measure equality before the law, and a clear recognition by the white race of the legal and human rights of their colored brethren. The colored race is here to test the white man's qualities of wisdom, humanity, and justice the nation over. After all, it is the white man who is on trial, because at present he must answer "Yes" to the question, "Am I my brother's keeper?"

---

[39] Note Lander, 52-53; Riggs to Tillman, 2 Sept. 1914, 10 June 1918; Riggs to Corcoran, 3 June 1918; and especially Riggs to Johnstone, 29 Aug. 1912, in CU President's papers, Riggs.

[40] For example, Riggs to Wilkinson, 27 July 1914; and Long's letter to Riggs, 22 June 1914, on the problem of reaching the black tenant in South Carolina, in CU President's papers, Riggs.

Education of all the people, white and colored, must help solve this great race problem, which in the shade of ignorance assumes the outlines of a menace. Education will teach the negro that his natural home is in the land of cane and cotton, that his natural calling is the one which lies nearest to Mother Nature's heart, that his interests are identical, not antithetical, with those of his white neighbors, and that in the South after all resides an affection for him that nowhere else is to be found.[41]

The Impact of the European War

Riggs's success in guiding Clemson did not occur without difficulties. These were mainly financial in nature, stemming in large part from the war in Europe which, even before America's entry in April 1917, adversely affected the college. Riggs also believed that American involvement in the conflict was responsible for the greatest problem he faced during his presidency, the student walkout or rebellion of 1920. Already during 1914 he expressed deep concern at the effect of the war on the school's finances, and specifically its impact on monies Clemson received from the state's fertilizer tax and on the credit available to the college from banks.[42] Clemson's critics had traditionally denounced the tax as a much-too-generous source for the school's income, but during the war the demand for cotton and other agricultural goods produced by the state declined, forcing a drop in the revenues from the tax.

Consequently, while work on the athletic field was continued, but by labor contributed by the students, and construction on the YMCA, funded largely by Rockefeller monies, began in January 1915 and was completed the next year, Riggs instituted strict economies elsewhere. Despite the austerity, the college's operating expenses, dependent as they were on the fertilizer tax, remained unstable. By 1915 Riggs even contemplated the prospect of having to request an appropriation from the general assembly. But in the end Clemson did not have to depend on the legislature for monies and possibly abandon the school's unique and controversial source of funding, the fertilizer tax. Instead the college was forced in 1915 to bor-

---

[41]See his "Address at Orangeburg," 30 July 1919, in CU President's papers, Riggs.

[42]Riggs to Ivy M. Mauldin, 10 Sept. 1914, in ibid. He wrote the board in his "Report of the President of the College," 1 Sept. 1914, 328, that "the European war . . . will likely so reduce the prospective income of the College derived from the fertilizer tax as to make impossible the developments planned. . . . The financial situation is fraught with great danger. . . . "

row $62,400 with the general assembly's consent, to continue operation.[43]

America's entry in the war produced even greater changes. Riggs, while delivering the commencement address in April 1917 at his alma mater, Auburn, interrupted his prepared remarks with an eloquently patriotic appeal, full of Wilsonian flourishes and sentiments about the war's effect. The conflict, he prophesied, would alter the nature of American society, transforming the country from a "political" into a "social and industrial" democracy, because the men who "mingled their blood on a common battlefield will demand all that such a sacrifice portends. . . . The time will come when as a result of this great struggle we shall have a realization of the true vision of Democracy as a land of *more* than equal suffrage—a land of equal justice before the law, a land of the open door to every man, and every woman too."[44]

Riggs repeated such remarks a few weeks later at Clemson's graduation exercises, emphasizing that forty-one members of the college's 1917 class had already entered officers' training camps and that agricultural and engineering schools would play a critical role in the war effort. In extolling the response of the "war class" of 1917 to President Wilson's call to "make the world safe for democracy," he reminded his listeners: "Modern wars must be fought by all the people. Behind the soldiers must stand the engineers and chemists, and behind all these, the man with the hoe. . . . In all the lines of technical endeavor, we shall find Clemson men doing their part."[45]

The war's effect on Clemson was immediate. Enrollment dropped to 662, the result of the college's students in uniform and of numerous others being forced to return home to help on farms. The war also produced changes in Clemson's faculty, including the hiring in 1918 of Rosamond Wolcott, one of the first women faculty members. Scholastic standards were also lowered, as the trustees empowered Riggs to shorten the semester.[46] A scarcity of goods, producing higher prices, aggravated the school's financial difficulties.

Particularly disruptive was the location on the campus of a training school for enlisted men, the Student Army Training Corps (SATC).

---

[43]Note Riggs's report to the South Carolina general assembly, 18 Dec. 1918; Riggs to A. C. True, 12 Sept. 1914; and Riggs to Johnstone, 12 Sept. 1914, in CU President's papers, Riggs.

[44]See his address in *The Auburn Alumnus*, 5 (Aug. 1917): 111.

[45]Riggs, "Graduating Exercises 1917," in CU President's papers, Riggs.

[46]Note in ibid., Riggs to trustees, 3 Apr. 1918; and Riggs, "Address to Seniors," 15 Sept. 1919.

Clemson, in return for a subsidy from the government, housed and fed the corps and provided its members with instruction in agriculture, chemistry, and engineering. Although the SATC forced the college to upgrade the mess hall, even raising the cost of food for the cadets, it proved injurious to the academic program. "The students have done practically no serious College work," Riggs lamented in November 1918 to R. A. Pearson, the president of Iowa State College. Riggs attributed the problem to "the mental attitude of the students, which has made them feel, and properly so, that the military work was the first consideration."[47]

But the most dramatic dislocations of Clemson life caused by the war came at its end in 1918 and 1919. Not only did an influenza epidemic strike the college, resulting in two deaths and the brief closing of the school, but Riggs departed suddenly on 13 February 1919 for France and six months of postwar service with the Army's overseas educational commission. The president expressed reservations about leaving the college at such a critical time, but the board of trustees encouraged him to participate in the commission's work.[48] The board named Samuel B. Earle, the head of the engineering department, as acting president. Riggs left Earle detailed instructions on how to govern the college, particularly regarding disciplinary matters and the upcoming 1 April, which Riggs feared might prompt disruptive "April-fool pranks" by the cadets.[49]

Riggs's absence in Europe had far-reaching consequences for Clemson. His fears of student unrest were not misplaced. The student walkout or rebellion of March 1920 had its origins in the previous spring, while Riggs was in France. Already during 1919 there had been disturbances at the University of South Carolina and elsewhere. The war had weakened both the academic program and military discipline at Clemson, a situation which, Riggs warned the seniors on 15 September 1919, would change.[50] Indeed, in the expectation that 1920 would produce readjustment and reform, Riggs welcomed the return to Clemson, following a three-year absence, of J. M. Cummins, by then a colonel, as commandant. Cummins, Riggs believed, would help restore the authority that the war had undermined. That was not to be the case, however.

---

[47]Riggs to Pearson, 18 Nov. 1918, in CU President's papers, Riggs.
[48]The main documents in ibid. are Riggs, "Report to Board of Trustees," 3 Apr. 1918, 6 Feb. 1919; Riggs to Pearson, 17 Dec. 1918; Riggs to Rawl, 18 Nov. 1918.
[49]Riggs's long "Confidential Memorandum for Acting President S. B. Earle," 13 Feb. 1919, is in CU President's papers, Riggs.
[50]A copy of Riggs's speech to the seniors in the chapel, 15 Sept. 1919; and Riggs to Wannamaker, 23 Mar. 1920, are in ibid.

The Walkout of 1920 and Aftermath

On 10 March 1920 most of the freshman and sophomore classes, which comprised more than 400 of the 779 cadets at Clemson, left campus and returned home. The causes of the rebellion were complex and included the perennial complaints that had prompted similar previous episodes in the college's history: discontent with military discipline, unhappiness with the food, and a feeling that cadets judged in violation of military regulations had been treated unfairly. The war, by creating a distaste for military discipline and authority generally, had intensified the grievances. There was also a perception that Riggs, consumed by his duties as president, had lost touch with the student body.[51]

Several sparks ignited the walkout. Two cadets who refused to serve meals in the mess hall were punished, and two other students were dismissed for disregarding their restrictions while under arrest for other offenses. When confusion broke out in the guard room, the commandant ordered the cadets to their rooms, an order which they obeyed. Amid the disturbances, however, some cadets symbolized their defiance by prominently displaying red badges and yelling "Bolshevik." Two days later the freshman and sophomore classes met without authorization on the athletic field and then marched to the president's office. There Riggs refused to reinstate the expelled cadets and advised the latter either to appeal to the board of trustees or to request a rehearing from the faculty's discipline committee.

When the students then left the campus, Riggs took steps to contain the revolt. He issued a special release to the press, presenting the administration's version of what had happened and indicating that the affair would be referred to the board. He also met with the junior and senior

---

[51]See the statement to Riggs made by L. G. Southard, a Spartanburg attorney who later counseled Riggs on the latter's defense against this and similar charges by the students, 18 Mar. 1920, in CU President's papers, Riggs. This is confirmed by the letters to Riggs, also in ibid., from former students such as W. C. Herron, 5 Apr. 1920, who said that during his time at the college "there did seem to be a certain lack of confidence in the administration." Another graduate, Joseph Tenhet, told Riggs even more bluntly on 5 Apr. 1920 that he thought some of the president's policies were poor, emphasizing that "many of your dealings with the students have been worse than high-handed; they have been unscrupulous." Both letters were in response to an appeal from Riggs prior to the investigation of him by the board for a candid appraisal of himself and his administration. Riggs expressed shock at Tenhet's remarks, although of the twenty-five graduates he wrote, only Tenhet responded unfavorably. On the other hand, the most recent graduates believed he was "autocratic," while his greatest supporters were the "old boys."

classes to hear their complaints,[52] and announced shortly thereafter that semester examinations would be omitted and school dismissed until 21 March. This would "enable students," he said, "to get a chance to relieve their minds of the present tension and . . . individual opinions on the matters which have recently disturbed them." On 13 March the president offered his resignation to the board, although he was confident that the trustees would not accept it. Three days later, moreover, he requested that the board conduct "a thorough investigation" of his office "in order that the atmosphere be thoroughly cleared." These were astute moves on Riggs's part to reinforce his own position. The board supported him and his handling of the incident, declaring it better to close the college than permit an open defiance of the authorities.[53]

Having assured himself of the board's backing, Riggs laid down the conditions on which the students would be allowed to return. Those who had participated in the walkout had to return by 21 March; furthermore, both they and their parents had to sign pledges to abide by the college's code of discipline. Most accepted the terms, and by 23 March all but twenty-four had either returned or received temporary leaves. Riggs greeted the cadets by addressing them in the chapel and stressing his commitment to Clemson and its future. "My dream has been to see Clemson College," he declared, "the greatest and best A[gricultural].M[echanical]. College in the South."[54]

The arrival of the students back on campus, however, did not end the crisis for Riggs. Although he was persuaded that the college's battle in overcoming the incident had been won, he informed the board chairman, Johnstone, of his belief that there was "a deep-seated conspiracy" behind the walkout "to result in my overthrow." Alluding to a meeting of 50 angry parents in Columbia and to criticism of Clemson in *The State*, he warned the trustees, "We have plenty of trouble ahead, and every member of the Board must gird up his loins for a fight." Both Riggs and Cummins,

---

[52]Riggs, "Memorandum of Meeting of Junior and Senior Cooperative Committees with President W. M. Riggs, March 10, 1920," in CU President's papers, Riggs.

[53]Note in ibid., Riggs, "Special Report to the Board of Trustees," 13 Mar. 1920; and Riggs to Johnstone, 16 Mar. 1920.

[54]See his talk in the chapel, 22 Mar. 1920; and Riggs, "To the Parents of Students," 16 Mar. 1920, in CU President's papers, Riggs. One parent in particular, D. L. McLaurin, a state legislator, complained on 20 Mar. that Riggs and the trustees "take the position that our boys are in a prison camp." He declared that "if Clemson is to continue as this kind of a school, I think the time has come when we should withdraw State aid, and allow the president and the trustees to run their military camp." McLaurin regarded himself as forced to sign the pledge.

desiring to restore discipline and silence their critics, asked the board for a public inquiry into the charges and complaints from the students against them.⁵⁵

The board agreed and held a hearing in the college chapel on 8 April 1920. Riggs, supported by numerous witnesses from the administration, faculty, the student body, and alumni, denied allegations that he had refused to improve the food in the mess hall, that he had neglected the students and lost their confidence, that discipline had been unusually harsh, and that the college's hospital facilities and fire protection has been unsatisfactory.⁵⁶ On 11 April the trustees published their report, which expressed the board's "very fullest confidence in the veracity, integrity, and loyalty of President Riggs, both to the College and its students." The board accepted his view on each point and, like him, explained the walkout as the consequence of a misunderstanding.

Although Riggs had triumphed in the crisis, he remained bitter at what had occurred and what he believed had maligned both him and Clemson. When he addressed the students in chapel on 12 April, he expressed his "feelings of indignation" at the cadets who had not attended the board's hearing but who, during the walkout, "had placed in jeopardy the reputation of the President of the College." He warned his listeners that they must "obey the rules of the College" or withdraw from it. In the following weeks the discipline committee dismissed the student president of the YMCA for falsifying an official report, and Riggs removed several faculty members ("kickers" as he called them) for disloyalty to him during the rebellion. Riggs also revised the procedure used by the students to file grievances against the school.⁵⁷ He never forgave what he termed "the Bolshevik

---

⁵⁵Riggs to Johnstone, 23, 31 Mar. 1920; and Riggs to Wannamaker, 23 Mar. 1920, in CU President's papers, Riggs.

⁵⁶The testimonials on Riggs behalf were nearly all favorable. He had earlier solicited statements from former students regarding himself and his administration. See in CU President's papers, Riggs; and n. 50 above. Riggs's brief summary of the walkout and its results is in his "Report of the President of the College," 1 Dec. 1920, in *Fifty-Second Annual Report of the State Superintendent of Education of the State of South Carolina, 1920* (Columbia SC: Gonzales and Bryan, State Printers, 1921) 6-7.

⁵⁷See Riggs, "Substance of an Address by President Riggs to Students in Chapel. April 12, 1920," in CU President's papers, Riggs. R. S. Crosman, an assistant professor of civil engineering, who had arrived at Clemson in Sept. 1919, was discharged by the board on 20 Apr. 1920 for his "disloyalty to the administration." Note, in the same collection, Riggs to Crosman, 1 May 1920. Riggs was especially bitter toward faculty dissidents; as the same files show, following Crosman's removal, Riggs informed W. P. Goodson of Winthrop on 21 Apr. 1920 that he expected at the board's meeting in July that "we will get the heads of five or six other disloyal hounds who have had a part in what has gone on."

Class of 1920" for the walkout, and in his meeting with the students on 29 March 1923, in which he reflected on the "tradition" of revolt at Clemson, he declared that "the College cannot allow these disorders to grow, eventually to destroy the College."[58]

Other changes that he introduced to restore order after March 1920 indicated that Clemson was beginning to take on the semblance of a modern university and to move away from the small, insulated "family" structure that had dominated the school. In August he named D. H. Henry, professor of chemistry, as director of the department of student affairs and assistant to the president. Riggs apparently intended Henry's appointment to answer the students' complaints that the president had neglected them. Furthermore, even before the walkout Riggs had realized the growing impossibility of his office handling every administrative detail of the college. As the students' resentment against the administration subsided and their esteem for Riggs reemerged, he initiated other changes, including upgrading food and conditions in the mess hall and revising the discipline committee's procedures.[59]

During 1922 and 1923 evidence mounted that he had regained the students' affection. They feted him on numerous occasions, including celebrating his fiftieth birthday and the twenty-fifth year of his connection with Clemson.[60] Still relatively young, he continued his demanding work schedule, despite warnings from others that he should slow his pace. On 22 January 1924 the college and state were stunned at the news that Riggs had died suddenly while attending a meeting of land-grant college officials in Washington, D. C. No one realized that he had suffered the previous weeks from severe pains in his chest; while in Washington he was seized by a severe coughing and choking spell that he did not survive. His body was returned to the campus for burial on Cemetery Hill.

Newspaper reports of his death referred to Riggs as "Clemson's greatest president." *The Tiger* remarked a few days later that he had "literally worked himself to death." Tributes and resolutions honoring him poured into the

---

[58]Riggs, "Substance of Address by President W. M. Riggs to Student Body in Chapel. March 29th, 1923;" and Riggs to Cummins, 31 July 1922, in CU President's papers, Riggs.

[59]See Riggs, "Confidential Inquiry," a letter sent to former students requesting their opinions on changes in military discipline and government; Riggs, "Substance of Remarks by President to the Senior Class after Chapel on October 13, 1920;" Riggs's special report to the trustees on 13 Mar. 1920, in which he conceded that there was a problem and called for "some reorganization;" Riggs, "Extract from President's Report to Trustees. July 4, 1922;" and Riggs to Earle, 16 Apr. 1921. All documents are in CU President's papers, Riggs.

[60]For example, *Greenville Piedmont*, 26 Jan. 1923; T. R. Cothran to Riggs, 10 May 1920; and Riggs to H. C. Tillman, 9 June 1921, in CU President's papers, Riggs.

college. Typical was that of Q. B. Newman, one of Riggs's former students, who called the president "the greatest influence for morality I have ever known. . . . And when I think of the thousands of boys who have drawn their principles and conduct from him at their most receptive periods, I have no hesitancy in expressing the belief that he was the greatest force and influence for personal righteousness that our state has produced in my lifetime."[61]

Under Riggs's authoritarian, but enlightened, leadership, Clemson College had grown from a small, troubled school into an important land-grant institution. His legacy—in military discipline, loyalty to the college, public service, and athletics—proved a lasting one. Perhaps most significant, however, he had strengthened the Clemson presidency, having given it a new authority and dignity both on the campus and among the public.

---

[61]Newman to Mrs. Riggs, 1 Mar. 1924, CU President's papers, Riggs; Earle, "In Memorium, Walter Merritt Riggs," 16 Apr. 1926, CU Faculty files, Earle; and *The Tiger*, 1 Feb. 1924.

• *President Samuel Broadus Earle, 1919, 1924–1925* •

· 8 ·
THE CONSERVATIVE CARETAKER SAMUEL BROADUS EARLE, 1919 and 1924–1925

Susan Duffy

The seventh man to lead the Clemson Agricultural College, S. B. Earle, served little time as its president. Earle was the acting president of the college on two occasions: the first time for six months in 1919, and the second for approximately eighteen months during 1924 and 1925. However, he surpassed other presidents in longevity, retiring from the college in 1950 after 48 years of service to it and celebrating his 100th birthday at Clemson in 1978. Earle is the only chief executive at Clemson to retain the title of "acting president." In 1919 this director of the college's engineering department, once described as "a man of very good and conservative judgment," served as the college's caretaker by meticulously obeying the instructions left him by the school's president, W. M. Riggs, in maintaining discipline and order on the campus. However, his term as acting president five years later, while it was smooth and effective in many respects, was marred by turmoil. Not only did his appointment help stir the latent conflict between the strongest departments at the college, agriculture and engineering, but the Clemson students staged their most disruptive walkout in the school's thirty-year history.

The Road to Clemson

A native of South Carolina, Samuel Earle took pride in the fact that his ancestor, John Earle, had emigrated from England to Virginia in 1650 and that his great-grandfather, Judge Baylis Earle, moved to South Carolina around 1750 and was the first judge of Spartanburg county.[1] Earle was born in Gowansville on 11 March 1878, the son of Thomas John Earle, a Baptist minister who also operated a small academy, and Eliza Jane Kennedy. At fifteen he enrolled in Furman University, as four of his brothers had before him. Tradition, however, was not the sole reason for his attending Furman. He cited the discount offered by the school to children of Baptist ministers as another factor that influenced his choice.[2] There his coursework included Latin, Greek, German, and French, in addition to English, chemistry, logic, history, civics, psychology, and extensive training in mathematics. He graduated from Furman with a bachelor of arts degree in 1898 and a master of arts in language and math a year later. By his own admission, he did not know what he wanted to do upon graduation. "I read a little about engineering," he told an interviewer in 1968, "understood that mathematics knowledge was needed, so went to Cornell where I graduated in mechanical engineering with a statement that I had specialized in electrical."[3]

After leaving Cornell with a master of engineering degree in 1902, Earle was offered positions with the General Electric company and Westinghouse before accepting an appointment at Clemson for a salary of $1,500. Although not intending to teach, he did so because his mother wished for her son to remain in the South and because he "owed" for his education at Cornell.[4] Teaching a variety of courses in mechanical engineering, he rose quickly to the rank of associate professor. According to George Aull, for many years head of the agricultural economics and rural sociology department and who knew Earle for nearly sixty-five years, the latter "always gloried in the performance of certain machinery around. He had one machine that generated electric current and it had been running since the College opened almost and he was so proud of that thing that he would always take the Trustees to show them this."[5] He also had one of

---

[1]See "Samuel B. Earle," entry written for *Biographical Encyclopedia of the World* (1943) in microfiche, Clemson University College of Engineering (hereafter cited as CUCE) papers, Special Collections, R. M. Cooper Library/Clemson University (hereafter cited as RMCL/CU).

[2]*Greenville News*, 14 Jan. 1976.

[3]S. B. Earle interview with John Allen, 8 Mar. 1968, Clemson University (hereafter cited as CU) Faculty files, Earle, RMCL/CU.

[4]See Earle to Christie Benet, Jr. (chairman of the CU board of trustees), 30 June 1950; and "Data on Teacher and Office Card," completed by Earle on 14 Jan. 1911, in Faculty files, Earle.

[5]George Aull interview with Susan Duffy, 10 July 1986, audiotape and transcript in RMCL/CU.

the first automobiles in Clemson and would often be seen driving with his wife, Susan Hall Sloan, whom he married in 1908 and with whom he had a son, Samuel Broadus Earle, Jr.

When W. M. Riggs became president of Clemson in 1910, Earle was promoted to professor and succeeded Riggs as director of the engineering department. He was also placed in charge of the college's heat, light, power, and sewage systems, which he oversaw until 1925. His projects were numerous, and evidence of his work is still found on the campus today. He built the first cold storage plant in the mess hall, the filter plant on what was then Hunnicut creek, and added boilers to the power station. By installing a turbine he helped modernize the campus and change the electrical system from direct to alternating current. Earle also designed the lighting, heating, and plumbing in the Young Men's Christian Association building (now the Holtzendorff Center) and helped install the swimming pool there. With Rudolph Lee of the architecture department, Earle designed the engineering shop building and other laboratories and classrooms. They remodeled the old chapel and contributed to converting the agricultural building, which stood on the site of the present Sikes Hall, into a library after the agricultural building was destroyed by fire in 1925.[6]

1919
Following Carefully Prescribed Instructions

During 1919 President Riggs was invited to serve as one of the directors for the army overseas educational commission in France. He tapped Earle to serve as acting president during his absence. "I refused," Earle recounted in 1969 about the appointment, but "Dr. Riggs said if you don't do it, I won't go."[7] Riggs justified his choice to the college's board of trustees by calling him "a man of good and very conservative judgment, liked and respected both by Faculty and students. The College could not be left in safer hands."[8]

On 13 February 1919 Riggs, to assist Earle and yet maintain a controlling hand, left for his replacement nine pages of "confidential memoranda." The directive carefully outlined the potential problem areas for the six months Earle would be acting president and stipulated various

---

[6]During World War I he supervised vocational training on campus, and in World War II he was in charge of civilian pilot and various defense training programs. See Faculty files, Earle; and CUCE records. Note also the Alumni Records, S. B. Earle, in Special Collections, James Duke Library, Furman University.

[7]Earle/Allen interview, 8 Mar. 1968, CU Faculty files, Earle.

[8]Riggs to the trustees, 6 Feb. 1919, CU President's papers, Riggs, RMCL/CU.

courses of action he should take. Earle's role as acting president, therefore, was merely a ceremonial one. Riggs, who was noted for control of nearly every aspect of the college, was still very much the president during his absence, and Earle was not to deviate from the rigorously prescribed instructions that he received. Fortuitously, there seemed not to have been any matter that caused him to improvise on Riggs's script.

According to Riggs's memorandum, Earle faced the problem of having the quarantine on campus, imposed during the influenza epidemic that swept the college in 1919, lifted as quickly as possible. Earle was also instructed to "work on the design of farm structures" so that Riggs, on his return, might publish a "bulletin on Farm Barns suitable to South Carolina." Riggs, however, left the most detailed orders for the many presidential duties that were paternalistic in nature, especially apprising Earle of how to handle faculty and students. The president left no doubt that his replacement was not to tolerate troublemakers or persons who refused to cooperate with the administration and trustees.

Earle, for example, was ordered to dismiss a staff member, Elias Earle, who was apparently applying for a faculty position. Riggs declared that "members of the Board . . . would likely object to our putting him on the faculty" because "of his fight on the College when he ran for the Legislature in Oconee County." If placed on the faculty, Riggs added, Elias Earle "would at once join the now diminished group of Bolshevists" who were causing a stir on the campus.[9] Regarding an instance of feuding faculty, Riggs told the acting president about a botany professor, R. C. Faulwetter, who had taken a door belonging to a colleague and "sawed it off and used it to cover an opening in which he had stored some of his property." If Faulwetter refused "to do what is right," Earle was not to allow him to return. In another case Earle was advised that a coach, Edward Donahue, who was "too much of a free lance," was to do weekly reports and attend chapel and faculty meetings.

Riggs spent even more time advising Earle on how to deal with the students. Earle was to inspect the barracks immediately after the cadets' departure from campus "to see [in] what condition the furniture, etc. has been kept." Regarding disciplinary matters, Earle was not to "hesitate to veto or modify the sentence of the Discipline Committee." He was told that "it would be best" in dealing "both with students and faculty, to take a 'no' rather than a 'yes' attitude" because, Riggs advised him, "it is better to refuse first and afterwards grant, than to grant and then take back." Riggs

---

[9]"Confidential Memoranda for Acting-President S. B. Earle," 13 Feb. 1919, CU President's papers, Riggs.

hastened to add that he "knew [Earle's] conservative judgment [would] approve of this advice."

He particularly cautioned Earle regarding 1 April, which had been a difficult day for previous Clemson presidents. Earle was told to "make it plain" to the senior cooperative committee that there were to be no April Fools' pranks or "repeat of the foolishness of the early days." He was also to alert the commandant to potential troubles, avoid tricks being played at the chapel service, and provide for guarding the bell tower and the whistle at the power station.[10] These instructions, followed by others on how to handle the college's board of visitors and prepare for commencement and the spring meeting of the trustees, were to be undertaken in addition to his work as director of engineering.

Earle accepted his task graciously, even though his salary remained the same despite the extensive new duties.[11] He informed Riggs, who returned to the college in July to resume the presidency, that he had accepted the position because "you asked me to do so, and I felt it might be my duty." Earle had followed his superior's instructions and encountered no major campus incidents. "I do not think there has been much of a Bolshivick [sic] spirit in the corps as a whole," he told Riggs, "though there may have been some few individuals." Nevertheless, Earle reported that "considerable unrest" had existed during his acting presidency.[12] Apparently the college had only narrowly averted a revolt against the military discipline of the commandant, Captain H. F. McFeely. Tension resulted from the remnants of the influenza epidemic, numerous vacancies on the faculty caused by the needs of America in World War I, and the presence on campus of many ex-soldiers and officers who had returned from the war and found the routine of cadet life irksome.[13]

---

[10]Ibid.

[11]See Riggs to Earle, 7 July 1919; and Earle to Riggs, 1 July 1919, CU President's papers, Riggs.

[12]Earle to Riggs, 1 July 1919, CU President's papers, Riggs.

[13]Accounts of the trouble are scarce. Riggs, however, had reported later to the trustees that "the mass-psychology of the student body was unsatisfactory. It had been so the session before, and during the spring of 1919, while I was in France, an open rebellion against the military discipline under Capt. McFeely was barely escaped." See his "Report of the President of the College," 1 Dec. 1920, in *Fifty-Second Annual Report of the State Superintendent of Education of the State of South Carolina, 1920* (Columbia SC: Gonzales and Bryan, State Printers, 1921) 6. On another occasion, he had declared: "Taking the session of 1918-1919 as a whole, it was probably the most unsatisfactory in the history of the institution." Note his "Report of the President of the College," 1 Dec. 1919, in *Fifty-First Annual Report of the State Superintendent of Education of the State of South Carolina, 1919* (Columbia SC: Gonzales and Bryan, State Printers, 1920) 20.

This probably explained Earle's later statement to Riggs that it was the onerous responsibility to maintain discipline that kept "the President continually on a strain."[14] His brief administrative success and loyalty to Riggs, which the latter acknowledged with "gratitude and appreciation" and rewarded with a salary increase, had resulted from his lack of pretension and from his ability to cooperate with and motivate subordinates. George Aull, editor of the college newspaper, *The Tiger*, when Earle was acting president in 1919, observed in a 1986 interview that Earle "just had a good way that the people were glad to do things for him. They liked him."[15]

Earle remained after the summer of 1919 as head of engineering, which also included architecture. The department continued to grow. He urged the greater development of civil engineering, with more emphasis on "highway work," and pushed for more competitive salaries for all engineering professors. His assessment for Riggs of various faculty members in 1919 revealed that the department had hired one of Clemson's first women professors—Rosamond Wolcott, who replaced her brother in architecture while he worked for the government. Manpower shortages caused by the world war, which had ended during the previous year, had brought the first women to the previously all-male faculty. Earle, however, appeared uncertain about his own feelings regarding this development. He described Wolcott as "a very conscientious girl fully qualified to do the work. . . . She was here only for the year and I am not quite sure that it would be wise to continue women teachers, though if we did I am sure Miss Wolcot would be an excellent one for the place."[16]

1924-1925
Administering Unrest

On 22 January 1924, while on a business trip, President Riggs died. Two days later the Clemson trustees appointed Earle "Acting President P[ro]. T[empore].," authorizing him "to administer all the affairs of the

---

[14]Earle to Riggs, 21 July 1919, in CU President's papers, Riggs.

[15]Aull/Duffy interview, 10 July 1986; and Riggs to Earle, 7 July 1919, in ibid. For Riggs's further praise of Earle, see Riggs, "Report of the President," 1 Dec. 1919, 7-8.

[16]Quoted from Earle, "Budget and Report for Engineering Department, Fiscal Year July 1, 1919," in CU President's papers, Riggs. Apparently Wolcott, who received a degree from Cornell in 1917, was one of three women appointed to the faculty by the fall of 1918. The others were Mary Evans in botany and Mabel Stehle in entomology and French; see Wright Bryan, *Clemson: An Informal History of the University, 1889-1979* (Columbia SC: R. L. Bryan, 1979) 192.

Samuel Broadus Earle (acting) 1919 and 1924-1925   Kate Salley Palmer

College . . . until otherwise ordered" by the board.[17] Although his term in 1919 made him the logical, if not the only acceptable, choice for the position, there were some who felt that others would have been suitable as well. A member of the college's board of visitors, for example, while praising Earle's ability, preferred David W. Daniel, a professor of English and director of the academic department, and called Earle "one of the best actors that I know of."[18] More significant, however, was the fact that Earle, an engineer, had succeeded Riggs, another engineer, and this posed problems for those who felt that agriculture was being superseded at Clemson.

There had always been a rivalry between the agriculture and engineering departments but, according to George Aull, the appointment of

---

[17] The terms of his appointment also directed him to "sign all papers authorized by the Bylaws of the College, and to perform all duties incident to the President's office." See microfilm, reel 2, "Minutes of Board of Trustees," (1908-40), 24 Jan. 1924, RMCL/CU.

[18] See the undated (but is 1924) clipping, "A Few Notes Concerning Clemson College," by T. H. D., in CU President's papers, Earle (acting president), RMCL/CU.

successive presidents from engineering "had aggravated the discussion."[19] Earle was not only aware of the rift, but extremely sensitive to it. Soon after he assumed his new office, he drafted an angry letter to R. M. Cooper, a powerful member of the trustees. It is doubtful that he sent the letter, but the draft, in Earle's hand, revealed not only the dissension surrounding the subject, but a different side to Earle's normally mild mannered personality. It also illustrated that, despite his apparent conservative judgment and willingness to follow faithfully the board's policies, he harbored bitter differences with at least one of the trustees.

Having heard that Cooper had stated publicly that "too much emphasis is being put on Engineering and too little on Agriculture" at Clemson, Earle challenged him to "bring your complaint before the Board . . . and let us have a frank and full [thrashing] out of the matter." He charged that Cooper, who was "not a [product] of Clemson," possessed "only a very superficial and inadequate knowledge" of the college, and particularly of engineering.[20] Indicating his further dislike of the trustee's views, he jotted at the bottom of the letter that Cooper, if given his wish, would "dismantle Eng. and [Text] depts." at Clemson and "pass a law compelling boys to take agriculture." Finally, Earle appeared to consider what he would do should Cooper persist. "If I believed," he mused to himself, "that a Trustee was doing something [detrimental] to College or embarrassing the Board when harm might result would it be proper to [charge] such member [before] Board."[21]

This incident, although dramatic, was not representative of Earle's relations with the trustees. No evidence exists that the letter was sent or that an open feud developed between him and Cooper. On the contrary, his politic handling of the board encouraged it to respond favorably to the recommendations and requests he presented it, many of which have had a long-term influence on Clemson. When the board met on 10 July 1924 he sought its approval for upgrading the college's broadcasting station, establishing an engineering experiment station, and conferring a bachelor of science degree on students who had completed three years of work at Clemson and gone on to receive a degree at the Medical College of South

---

[19]According to Aull: "There always had been [a rivalry]. . . . There had been some talk, no one took it very seriously, that the engineering was ruling. . . . The school was a land grant school. . . . The Clemson Agricultural College. And right off the bat almost, the engineers began to get more money." See Aull/Duffy interview, 10 July 1986.

[20]Earle to Cooper, [?] Jan. 1924, CU President's papers, Earle (acting president). Bracketed words are those that are difficult to read accurately.

[21]Ibid.

Carolina. The trustees agreed to his request to set aside "certain wooded lands on the college property . . . as demonstration forests to be maintained for educational and demonstration purposes," and the board approved his proposal to replace the division of rural sociology with one in agricultural economics.[22]

Most interesting about the meeting, however, was an item that Earle presented to the board "without recommendation": a petition from the Clemson students, which included a proposed constitution and bylaws, to form a popularly elected student government. This was the earliest formal attempt to establish such an institution. The board, unwilling to act on the proposal immediately, appointed a subcommittee of trustees and charged Earle with naming three professors who, together with the subcommittee, would study the issue and report to the board at its next meeting.[23] However, the issue did not appear on the agenda when the trustees met three months later. The board was obviously not prepared to end military government at the college, and whatever inroads into self-governance the students made during 1924 were lost until after World War II. The next meeting of the full board occurred in an emergency session on 20 October 1924 to consider the matter of the student walkout.

The student walkout during that month was the largest of the long series of such incidents that had begun in 1902. Because of the walkout's disruptiveness to the campus and the unfavorable public attention it drew to the college, it was also the most trying event of Earle's acting presidency. It began during the evening meals on Saturday and Sunday, 11 and 12 October 1924, when the cadets complained about bad food, alleging that they had been served wormy and moldy sausages and spoiled chicken. From the beginning of their protest, the students received only mild sympathy from Earle. With some insight he informed the president of the trustees, Senator Alan Johnstone, that there was nothing "seriously wrong with the mess hall" and that "the boys [were] as sometime in the past, using that as a disguise for other complaints."[24]

Nevertheless, he promised a committee of the senior class on 13 October that he would investigate the food, but matters worsened when a cadet, R. F. "Butch" Holahan, was sent by the seniors to the commandant, Colonel Otis R. Cole, to request permission for the class to hold a

---

[22]See "Minutes of Board," 10 July 1924.

[23]Ibid. Note also the draft of "Constitution and ByLaws of Student Government," undated, in CU President's papers, Earle (acting president).

[24]He did not identify what such complaints were, however; Earle to Senator Alan Johnstone, 14 Oct. 1924, in CU President's papers, Earle (acting president).

meeting. Permission to meet was granted, but the unfortunate messenger, Holahan, was accused by Cole of having "liquor on his breath" and immediately taken before the discipline committee, which decided to suspend him for a year. On the morning of 14 October Earle informed Holahan, who was the senior class president, captain of the football team, and one of the most popular students on campus, of his dismissal. When Earle refused to allow the seniors to meet regarding the Holahan case, they did so without permission on Riggs Field, where Clemson athletic contests were played. They drafted a petition that demanded more and better food; the resignation of the mess officer, J. D. Harcombe; the services of a matron at meals; and reinstatement of Holahan.

When Earle rejected the seniors' demands, agreeing only to continue investigating matters pertaining to food, approximately 500 cadets left the campus in protest on the evening of 14 October. Earle asked for, and received, a meeting of the trustees, who praised the acting president for refusing "to surrender to the senior class the authority conferred upon him" by the board.[25] The latter's punishment was harsh. Twenty-three students were dismissed and 112 suspended. Sixty-five received honorable discharges from various classes, and thirty-six students, unwilling to serve the punishment that faced them on their return to the college, withdrew. The incident had affected nearly every student, and for those who did return there was a lingering undercurrent of discontent.[26]

Press accounts of the walkout were sensational and widespread, ranging from the nearby *Anderson Tribune* to papers in Kansas City and New York. Earle, although chagrined by persistent letters to the newspapers from parents and alumni critical of the college, chose not to reply in the hope that the disgruntled "will stop writing."[27] This may explain in part why Earle managed to retain public support in the wake of the incident while the students and trustees were subjected to harsh denunciation in several

---

[25]Quoted in Bryan, 108, which contains an extensive discussion of the walkout. See, furthermore, Earle to the trustees, 15 Oct. 1924, in CU President's papers, Earle (acting president). Additional sources in RMCL/CU include *Report of Board of Trustees Regarding the "Walk-Out" or "Strike" of Students on October 14, 1924* (Clemson, 1924); "Clemson University Student Demonstrations," a scrapbook file of clippings, CU Clippings file; a folder titled "Walk-Out of 1924," Littlejohn papers, folder 174; and the trustees's lengthy deliberations on the incident, "Minutes of Board," 20 Oct. 1924.

[26]According to Bryan, 110: "Almost every cadet still on campus had lost from daily association one or more of his closest friends." See also Earle to R. I. Manning, 3 Nov. 1924, in CU President's papers, Earle (acting president).

[27]Note, for instance, Earle to H. C. Twiggs, 10 Nov. 1924, CU President's papers, Earle (acting president); and clippings from the newspapers in the same collection.

papers. However, letters to the acting president from Clemson alumni summarized the criticisms repeated most often. They identified three primary causes of the walkout: the system of military discipline, lack of student government, and mess hall conditions.[28]

Following the walkout there was a gradual relaxing of the strict military regulations that governed the campus, and mess hall conditions underwent a few cosmetic changes. However, student government did not emerge from the ashes. More concerned about quelling the criticism, Earle invited the members of the South Carolina general assembly to visit Clemson during November and December 1924.[29]

Less than ideal circumstances also characterized the remainder of Earle's term as acting president. In the first week of April 1925, a fire completely destroyed the agricultural hall. His plan to rebuild the hall as a library and erect a new agricultural building included an unsuccessful effort to recruit funds for the project from Bernard Baruch, the philanthropist.[30] Nevertheless, Earle's hand was clearly evident in the eventual completion of both structures.

* * * *

It had to be with a sense of relief for Earle when, three weeks later, his acting presidency ended with the appointment of E. W. Sikes as Clemson's new president. Sikes officially assumed his duties at the trustee's meeting on 10 July, but not before the board had passed a resolution praising Earle's service in the face of a "herculean task beset with trials of unusual difficulties.[31] Earle continued as director of engineering and, in July 1932, was appointed dean of the school of engineering, a position he held until his retirement in 1950. It was in that capacity that he made his most

---

[28]Relevant sources in RMCL/CU are A. L. Shealy, W. E. Stokes, and J. E. Johnson to Earle, 17 Oct. 1924, CU President's papers, Earle (acting president); and the board of the CU alumni association to Earle contained in "Minutes of Board," 12 Dec. 1924.

[29]According to a letter from his secretary, Margaret Sadler, to R. E. Currin, 10 Nov. 1924, in CU President's papers, Earle (acting president): "He [Earle] is in hope that a large number will accept the invitation and thinks many wrong impressions can be dispelled by a visit to the grounds and a visit to all points of interest at the College." Regarding the trustees's views against student government, see Bryan, 111.

[30]Earle worked through one of the trustees and United States congressmen from South Carolina, A. F. Lever; Earle to Lever, 22 May 1925, CU President's papers, Earle (acting president).

[31]"Minutes of Board," 14 July 1925.

significant contributions to Clemson. While he may have been chosen to serve as acting president because of his conservative judgment and loyalty to the trustees, he proved to be remarkably liberal and broad-minded in his conception of what made a good engineer.

The most important qualities for an engineer, he believed, were personality, enthusiasm, culture, patience, and knowledge of the subject.[32] In his presidential address in 1938 to the Society for the Promotion of Engineering Education, he urged a vigorous study of the humanities by engineering students, declaring: "It is the duty of the college not only to train men who will become capable engineers, but men who will take an interest and leading part in our social and economic readjustment. . . . [The engineer] should be able to converse at least with some intelligence about music, art or literature as well as economics and politics."[33] Earle also worked tirelessly to keep engineering students in the South by establishing a network of contacts among textile mills and power companies with which Clemson graduates could seek employment.[34]

After his retirement in 1950, Earle retained an active interest in the development of the engineering program at Clemson. He received numerous awards from professional organizations, including an honorary degree from Clemson and induction into Furman's Hall of Fame. The most profound and enduring tribute, however, occurred with the dedication on 6 November 1959 of a new chemical engineering building, named The Samuel Broadus Earle Hall. Not only did the funding for the building, provided by the Olin foundation, represent the largest grant ever received by the Clemson Agricultural College, but it was the first time in the school's history that a living person was honored by having a campus building bear his name.

---

[32]American Society of Mechanical Engineers, "Questionnaire," in microfiche, CUCE papers.

[33]See "The Cultural and Professional Phases of Engineering Education," presidential address presented at the 46th annual meeting of the society, College Station, Texas, 27-30 June 1938, in *The Journal of Engineering Education* 39 (1938): 7, 8, 10.

[34]He wrote to Benet on 30 June 1950, in Faculty files, Earle: "I am glad that the trend has been such that we are now placing a large number of our graduates in the State and in the South. I believe it was the class of 1948 I checked and found that 44% of the graduates remained in South Carolina and 77% in the South, and many of those who went North for further training would eventually come back to this section."

• *President Enoch Walter Sikes, 1925–1940* •

· 9 ·

THE PLOWBOY SCHOLAR ENOCH WALTER SIKES, 1925–1940

Bruce Yandle

Appointed the sixth president of the Clemson Agricultural College in July 1925, E. W. Sikes served in the office longer than any of his predecessors. Despite his rural background and nickname of "ploughboy," given him by Clemson students because of his slow, plodding gait,[1] Sikes was nonetheless one of the school's most qualified chief executives. A tall, large-boned, and solidly built man, he arrived on the campus with an established reputation as a scholar, educator, politician, author, orator, and churchman. Faculty and staff remembered him as a kind and gentle man, deeply religious, dignified but not forbidding, and willing to listen to others' ideas and problems.[2]

---

[1] Sikes referred to the nickname in an eight-page, undated "Autobiography" that he wrote, which is in the Clemson University (hereafter cited as CU) President's papers, E. W. Sikes, Special Collections, R. M. Cooper Library/CU (hereafter cited as RMCL/CU). Virginia Shanklin, Sikes's secretary, confirmed the origin of the name in an interview with the author on 3 Nov. 1986.

[2] These impressions were drawn from interviews with various persons who were at Clemson during Sikes's administration and still reside in the city: Shanklin, 3 Nov. 1986; George Nutt, retired director of the college's cooperative extension service and a faculty member, 22 Sept. 1986; G. E. Metz, faculty member and registrar, 4 Nov. 1986; Tom Milford, a student, 22 Sept. 1986; and Mrs. John T. Bregger, the widow of a U.S.D.A. scientist assigned to Clemson, 10 Nov. 1986. In addition, these contemporaries commented about the blue color of Sikes's face as he grew older, a condition that was both striking and obvious. The pigmentation was apparently not associated with organ failure or weakness but, according to Robert Burley (a physician at the CU Redfern medical center and who was a small boy living in Clemson during the Sikes years), may have been argyria, which resulted from the use of silver nitrate medication, commonly found in nose drops in the 1920s. Silver becomes deposited in the tissue and gives a blue tint to the face.

The challenges he faced during his fifteen-year presidency called on all his skills. When he arrived at Clemson, the school had a notorious history of student disorders and unrest. However, not only were there no such disruptions between 1925 and 1940, but the college's enrollment increased from 1,087 students to 2,227. The faculty grew from 83 to 163, but the number of those holding graduate degrees remained one of the lowest among land-grant colleges. New buildings were erected and old ones improved. The school obtained accreditation in 1927 from the Association of Secondary Schools and Colleges of the Southern States and, although the college struggled to do so, retained the standing. The number of graduates nearly doubled, and ten new bachelor's degree programs were added to the nine that existed when Sikes became president. Furthermore, the first graduate degrees were offered, and Sikes significantly restructured the academic administration.[3] Remarkably, most of these accomplishments occurred during the difficult era of the Great Depression.

Early Years

Sikes, the fourth of ten children, was born in 1868 in rural Union county, North Carolina, near the small town of Monroe and fifteen miles from the nearest railroad.[4] A country boy whose first lessons were learned in the community's one-room log schoolhouse, he was later sent to a boarding school, where he became enamored with words, the debate team, and regular Friday declamations. The first of his family to advance beyond high school, Sikes attended Wake Forest College where he starred as a guard on the school's first football squad and developed a reputation as a speaker and a student of Latin and Greek.[5] After graduating from Wake

---

[3]Data were obtained from Sikes's annual reports as president, several of which are cited herein, to the Clemson College board of trustees. Information was also taken from his "Autobiography," CU President's papers, Sikes. In 1925 the college claimed 2,369 graduates; when the Sikes period ended, 2,780 had been added to that number.

[4]The details of Sikes's early years and time at Wake Forest College are in his "Autobiography," in CU President's papers, Sikes.

[5]Information about Sikes's accomplishments at Wake Forest is from ibid.; and an interview with the registrar, Wake Forest University, 30 Oct. 1986. Sikes's speaking abilities are always recalled by his contemporaries. He established a custom of giving a "charge" to each Clemson graduating class, a short, inspirational talk that came before the graduation speaker's address. These were printed in small booklet form and distributed to students and friends. Shanklin recalls that Sikes took his final draft of speeches and arranged for his chauffeur to drive him and Mrs. Sikes into the country so that he could practice the addresses; Shanklin/Yandle interview, 3 Nov. 1986. Copies of each "Charge to the Graduates" are in the CU President's papers, Sikes.

Forest in 1891, he remained at the college for three years as director of the gymnasium, coach, and athletic director.

He entered the doctoral program at Johns Hopkins University in 1894 and three years later completed studies in history, government, and economics. While a student at the Baltimore school, Sikes was impressed by Woodrow Wilson, one of his major professors. Sikes's doctoral dissertation, entitled "The Transition of North Carolina from a Colony to Commonwealth," focused on his home state and region. From Johns Hopkins he returned to Wake Forest, where he organized a department of history and economics and married Ruth Wingate, the daughter of a former president of the college. Except for receiving a leave during which he ran successfully for a seat in the North Carolina senate and served there for a year, he remained until 1916 a faculty member and then dean at Wake Forest.

Sikes built his reputation as a college administrator, however, when he served from 1916 to 1925 as president of Coker College, a Baptist woman's school in South Carolina.[6] By 1920 Sikes had doubled the value of the college's endowment, eliminated the preparatory and nondegree programs, encouraged the formation of a student government, tightened entrance requirements for incoming students, and seen enrollments move higher. Under his leadership Coker College gained accreditation in 1923 from the Association of Colleges and Secondary Schools of the Southern States, an achievement which, for example, Clemson had not yet attained.

His years at Coker made him widely known in South Carolina, especially among members of the Baptist associations that supported the college. Involving himself actively in public and civic affairs, he served as governor of Kiwanis International for the Carolinas and, during the final years of World War I, spoke across the state for the American effort in the conflict. As a public speaker few could match him. A Clemson professor would later describe Sikes as "one of the greatest platform orators I ever heard." Sikes was thus widely known and much in the popular eye, someone who might significantly improve the public image of a state college. Perhaps it was more in recognition of Sikes's reputation than an important statement about Clemson's future that Governor Richard I. Manning himself, also a life member of the college's board of trustees, announced on 27 December 1924 the election of Sikes as the school's new president.

---

[6]The discussion of the Sikes years at Coker that follows is from William Salter Parrish, "A History of Coker College" (M.A. thesis, University of South Carolina, 1938) 86-108. The author expresses appreciation to Gordon Gourlay, Coker College librarian, for providing this and other materials related to the school.

Clemson
The College and Town in 1925

Prior to Sikes's arrival at Clemson, the college had become notorious for student strikes, walkouts, and insurrections.[7] There had been troubles in 1902, 1908, and 1919-1920. Stories about the school's difficulties were commonplace in the state's newspapers, and public pressure to resolve the problem was becoming evident. The most disruptive student walkout had occurred in October 1924 while S. B. Earle, head of the engineering department, was acting president. Sikes's appointment as the new president did not please everyone. Some were concerned at the choice of a woman's college president to lead an all-male school, and of one educated in the liberal arts for a scientific and technological institution. Sikes later suggested in a brief autobiographical sketch that his selection was based partly on the expectation that he would end Clemson's troubles and move it forward.[8] His strong skill in public relations may also have attracted the college's trustees, who wanted him to spend time speaking to as many groups outside the school as possible.[9]

He assumed the management of a college with 1,087 students, many of whom were from Anderson, Pickens, Greenville, Spartanburg, and Oconee counties.[10] The cost for the typical student was $239.40 per year, which included $40 for tuition for the in-state student. The school had fourteen administrators and eighty-five faculty members, of which only twenty-four percent had master's degrees and six percent the doctorate. Almost a fourth were graduates of Clemson. The average salaries of faculty in 1926 ranged from $2,851 for the rank of professor to $1,573 for an instructor. A salary roll from 1928-1929 showed a disparity among the disciplines. The highest paid full professor in engineering received $3,600; his counterpart in arts and sciences earned $3,000. The president earned

---

[7]Accounts of the problems with students are found in Wright Bryan, *Clemson: An Informal History of the University, 1889-1979* (Columbia SC: R. L. Bryan, 1979) 106-12; and Rebecca McKinney Hale, "Clemson Agricultural College: Years of Transition, 1925-1929" (M.A. thesis, Clemson University, 1984) 16-22. For the comment on Sikes's oratory, see Gaston Gage, "The Past Presidents of Clemson College," a paper read to the Clemson Forum Club, 25 May 1948, Gage papers, folder 28, RMCL/CU.

[8]See Sikes, "Autobiography," CU President's papers, Sikes. For the criticism regarding the choice of Sikes, note Bryan, 112.

[9]As suggested by Hale, 22.

[10]See E. W. Sikes, "Report of the President of the College," 1 July 1926, in *Thirty-Seventh Annual Report of the Board of Trustees of the Clemson Agricultural College to the General Assembly of South Carolina, 1926* (Clemson SC: Clemson Agricultural College, 1926) 8, 21-33.

$9,000 annually, and the head coach was paid $6,000. Stenographers were paid $100 a month.[11]

In 1925 buildings on the Clemson campus were concentrated around Tillman Hall. The present Sikes Hall was standing, and a main campus road passed by Hardin Hall and the engineering building, which was called Mechanics Hall. The school owned fifty-eight houses and apartments, scattered to the rear and alongside the college buildings, that were rented to faculty and staff at very low rates.[12] The Trustee House was used frequently by visiting trustees, who were met at the railroad station in a horse-drawn surrey and wheeled to campus.[13] The Calhoun mansion was still occupied by relatives of the Calhoun family, but rooms in the house were sometimes rented to Clemson cadets. The Clemson Hotel, located at the site of the present Clemson House, provided rooms and apartments for faculty, and today's College Avenue was not only the main street of downtown Clemson, but a dirt road connector between Greenville and Atlanta. The only paved sidewalk on campus connected Tillman Hall with the agriculture building, now Sikes Hall, and passed by the water fountain and concrete benches that had been given to the college by the class of 1917. Faculty children used the sidewalk for skating and riding tricycles, and President Sikes could frequently be seen talking and playing with them.

When he walked from his office in Tillman Hall to town, the president passed the old textile building, today's Godfrey Hall, and the Young Men's Christian Association (YMCA) building, then crossed the Seneca highway and passed Sloan's mercantile store. Turning to walk toward the center of town, which was only a block from the corner, Sikes passed Crawford's pressing club, the local dry cleaner. L. C. Martin's drugstore, which arranged to sell textbooks and supplies to the students during Sikes's administration and where students ordered class rings, was located next door. Proceeding further, Sikes would pass the community store, a grocery that had been organized by the faculty and located in the lower half of the Masonic building. If he crossed today's Earle Street, he would have been in front of the Fort Hill Depository, Clemson's only bank and the last building on that side of College Avenue.

Located on the other side of the street was Clinkscales livery stable, where mules looked out of open stalls at passersby. Another clothing shop was on that side of the street, and Judge Keller's store occupied one cor-

---

[11]Note the "Salary Roll for 1928-29," Sept. 1928 (?), CU President's papers, Sikes.

[12]The figures are in a memorandum from J. C. Littlejohn to Sikes, 1928, in ibid.

[13]This and the discussion that follows are based on Shanklin/Yandle interview, 3 Nov. 1986.

ner. Beyond the downtown were several churches and a busy railroad station that served as the transportation hub for students, faculty, visiting trustees, and anyone else who visited the college. Since the roads left much to be desired, few people traveled by car.

Economic Changes and the New Trend in Education

During the last half of the 1920s, Clemson College was slowly affected by major alterations in higher education that were ocurring in America. The changes at the college also resulted from the leadership of President Sikes. The country still experienced the post-World War I economic boom. Agriculture, by providing foodstuffs to a war-torn Europe, enjoyed golden years. There was a free spirit in the air. Incomes rose; old restrictions on behavior were modified. While the national mood reflected the prosperity, the South, including South Carolina, made a transition from low-income-producing agriculture to manufacturing. Textile manufacturing had expanded in the South at the end of the war, with many plants built in South Carolina where an abundance of cotton and a large pool of trainable labor existed. The latter could move easily from the thousands of small farms in the state to the scattered cotton mills being built in rural areas.[14]

Despite such changes, agriculture was still the dominant feature of the state's economy.[15] South Carolina remained poor, ranking in 1929 near the bottom of the United States in per capita income; the state's income level fell even more throughout most of Sikes's years as president at Clemson. When he arrived at the college the state had a population of 1,718,000, of which fifty-one percent was white. The dual color school system was the standard across the South, and the appropriations for public schools showed just how deep the disparity was between the two races.

---

[14]In 1923 there were 16.5 million spindles at work in Southern textile mills and 18.9 million in New England, which had been the center of textile manufacturing for almost two centuries. That same year cotton goods accounted for 67.6 percent of the value of all manufactured goods produced in South Carolina and about the same share of employment in manufacturing. See Jack Blicksilver, *Cotton Manufacturing in the Southeast: An Historical Analysis* (Atlanta: Bureau of Business and Economic Research, Georgia State College of Business Administration, 1959) 52, 91; and "The Carolina Economy," University of South Carolina Bureau of Business and Economic Research, 1958.

[15]Better than half the working population was employed on the 173 thousand farms in the state, a number that declined continuously thereafter; see "Carolina Economy." Charleston, with a population in 1920 of 67,000 was the largest city in the state; 83 percent of the state's population lived in the country. Note *The Statistical Abstract of the United States, 1925* (Washington DC: U. S. Department of Commerce, 1926).

In 1929 payments for the education of white children averaged $80, while expenditure per black child was $11.25.[16] Unpaved roads, moreover, were standard for South Carolina: of 64,409 miles of road in 1924, only 365 had a hard surface.[17] Higher education also operated on a relatively small scale, with the twenty-three colleges in the state enrolling about 6,400 students in 1924.

On a national level, the spirit of rising expectations that swept the country helped stimulate a new trend in higher education. Attention focused on the individual student, education of the whole person, greater choice and flexibility in courses of study, and less regimentation. Clemson, however, was less affected initially than many other colleges. It remained a military school, where cadets were not allowed to leave their rooms in the evening or the campus on weekends. The college regulated practically every aspect of student life. Rules set study hours in the evening (when students were not allowed to speak), forbade the possession of civilian clothes, required daily chapel attendance at 8:00 a.m., and made the towns of Seneca, Central, Anderson, and Pendleton off limits.

In some instances the regimented life had its pluses, even for the students. Payments of tuition provided all the necessities—food, clothing, and shelter. The military, moreover, was an equalizer. Everyone, rich or poor, wore the same clothes, had the same meager possessions, and followed the same schedule. "When a student makes his full payment to the treasurer," President Sikes described in his annual report to the trustees in 1931, "that student is entitled to a complete outfit of clothing . . . admission to all classes and laboratories of his chosen course . . . heat, light, and water . . . hospital facilities. . . . The student is entitled to membership in the Y.M.C.A and subscription to the student newspaper. He also has the privilege of free banking service at the treasurer's office."[18] Another advantage of the military life was the spirit it produced among the cadets, who were drawn together by force of a common adversary, the commandant.

However, what had worked in the past no longer seemed to fit the mood of the 1920s. The walkouts and disruptions had shown that Clemson students were unwilling to accept all the rules. The associated hazing also no longer seemed appropriate for the times. The problem was illustrated in a

---

[16]See "General Statistics on South Carolina," State Development Board, June 1958.

[17]Data here are from *Statistical Abstract, 1925*.

[18]E. W. Sikes, "Report of the President of the College," 31 Dec. 1931, in *Forty-Second Annual Report of the Board of Trustees of the Clemson Agricultural College to the General Assembly of South Carolina, 1931* (Clemson SC: Clemson Agricultural College, 1931) 18-19.

letter of 4 October 1927 from a cadet to his father, which the latter passed along to Sikes: "All we freshmen do is wait on old boys from six in the morning until twelve at night. . . . I am sick and tired of it. I suppose you have been reading articles editorials about hazing up there. Only thirty boys were found bruised severely. If this is college I don't want it."[19]

Not only was Sikes aware of such problems, but evidence suggests that he knew of the changes in higher education nationally and that, when he assumed the presidency at Clemson, he may have envisioned altering the direction of the college. He compared it to counterparts in other states and soon learned that adjustments had to be made. A report of 4 October 1927 from F. H. H. Calhoun, the director of resident teaching at the college, indicated that Clemson stood second among agricultural schools in the country in the number of units in military science and tactics, and that only two other schools required drill for students in their junior and senior years.[20] Although the military tradition held firm, there was ample room for change in the many student regulations. For example, to the delight of the cadets, who were ordered to rise each day at 6:00 a.m., Sikes allowed them to go to bed earlier; the older restriction forbidding them to be in bed before 10:30 p.m. was changed to 7:30. The president, moreover, permitted students to have civilian clothes in their rooms, abolished daily chapel, removed places that were "off limits," did away with silence after the playing of taps, and allowed students to visit other dormitories.

In 1927 Sikes also permitted national honorary fraternities to establish chapters on the campus, a move designed to reward outstanding scholarship. He even took up the cause of the students to obtain Greek-letter social fraternities, which state law precluded at the time. In 1932 he proudly listed in his annual report to the trustees, as part of a section titled "The Individual Student," the many national honor societies at Clemson and described honors day, an event that has continued to the present. The report also noted, however, that other types of students received attention at the college. A faculty committee on deficient students augmented faculty advisers in assisting students, and a reexamination and promotion committee dealt with serious problems faced by students who did border-

---

[19]See the letter from the father, John W. Conder, to Sikes, 4 Oct. 1927, CU President's papers, Sikes. The student remained at Clemson, however, apparently because of the following advice he received in a telegram from his father: "Letter received. Would you be one out of twelve hundred to quit and be bluffed out by a bunch of rough necks. You would never be worth a tinker's damn if you were to quit at this stage. Act within your rights and defend them to the best of your ability and allow no one to impose upon you any further and I am with you on that as long as I have a dollar or any strength left."

[20]Calhoun to Sikes, 4 Oct. 1927, in CU President's papers, Sikes.

line classwork. Sikes's focus during the first years of his presidency on individual students and their problems carried over to the faculty. He met monthly in his office with newly hired professors and took time to work personally with many others.[21]

That Sikes possibly held a vision of a new college was also supported by the extensive changes he introduced in the curricula, programs, and structure of the college. During his first year as president, ninety-four percent of the student body was from South Carolina; fifty of the 146 graduating seniors received degrees in agriculture, twenty-nine in electrical engineering, and thirty-two in textiles.[22] The diplomas reflected the state's economy. By 1939, fifty-three of the 282 graduating seniors received degrees in agriculture, forty-seven in agriculture education, forty-three in textiles, and forty-one in general science, the equivalent of a program in arts and sciences. The last category of diplomas reflected a significant change in curriculum development and structure of the college.

As part of Sikes's efforts to obtain accreditation for the college, in 1926 the department of arts and sciences was formed and modern languages was added as an area of study. Moreover, the agriculture department began programs in agricultural economics and poultry science, a physical education department was created, and the textiles department added studies in textile research and testing. In 1928 the two-year programs were dropped and the textiles curriculum moved from vocational training toward engineering and process management. During the year the college offered its first graduate programs when it listed master of science degrees in agronomy, agricultural economics, education, horticulture, zoology, and entomology. From 1929-1933 a master of science degree was introduced in textile chemistry and dyeing along with a new bachelor of science program in agricultural engineering. New professional degrees in civil, electrical, and mechanical engineering were added, and so were courses in religion in the department of arts and sciences.

Sikes also led a major restructuring of the college in 1933, one that left an imprint still apparent today. The programs of the college were formed

---

[21]Note E. W. Sikes, "Report of the President of the College," 31 Dec. 1932, in *Forty-Third Annual Report of the Trustees of the Clemson Agricultural College to the General Assembly of South Carolina, 1932* (Clemson SC: Clemson Agricultural College, 1932) 12-13; and Bryan, 112-14.

[22]S. B. Earle, "Report of Acting President of the College," 1 July 1925, in *Thirty-Sixth Annual Report of the Board of Trustees of the Clemson Agricultural College to the General Assembly of South Carolina, 1925* (Clemson SC: Clemson Agricultural College, 1925) 13-14. The discussion of changes in program and curricula that follows is based on data drawn from similar reports for the noted years. See, moreover, Bryan, 114-15.

into six schools: agriculture, engineering, chemistry, general science, textiles, and vocational studies. The latter administered programs in several areas of education: agricultural, industrial, textile, and general education.

Finances and the Great Depression

Obtaining money for Clemson, a common problem for most university presidents, constantly plagued President Sikes. The college had received its first state appropriation from general funds in 1922. Previously the school operated on student fees and the proceeds of a tax collected by the state from the sale of fertilizer.[23] Consequently, the school's fortunes were tied to those of the agricultural community. When farmers prospered, Clemson did well; when farming suffered, so did the college.

History revealed that the proceeds of the fertilizer tax had fluctuated significantly, from a low of $155,000 in 1914 to a record high of $313,000 in 1919.[24] When tax receipts fell consecutively in 1915 and 1916, the college received loans from the state. After receipts dipped again in 1921 and 1922, the state finally provided direct appropriations to supplement the tax and continued the assistance thereafter. But the tax remained the largest source of funds and fluctuated with the agricultural economy. Sikes's struggle with the tax, however, encountered its most serious test when the Depression hit South Carolina.

Some writers have suggested that the Great Depression had little effect on the South because the region already suffered from a depressed economy. Although it was true that incomes did not fall as much in the South as in the nation as a whole, the problems faced by South Carolinians and Clemson were nevertheless severe. Per capita income in South Carolina fell from $270 in 1929 to a low of $157 in 1932.[25] The state did not regain its 1929 income level until 1939. Its government, like many others, defaulted on bonds (although full restitution of debt was made later) and Clemson College found itself strapped for cash.

The problems faced by the College were reflected vividly in several ways. Enrollments declined from a record high of 1,336 students in 1930-

---

[23]A table listing annual college budgets, the proceeds of the fertilizer tax, and state loans and eventual appropriations is found in S. B. Earle, "Report of the President of the College," 20 Dec. 1924, *Thirty-Fifth Annual Report of the Board of Trustees of the Clemson Agricultural College to the General Assembly of South Carolina, 1924* (Clemson SC: Clemson Agricultural College, 1924) 10-12, 43-45.

[24]Ibid.

[25]The figures are taken from the volumes of *The Statistical Abstract of the United States* (Washington DC: U. S. Department of Commerce, 1929-1932).

Enoch Walter Sikes 1925-1940   Kate Salley Palmer

1931 to 1,108 two years later. Sikes, in his report of 1931 to the trustees, emphasized the sharp reduction in the monies from the fertilizer tax earmarked for Clemson. From receipts of $209,000 in 1925-26, the level had fallen to $150,000, and estimates for 1931-1932 set the proceeds at $100,000.[26] Farmers were buying much less fertilizer because the price of cotton was falling rapidly. A portion of the tax revenues was used by Clemson to fund fertilizer and livestock testing and other services. Prospects for continuing such programs, however, appeared bleak, as did support for general faculty research and quality teaching. "The man who can not and does not keep pace with progress," the president argued in presenting the school's plight to the trustees, "has no place on the faculty of a college like Clemson." But also of pressing importance was the state law requiring that 220 scholarships of one hundred dollars each for students in agriculture and textiles at the college be funded from the fertilizer tax revenues.[27]

---

[26]Sikes, "Report of the President," 31 Dec. 1931, 10.

[27]Ibid., 9, 11, 17. See also the undated memorandum from Sikes, "Why Appropriations for Clemson College Should Not be Reduced," CU President's papers, Sikes.

Sikes thus found himself in a difficult situation. Reporting to the board in 1932, he emphasized that because the financial crisis could destroy much of the college's progress of the last six years, the time had arrived to determine what kind of school Clemson would be. Hardly had the ink dried on his report, however, when the troubles deepened. To remain within the budget of 1932 that was $98,000 or twenty-five percent less than the total appropriations and revenues of 1930, the president and trustees implemented salary reductions that ranged from five to twenty percent and slashed equipment purchases and supply budgets. As the even harder times of 1933 hit the college, Sikes found no choice but to cut salaries again, putting a one-third reduction into effect. The situation only improved slightly in the spring, when the president instructed the faculty "that the College will be able to modify [the] reduction and pay teachers and officers an additional $25 per month."[28]

Nevertheless, Sikes told the trustees on 1 July that the college's "chief problem" was still "financial, the effort to end the year with a balanced budget and with no outstanding obligations." Not only did he report the reduction of salaries but, even in the face of the hard times confronting cadets and their families, he noted that the college had raised its tuition from $40 to $60 for in-state students.[29] Another severe difficulty resulting from the Depression was trying to retain good faculty and attract replacements. For example, the head of the college's extension service, W. W. Long, emphasized to Sikes that, while the service sought to keep its key officials, its sharply declining budget would likely force reductions in its staff to one in each special area.[30]

Although budget cuts and reduced programs helped the school continue its operation, there was little aid initially for students who had no money. President Sikes, the faculty, and other townspeople made countless efforts to assist cadets as the latter stretched their spending money to remain in school. Sikes's secretary, Virginia Shanklin, remembered how the president in 1934 personally aided a cadet to remain in school; the student possessed only five dollars and a white linen suit to his name but

---

[28]See the president's memo to teachers and officers, 26 May 1933, provided the author by G. E. Metz.

[29]E. W. Sikes, "Report of the President of the College," 1 July 1933, *Forty-Fourth Annual Report of the Board of Trustees of the Clemson Agricultural College to the General Assembly of South Carolina, 1933* (Clemson SC: Clemson Agricultural College, 1933) 5.

[30]Note the undated memo from Long to Sikes, CU President's papers, Sikes.

was determined to receive his Clemson diploma.³¹ G. E. Metz, a faculty member and the registrar, recalled that the federal government's New Deal programs significantly rescued hard-pressed students.³² The Federal Emergency Relief Administration and the National Youth Administration provided funding for students to work part-time on campus, much like today's work-study programs. The cadets were paid thirty cents an hour for their work. The New Deal had arrived at Clemson, and there was finally ample money to go around.

The New Deal programs, furthermore, brought bricks and mortar to Clemson. With aid from the Works Progress Administration, the college erected four new dormitories that provided rooms for 420 cadets and relieved a serious shortage of housing. Federal assistance also supplied the means for Clemson to construct an agricultural building (named Long Hall), something Sikes had sought for years.³³ He often commented how strange it was for an agricultural college not to have an agriculture building. The South Carolina general assembly, however, would not act. Although funds finally came from Washington, action was still required of the assembly, which had to grant its permission for the construction of federally funded projects on state land.

Not only was Long Hall constructed, but as federal money poured in, a new textile building, today's Sirrine Hall, was erected. Federal funds also helped pave campus streets, build a new dairy barn, and increase agricultural research and extension services. Moreover, under the imaginative and energetic leadership of George W. Aull, a Clemson graduate and chairman of the department of agricultural economics and rural sociology, the college participated in the New Deal's land purchase and development program and ultimately acquired 29,625 acres of privately owned farmland in the immediate vicinity of the campus. What is today the

---

[31] Shanklin/Yandle interview, 3 Nov. 1986. To help the cadet, Sikes inquired of the local Episcopal minister whether the church needed a part-time janitor. The church hired the student, but that did not provide him with enough money. The student then asked about working with the waiters, all of whom were black, at the Clemson Hotel. The kitchen supervisor refused, maintaining that she did not wish to have a white cadet working with the black help. The student, however, persisted and finally broke the color line. The job kept him in school, and at the time of his graduation, he had become the majordomo of the hotel.

[32] Metz/Yandle interview, 4 Nov. 1986.

[33] The struggle to gain funding and legislative permission for the construction of Long Hall and other buildings is recounted in *The 1936 Taps: Annual Publication of the Corps of Cadets at Clemson* (Clemson College SC, 1936) esp. the sections titled "The Administrative Year" and "Clemson's New Buildings Under the WPA Program."

Clemson forest was then worn-out, eroded land. Aull served as supervisor of the project for the federal government during 1934-1936, but thereafter the management changed and some college authorities cooled on its assuming responsibility for the land.

Among them were President Sikes and James C. Littlejohn, the school's business manager. However, the trustees accepted in July 1939 the long-term lease on the land offered by Washington, which remained in effect until the government in 1954 deeded the land to the college.[34] Although Sikes's support of Clemson's receiving title to the largest New Deal benefit for the school appeared to waver by the end of the 1930s, his legacy and the New Deal were nevertheless entwined. Possibly because of the influence of his former professor, Woodrow Wilson, Sikes called himself a "Progressive Democrat." He was never uncomfortable with the efforts of the federal government to assist Clemson, but instead welcomed them.

While federal programs brought great assistance to Clemson, however, they did not provide for sorely needed improvements in the faculty. By 1939 the college's hard-won accreditation was in jeopardy,[35] Discussions with officials from the Association of Secondary Schools and Colleges highlighted continued weaknesses in the faculty. Only twenty percent held doctoral degrees, which ranked Clemson second from the bottom among land-grant schools; the percentage with master's degrees was the lowest of such schools. Moreover, funding for the library was inadequate: the seventy cents budgeted per student for books had to be raised to three dollars. Sikes, with the trustees' support, both gained the library monies and addressed the faculty problems. He especially required professors under forty-five years of age to continue their education in the summers or while on leave until they earned advanced degrees.[36] His program and additional funds found to support it satisfied the Association, saved accreditation, and steadily improved the quality of the faculty.

---

[34]The federal government stipulated that it would retain mineral rights to the land and that the latter should be used only for educational and public purposes; an extensive discussion, including mention of Sikes's role in the project, is in Bryan, 118-21. See, too, Robert T. Sorrells, "The Clemson Experimental Forest: Its First Fifty Years," College of Forest and Recreation Resources, Clemson University, 1984.

[35]This problem and the following discussion is based on a memorandum from Sikes to the faculty, 24 July 1939, CU President's papers, Sikes.

[36]What was now required of the faculty, however, had been encouraged by Sikes since the beginning of his presidency; see, for instance, "Newsletter No. 7," 4 Oct. 1928, in ibid., which noted that "a number of the members of the Clemson faculty have taken graduate work at various institutions in this country and abroad during the summer."

Despite such problems, major figures in Clemson's history served on the faculty and staff and in the administration during Sikes's years. Buildings on today's campus bear some of their names (including that of Sikes): R. N. Brackett was head of chemistry; William W. Long directed the agricultural extension service; J. D. Harcombe was mess officer; H. W. Barre supervised experiment station research; D. W. Daniel headed the English faculty; S. M. Martin was professor of mathematics; W. E. Godfrey was professor of physics; James C. Littlejohn was the business manager; Rudolph E. Lee was professor of architecture; and S. R. Rhodes was professor of electrical engineering. Moreover, the board of trustees included S. A. Burns, Alan Johnstone, A. F. Lever, and R. I. Manning.

Episodes in the Sikes Administration and Retirement

Beyond the administrative difficulties Sikes confronted as a consequence of his office, and later of the Depression, he faced his share of day-to-day problems. For instance, when the solicitor of the tenth judicial district in Anderson alleged in October 1927 that whiskey was being sold by "outsiders" and consumed in the college's YMCA, Sikes—a teetotaler—increased police surveillance to halt the illegal activity.[37] Also at the beginning of his administration, the president and his business officer, Littlejohn, concerned themselves with placing the Clemson College Hotel, today's Clemson House, on a sound financial basis[38] and with replacing major losses to college property resulting from fires. During the night of 1 April 1925, immediately following the visit of the newly appointed Sikes to Clemson to acquaint himself with the campus, the agricultural hall (now Sikes Hall) burned. Since the exterior of the building was not severely damaged, the structure was rebuilt to house the library. Twelve months later, the old mechanical hall that had housed engineering since the earliest days, was lost to fire.[39] Plans for the construction of a new engineering building, Riggs Hall, were begun soon by Rudolph E. Lee, and the cornerstone was laid in November 1927.

---

[37]L. W. Harris to Sikes, 3 Oct. 1927, in CU President's papers, Sikes.

[38]See Littlejohn to Mrs. N. T. Pickens (manager of the hotel), 4 Oct. 1927, in ibid. Littlejohn and Sikes, after reviewing the hotel's financial records, learned that it was losing $1500 annually. At the time room and board for a month cost $31.

[39]Fire companies from as far away as Greenville arrived to fight the blaze in June 1926, during which J. F. Burns, one of the firemen, perished. The trustees quickly passed a resolution providing that Burns's three small sons would be given educations at Clemson when old enough to attend the college. See W. C. Cothran (a Greenville attorney representing Burns's widow) to Sikes, 19 Nov. 1927, in CU President's papers, Sikes.

Athletics also received Sikes's attention. A former star lineman of the Wake Forest football team, he took a keen interest in Clemson's athletics program. Apparently the successful but brief years of John W. Heisman as football coach at Clemson (1900-1903) had not established a winning tradition at the college.[40] The 1925 squad, coached by Bud Saunders, had won only one game out of eight, losing to Presbyterian, Auburn (then the Alabama Polytechnic College), Kentucky, the University of South Carolina, Wofford, Florida, and Furman. The lone victory, by the hardly decisive score of 6-0, was against The Citadel. Although the team improved slightly the next year, winning two games, the school's athletic program was $8,000 in debt, which contributed to the cancellation of Saunders's contract.[41]

Sikes, concerned about the college's miserable record, asked F. H. H. Calhoun, the director of resident teaching and chairman of the school's athletic council, to investigate the problem. Calhoun responded with a lengthy letter that gave a detailed and sad analysis of the prospects. He listed eleven reasons for Clemson's football woes, which included the school's isolated location; indifference on the part of the alumni; a lack of school traditions; the difficulty of the academic programs; no gymnasium or courses in physical education; insufficient school spirit; and the fact that the school did not encourage "the buying of high school players," a practice that had been discontinued at the college but not by its rivals.

Calhoun especially discussed the alumni, who were critical of Saunders. "Individually alumni are most charming people," he told Sikes. "Collectively they are a nuisance and often a menace. . . . I am firmly convinced that these alumni want to help the college, but their idea of so doing seems to be by holding thumbs down at the end of an unsuccessful football season."[42] With regard to "buying" players, Calhoun added:

> Whether we approve or deplore this practice, we can never meet a situation by refusing to face facts. I am of the opinion that it is now impossible for a college which does not go into the business of buying players to compete with those who do. . . . I have heard of men selling a pair of suspenders for $200, or a belt for $300, or who were given several hundred dollars during the football season for a few hours of nominal work a month.[43]

---

[40]The data on Clemson's records are in Joe Sherman, *Clemson Tigers: A History of Clemson Football* (Columbia SC: R. L. Bryan, 1976) 206-14. See, moreover, Bryan, 206-207.

[41]See the 5 Oct. 1927 note, unsigned, detailing the athletic association's deficit, CU President's papers, Sikes; and Sherman, 27.

[42]Calhoun to Sikes, undated, CU President's papers, Sikes.

[43]Ibid.

Clemson's new coach in 1927, Josh Cody of Vanderbilt, quickly produced three winning seasons in a row. A new feeling of optimism swept the campus. For example, *The Clemson Alumnus* proudly announced in its November 1927 issue the college's recent 3-0 victory over Auburn, the first such triumph over that major rival in twenty-one years. The magazine praised Cody for "leading the Tigers out of the morass into which they have plunged."[44]

In 1930 President Sikes separated the athletic program from the physical education department and began to search for ways to improve the school's football image. Clemson moved into prominence when Jess Neely, the coach at the University of Alabama who had just won the Rose Bowl, was hired for the 1931 season. Neely brought with him an assistant coach, a player on Alabama's championship team named Frank Howard. Despite the new talent, the college's football team suffered for several more years, but hit its stride in 1934 and won the Cotton Bowl in 1940. All of Calhoun's prophesies were turned upside down.

One phenomenon that Calhoun could not have predicted was the formation in 1934 of IPTAY, which stood originally for "I Pay Ten a Year." After what Neely called "seven lean years" of Clemson football, word circulated that the college needed financial support for athletics.[45] A small group of the school's alumni in Atlanta conceived an organization for that purpose and established IPTAY. With Neely's help, 162 members were enrolled during the group's first year, each paying ten dollars, but some suffering from the effects of the Depression did so with post-dated checks, turnip greens, sweet potatoes, and fresh milk.[46]

President Sikes's interests, however, extended beyond football players and athletes to all students, "the boys," as he called them. In his view every Clemson cadet was equal. He rejected anything that he believed would magnify the differences, such as the request in 1939 that Clemson form an affiliation with the National Conference on Christians and Jews. He wrote to one of the Conference's leaders: "There is no Gentile, Jew, Protestant, or Catholic on the campus of Clemson College. For fear that a distinction might be made I think it best not to raise the issue." However, despite his vigorous support of the YMCA on campus and the teaching of religion courses, he protested to the Conference "against a Jewish Vet-

---

[44]See *The Clemson Alumnus* 1:10 (Nov. 1927), copy in RMCL/CU; and on Cody, Sherman, 28-32.

[45]Note *IPTAY: The First Fifty Years*, ed. Harry S. Gault (Clemson SC: Clemson IPTAY Club, 1984) 4-5; Bryan, 209; and regarding Neely, Sherman, 33-74.

[46]Gault, 4; and Sherman, 71-73.

erans' Journal which is sent here for distribution." While others might be interested in the movement, Sikes concluded, Clemson had no need for it.[47]

Toward the end of his presidency, he responded to an inquiry from a sixth grader in nearby Anderson who apparently had asked about Sikes's life and what explained his success. In a letter to the youth Sikes not only discussed his career, but offered several "lessons" that he had learned from his experiences. "Don't be afraid of hard work" or "afraid to take part in games," he wrote. "Choose your friends with care and wisely," he continued, "and be loyal to them." Sikes concluded by advising the student to appreciate his parents and urging him to observe "the teachings of the New Testament as to right and wrong."[48]

Upon his retirement on 1 July 1940, Sikes assumed the title of president emeritus and lived in the Clemson community. He looked forward to spending his final years engaging in research and writing on South Carolina history, working in Baptist organizations, and maintaining contact with his many friends and colleagues. Such activities, however, occupied his time for less than a year; on 8 January 1941 he died quietly and without apparent warning. The papers left on his desk that day were carefully saved and stuffed away in an envelope. A random collection, they included fragments of poetry, writings on the history he was preparing, and names and addresses of people with whom he was corresponding. The notes reflected his lifelong interest in people, words, and the region where he had lived and worked.

Sikes had contributed significantly to the development of Clemson College, providing the school with fifteen years of stability and guiding it through the gruelling challenges of the Depression. The public image of Clemson, which had suffered with the last walkout at the college in 1925, had improved steadily. But most significant, Sikes not only found the funds with which to construct new buildings on the campus, he had expanded and enhanced the academic program of the college.

---

[47]See Sikes to Arthur H. Compton, 15 Jan. 1939, in CU President's papers, Sikes. According to Compton's previous letter to Sikes, 12 Jan. 1939, the conference's goal was "to persuade American college students of the necessity of understanding and cooperation among Catholics, Jews, and Protestants and to assist them to a fuller appreciation of the distinctive contributions to American culture which the various racial and religious groups are making." Of the YMCA, Sikes had once written: "This organization continues to render an invaluable service to the College community and students. . . . Catholics, Lutherans, and Presbyterians, while without a church, use the building." See his "Report of the President," 1 July 1933, 8.

[48]Sikes to James Bagwell, 5 Apr. 1940, CU President's papers, Sikes.

• *President Robert Franklin Poole, 1940–1958* •

• 10 •

THE GENTLEMAN MANAGER ROBERT FRANKLIN POOLE, 1940–1958

James C. Hite

On 1 July 1940 a tall, ruddy-faced man with pale blue eyes and thinning hair sat down behind the desk in the corner office on the first floor of Tillman Hall. R. F. Poole was forty-seven years old, the father of five children, a Presbyterian and Rotarian, and beginning a job he would hold for just twenty-four days short of eighteen years. He was the seventh president of what was then known as Clemson Agricultural College.[1] A scholar and gentleman whose style of leadership made him more akin to the Old South rather than the New, he presided over the college's survival of World War II and its aftermath. The school changed quickly from a military to a civilian, coeducational one, but without the serious unrest of previous times.

What did not change, however, was the rigorous defense by Clemson leaders, including Poole, of the college's policy of racial segregation, which received several initial but mild challenges. By the 1950s the problems confronting the president began to overwhelm him, as shown by his failure to perceive the dangers to the campus posed by the Hartwell Dam project. The college's ruling board of trustees, eager to adapt Clemson to the rapid economic and social changes transforming the South, established administrative changes alien to Poole and implemented a new policy aimed at forcing him and other persons, whom the board believed had been at the college too long, to retire.

---

[1] See "Robert F. Poole," *Who Was Who in America*, 4 vols. (Chicago: A. N. Marquis, 1960) 3:693.

From Graduate to President of Clemson

Poole was no stranger to Clemson. He had come to the college in 1912 from a farm in Laurens county to take advantage of a scholarship he had received to study botany. He had done well as a student. The 1916 catalogue of the college listed his name among the students earning academic honors.[2] He was also elected vice president of the Columbian Literary Society and the Laurens County Club. The college yearbook for his senior year said of him: "By his amiable disposition, 'SARGE' has won many friends." Then, with perspicuity rare in yearbooks, the 1916 *Taps* added: "In the near future, we would hear of him as the 'eminent' botanist, 'DR. POOLE.'"[3]

Although the Pooles were not a part of the low-country aristocracy of South Carolina, they were an old and respected family in the Carolina Piedmont, possessing some of the most fertile land in Laurens county. The first Poole had purchased land in 1788 in the same rural area where R. F. Poole was born, had run a wheat and corn mill on Buckhead creek, and built a Methodist church called Poole's Chapel.[4] The Clemson president's father, Ula Barto Poole, had married Lila Yeargin, a school teacher and member of another prominent local family. In the years just before the birth of R. F. Poole, his mother's kinswoman, Mary Yeargin, had played an instrumental role in founding Winthrop College as a place of higher education for women in South Carolina.[5]

Young R. F. Poole had grown up on his father's farm on Warrior's creek, a few miles east of Gray Court. He was the eldest of seven children and, except for the death of his mother when he was thirteen years old, there seems little in his childhood that was greatly different from that of thousands of farm children growing up in the Piedmont during the early years of the twentieth century. He awakened every morning at 4:00, milked two cows, and then, after breakfast, walked three miles to a two-room school. When he had time away from farm chores, he liked to hunt and

---

[2] Clemson College, *Catalogue 1916-17*, 50-51, defined the honor that Poole, the holder of a scholarship, received: "That a student attaining this standard shall have no failures, no work to make up, and less than twenty demerits at the close of each term during the session."

[3] *Taps '16*, the Clemson annual yearbook, also remarked that Poole "is a big husky fellow. . . . He came to Clemson in the fall of 1912, 'through Greenville.' Since then, he says Heaven and Greenville are one and the same place."

[4] See Julian S. Bolick, *A Laurens County Sketchbook, with a Brief Sketch of the Development of Laurens County by Edna Riddle Foy* (Laurens SC: Privately printed, 1973) 5-6.

[5] Ibid.

fish, leisure activities he pursued for the rest of his life. Later Poole recalled that he spent time during his youth serving as chauffeur for an uncle who was a country doctor and flirted briefly with the idea of becoming a doctor himself. But it was a notion that fled by quickly. Except for that passing fancy, Poole said, his interests had been always in becoming an agriculturalist.[6]

After his graduation from Clemson, Poole went north for graduate study, receiving the master of science degree at Rutgers in 1917. He was called into the army when the United States entered World War I and assigned to a unit experimenting with the use of aerial photography. Eventually the military duty took him to France and Germany, giving the young man not only an opportunity to see something of Europe, but to experiment with a new scientific tool.[7]

Discharged from the army, Poole returned to Rutgers to complete study for the doctor of philosophy degree in plant pathology, which he was awarded in 1921. During the 1920s, first as a member of the Rutgers faculty, and later as a professor at North Carolina State College, his studies of the sweet potato built him a reputation as an outstanding young scientist.[8] But his heart always had been in South Carolina, and with his appointment at Clemson in July 1940 he was home again.

Physically Poole was an impressive man. It was not that he was handsome; his face was rather plain and his nose too large. But he had a large frame, and while by the time he arrived as president at Clemson he had begun to put on a paunch, he possessed what theater people call "presence." Even in photographs of Poole with others, the eye was almost invariably drawn to him, a large, sad-eyed man in a baggy suit who radiated warmth and good humor. Yet his selection as Clemson's president was not without whispers that he was chosen because of his family connections.

When E. W. Sikes announced in 1939 that he would retire as president at the end of June 1940 and the college's board of trustees began the search for a new chief executive, three candidates for the job emerged. The first was James C. Littlejohn, the powerful business manager of the college. He was a man of proven ability who knew the "ins" and "outs" of the school's operations. When later, in 1943, students complained to him that the food being served air corps cadets stationed for training at Clemson was better than the food being served regular Clemson students, he

---

[6]See the public service award, the "Scroll of Honor," presented to Poole by the *Anderson Daily Mail,* which was published in the student newspaper, *The Tiger,* 15 Jan. 1942.
[7]Ibid.
[8]*Who Was Who,* 3:693.

replied brusquely, "They're paying for it." They were. The federal government was paying one dollar per head per day for the food served the air corps cadets, while regular Clemson students were paying only sixty-five cents per day. Littlejohn's reply, however, was not the type that won him warm friends.[9] He was respected, admired, and perhaps even feared, but he also had antagonized a number of faculty members and, doubtlessly, powerful people beyond the campus. Moreover, he lacked advanced degrees, and there was a strong feeling that the president of the college should hold the academic credentials that would be expected of a senior member of the faculty. Littlejohn's candidacy probably was doomed from the start, and he was sensible enough to remove himself from further consideration very early in the search for president.[10]

The second candidate was Sidney B. Hall, state superintendent of public instruction in Virginia. Hall possessed impressive academic credentials and a great deal of administrative experience. A native of Great Bridge, Virginia, he was forty-five years old. At the College of William and Mary, where he received a bachelor's degree, he had obtained Phi Beta Kappa honors. He held a master of arts degree from the University of Virginia and a doctor of education degree from Harvard. But except for three years as professor of secondary education at the Peabody College for Teachers, Hall had no experience in higher education.[11] Perhaps more important, he had no experience with land-grant colleges and no ties to agriculture.

The trustees could not fail to notice, however, that R. F. Poole had twenty years of experience in strong, well-regarded land-grant colleges as a researcher, teacher, and administrator. He had published 130 scientific papers and articles, one of which had been selected as the outstanding technical bulletin produced at any American agricultural institution in 1930. For the past ten years he had been chairman of the committee supervising the graduate programs at North Carolina State, in effect (albeit without the title) dean of the graduate school.[12] On paper Poole was at least as well qualified as Hall.

Poole also offered other attractions as a potential president for Clemson. Not the least of these was his possession of a Clemson degree. No

---

[9]Wright Bryan, *Clemson: An Informal History of the University, 1889-1979* (Columbia SC: R. L. Bryan, 1979) 130.

[10]See *The Tiger*, 27 Mar. 1940.

[11]Ibid. reported Hall as a candidate considered by the trustees. The biographical information on him is from *Who's Who in America*, 21 vols. (Chicago: A. N. Marquis, Co., 1940) 21:1139.

[12]From the "Scroll of Honor" in *The Tiger*, 15 Jan. 1942.

graduate of the college had ever served as president, and the appointment of an alumnus would have advantages in dealing with the growing body of alumni. Almost three-fourths of South Carolina's population remained on farms in 1940,[13] and such persons had proprietary interests in Clemson. At least half of the agenda items at board of trustee meetings involved agricultural programs administered by the college. Poole, as the son of a South Carolina farmer and as an agricultural scientist of distinction, would be able to speak to the state's important farm constituency with undeniable credibility, if not always in standard English grammar.

Finally, Poole had made a fortunate decision in choosing a wife. After he had completed his doctorate at Rutgers and been employed by the New Jersey agricultural experiment station as an associate plant pathologist, he had traveled to Abbeville to marry Sara Margaret Bradley. She was a young woman of beauty and charm, and doubtlessly it was her own special qualities that attracted the young plant pathologist to her. They were characteristics that endeared her to students and faculty at Clemson during the long years she lived on the campus, first as the president's wife and later as his widow. But she was also the niece of both W. W. Bradley who, in 1940, was chairman of the Clemson College board of trustees, and of Professor Mark E. ("Prep") Bradley, one of the school's venerable faculty members.

Her connection to the trustees caused tongues to wag when the board announced on 22 March 1940 that R. F. Poole had been selected as successor to Sikes. Perhaps it was true that this tie caused the board to give more attention to Poole as a potential president than he might have received if he had a wife without kin in important places at Clemson. There were other Clemson alumni with equally distinguished academic achievements. Yet the evidence was overwhelming that, of the three men mentioned in the press as possible successors to Sikes, Poole was objectively the best qualified for the position. Moreover, despite the gossip that may have circulated, the announcement was well received in the South Carolina press and among Clemson alumni and students. According to the *Anderson Daily Mail,* which presented Poole with a public service award in January 1942, "Dr. Poole and Clemson College grew up together."[14]

---

[13]See, for instance, the diagram, "Urban and Rural Population of South Carolina: 1790 to 1940," in U. S. Department of Commerce, Bureau of the Census, *Sixteenth Census of the United States: 1940,* vol. 1, *Population: Number of Inhabitants* (Washington DC: U. S. Government Printing Office, 1942) 975.

[14]"They are continuing to grow together," the *Daily Mail* added in its award, "for no other man is better qualified than he to fill the position of the college's chief executive." See the paper's "Scroll of Honor" reprinted in *The Tiger,* 15 Jan. 1942.

The public viewed him as a Clemson man who had made good and was returning to his alma mater to lead it to new heights.

Leading a Sleepy Country College

The college that Poole returned to in July 1940 was not significantly different from the one he had left in the summer of 1916. It was bigger—there had been 802 students at Clemson in 1915-1916; enrollment in 1940-41 was 2,381.[15] The school also had made some qualitative progress, and a few of the faculty, mostly those connected to the agricultural experiment station who had opportunities for research, were acquiring national reputations.[16] However, Clemson was still a sleepy country college in a sleepy Southern village miles and miles from the rest of the world.

Many of the faculty and others who had been prominent at the college when Poole was a student retained their stature when he returned as president. These included Littlejohn who, for all practical purposes, was the "prime minister" at Clemson, and S. W. Evans, the college treasurer and secretary of the board of trustees. Professor F. H. H. ("Rock") Calhoun kept his finger on chemistry and geology; Professor S. M. ("Major") Martin still presided over mathematics; Professor Samuel B. Earle was dean of engineering; and the venerable D. W. Daniel, although officially retired, was retained to keep the academic programs on an even keel.

In the minds of most Clemson alumni, these men embodied the college. A photograph made shortly after Poole's return showed nine faculty members with an average of forty-seven years of service to the college. Many had taught the new president when he was a cadet, and he always showed them the utmost deference. Speaking to visitors in his office, Poole picked up a group photograph of the college faculty from 1912, his first year as a student, and declared, "These, and a few others like them, are the men who made Clemson great."[17]

The physical resources at the college, however, had not grown as rapidly as the enrollment. The library remained seriously deficient. It had contained 17,557 books in 1916, and only 28,000 in 1940.[18] There had been four recent buildings—Long, Riggs, and Sirrine halls and a new barracks—constructed with federal assistance by New Deal programs, and the amphitheater, a gift of the class of 1915, was completed in 1940. During

---

[15]See *Catalogue 1916-17*, 25; and Clemson Agricultural College, *Catalog Number, 1940-1941*, 251.

[16]Bryan, 122.

[17]Ibid.

[18]Compare the figures in *Catalogue 1916-17* and *Catalog Number 1940-1941*.

the 1930s Clemson also had acquired management over thousands of acres of surrounding land purchased by the Farmer's Resettlement Administration and referred to as the "land-use" project.[19] Despite the changes, however, a comparison of photographs of the school in the 1916 and 1941 *Taps* reveals that the intervening quarter century had not changed the physical appearance of the campus very much.

Poole appeared to have a good general grasp of what needed to be done at Clemson. He outlined his objectives to the press shortly after assuming office. His job, he told the *Anderson Daily Mail*, was to be a coordinator. He would attempt to improve and expand the physical plant, better the faculty, encourage scholarship and research, and move larger numbers of students to other institutions for graduate work, all aimed at broadening the scientific manpower and knowledge base for attacking the chronic problems of poverty in South Carolina and the region.[20] Poole knew the strengths and weaknesses of the Clemson faculty. While it contained, as Wright Bryan observed, many good, and a few great, teachers,[21] many lacked advanced degrees and the percentage holding doctorates was embarrassingly low. With the advances in science, Clemson was in danger of falling behind the pace that a land-grant college of good reputation needed to sustain, and Poole, with his experience at Rutgers and North Carolina State seemed to understand that.[22]

What is unclear is whether he possessed a well-developed and realistic strategy to achieve his objectives. His private papers and newspaper clippings from the time show that he had no interest in, or appreciation for, the management challenges that might exist at Clemson. In the interview with the *Daily Mail*, in which he outlined his goals for the college, he also explained his normal daily routine, which did not appear to suggest an intense involvement in the school's management.

He said that he arrived at the office between 8:00 and 9:00 a.m. and went through his mail. Then he held open house for students, faculty, and visitors and went home for lunch at 1:00 p.m. He returned to the office after lunch, but usually finished his day there by the early afternoon. From 5:00 until 6:30 p.m. each day, Poole explained, he visited some part of the campus—perhaps the dairy barn or the athletic fields. While he usually carried a briefcase home in the evenings, those who worked closely with him saw little evidence that he consulted what it contained at night.

---

[19]Bryan, 118-21.
[20]See "Scroll of Honor" in *The Tiger*, 15 Jan. 1942.
[21]Bryan, 122.
[22]Ibid., 122-23.

He spent many evenings attending meetings of various campus organizations. He maintained, moreover, a busy schedule speaking to groups in the state and to Clemson alumni clubs everywhere, an activity he much enjoyed. Poole added that he also found time to cultivate a garden, growing vegetables, dahlias, and chrysanthemums, and to continue his research on foliage diseases.[23] It was the schedule of a gentleman and a scholar, but one that suggested that the details of running the college were left to others.

If his activity as president was more relaxed than that of his successors, he shared with them a need to reassure the larger Clemson family of his support for athletics. In his first public appearance after being named president-designate at Clemson, he told 250 members of the alumni club in Columbia that he appreciated the value of sports to any college.[24] The comment indicated that Poole was not without an understanding of the political realities that he faced. It undoubtedly relieved some Clemson supporters who must have been waiting for such words from the new president.

His early remarks about college athletics provided revealing insight into the man. As a student he had made the Clemson football team the hard way, playing "class" football his freshman year and being a member of the "scrub" football team as a sophomore. He did not win his block "C" until he was a 167-pound senior end. The 1916 *Taps* declared: "After existing for two uneventful years, 'SARGE' decided to show them that he could play football as well as he could [do] anything else."[25] With such a background there was no reason to doubt the sincerity of his early endorsement of college sports. However, soon after the United States was drawn by Pearl Harbor into World War II, the Columbia newspaper, *The State*, observed that "Doctor Poole believes that the calling of varsity athletes might be a blessing in disguise for colleges since it might be the means of returning football to the students."[26]

Poole worried that college football was changing from the student game he had known into the entertainment business it has subsequently be-

---

[23]Note "Scroll of Honor" in *The Tiger*, 15 Jan. 1942.

[24]Undoubtedly Poole's interest was genuine, although he had to be encouraged by the widespread following that Clemson sports already possessed. For example, according to *The Tiger*, 10 May 1940, the Clemson football coach, Frank Howard, spoke briefly at the alumni meeting and showed films of the college's victory in the Cotton Bowl during the previous season. The student paper also remarked proudly, "As a member of the class of '15, Dr. Poole participated in the athletic program, being a member of the football team."

[25]See *Taps* '16.

[26]*The State* (Columbia SC), 13 Jan. 1942.

come. Yet at no time in his presidency was there evidence that he took steps to set things right. Indeed, within months after assuming his office, Poole recommended to the trustees that the college construct a 15,000-seat stadium. He told *The Tiger*, the student newspaper, that such a structure would draw "name football teams like Tennessee, Kentucky, and Tulane to South Carolina." It also would, he added a bit disingenuously, be used by farmer organizations, singing conventions, and other large groups that regularly met at Clemson.[27] The foundations for the present 80,000-seat Memorial stadium, therefore, were laid by a president who seemed to possess genuine, if infrequently spoken, concerns that college football was in danger of running out of control.

The War Weakens the Military Tradition

Regardless of the ideas Poole may have brought with him about the leadership he would provide Clemson, events in the larger world soon began to shape the agenda. Just seventeen months after he assumed the presidency, the Japanese attacked Pearl Harbor and pulled the United States into the World War. Always noted for his calmness (he never seemed to be rushed or flustered, the *Daily Mail* remarked), Poole called the students together and urged them to "maintain stability and poise, and await such time as you may be needed before abandoning educational opportunities."[28] Most of the students remained in school, but soon *The Tiger* reported the deaths of alumni on active duty and speculated on the whereabouts of others, such as Henry D. Leitner ('37) and Beverly ("Ben") N. Skardon ('38), both known to be with General Douglas MacArthur in the Philippines.[29] Indeed, Clemson furnished more officers to the army during the first two years of the war than any other American institution except Texas A&M.[30] Poole was prescient enough to see that most college men would soon be at war and that his immediate job was to find the best use of the college's facilities in the war effort.

Poole directed his efforts during the next four years toward that end. He urged the military to use colleges to teach math, physics, and other basic courses.[31] The appointment of James F. Byrnes, a member of the Clemson trustees, to oversee all war mobilization efforts for the United

---

[27]*The Tiger*, 3 Oct. 1940.
[28]*Anderson Daily Mail*, 9 Dec. 1941.
[29]*The Tiger*, 6 Mar. 1942.
[30]See *Anderson Independent*, 23 May 1943.
[31]*The State*, 13 Jan. 1942.

States, gave Poole special access to high officials in Washington, and the board gave him "blanket authority" to work with the federal government in the war effort in whatever fashion seemed most appropriate.[32]

In 1943 the basement of Sirrine Hall was turned over to the Army Signal Corps and the first contingent of a thousand Army Air Corps cadets arrived on campus for flight training (using the Anderson airport). By July 1943 all able-bodied students of military age had left the campus. Their places were filled with aircrew students of the Army Air Corps and a unit of the Army Specialized Training Program (ASTP). Clemson had gone to war.[33] Many members of the college faculty also were away on military leave. Some who remained served as instructors in the various military programs on campus. Wallace T. Ferrier of agricultural economics, for example, was detailed to teach navigation to Air Corps cadets, and James M. Stepp, also of agricultural economics, was assigned to teach history in the ASTP program.

Poole kept his renowned composure throughout this monumental transformation. His prestige in Washington undoubtedly increased because of his close ties to Byrnes. He traveled often to the nation's capital to confer with government officials on the problems of colleges and universities in dealing with the war effort. He was also elected president in 1943 of the Southern Association of Colleges, a position that made him a representative of higher education in the region and that also increased his prestige in Washington. However, there is little to suggest that Poole ever became involved in the details of administration, leaving those to Littlejohn and others and becoming active only in situations where the prestige of Clemson's president was needed to deal with the problems.[34]

By the spring of 1944 the shape of the war's eventual outcome was becoming evident, and the trustees at their meeting on 7 April first discussed plans for the return of servicemen. The board approved a recommendation that the college survey "practical courses" that it might offer them. Who presented the recommendation and the extent to which Poole played a role in it is not clear.[35] Yet at the close of 1944 and beginning of 1945,

---

[32]Bryan, 128.

[33]Ibid., 128-30.

[34]There is nothing in Special Collections, R. M. Cooper Library/Clemson University (hereafter cited as RMCL/CU) that suggests otherwise. See the clipping from an unknown newspaper in microfilm, "Robert Franklin Poole Scrapbooks, 1940-1959," reel 2, in Poole papers, RMCL/CU.

[35]See microfilm, reel 3, "Minutes of Board of Trustees" (1940-62), 7 Apr. 1944, RMCL/CU.

it was apparent that it would take several years after the end of the war before Clemson could return to normal operations. Preparing for the return of servicemen was almost as great a challenge as making the transformation to a war footing.

However, Poole did little to involve himself in the management problems arising from the postwar influx of ex-servicemen into Clemson. Apparently most of the work in finding housing and classroom space to accommodate the 2,700 students expected in 1946 was left to Littlejohn. The trustees also took the initiative at the end of 1945 in contacting South Carolina's senators, Olin D. Johnston and Burnet R. Maybank, to secure their influence in obtaining surplus government housing for use by veterans, many of whom were married.[36] Moreover, Littlejohn's brother, Major General Robert M. Littlejohn, a former Clemson student, supervised for the government prefabricated housing that was intended for shipment to England. Through that connection Clemson secured the "prefabs," small bungalows that for twenty-five years after the war, until they were removed to make way for Littlejohn Coliseum and Barre and Lehotsky Halls, served as housing for a generation of married students.[37] Poole's personal role in solving the housing problem apparently occurred after the major crisis was over. In July 1949 he testified before the committee on banking and commerce of the United States Senate in support of the Sparkman bill, which provided loans to colleges and universities for student and faculty housing.[38]

The Clemson president, however, was busy with other matters pertaining to the college's development. On 24 May 1945 he told the Southern Association of Science and Industry, meeting in Columbia, that the postwar industrial development of the South would depend on cooperation between industries and graduate schools.[39] A month later, at the meeting of the trustees, he secured approval for the establishment of a graduate school at Clemson, in which would be offered the degrees of master of science, applied masters (that is, professional degrees, such as the master of education), and doctor of philosophy. At the same meeting the trustees approved the creation of a school of commerce "for the purpose of teaching business principles related to agriculture, engineering and tex-

---

[36]Ibid., 23 Oct. 1945.
[37]Ibid., 24 June 1946.
[38]*Greenville News*, 18 July 1949.
[39]*Charleston News & Courier*, 26 May 1946.

tiles." Consent was also granted for a professorship of forestry in the agriculture department.[40]

Although it is unclear how much of the impetus for such change at Clemson came from its president and how much from the trustees, the immediate postwar years witnessed rising expectations about the college's future. The board approved at its October 1946 meeting the construction of Brackett Hall as a new home for chemistry and the building of a new heating plant for the campus.[41] The *Anderson Daily Mail* reported in November that Poole had informed the state budget commission that Clemson needed eight million dollars to build facilities to accommodate a permanent enrollment of 4,000.[42] Whether or not Poole framed the recommendations acted on by the trustees, it is obvious that they were in keeping with the goals he had outlined for his presidency soon after assuming the office six years before, and it seems probable that he was the moving force behind them.

There were problems, however, that foreshadowed the challenges Clemson would face during the 1950s. The returning servicemen were not inclined to accept the military discipline that was part of the Clemson tradition. Poole's attitude toward the military aspect also appeared ambivalent. A few weeks after he became president in July 1940, he spoke to the South Carolina Council of Farm Women in Rock Hill and praised military training "because of the discipline it affords. All of us need some discipline in our lives."[43] Two years later he quashed rumors alleging that, because of America's manpower needs in the war, Clemson would establish a drastically changed curriculum that would permit students to graduate early.[44] However, faced with the postwar reality of hardened veterans

---

[40]See "Minutes of Board," 16 June 1945. A school of commerce, however, was not established until the creation of the college of industrial management and textile science in 1966.

[41]Ibid., 29 Oct. 1946.

[42]An editorial in the paper, 8 Nov. 1946, which supported the huge request, declared: "He is probably conservative in his estimate."

[43]This statement resulted as part of his emphasis in the speech on national defense. "We may all be pacifists at heart," he said, "but we want to be able to defend ourselves." In a reference to the war in Europe, he added that "Clemson College is thoroughly American and we will not tolerate the teachings of any 'isms' to our boys." See *The Tiger*, 14 Aug. 1940.

[44]In defending his view, he proudly stated to *The Tiger*, 15 Jan. 1942: "From 1930 to 1940 inclusive, 1,984 officers were graduated at Clemson. In addition to these, a large number completed the advanced R.O.T.C. course and all members of the student body have had sufficient training to make potential officers and capable non-commissioned officers. This is a very significant fact which indicates the soundness of the institution in its present procedures."

who questioned Clemson's military traditions, he appears to have persuaded the trustees to excuse veterans from most of the routine exercises the cadets had been expected to suffer through. The board approved a "liberal attitude" whereby veterans did not have to participate in reveille, drill, and "certain other formations." According to Wright Bryan, this was the beginning of the end of the military organization of Clemson.[45] In fact, never again was it a genuine military school.

Poole also had to face a potential revolt by the veterans over the long-established arrangement for the sale of textbooks. For many years the L. C. Martin drugstore in downtown Clemson had held a monopoly on the sale of such books to Clemson students. The store was owned by Pickens S. ("Doc") McCollum, a power in Pickens county politics and the Democratic party. While McCollum had enjoyed some popularity with Clemson students, his control over textbook sales angered the veterans, and they complained loudly to President Poole.

The problem reached a head when Leonard Crawford, a local Clemson resident and veteran, sought to establish his own bookstore in competition with McCollum. Crawford found, however, that he could not accept veterans' requisitions for books because of an agreement between McCollum and the college assigning that right solely to the Martin drugstore.[46] Crawford undoubtedly was interested in making money for himself, and, at least in part because he was also a veteran, the returning servicemen on campus supported him.

Someone—whether the veterans or someone else, is not clear—suggested forming a student cooperative to operate an alternative bookstore. A committee of veterans was formed to examine the idea, and Ferrier and Dairy Professor B. E. ("Big Ben") Goodale were persuaded to work with the group. While Poole's role in putting the committee together remains uncertain, the president nevertheless arranged for it to meet with the trustees on 20 June 1947.[47] The board, accepting the committee's appraisal that a student cooperative would be economically unfeasible because of the debt involved in handling veterans' requisitions, authorized Poole to begin the creation of a college-owned bookstore to replace the Martin drugstore. The new venture, of course, was also a monopoly, but the board ordered that it was to price books as low as possible, consistent

---

[45]Bryan, 131.
[46]*The Tiger*, 27 Jan., 18 Sept. 1947.
[47]Ibid., 18 Sept. 1947.

Robert Franklin Poole 1940–1958   Kate Salley Palmer

with covering its operating expenses.[48] Although some cadets remained dissatisfied and a student cooperative bookstore operated briefly during the autumn of 1947,[49] the crisis was weathered and, while students were (and still are) peeved at the prices they must pay for books, there was no more unrest.

The other major problem that arose at the end of the 1940s involved racial integration at Clemson. In 1948 the college received letters from Spencer M. and Edward Bracey, students at South Carolina State College in Orangeburg, inquiring about admission to Clemson. The Braceys wished to study engineering. Clemson was filled and overflowing with white students at the time, but even if it had not been, it was unlikely that the school, steeped in the tradition of racial segregation, would have consid-

---

[48]See "Minutes of Board," 20 June 1947. It is not clear if a college bookstore was established. Such a store was again recommended at the board meeting on 18 June 1954, but action on the proposal was deferred at the meeting on 25 Oct. 1954.

[49]According to *The Tiger*, 18 Sept. 1947, one of the directors of the cooperative referred to it "as an insurance plan . . . insurance against high rates, mal-treatment and unfair practices."

ered the applications of the black students. However, Poole presented the matter to the trustees, but he took no part in the board's discussion of it on 18 June 1948, except "to read correspondence relative to [the] application of Spencer M. Bracey." One trustee, Ben T. Leppard of Greenville, closed the deliberations by declaring "that public opinion and time would likely bring about a solution of the problem."

Nevertheless, two letters, essentially identical except for the details applying to each of the Braceys, were drafted at the meeting to be sent over Poole's signature in reply to the inquiries. The letters, although highly civil in tone, noted that there was no space available for additional students at Clemson, that the Braceys currently were enrolled at South Carolina State, that the policy of the state was "to furnish separate but comparable facilities for the education of the white and Negro races," and that South Carolina State College was established to meet the needs of blacks. "As long as this policy is maintained," Poole wrote the Braceys, "the Board of Trustees of this institution does not feel that it has the right to consider the application of a Negro student for admission to a white institution."[50]

The board, however, did not merely turn the Braceys away. Whether to protect itself from possible legal action or to ease the pangs of conscience, it approved a three-part proposal submitted to it, after some discussion, by President Poole. In addition to recommending the letters described above, it agreed to "memorialize" the state's general assembly to provide adequate funding for South Carolina State and urged the latter's board of trustees to use wisely its share of the state's land-grant monies from the federal government.[51]

Although the Braceys apparently made no further attempts to enter Clemson, the issue of racial integration was far from settled. Problems associated with mixing of the races arose again several times before the Poole administration ended. A second incident occurred much later and involved a black member of the North Carolina State College band. On 5 October 1957 Clemson played North Carolina State in football at Memorial stadium in Death Valley. The State band accompanied its team and the black bandsman ate in the Clemson dining hall with fellow band members. As might have been expected, the news of this breach of long-established Southern practice spread quickly. A petition from Florence county containing two thousand signatures was sent to Governor George Bell Timmerman, demanding that steps be taken to assure that such mix-

---

[50]"Minutes of Board," 18 June 1947.
[51]Ibid.

ing of the races not occur again. Reports that the young black man in question was also a member of the State tennis team that was scheduled to play Clemson in the spring complicated the matter even more.[52]

Poole immediately contacted officials at the Raleigh school and informed them that state policy in South Carolina prohibited a mixing of the races such as had occurred at Clemson in October. He indicated, moreover, that the Clemson tennis team would be prohibited from playing North Carolina State if the latter's team included black members.[53] The consequence was that the schools did not play each other in tennis during the the spring of 1958.[54] Although the storm blew over, it was obvious that pressure on Clemson would continue to grow, as on all Southern institutions, to find a new racial accommodation.[55]

Toward a Civilian and Coeducational School

Much of the optimism prompted by the record enrollments at Clemson during the immediate postwar years soon ebbed. After the wave of returning servicemen crested, the number of students at the college declined. It peaked during the 1947-1948 academic year at 3,756, but by 1953-1954 it was down to 2,910.[56] A new generation of students, faced with the military draft upon graduation, was less than enthusiastic about attending a school where uniforms were required and military discipline was enforced. The nature of the problem became clear during 1954-1955 when, although all students had to wear uniforms, those who had satisfied their basic Reserve Officer Training Corps (ROTC) or other military obligations were allowed to opt out of the corps. One thousand of 2,500 chose to do so.[57] Moreover, the all-male student body was an increasingly negative factor in attracting students to the campus.[58]

---

[52]See *Raleigh News and Observer*, 17 Oct. 1957.

[53]Ibid.

[54]Telephone interview with Robert Bradley, CU sports information director, 24 Nov. 1986.

[55]"Minutes of Board," 20 Oct. 1955, indicated that an application had been received from William Edward Green, another student at South Carolina State College who wished admission to Clemson. Poole was told to handle it like the Bracey matter.

[56]The figures are in Cresap, McCormick, and Paget, "Clemson Agricultural College Survey of Administrative Management," vol. 1, "Top Organization and Administration," Apr. 1955 (hereafter cited as CMP Report), II-3. A copy is in RMCL/CU.

[57]See, for example, *The Tiger*, 9 Sept. 1954.

[58]According to Bryan, 131: "Wiser heads realized that continuation of military life and government would result in dwindling enrollments and thus curtailed resources. Clemson would be less effective in the prime purposes set forth by Thomas G. Clemson, to provide scientific and technological education."

If President Poole had ever possessed the initiative in dealing with Clemson's problems, there was evidence that it began slipping from his grasp at the beginning of the 1950s. Charles E. Daniel, a native of Elberton, Georgia, and elected to a life term on the board of trustees in 1949, provided the principal leadership in urging that Clemson reexamine its future. Daniel had moved to Anderson as a young man and became involved in the construction business, eventually establishing his own firm and later relocating in Greenville.[59]

Daniel was the prototype of the new breed of postwar business leaders in South Carolina, intellectually gifted, energetic, far-sighted, and civic-minded. Furthermore, he possessed a strong pecuniary interest in the growth and economic development of the South since his firm expected to play a major role in constructing the facilities that expansion would require. In that commitment to Southern economic development, he and Poole shared the idea that Clemson could be a major force in a regional awakening. Daniel threw his legendary energy into his duties as a Clemson trustee, and the minutes of board meetings during the 1950s revealed that he became the de facto leader among the trustees.

Daniel's company played a prominent role in the physical reshaping of the Clemson campus which, given his position as a trustee, aroused enough controversy to threaten his membership on the board.[60] More significant for Poole's presidency at Clemson, however, was Daniel's influence in transforming the administration of the college and in the decision in 1955 to convert it into a civilian and coeducational institution. During the previous year, at Daniel's urging and funded by a $20,000 gift from his foundation and $20,000 from state money, the trustees employed the New York consulting firm of Cresap, McCormick, and Paget to survey the administrative management of Clemson.[61] A final report in June 1955 strongly criticized the mixture of administrative responsibility that had developed without much planning at the college. The firm, moreover, castigated the involvement of the trustees in details of the school's operations.[62]

The new organizational plan recommended and adopted by the trustees provided for a dean of the college to supervise academic affairs; a dean

---

[59]See "Charles E. Daniel," *Who's Who in America* (Chicago: A. N. Marquis, Co., 1958) 29:612.

[60]See the Daniel papers, RMCL/CU.

[61]Bryan, 132; and C. E. Daniel to Poole, 3 July 1954, in ibid.

[62]See CMP Report, II-5 to II-8, which observed: "Without a clear distinction between policy and administration, the roles of the Trustees and the administration become intermingled and interfere with each other's effectiveness."

of students to assume an expanded role in student affairs previously performed by the commandant of cadets; a comptroller to take over the responsibilities held by the retiring Littlejohn; and a vice president for development to guide alumni affairs, college planning, and fund-raising activities. These persons reported to the president and comprised his advisory body or college "cabinet." All other college officials reported to one of the four above, depending on the subordinate's area of responsibility.[63]

The trustees supported the recommendations with enthusiasm and authorized Poole to implement them.[64] The president said nothing about his personal feelings regarding the changes, but he loyally carried them out. He hired Melford A. Wilson, executive director of the South Carolina employment security commission, as comptroller with considerable latitude to reorganize the college's financial administration and budgeting. Francis Marion Kinard, an English professor, became dean of the college, and Walter T. Cox, graduate of Clemson in 1939 and formerly assistant to the president and director of alumni affairs, was appointed dean of students. When Poole announced to the board in October 1955 that the new cabinet-level posts, except for that of vice president for development, had been filled, the trustees praised the results as "magnificent."[65]

The Cresap, McCormick, and Paget (CMP) study dictated the basic administrative structure of Clemson that endured, with only minor modifications, for more than twenty years. It also contributed decisively to changing Clemson into a civilian and coeducational school. Already in April 1954 some trustees had suggested that the college become a civilian institution. T. Wilbur Thornhill recommended to fellow board members that non-ROTC students be allowed to wear civilian clothes, a move tantamount to abandoning the military tradition. Governor Byrnes supported Thornhill's idea, noting that conditions were changing and that Clemson would have to do similarly to remain competitive. Surprisingly, however, given his usual support of change at the college, Charles Daniel disagreed and voiced an attachment to the military training. While no vote was taken at the meeting of the board on 20 April 1954, the consensus among its members was that the military requirements should remain.[66]

That agreement eroded rapidly during 1954. At their autumn board meeting, the trustees voted to admit women to Clemson the following

---

[63]Ibid.

[64]Bryan, 133-34.

[65]Ibid. According to "Minutes of Board," 17 June 1955, "Dr. Poole expressed himself as favorable" to the board's adoption in principle of the CMP report.

[66]"Minutes of the Board," 20 Apr. 1954.

January. Coeducation was incompatible with maintenance of the cadet corps. The final decision to bite the military bullet was made officially on 18 July 1955, when the trustees accepted the CMP recommendation that a "civilian two-year military training program similar to most land-grant colleges should be substituted for the required military training now in effect."[67] The trustees instructed Poole to implement the change in whatever manner seemed best to him, but the minutes of the board's meeting mentioned no discussion surrounding the vote.[68] Undoubtedly, if no debate occurred during the meeting, plenty had gone on informally during the months and weeks before it.

As Poole wrestled with putting the new administrative structure into place and with the controversies that arose from abandoning the traditions connected with the male-only, military Clemson, a third major problem intruded. This was the possible flooding of a substantial portion of the campus by the new Hartwell Lake. Congress had authorized in 1950 the Hartwell project of U. S. Army Corps of Engineers. It included construction of a dam on the Savannah river and a multipurpose 55,950-acre reservoir with a shoreline of 952 miles. At a normal surface height of 660 feet above sea level, almost one hundred miles of the lake bordered lands of Clemson College.[69]

As plans for the project had become public in 1950, the Clemson alumni association appointed a committee to investigate its ramifications for the college. A report by the committee indicated serious adverse consequences. If the lake flooded, water would cover Memorial stadium as well as cause the loss of a hydraulics laboratory, more than 40 college houses, a barracks, and the cabin that belonged to the Young Men's Christian Association. Moreover, much of the land near the campus used for agricultural research would be lost, pasture would be separated from the existing dairy barns, making the latter useless, and the water would endanger other campus buildings.[70]

Neither Poole nor the trustees gave the alumni committee's report much attention until 1955. On 17 July the board postponed action on a resolution presented by Thornhill that condemned the Hartwell project, although building of the dam had already begun and time was running out for Clemson to alter or halt the construction. State Senator Edgar A. Brown, one of the most influential members of the board, publicly sup-

---

[67]Ibid., 18 July 1955.
[68]Ibid.
[69]Bryan, 146-47.
[70]Ibid.

ported the project, and some concern existed among the trustees that Thornhill's proposal would place the powerful politician in an embarrassing position. Not until November 1956 did the board bestir itself to protect the college's interests.[71]

Of major relevance to this study is whether President Poole was derelict in his responsibilities in not sooner bringing the Hartwell affair to the urgent attention of the board. Robert C. Edwards, who came to Clemson in 1956, largely as a result of the urging of Charles Daniel, to assume the new post of vice president for development, found that Poole and his associates had done little to prepare the college's case for dealing with the Corps of Engineers.[72] Poole had given responsibility for the matter to H. E. ("Pop") Glenn, the director of planning in the new development office and a former professor of civil engineering, but Glenn's effort had been a feeble one. Edwards, with his characteristic drive and energy, took on the problem as his first significant task, and Poole provided him the support that he needed to succeed eventually in shaping an acceptable arrangement with the corps. However, it is difficult to escape the conclusion that Poole failed to give the affair the attention that it deserved. This lapse, while perhaps explicable in the context of the many changes at Clemson that Poole was faced with implementing at the time, could have resulted in dire consequences for the college.

The Trustees Seek Poole's Retirement

It seems that from 1953 or 1954 until the end of his life, Poole was increasingly overwhelmed with problems that he did not know how to resolve. The talents required were those that today would be called modern management skills, particularly the ability to select reliable, competent subordinates and delegate responsibilities while retaining general control and direction of the organization. Clemson had functioned reasonably well during Poole's presidency because Littlejohn, the business manager, had attended to the mundane administrative matters required to keep the college operating. He retired in 1955, however. Apparently Daniel saw the

---

[71]Ibid., 148-49. Some longtime Clemson faculty attributed the slowness to act on the Hartwell threat to the unwillingness of Poole and Littlejohn to offend trustee chairman, Senator Edgar A. Brown. Both Ernest M. ("Whitey") Lander, Jr., today alumni professor emeritus of history, and James M. Stepp, presently alumni professor emeritus of agricultural economics, took public positions questioning the merits of the Hartwell project and were advised by Poole that their positions were offensive to Brown and likely to have adverse consequences for the college.

[72]Ibid.

problem, and his insistence on the CMP management survey may have been intended to provide Poole with much-needed assistance.

If that was the trustee's objective, however, it did not succeed. The college implemented the CMP recommendations but, to a person as intelligent as Poole, the experience of dealing with such "management engineers" must have been frustrating. They spoke a language and came from an urban culture that were foreign to him. The skills they possessed were those that he must have realized he could never have. To acquire them Poole needed to become a different person than he was and, already sixty-two years old, that was beyond question. He was a respected plant pathologist and agrarian gentleman with a genial nature, orthodox Southern philosophy, and idealistic dreams about the future of his alma mater. Poole was the type of person that John Donald Wade wrote about in "The Life and Death of Cousin Lucius," his piece for the famous Southern book on agrarian philosophy, *I'll Take My Stand*.[73] Although there was much to admire in this Clemson president, he was not the kind that the college would need at its helm while a new, industrialized South Carolina unfolded around it.

Of Daniel's role in Clemson's affairs in the 1950s there are much less kind interpretations. For example, he may have recognized Poole's deficiencies and sought to rid the college of him. However, a direct attack on Poole by Daniel or anyone else could not have been successful. Poole enjoyed too much prestige, both in the state and nationally. He had served as president of the Southern Association of Agricultural Workers in 1948, and three years later the Association of Land-Grant Colleges and Universities elected him its head. He had played a key role, moreover, in establishing the national 4-H Club foundation and the national 4-H Club center in Washington. The prestigious American Association for the Advancement of Science had selected him one of its fellows. To many South Carolinians, and indeed to agriculturalists and educators in the land-grant schools across the nation, Poole was one of the most eminent and admired educators, scientists, and philosophers of his day. He was also popular with the Clemson students and alumni, although less so with the faculty.

It would take a major flank attack, therefore, to force Poole to retire. A new policy adopted by the trustees that took effect on 30 June 1957, however, was such an assault. The board decreed a retirement program mandating that all Clemson employees, academic and staff, must retire at

---

[73]John Donald Wade, "The Life and Death of Cousin Lucius," in *Twelve Southerners, I'll Take My Stand: The South and the Agrarian Tradition* (New York: Harper, 1930) 265-301.

the age of sixty-five.[74] The policy resulted indirectly from the CMP report and from the general feeling that there was much "deadwood" among the college's employees. Clearly the policy was not aimed solely at Poole, and he paid little attention to its implications for him when it was adopted. While sixty-five had been the nominal retirement age at Clemson, it routinely had been waived in the past. Retirement benefits for college employees were meager, and there had been a practice of allowing those who wished to continue working to do so. Sikes had served as president until he was 72, and David W. Daniel, the former dean of the school of arts and sciences, had been called back as an emeritus professor to serve well into his seventies. Possibly Poole thought he would be afforded the same opportunity. His subsequent behavior suggested that he had not planned to retire at age sixty-five.

However, at the beginning of 1958 the president realized that the mandatory retirement policy would also apply to him. An article appeared in the *Columbia Record* reporting that Poole, who would be sixty-five years old in December, was considering retirement. He quickly dismissed the story as untrue, but eagerly sought its source and made inquiries of his friends. Robert M. Cooper, then chairman of the trustees, denied to him on 19 February that he knew how the paper had received such information. Although Cooper maintained his innocence in the affair and mentioned that "I do have a sneaking idea" about who the source might be, he gave Poole no names.[75] Moreover, the editor of the *Record*, Henry F. Cauthen, shed little additional light on the matter. He refused to disclose the source for the paper's story, but informed Poole that it "came from one very close to you, but not from any official, or board member or anyone else connected with Clemson College." Cauthen added: "We regarded the information as absolutely authentic."[76]

Although sometimes slow to act, Poole was not slow of mind. Despite reassurance from the speaker of the state House of Representatives, Solomon Blatt, that Poole was "a member of the Barnwell Ring" and that he need not step down at Clemson until "you get ready to retire of your own

---

[74]The board had established the new policy eight months before, but it went into effect in June 1957, see "Minutes of Board," 29 Oct. 1956.

[75]Cooper to Poole, 19 Feb. 1958, CU President's papers, Poole, RMCL/CU; and *Columbia Record*, 13 Feb. 1958, which stated that a "source close to the school revealed the impending retirement" of Poole. The president informed the *Charleston News & Courier*, 14 Feb. 1958: "There has been no definite time (for retirement) set by either myself or the Clemson Board of Trustees. I'm not particularly interested in retirement right now, I'm not sure what will happen."

[76]Cauthen to Poole, 20 Feb. 1958, in CU President's papers, Poole.

free will and accord,"⁷⁷ the president realized that his only options were the dates prescribed for his retirement by the board's new policy. He could leave at the end of 1958 or remain until 30 June 1959, but he would not be exempted from the policy. At his request, John B. Gentry, the college's personnel director, inquired of the state retirement system what Poole could expect for a pension, but apparently no commitments were made.⁷⁸

Unfortunately, chance intervened and made Poole's decision for him. He died suddenly on 6 June 1958, after suffering a heart attack.⁷⁹ The news surprised and shocked the Clemson community and the state, particularly since he had seemed healthy and hearty had no history of heart problems. Some who knew Poole well and worked closely with him but who refused to be quoted, believed that he went to an early grave because persons like Charles Daniel overloaded him with work. Although that is a possible reading of the facts, which are not entirely clear, it was not the only one. Nor is it fair to the memory of either the president or Daniel. Others maintained that Poole went to an untimely death because the tasks he faced distressed and overwhelmed him. That situation would have prevailed, they said, even if Daniel had not been a player in the game. According to their view, Daniel did not create the problems that confronted Poole, and they would have posed a considerable challenge to a young, accomplished manager. Poole's confidence had been undermined by his dealings with the "management engineers" from CMP, and he had reached an age when his energy was waning. He possessed little natural talent as a manager, and the work required to compensate for his limitations was too much for his heart.

Whatever his deficiencies as Clemson's president (and he would be other than human if he had not had some), Poole was an honorable, well-loved person who did his best to make his alma mater into an exemplary

---

⁷⁷Blatt to Poole, 17 Feb. 1958, in ibid. Blatt was from Barnwell. He and fellow townsman, Edgar Allen Brown, were key figures in a group of South Carolina Democrats known as the "Barnwell Ring." This was a loose alliance of old-guard conservatives devoted to two principles: fiscal responsibility and small-county rule in South Carolina. On national issues, the Ring, more consistently loyal to the Democratic administration than the ex-Dixiecrats, was frequently out-voted in the state. See, for example, W. D. Workman, Jr., *The Bishop From Barnwell: The Political Life and Times of Senator Edgar A. Brown* (Columbia SC: R. L. Bryan, 1963) 99-129; and Ernest McPherson Lander, Jr., *A History of South Carolina, 1865-1960,* 2nd ed. (Columbia SC: University of South Carolina Press, 1970) 193.

⁷⁸Gentry to Tatum W. Gresette, 25 Apr. 1958, CU President's papers, Poole, which noted defensively: "This does not mean he [Poole] is planning to retire. . . . "

⁷⁹See *Anderson Independent,* 7 June 1958.

land-grant college. Consciously or not, he adopted traditional Clemson figures like David W. Daniel as a role model. That was not the ideal of a modern manager, but of a traditional Southern leader who made things happen by persuasion and appeal to common values. Modern managers are seldom gentlemen, and Poole was a gentleman. By the end of the 1950s this made him an anachronism as a college president, particularly as head of a rapidly changing and expanding land-grant institution in a region undergoing massive social and economic transformation.

Yet in many ways, based on a realistic assessment, Poole must be judged a successful president for Clemson. The college weathered the crisis of World War II and its aftermath and emerged academically stronger and with an enhanced reputation in the state and region. Had he retired in 1950, Poole might easily be remembered as one of Clemson's great chief executives. He gave the college and South Carolina visibility in important academic circles at the regional and national levels. Major additions were made to the campus. Moreover, he avoided the serious unrest that had plagued some of his predecessors. These were considerable achievements with which, despite his lack of direct involvement in them, he should be credited.

• *President Robert Cook Edwards, 1958–1979* •

• 11 •
A TAKE-CHARGE BUSINESSMAN ROBERT COOK EDWARDS, 1958–1979

Stephen H. Wainscott

The presidency of Robert Cook Edwards, the eighth and longest-serving chief executive of Clemson, changed the school dramatically. Edwards's leadership and the new demands of American society, politics, and education in the late twentieth century transformed Clemson from a small, segregated agricultural and military college for men into a coeducational, racially integrated university with a diversified curriculum.

When the Clemson board of trustees moved Edwards from acting president to president in 1959, there were 3,500 students enrolled in compulsory military training; a faculty of 300, only one-third of whom held doctoral degrees; and an old-fashioned curriculum organized into four "schools." By 1979 and Edwards's retirement, the student body numbered 11,000; more than two-thirds of the 1,000 faculty held terminal degrees; the four schools had mushroomed to nine colleges; participation in the military course had become optional; and students could choose what they wished to study from more than sixty majors. The Edwards years also added to the physical facilities of the campus. Monuments to the career of the man affectionately known as "R. C." included the R. M. Cooper Library, Strode Tower, the Daniel classroom building, Redfern Student Health Center, Rhodes Engineering Center, Littlejohn Coliseum, and numerous dormitories.[1]

---

[1]Wright Bryan, *Clemson: An Informal History of the University, 1889-1979* (Columbia SC: R. L. Bryan, 1979) 142-43; and *Anderson Daily Mail*, 11 May 1979.

The transition was not always easy. In 1956 Edwards had barely settled into his position at Clemson as vice president for development when the physical existence of the school was threatened by a Corps of Engineers design for a dam project that marked more than 9,000 acres of college lands for flooding. During the 1962-1963 school year the attention of the state and, to a large extent, the entire nation was riveted on Clemson as Harvey Gantt became the first black enrolled at the college. In 1975 findings of improprieties and illegalities in the men's basketball program tarnished the school's reputation for integrity in intercollegiate athletics.

From Textile Executive to Clemson Vice President

Edwards was born in Fountain Inn, South Carolina, the son of John T. and Effie Cook Edwards, on 25 March 1914. An industrious youth with normal boyhood interests, he won a scholarship to the Clemson Agricultural College after completing only the tenth grade.[2] At age nineteen Edwards graduated with a bachelor of science degree in textile engineering and a commission as second lieutenant through the college's mandatory military program. Known as "Smokey" to his college friends, Edwards quickly earned the respect of classmates for his energy and enthusiasm. His senior picture in *Taps*, the student yearbook, carried the motto, "Determination makes dreams come true."[3]

Beginning his career in textile manufacturing with J. P. Stevens in Greenville, Edwards moved steadily up the corporate ladder. Along the way he wed Louise Odom in May 1935, a marriage that produced a son, Robert C. Jr., and daughter, Nancy Louise. After serving in the army during World War II, Edwards began a career in textiles. In 1946 he landed a position as plant manager of Abbeville Mills, a division of the emerging corporate giant, Deering-Milliken.[4] Through his boss and textile magnate, Roger Milliken, Edwards cultivated a close friendship with Charles E. Daniel, the founder of a large construction company and, beginning in 1949, a life member of the board of trustees of Clemson.

While making a name for himself at Deering-Milliken, Edwards retained close ties to his alma mater, serving as president of IPTAY, Clemson's athletic booster club, during 1954-1955. He declined an offer from the college to become dean of the school of textiles, but in June 1956,

---

[2]See the student newspaper at Clemson, *The Tiger*, 10 Apr. 1979.
[3]*Clemson Alumni News*, July 1956, May 1959; and *Greenville News*, 10 Sept. 1978.
[4]*Greenville News*, 10 Sept. 1978; *The Tiger*, 20 Apr. 1979; and R. C. Edwards interview with S. H. Wainscott, 25 Feb. 1987.

when Clemson beckoned again with an offer more to his liking and talent, he returned to the college. He accepted an appointment as vice president for development, a newly established position at the school.[5] The office had resulted from a major study and review of the college's administrative and "nonacademic" activities, suggested by such trustees as Daniel and James F. Byrnes and conducted for the board by a New York-based consulting firm, Cresap, McCormick, and Paget (CMP).

In July of 1955 the board had directed the college's president, R. F. Poole, to implement the CMP report. This subsequently became the most important policy decision in Clemson's history, because it was a crucial step in the dramatic transformation of the school from a college into a university. The study had revealed significant problems at the college, including the excessive involvement of the board in administrative details, the inordinate number of administrators reporting directly to the president, poor admission and graduation standards, and low faculty salaries. The changes recommended by the CMP survey were as sweeping as the criticisms were severe. It called for a thorough reorganization of the college's administration, reducing the number of officers reporting to the president from twenty-five to four, one of whom was the new vice-president for development, the post filled a year later by Edwards. In addition, the CMP report proposed that required military training be discontinued, that the college open its doors to women, that entrance requirements for students be strengthened, and that faculty salaries be increased.[6]

Many officials at Clemson, including the gentlemanly but tradition-bound Poole, who had served as president since 1940, had difficulty accepting such a radical change from the college's past. Poole's lack of resolve in implementing the changes frustrated trustees such as Byrnes, Daniel, and State Senator Edgar A. Brown. If the CMP report were to avoid collecting dust on the president's shelf, they would have to find a "real trash mover."[7] Their choice for carrying out the report's recommen-

---

[5]See microfilm, reel 3,"Minutes of Board of Trustees" (1940-62), 11 June 1956, Special Collections, R. M. Cooper Library/Clemson University (hereafter cited as RMCL/CU); and Joseph C. Ellers, *Getting to Know Clemson University is Quite an Education* (Columbia SC: R. L. Bryan, 1987) 32.

[6]"Minutes of Board," 1 July 1955; and Cresap, McCormick and Paget, "Clemson Agricultural College Survey of Administrative Management," 4 vols., 30 Apr. 1955 (hereafter cited as CMP report). A copy is in RMCL/CU. For the recommendation to discontinue the military requirement, see CMP report, vol. 3, "Student Affairs," IX-8.

[7]In the words of Senator Brown, in W. D. Workman, Jr., *The Bishop from Barnwell: The Political Life and Times of Senator Edgar A. Brown* (Columbia SC: R. L. Bryan, 1963) 279-81; and Edwards/Wainscott interview, 25 Feb. 1987.

dations was Edwards. As vice president for development he oversaw fundraising and supervised public and alumni relations. However, according to the CMP report, his principal responsibility—the one that would have a critical bearing on putting the report into operation—was to "originate and coordinate all studies affecting the component units in such areas as enrollment, building planning, long-range finance, and the role of each of the component parts of the system."[8]

Some elements of the "old guard" at Clemson, mainly Poole loyalists, viewed the new vice president with suspicion and even fear. Although an alumnus, Edwards was, at least by vocation, an outsider. Rumors surfaced that he was a hatchet man brought on board to move bodies as well as trash.[9] Although Edwards later denied the tag of hatchet man, he admitted that the perceptions of him as such were not unreasonable. In those days, he maintained, chains of command were not always clear and many administrators considered themselves autonomous. Department heads drove cars furnished by the college and often looked on their departments as their own personal kingdoms. But that would end if the CMP reforms were adopted. Naturally those who felt threatened viewed Edwards with anxiety.[10]

Protecting Clemson from Disaster: The Hartwell Project

Even if these concerns had been justified, Edwards could find little time for head-hunting. Barely had he settled into the Clemson job when he found himself coordinating an effort to save the college. The United States Army Corps of Engineers had revealed plans for a dam and reservoir which, if constructed as designed, would literally turn Clemson into an island. The proposal for the construction of the Hartwell Dam and Reservoir, a multipurpose project for electric power generation, flood control, and recreation, first surfaced in 1940. The idea attracted many in the state who still yearned for liberation from the remnants of the Depression. The plans underwent several revisions before being given final approval by the United States Congress in 1950. Because few details of the project existed until then, it had encountered little serious opposition.

That began to change when plans called for a dam at an elevation of 660 feet to be constructed on the Savannah River near Hartwell, Georgia.

---

[8]CMP report.
[9]Ellers, 32.
[10]Edwards/Wainscott interview, 25 Feb. 1987.

Initially, it was proposed that approximately 9,000 acres, much of it on Clemson College property, would be flooded.¹¹ The board of trustees, while accepting reports during 1949-1951 regarding anticipated floodlines and the potential threat of the project to the college, showed little concern, but authorized President Poole to "negotiate" with the Corps of Engineers to keep the reservoir pool below 640 feet.¹²

Between 1951 and 1955 opposition to the Hartwell project gathered momentum. A vigorous debate at the board's meeting on 17 June 1955 between trustee T. Wilbur Thornhill, a strong advocate of soil conservation and an opponent of the dam, and Edgar Brown, who supported it, revealed the trustees' critical lack of understanding of the project's threat to Clemson. A resulting study for the board by Lockwood-Greene, an engineering firm in Spartanburg, confirmed many of the dam opponents' worst fears. The reservoir would flood 9,000 acres of Clemson property, including 1,600 acres of priceless bottom lands critical to the college's agricultural experiment programs. Many campus buildings and facilities would have to be relocated; in addition, it was determined that the football stadium would be flooded.¹³

The board, finally persuaded that Clemson's survival was at issue, adopted the Lockwood-Greene report at its meeting on 11 June 1956, the same meeting at which it confirmed Edwards's appointment as vice-president for development. Shortly thereafter the board asked the Corps of Engineers to lower the height of the dam to 610 feet above mean sea level or to consider diverting the Seneca River channel away from the campus and valuable bottom lands.¹⁴ Edwards hardly had enough time to arrange his new office when the Lockwood-Greene report and the board's recommended options landed on his desk. Almost from the outset it was understood that Edwards, not President Poole, would be the coordinator of the strategy to protect Clemson's interests in the Hartwell matter. Soon Edwards's office became the central repository of virtually all information related to Hartwell.¹⁵

---

¹¹Ellers, 34.

¹²"Minutes of Board," 11 Oct. 1949; 16 June, 24 Oct. 1950; 8 May, 11 June 1951.

¹³See Lockwood-Greene Engineers, Inc., "The Clemson Agricultural College of South Carolina: Comments Regarding Hartwell Dam Project," Relocation item no. 4, 1, Clemson University (hereafter cited as CU) Archives file, Hartwell Dam, No. 1 (Dec. 1948-Dec. 1956), RMCL/CU; "Minutes of Board," 17 June 1955; Edwards/Wainscott interview, 25 Feb. 1987; and Workman, 289.

¹⁴Brown to Col. T. DeF. Rogers (district office of Corps of Engineers, Savannah, Ga.), 29 June 1956, CU Archives file, Hartwell Dam, General Correspondence, RMCL/CU.

¹⁵Edwards to Silas C. McMeekin, 29 Apr. 1957, CU Archives file, Hartwell Dam, General Correspondence, 1955-57, RMCL/CU.

Edwards played a key role in organizing the college's strategy. He carefully sought to establish unity among the board on what to do, particularly by counseling Thornhill, the trustee most opposed to the dam, against making "a frontal attack on the [Hartwell] project."[16] By the end of October 1956 the momentum had shifted to Clemson. The board, at the suggestion of Edwards and public information officer Joe Sherman, initiated a public relations offensive. Coordinated by Edwards, the campaign was launched with a news release that outlined Clemson's suggestions for modification of the dam and reservoir.[17]

Two weeks later the South Carolina congressional delegation visited the campus at the invitation of the board. During the group's tour of the lands targeted for flooding and its meeting at the Clemson House with the trustees and representatives of the college's administration, the contours of an eventual compromise began to emerge. Amid reports that the Corps of Engineers was considering diverting the Seneca River, Clemson officials agreed that, as long as there could be assurance that the college's precious bottom lands would be protected, the school would "not oppose the construction of the dam."[18] The congressional delegation urged the board to send a formal petition to the delegation requesting its assistance in the matter.

Despite the efforts of the board to achieve a consensus on strategy, divisions remained among the trustees over whether Clemson should support construction of the project. At the board's meeting on 28 November 1956, a letter was read from an absent and ill Senator Brown urging his colleagues to press the Corps for acceptance of the diversion plan and reimbursement for Clemson's losses. The hardliners, however, were unmoved. Thornhill and Paul Sanders called on the board to "protest against the construction of this dam."[19]

The impasse was broken with the presentation to the board of an alternate resolution, drafted by Edwards with the legal advice of Clemson's attorney, William L. Watkins. It proposed that either the height of the dam "be lowered to 610 feet" or that the Seneca River be diverted "around the important lands of the college." The resolution also called for "any other modification of the plans" that would spare the bottom lands from

---

[16]Edwards to Thornhill, 24 Oct. 1956, CU Trustees file, Thornhill, RMCL/CU.

[17]"Minutes of Board," 29 Oct. 1956.

[18]See "Meeting of the Board of Trustees and the South Carolina Congressional Delegation," 19 Nov. 1956, 7, 13, in CU Archives file, Hartwell Dam, Congressional Delegation, RMCL/CU.

[19]"Minutes of Board," 28 Nov. 1956.

inundation and for Clemson to be "fully reimbursed for any and all developing damages."[20] Following discussion regarding the board's past inaction on such an important issue, during which Byrnes confessed to "sins of omission" and Daniel lamented that he "just didn't know what to oppose," the Edwards resolution was adopted with only Thornhill dissenting.[21]

The showdown occurred on 20 December when the trustees, college administration, and congressional delegation made their case to the Secretary of the Army and the chief of the Corps of Engineers. Edwards played a crucial role at the meeting, officially presenting Clemson's policy and summarizing its primary objective of saving lands that "we feel cannot be evaluated in monetary terms."[22] The Corps agreed in principle to what became known as "Plan X," the proposal that was eventually put into effect. It called for a "modified diversion" of the Seneca River and the construction of dikes at an elevation of 675 feet to protect the "campus proper" and save the bottom lands to "enable the college to fulfill its functions."[23]

Although the Corps agreed to Plan X, persuading the army's engineers to put it in place was another matter. Ensuing discussions between Clemson officials and representatives of the Corps were difficult and frustrating. After a meeting on 29 January 1957, Edwards wrote in a "confidential memorandum for the record" that the discussion resembled an interrogation in which college spokesmen were treated as "hostile witnesses being subjected to cross-examinations."[24] In the end, however, both parties agreed to a settlement of $1,150,000, which Clemson used to purchase the lands for the present-day Simpson Agricultural Experiment Station.[25]

In retrospect, it is difficult to understand how the design for the Hartwell Dam and Reservoir could have been conceived with such disregard for its impact. Edwards and Brown blamed the bureaucratic arrogance and insensitivity of the Corps of Engineers.[26] But a more serious question was

---

[20]Ibid.

[21]Ibid.

[22]Note "Meeting of Clemson Board of Trustees, Administration, South Carolina Congressional Delegation with Representatives of the Secretary of the Army and Chief of U. S. Army Corps of Engineers, Clemson House, December 20, 1956," CU Archives file, Hartwell Dam, General Correspondence, 1955-57.

[23]Ibid.; and Workman, 291-292.

[24]Edwards, "Confidential Memorandum for the Record," undated, CU Archives file, Hartwell Dam, General Correspondence, 1955-57.

[25]Ellers, 39.

[26]Workman, 292; and *Columbia Record*, 11 May 1979.

why it took so long for Clemson officials to comprehend the danger the dam project posed to the college. Part of the answer, Edwards claimed later, was that people believed erroneously that Dwight Eisenhower's replacement of Harry Truman in the White House meant the end of Democratic "pork barrel" projects and of an era when the Corps of Engineers "just loved to build dams."[27]

The heart of the problem, however, was closer to home. In many ways the failure of Clemson to respond to the challenge in a vigorous and timely fashion was symptomatic of the administrative and managerial problems revealed by the CMP report. Of these, perhaps the most frustrating in Edwards's view was "getting the Board to be a Board."[28] Indeed, a casual survey of the board's minutes prior to 1955 shows the trustees absorbed in matters such as approving leaves of absence and class schedules. Once, in a seemingly interminable blaze of executive minutiae, the board authorized the sale of sixteen obsolete microscopes used in a bacteriology laboratory and approved the hiring of an assistant turkey specialist for the York County extension office.[29] With the trustees constantly meddling in the administrative routine of the college, the board's inability to focus on the Hartwell threat and other important long-range matters became, if not excusable, somewhat understandable.

Related to this, maladministration within the college itself deprived the institution of a crucial early-warning function. With lines of accountability vaguely defined and/or misunderstood, the various college departments and administrative units operated as isolated, self-serving empires with little common purpose. Hence, it was virtually impossible to fix in any one person or office primary responsibility for monitoring the march of events related to the growing Hartwell crisis.

The New President and New Era

By March of 1958, as the crisis atmosphere of the Hartwell controversy subsided and Edwards neared the end of his second year in the Clemson administration, plans were developed by President Poole to initiate a search for the president's successor.[30] Poole had made no formal announcement of a retirement date. However, after a presidency of nearly eighteen years, a growing sense had developed among some members of

---

[27]Edwards/Wainscott interview, 25 Feb. 1987.
[28] Ibid.
[29]"Minutes of Board," 29 Oct. 1946.
[30]Frank Jervey (president of CU Alumni Association) to Thornhill, 2 June 1958, Thornhill papers, RMCL/CU.

the board that the time had come for a new generation of leadership. Such an objective was in part the reason for the board's policy that took effect on 30 June 1957, requiring Clemson officials to retire at age 65.[31] The question, therefore, was not whether Poole would retire but when.

The search committee had barely been formed when Poole died suddenly from a heart attack on 6 June 1958, during an alumni reunion weekend on the campus. Although a consensus quickly emerged among the trustees that Edwards would be named as Poole's replacement, no sentiment existed on the board for installing him as permanent president. Indeed, when the board assembled on 8 June it was publicly announced that Edwards had been named acting president under the "mutual understanding that he is not to be considered for the permanent position."[32] To underscore the temporary nature of the appointment, board chairman Cooper informed his colleagues on 11 June that after a "very satisfactory talk with Bob, I frankly do not believe he has any ambition ever to be President but he is desirous of serving Clemson to the best of his ability."[33]

The circumstances surrounding Edwards's selection as acting president remain hazy. It has been alleged that the board decided on the interim appointment because of rumors that Edwards was being groomed for the presidency by Charles Daniel. Edwards, however, later denied that he ever contemplated becoming president and instead maintained that he was told, not asked, by the board to become president.[34]

Whether the claim is true is unclear. The question, however, remains: why Edwards? First, his take-charge manner in handling the Hartwell negotiations had impressed the trustees and won their confidence. Furthermore, the fact that when Poole died Edwards was the only administrator with the rank of vice president made him a leading candidate for the presidency. Another factor was that while serving as acting president, Edwards made believers of the few trustees, such as Brown, who doubted his abilities or questioned his ambitions. Edwards reached final terms on the Hartwell settlement, dealt with the politically sensitive matter of separating the architecture program at Clemson from the college of engineering, and reactivated implementation of the CMP recommendations, which had been stalled during the final days of Poole's administration. The trust-

---

[31]Regarding the establishment of the new policy, see "Minutes of Board," 29 Oct. 1956.

[32]Ibid., 8 June 1958; and telegram, Thornhill to Cooper, 6 June 1958, Thornhill papers.

[33]The board later set his new salary at $13,500; "Minutes of Board," 20 June 1958. See, moreover, Cooper to board of trustees, 11 June 1958, copy in Thornhill papers.

[34]Edwards/Wainscott interview, 25 Feb. 1987; and Workman, 282.

ees, at their meeting on 9 April 1959, unanimously approved Brown's motion that Edwards be chosen permanent president of the college.[35]

Outside the board of trustees, reaction was mixed. No one faulted Edwards personally. Almost universally newspaper editorials described him as a "dynamic personality" and a man of unusual talent and energy. The raised eyebrows had mainly to do with his academic qualifications—particularly his lack of a graduate degree—for the top post at Clemson. "I think," a junior English major commented, "that he may have knowledge of his special field, management and executive, but I don't think he possesses the wisdom and insight of an academic leader." In other quarters there were disturbing questions about the sincerity of the Board's insistence, when it named Edwards acting president, that he would not be a candidate for the permanent position. The *Anderson Independent*, for example, wondered if the "purpose of discounting the Edwards candidacy was to avoid opposition to it," and the paper called the board's action "a sleight-of-hand performance" that would "help neither the college nor its new president."[36]

Despite the criticisms and reservations, which Edwards later maintained that he understood,[37] his appointment quickly ushered in a new era in the development of Clemson. Things would never be quite the same again at the school.

Integration without Violence: A Conspiracy for Peace?

The first significant issue to confront the new president involved the integration of the previously all-white Clemson College. In July 1959 a young black man from Charleston, Harvey B. Gantt, wrote to Clemson requesting information about the school's architecture curriculum.[38] Within a year and a half, Gantt applied for enrollment in the college, unleashing a struggle in the courts that ended with his admission to Clemson in January 1963. But while Edwards and other Clemson officials sought through legal measures to block integration, they appeared to recognize the probability of their defeat and worked to settle the affair peacefully. This stood in contrast to the violent turmoil during the fall of 1962 that

---

[35]"Minutes of Board," 19 Apr. 1959; and Workman, 282.
[36]See *Anderson Independent*, 11, 12 Apr. 1959.
[37]Edwards/Wainscott interview, 25 Feb. 1987.
[38]See *Gantt v. Clemson College et al.*, Civil Action 4101, U.S. District Court for the Western District of South Carolina, Plaintiff's Brief, exhibit no.1, in Gantt papers, RMCL/CU.

accompanied the effort of a black student, James Meredith, to enroll at the University of Mississippi.

Clemson's policy of racial segregation had been in violation of the law since 17 May 1954, when the United States Supreme Court issued in *Brown v. Board of Education* possibly the most dramatic and sweeping court decision of the twentieth century. The court's ruling was unanimous and unambiguous: "We conclude that in the field of public education the doctrine of 'separate but equal' has no place." Separate public schools for blacks and whites, the court ruled, were "inherently unequal" and therefore unconstitutional.[39] The legal foundations of racial segregation began to crumble. Southern reaction to the decision ranged from shock to hysteria. The region's instruments and tactics of "massive resistance" were varied. In South Carolina, the legislature, on the recommendation of an ad hoc committee appointed by the governor, John Bell Timmerman, and chaired by State Senator Marion Gressette, established numerous policies of defiance, including denying state funds to school systems that complied with a court order to desegregate.[40]

The complacency and self-delusion that existed in the state ended in January 1961, when Harvey Gantt applied for admission to Clemson College. Gantt was not the first black to seek acceptance to the institution.[41] He was, however, the most persistent. Although he had enrolled as an architecture student at Iowa State University, he applied three times during 1961 for admission to Clemson, but was refused by the college's registrar, Kenneth N. Vickery, and the dean of the school of architecture, Harlan McClure. While Gantt completed all the requirements for admission, both officials carried out the college's policy of segregation by presenting him with repeated hurdles designed to deny him enrollment.[42]

On 7 July 1962 Gantt's attorney, Matthew Perry, filed suit in the Anderson division of the Federal District Court for Western South Carolina.

---

[39]*Brown v. Board of Education*, 347 U.S. 483, 74 S. Ct. 686, 98 L. Ed. 873.

[40]Numan V. Bartley, *The Rise of Massive Resistance: Race and Politics in the South During the 1950s* (Baton Rouge: Louisiana State University Press, 1969) esp. 75-77, 116, 118.

[41]In June 1948 Spencer Bracey of Orangeburg sought and was denied entrance to Clemson; see Workman, 297-98. In July 1956 the applications of John L. Gainey and John Lonny Dease of Cheraw were rejected. Note *Charleston News and Courier*, 17 July 1956; and *Florence Morning News*, 27 July 1956.

[42]*Gantt v. Clemson College et al.*, Civil Action 4101, Plaintiff's Brief, exhibit nos. 3, 5, 6, 7, 9, 10, 11-13, 15-18, 20-23, Gantt papers; and *Greenville News*, 23 Aug. 1962. One of the reasons given for the denial was that Gantt received scholarship aid to attend Iowa State University from the South Carolina Regional Education Board. During this period many states maintained the all-white status of public colleges and universities through programs of tuition assistance for blacks to attend out-of-state institutions.

The case was heard before Judge Charles Cecil Wyche on 22 August. Gantt contended that he had been subjected to admissions standards at Clemson different from those applied to whites and that the school failed to act expeditiously in handling his application. These factors, the suit alleged, coupled with the college's "long-standing custom, supported by State law, of refusing admission of Negroes,"[43] were evidence that Gantt had been denied admission to Clemson on grounds of his race. On 6 September Wyche ruled that the facts and testimony presented in the case were "barren" of evidence to determine "whether there has been any discriminatory action on the part of the college." Accordingly, the judge denied Gantt's petition for a court order admitting him to Clemson.[44]

Gantt appealed the decision to the United States Court of Appeals, but the latter ordered the case remanded to the Anderson court. The result of the Anderson trial during 20-23 November was the same as before. Wyche rejected the plaintiff's contention that the college deliberately pursued a policy of barring blacks from admission. Throughout the judge's opinion Gantt was depicted as a recalcitrant who would rather file complaints and lawsuits than comply with established and reasonable application requirements. By contrast, Clemson officials were portrayed as agents of goodwill whose best efforts to cooperate with the plaintiff had been spurned. Alleging Gantt's claims of racial discrimination to be based on circumstantial evidence, Wyche dismissed the complaint.[45]

Gantt immediately appealed the decision. The Fourth Circuit Court of Appeals ruled on 16 January 1963 that he had been subjected to requirements and procedures not normally applied to other students, that Gantt's race had attracted more than coincidental attention from Clemson officials, and that Wyche had erred in his contention that no official policy of segregation existed at the college. Accordingly, the decision of the district court was reversed and Clemson was ordered to admit Gantt no later than 1 February.[46]

Attorneys for Clemson, on hearing of the ruling and acting on the suggestion of President Edwards, requested of the appellate court a stay of the integration order pending a final review of the case by the Supreme Court.[47]

---

[43]*Gantt v. Clemson College et al.*, Civil Action 4101, Plaintiff's Brief, p. 11, Gantt papers.

[44]*Gantt v. Clemson College et al.*, Opinion and Order, Sept. 1962, Gantt papers.

[45]*Gantt v. Clemson College et al.*, 208 F., Supp. 416 (1962), p. 6, Gantt papers.

[46]*Gantt v. Clemson College et al.*, No. 8871 U. S. Court of Appeals for the Fourth Circuit, 16 Jan. 1963, Gantt papers.

[47]*Gantt v. Clemson College et al.*, Application for Stay of Judgment of U.S. Court of Appeals for the Fourth Circuit, Jan. 1963, Gantt papers.

It was a futile gesture, but all along Clemson officials and political leaders had assured South Carolinians that no legal stone would be left unturned to keep the college segregated. On 21 January the Supreme Court denied Clemson's request for a delay, and the next day a somber Wyche ordered Clemson's compliance with the appeals court ruling.[48]

The story of integration at Clemson was only in part one of protracted legal maneuverings and court decisions. Equally important was how the college prepared for and adjusted to an outcome considered by many of its leaders to be inevitable. Even before the Gantt case went to court, Edwards had telephoned John K. Cauthen, the executive vice president of the South Carolina Textile Manufacturers' Association. In discussing Gantt, they agreed that every legal avenue should be pursued while making plans for peace. Of chief concern to Edwards was whether the business community would be supportive of the college's efforts to maintain law and order in the event that court rulings were unfavorable. Cauthen assured Edwards that business leaders would act in a more responsible way than had been the case in the Little Rock crisis of 1957, when the integration of the Arkansas capital's high schools had begun amid bitter protests from local segregationists. Edwards and Cauthen ended their conversation by agreeing to "feel around discreetly" for allies in their "conspiracy for peace."[49]

In September 1962, as the Gantt case wound its way through the courts, the violence at the University of Mississippi, which was quelled only by federal troops and marshals, caused South Carolina officials, including Governor Ernest Hollings, to speed up their timetable for constructing a plan for peace at Clemson. The proposal developed by the State Law Enforcement Division (SLED) was based on the lessons its chief learned from the Mississippi incident.[50] In addition, as Clemson lost its case in the courts, contact between Edwards and law enforcement officials became more frequent. Prior to Gantt's arrival on campus, a final security plan was carefully worked out, in which thirty SLED agents, forty state highway patrol officers, and a SLED aircraft would monitor the campus. A strict code of student discipline was established, granting the dean of

---

[48]See *Gantt v. Clemson College et al.*, Order in Compliance with Opinion Order and Mandate of the U. S. Court of Appeals for the Fourth Circuit, 22 Jan. 1963, Gantt papers; and David Redekop, "A Case Study of Court-Ordered Integration: Harvey Gantt Enters Clemson College," research paper for History 800, Clemson University, spring 1986, 15.

[49]Workman, 299.

[50]George McMillan, "Integration with Dignity," *Saturday Evening Post*, 16 Mar. 1963, 18.

students broad authority to expel from the college any students who instigated or participated in a riot. Special rules were also set forth restricting the movement and activities of the 200 press and television reporters who descended on Clemson the day before Gantt arrived.[51]

Shortly after noon on 28 January 1963, Gantt entered Tillman Hall and became the first black student at Clemson. The "mob" that many expected was actually a gathering of 200 generally well-behaved students who seemed more concerned about the wintry breeze at their necks than causing a disturbance. Soon Gantt made his way across campus for a conference with McClure, the architecture dean. Edwards, discovering by this time that most of the reporters had returned to the Clemson House, joined the meeting in McClure's office. He assured Gantt that there were no hard feelings, declaring that "the fact that the courts have ordered your ad-

---

[51]See "Confidential Outline of the Advanced Plan of Law Enforcement, Maintenance of Student Discipline and Arrangement for the Press," approved by Governor Hollings on 12 Jan. 1963, in Gantt papers, Security Plan for Gantt Enrollment.

mission to Clemson is moot. That's in the past. You're a Clemson student now, and I promise that you will be treated just like any other student."[52]

The ordeal was over. Except for punctured tires of three highway patrol cars and two visitors ordered off campus because of "bad talk," integration occurred at Clemson without incident or bloodshed. Edwards put what had happened into perspective by telling the press: "It is a historic day. We will let historians record whether it is a great day." The judgment came much sooner than Edwards expected. The next day newspaper editorials across the United States commended Clemson for keeping peace. Envious praise even came from the Greenville, Mississippi *Delta Democrat*, hardly a tabloid of integrationist sympathy: "The Palmetto State's leaders could have decided in favor of another Oxford; they chose progress of their state instead."[53]

Why was Clemson's rendezvous with integration a success story rather than a tragedy? Edwards, reflecting on the episode, insisted that Gantt himself deserved much of the credit for the peaceful transition, noting, "If Harvey Gantt had not been the great person that he was and is, the situation at Clemson would have been a lot different." When Edwards retired in 1979, Gantt returned the compliment, telling the press: "President Edwards was very fair to me. He seemed to be singularly interested in making sure the change was peaceful."[54] From another perspective, it could be argued that the maintenance of peace at Clemson was rooted in the sobering lessons of the times. The ugly incidents in Arkansas and Mississippi, if they served no other positive purpose, confronted Clemson with the brutal and inescapable reality that bitter-end resistance would fail.

However, even before the infamy in Mississippi, Clemson officials and public leaders had been quietly seeking to cut a deal with reality. How much they formed a "conspiracy for peace" is unclear, but since July 1961 several had quietly urged integration at the college without violence. Included among them was Edwards, who had the most direct stake in ensuring that the calm which had characterized Gantt's first day at Clemson would continue. The informal coalition also included Wayne Freeman, the editor of the *Greenville News*. Moreover, Cauthen and Charles Daniel took the initiative for nurturing support for integration from the state's economic leaders, arguing that fair treatment of blacks was not only an affirmative obligation, but that violence would be bad for business. Edgar

---

[52]Edwards/Wainscott interview, 25 Feb. 1987.

[53]See *Delta Democrat*, 29 Jan. 1963; *Greenville News*, 29 Jan. 1963; and *Anderson Daily Mail*, 29 Jan. 1963.

[54]*Charlotte Observer*, 11 Mar. 1979; and Edwards/Wainscott interview, 25 Feb. 1987.

Brown, who wished to wage the struggle in the courts but keep Clemson open regardless of the outcome, and outgoing Governor Hollings provided political leadership.[55]

Hollings, well respected in circles of the national Democratic party, helped convince the United States Attorney General, Robert Kennedy, that federal marshals would not be needed at Clemson. In this regard Hollings received valuable assistance from third district Congressman William Jennings Bryan Dorn who, on 25 January 1963, three days before Gantt's enrollment, hand delivered a letter to President John F. Kennedy. "The Clemson situation," Dorn assured Kennedy, "will be handled in such a way as to reflect honor upon local officials and the State of S. C. . . . I have the utmost confidence in Dr. Bob Edwards, Clemson's Board of Trustees, the student body, and in my people."[56]

A further example of Edwards's dedication to preserving tranquillity at Clemson and keeping the college open involved his interaction with Gressette, the chief architect of the state's segregation laws. Edwards later maintained that Gressette's commitment to law and order was unimpeachable. However, neutralizing the senator's potential for fomenting reaction was a serious concern, which appears to have surfaced in June 1962 when Edwards and the Clemson College attorney, Watkins, met in Columbia with Gressette and state Attorney General Daniel McLeod to discuss Clemson's legal strategy. According to Edwards, Clemson dictated its plans to the senator. "Never once did we ask the Gressette Committee what to do," Edwards recalled. "We always took the initiative and said 'this is what we're going to do.' "[57] Even Gressette appeared to recognize defeat. Although a few of his fellow segregationists in the state legislature angrily attacked Clemson officials for their alleged cowardice and "cringing and bowing before tyranny,"[58] Gressette did not do so. Peace remained at Clemson.

The University and Limited Enrollment

During the early years of the Edwards presidency, the civil rights revolution was one of many changes that affected Clemson and other college campuses. The trauma of the Vietnam War would be felt at the end of the 1960s, although not so intensely at Clemson as at other schools. Long be-

---

[55]McMillan, 17, 20; and Workman, 299.
[56]See Dorn to Kennedy, 25 Jan. 1963, given by R. C. Edwards to the author.
[57]Edwards/Wainscott interview, 25 Feb. 1987; and McMillan, 20.
[58]McMillan, 21.

fore most Clemson students had heard of Harvey Gantt or Ho Chi Minh, however, a much quieter revolution was occurring in the role and mission of higher education. Learning in America's colleges and universities reflected the nation's new fascination with science. The age of scientific discovery had arrived, prompted by the dawning of the atomic era at the end of World War II, by the Soviet Union's launching of the Sputnik satellite in 1957, and by President Kennedy's promise to reverse the nation's neglect of scientific and technological research.

These national and international trends contributed toward Clemson's development during the Edwards administration into a diversified educational institution. Until the mid-1950s the school's mission had been to advise and assist the state's farmers and prepare young men for military service. Ancillary programs such as the arts and sciences played a secondary role. However, with the board of trustees' acceptance in July 1955 of the CMP report, which had recommended abolishing the required military training, opening the college to women, and raising its academic standards, it became evident that not only the college's administrative structure but also its central mission would have to change. Academic emphasis now shifted from agriculture to engineering. Curricula in the sciences were added or upgraded. A college of liberal arts was established in 1969. Clemson also increased its graduate-level programs; the college's first doctoral degree was awarded in 1958. By the end of the 1970s almost one-fourth of the school's enrollment was post-graduate.[59] During the Edwards presidency, Clemson developed the tripartite mission for which it is known today: teaching, research, and public service.

Edwards, apparently because of his commitment to enhancing the influence of Clemson in the economic growth of the state, supported this expansion of the school's role. The broadened emphasis coincided with the campaign, begun already in 1956 by the alumni,[60] to change the name of the institution from Clemson Agricultural College to Clemson University. Following a meeting in January 1963, at which the governor, Donald Russell, and the presidents of South Carolina's public colleges agreed that "university" would more accurately reflect the kind of institution Clemson had come to be, Edwards moved to change the school's

---

[59]Bryan, 139, 255.

[60]On 1 June 1956, ten days before Edwards was named vice president for development at Clemson, the Alumni Corporation noted in a resolution that the college had "operated as a university in fact if not in name for 20 years" and had developed in addition to agriculture "very strong schools in arts and sciences and technology." See *Charleston News and Courier*, 4 June 1956.

name.⁶¹ He contacted the college's attorney, Watkins, who advised the president that changing the name could be a sticky legal matter because the name "Clemson Agricultural College" had been established by the will of Thomas Green Clemson. Consent to alter the name, Watkins said, would have to be obtained from all of Mr. Clemson's living descendants.⁶²

As Watkins soon discovered, finding such persons could be difficult. On 29 March 1963 he wrote to Edwards admitting to have "flunked Ancestry 1." Several limbs on Mr. Clemson's genealogical tree were missing. Months passed with no leads being found. In December an exasperated Watkins contacted Ernest M. Lander, Jr., a professor of history at Clemson with a special expertise in South Carolina's past, about the problem.⁶³ After a week of research Lander reported to Watkins that there was but one living descendant of Mr. Clemson, an army captain named Creighton Lee Calhoun, who at the time was on leave to study at the University of Wisconsin. Calhoun, when contacted, responded enthusiastically to the proposed change of name for Clemson College.⁶⁴

Although a court ruled on 28 February 1964 that the change from "college" to "university" would not constitute a breach of Mr. Clemson's will,⁶⁵ the legal struggle was far from over. Almost five months before the court's decision, Watkins informed Edwards that any name change would eventually require amending legislation, since the name Clemson Agricultural College had been established by an act of the South Carolina General Assembly. Edwards's campaign in the legislature began on 24 January, when he urged Representative Harold D. Breazeale of Pickens, chairman of the House Education and Public Works committee, to support the name change. "The accepted definition of a university," Edwards explained to Breazeale, "is an institution of higher education which is involved in teaching and research; which awards bachelor's, master's, and doctor's degrees; and which includes one or more professional schools as part of its organizational framework." In view of these criteria, the Clemson president concluded, "Clemson is in every sense a university."⁶⁶

---

⁶¹Telephone conversation with R. C. Edwards, 10 Mar. 1987.

⁶²Ellers, 51.

⁶³Ibid., 59; and Watkins to Edwards, 29 Mar. 1963, in CU Archives file, Clemson University, July 1, 1964, RMCL/CU.

⁶⁴Calhoun to Watkins, Vandiver, Freeman and Kirven, 4 Jan. 1964, in CU Archives file, Clemson University, July 1, 1964.

⁶⁵See in ibid., *Clemson College v. Creighton Lee Calhoun and Daniel R. McLeod*, Complaint for Declaratory Judgment, 3 Feb. 1964.

⁶⁶Edwards to Breazeale, 24 Jan. 1964; and Watkins to Edwards, 3 Oct. 1963, in CU Archives file, Clemson University, July 1, 1964.

On 20 February the bill proposing the change of name was debated in the House. While the bill passed easily, it was criticized vehemently for several hours during the discussion by A. W. ("Red") Bethea of Dillon, who protested that Clemson's recent attempts at modernization would open the floodgates of subversion. "I don't want to change a good conservative college into a big liberal university," the legislator shouted. In another expression of his outrage at Clemson's abandonment of tradition, he speculated that if the school had kept its compulsory military program, "I don't think that colored boy would be there now."[67] From the House Edgar Brown swiftly shepherded the bill through the Senate, and on 11 March 1964 the governor signed the measure into law.[68] Clemson was now a university.

What dramatized the school's new status the most was a rapid increase in its enrollment. During the fall semester of the 1964-1965 academic year, 4,588 students attended the university. A decade later the number of students surpassed 10,000.[69] As far as Edwards was concerned, Clemson would grow no more. In 1966 the decision was made that enrollment would be limited to 10,000. He fully supported the policy, always explaining it by maintaining that Clemson, unlike many other colleges or universities during the era of exploding enrollments in the 1960s, chose "to go the quality route instead of playing the numbers game."[70]

It appeared that Clemson's decision to restrict the growth of the student body was a simple choice motivated solely by a commitment to academic excellence. Yet there is evidence that the policy was also influenced by concerns about student unrest that characterized many college and university campuses during the 1960s and early 1970s. In retrospect, Edwards appeared to exaggerate the danger to Clemson, whose quiet, pastoral setting hardly provided an atmosphere for insurrection. Because of the "practical" orientation of the school's curriculum, student worries about career outweighed commitment to cause. Also the military legacy of the institution tended to nurture support for, instead of opposition to, American involvement in Vietnam. Clemson was in many ways a conservative in-

---

[67]*The Tiger*, no date; and *Greenville News*, 21 Feb. 1964.

[68]*General and Permanent Laws of South Carolina*, no. 803 (R868, H2186), 11 Mar. 1964, 185.

[69]Compare, for example, the figures in Clemson College, *Record*, 1965-66, with Clemson University, *Announcements*, 1974-75.

[70]Edwards/Wainscott interview, 25 Feb. 1987.

stitution in a traditionally conservative state. Disturbances at the college were, in fact, few and minor, resembling pranks more than rebellions.[71]

The board of trustees and administration wanted to keep things that way. In 1966 Edwards visited the University of California-Berkeley campus following the antiwar disturbances there. What he observed was in his judgment a factory of dissent rather than a center of learning. Determined that the mistakes of Berkeley would not be visited on the Clemson campus, he adopted a policy, approved by the board, of promising students that the reward for disruption would be a one-way ticket home. To demonstrate his resolve, when several activists approached the administration in November 1969 about the possibility of Clemson hosting a regional "peace moratorium," Edwards denied the request.[72]

A few years later he attended the conference in Chicago of the National Association of State Universities and Land-Grant Colleges. In the aftermath of the tragedy at Kent State University, in which four students were killed by national guardsmen during a protest against America's military intervention in Cambodia, the conferees discussed a number of challenges to higher education posed by national political events. Edwards, who administered a relatively tranquil institution, found the testimony offered by several of his fellow university presidents unsettling. The meeting crystallized even further his fears regarding the relationship between campus disorder and uncontrolled growth of enrollment and confirmed his belief that Clemson should limit its student numbers.[73]

Trouble in Tigertown

In virtually every category of comparison—physical appearance, personality, background, and management style—few Clemson presidents provided a more striking contrast than Edwards and his immediate predecessor, R. F. Poole. Yet Edwards, like Poole, exhibited a passion for athletics possessed by most of the presidents of Clemson. While Edwards viewed strengthening Clemson's teaching, research, and public service functions as his job, he received his greastest pleasure from Clemson sports.

His affinity for them was not surprising. During his student days he was manager for the Clemson football team, and during 1954-1955 he served

---

[71]In 17 October 1969, a group of students wearing black armbands chanted slogans denouncing the Vietnam war. However, their protests were drowned by refrains of "Dixie" sung by a larger contingent wearing red, white, and blue armbands and displaying signs that read "Peace Through Victory." See Ellers, 129.

[72]*Columbia Record*, 11 May 1979.

[73]Ellers, 130-31.

as president of IPTAY, the college's booster club. Still, his enthusiasm was unusual even by Clemson standards. He missed only one of the football team's 242 games during his presidency. While some thought it contrary to the reserved academic image of a college president, Edwards saw nothing wrong with running onto the field with the football team or substituting for the Clemson spotter in radio broadcasts at games.[74] Nor did he consider it a breach of presidential dignity to have orange tiger paws painted in his cheeks. Critics questioned the priorities of an institution whose football stadium seated more than seven times the school's number of students. But in Edwards's view, Clemson's athletic prominence deserved applause rather than apologies. Even in times of trouble with athletics, he maintained that both he and Clemson kept athletics and academics in proper balance.

When he became president in 1958, Clemson athletics consisted of eight intercollegiate sports, some of which were either barely competitive or operated under a "club" designation. When Edwards retired in 1979, the athletic program offered grants-in-aid to participants in ten men's and five women's sports. In 1958 Clemson football fans who were unable to attend games at Death Valley, could visualize touchdowns and fumbles by listening to radio broadcasts. Before the end of the Edwards years, Clemson athletic officials were negotiating multimillion-dollar television contracts not only for football, but also for basketball games. When Edwards attended his first game as acting president in 1958 (a 20-15 home victory over Virginia[75]), no one envisioned that in twenty years "overexposure" and "overemphasis" would be major concerns of universities regarding intercollegiate athletics.

During the Edwards era—as before and after—the crown jewel of Clemson's athletic program was football. Indeed, it seemed that the sole purpose of basketball, the school's other revenue-producing sport, was to offer a winter interlude between the season-ending football game with the University of South Carolina and spring practice. Not even the fact that Clemson's football teams won only fifty-three percent of their games and had nine losing seasons during 1954-1979 dampened the enthusiasm of Tiger fans.[76]

If football had always been the centerpiece of Clemson's athletic pride and joy, dishonor suddenly emerged in 1975 when improprieties in the

---

[74]Bryan, 143.

[75]See Joe Sherman, *Clemson Tigers: A History of Clemson Football* (Columbia SC: R. L. Bryan, 1976).

[76]Ibid.; and the Clemson University yearbook, *Taps*, for 1976-78.

men's basketball program were revealed. Compared to football's won-lost record, the basketball program, with only three winning seasons between 1953 and 1970,[77] was a source of embarrassment. Following three consecutive humiliating seasons, Edwards and the administration decided in 1970 that a coaching change was in order. Chosen to pump new life into the basketball program was Tates Locke, who had coached previously at the United States Military Academy at West Point and at Miami University of Ohio. His 1968-1969 Miami team played in the National Collegiate Athletic Association's (NCAA) postseason championship tournament, and Locke was named coach of the year in the Mid-American Conference. The next year Miami's Redskins went to the National Invitation Tournament (NIT).[78]

Locke seemed to be what Clemson needed to make its program competitive with the perennial basketball giants of North Carolina's "tobacco road." He was young and personable. At Army he had gained a reputation as a strict disciplinarian. He appeared to be the kind of coach who would understand his place; that is, he could be counted on not to challenge the hegemony of Clemson football. But best of all, Locke was a proven winner and, much like his new school, he was hungry for the limelight and success that more winning seasons could bring.

During his first three years at Clemson, Locke's teams won almost twice as many games as the three previous teams, but the composite record was still a losing one, 31-47. In 1973-1974 he produced Clemson's first winning season in seven years. The next year the team's record climbed to 17-11. Until then, only two teams in the school's history had amassed seventeen wins.[79] Basketball respectability had arrived at last. Fame and glory could not be far behind.

However, before that successful 1974-1975 season had begun, storm clouds gathered. In July 1974 rumors surfaced that several high school basketball stars had been offered illegal inducements to sign athletic grants-in-aid with Clemson.[80] By the end of the summer independent investigations were launched by the NCAA and the Atlantic Coast Conference (ACC). For nearly a year fantastic and often conflicting stories emerged about cash and other under-the-table gifts being given to Clemson basketball recruits and players.

---

[77]See the CU athletic department promotional brochure, "Tiger Revolution, 1975-76," in Lemon papers, RMCL/CU.

[78]Tates Locke and Bob Ibach, *Caught in the Net* (West Point: Leisure Press, 1982) 9.

[79]"Tiger Revolution."

[80]*Greenville News*, 4 July 1974.

Despite Locke's denials and what he claimed were attempts by the Clemson administration to blame jealous ACC opponents and an irresponsible press for the school's troubles, the storm would not pass.[81] Throughout the 1974-1975 season fresh allegations depicting an athletic program mired in scandal seemed to surface daily. The basketball team capped a successful season with an appearance in the NIT, but the pressure on Locke only intensified. On 20 March 1975 he submitted his resignation to director of athletics, H. C. ("Bill") McLellan.[82] Six months later, after an investigation of more than a year, the NCAA infractions committee released a report that found Clemson guilty of forty-one violations of NCAA regulations, most of which involved "significant benefits and inducements to prospective and enrolled student athletes." In most instances, the report detailed illegal payments or gifts provided to players or recruits with Locke's knowledge and/or direct involvement. By far the most serious violation was an offer by Locke to purchase a house for the mother of eventual professional basketball star, Moses Malone. The coach also offered to pay the utility bills for Mrs. Malone's new residence during the period of her son's enrollment at Clemson.[83]

For its sins, Clemson's basketball program received a three-year probation from the NCAA, during which the school was banned from post-season tournament play and prohibited from appearing on NCAA-sponsored telecasts. The number of basketball grants-in-aid the university could offer was also reduced. Finally, the NCAA directed Clemson to sever all relations with certain unnamed "representatives of the University's athletic interests."[84]

The aftermath of the NCAA investigation and report produced recriminations and accusations from Edwards, Locke, and other interested parties. Edwards, the rabid sports fan, reserved his harshest criticism for the press, especially the *Washington Post*. "I personally feel it is unfortunate," he declared, "that some newspapers have chosen to indict and convict Clemson." For many months, he asserted, the university had been the focus of "a deliberate attempt to discredit its intercollegiate basketball pro-

---

[81]Locke and Ibach, 28.

[82]The resignation letter is in ibid., 116-17.

[83]See the NCAA news release, "Clemson University Placed on NCAA Probation," 6 Oct. 1975, Lemon papers. Not only did Clemson lose the college recruiting war for Malone's talents, but the Petersburg, Virginia, basketball star signed a professional contract directly out of high school.

[84]NCAA, "Clemson University Placed on NCAA Probation," 6 Oct. 1975, Lemon papers.

gram."⁸⁵ On the other hand, the Clemson student newspaper, *The Tiger*, believed that McLellan should shoulder much of the blame. The paper, finding it "unacceptable and absurd" that a scandal of such proportions could occur without McLellan's knowledge, concluded that his "excuse is also his indictment."⁸⁶

Locke, in his backbiting account of the episode, maintained that he was made to take the fall by an administration that lacked the courage to control wealthy alumni who had been buying basketball players. However, Locke's claims sounded like the whine of a weak coach whose judgment was clouded by visions of glory in one of the nation's most prestigious basketball conferences. While the NCAA had shown that prominent Clemson boosters had contributed to the creation of an atmosphere ripe for scandal, it was Locke who was identified twenty-five times for breaking the rules. Whether valid or not, his search for a scapegoat crumbled under the weight of his own confession. "I didn't cheat because the Joneses did or because it made me a big man," he wrote after the affair. "I did it because I was tired of losing."⁸⁷

The President and His Legacy

Although many of the major developments and events at Clemson during the Edwards years would have occurred, if in altered form, no matter who had occupied the presidency, Edwards's personality and philosophy significantly influenced their course. To the casual observer he appeared to be a caricature often found in popular images of the South. In addition to his characteristic drawl, his handshakes were frequently accompanied by a zestful slap on the back. In his relations with others, he eschewed bureaucracy and formal procedure, preferring instead to settle his differences with people face-to-face.

On the other hand, Edwards's personality did not fit the stereotype of a Southerner. He possessed boundless energy and expected associates and subordinates to share his work habits. "He worked you hard," recalled his secretary Virginia Shanklin, "but he worked harder himself."⁸⁸ Moreover, although trained as a textile executive in the cold, impersonal world of profit and loss, Edwards nevertheless displayed emotions that seemed incongruous with the mentality of a business manager, particularly when asked what Clemson meant to him.

---

⁸⁵See his attack on the *Post* in *The Tiger*, 9 Oct. 1975.
⁸⁶Ibid.
⁸⁷Locke and Ibach, 61.
⁸⁸Quoted in Ellers, 64. Shanklin was Edwards's secretary from 1958 to 1965.

Equally important was the irony of his role in Clemson's confronting the realities and demands of the twentieth century. In guiding the institution through the most stressful era of its history, Edwards exhibited a fearlessness of the future that one would not expect of a person who held such traditional and conservative values. Part of his confidence may have resulted from his unusually close and harmonious relations with the board of trustees. A comparison of the minutes of board meetings during the Edwards and Poole administrations, for example, shows that meetings in the Edwards era were shorter and ran more smoothly. In one sense, the relative dispatch and lack of rancor with which the board operated was a reflection of Edwards's managerial style. He believed that the board should not be a debating society wherein solutions to problems emerged from its members' competing opinions. Instead, Edwards acted to keep the trustees fully informed in an attempt to achieve a broad consensus on policy prior to board meetings.[89]

At times trustee meetings ran so smoothly that the board was accused of being a rubber stamp for the administration.[90] Although the conclusion was not unreasonable, it was inaccurate for two reasons. First, despite Edwards's take-charge manner and commanding presence, trustees such as Charles Daniel, T. Wilbur Thornhill, Edgar Brown, and James Byrnes were strong personalities and not known for timidity. Second, the board's apparent deference to Edwards on administrative matters was more a reflection of the changing role of the board mandated by the CMP report than it was a willful capitulation to Edwards's wishes.

Edwards also developed a positive relationship with leaders of state government. Although he never expressed an interest in a political career for himself, he moved with ease among the leading public figures of the day. Much of his political acumen was acquired through his friendship with Edgar Brown, whose greatest contribution to Clemson was a long stewardship of the institution's interests—especially financial—in the state legislature.[91] Also, the two greatest crises of Edwards's presidency, involving the Hartwell Dam and integration, served as practical seminars in the art of politics. To some, Edwards's strength was his constant—and usually effective—presentation of Clemson's needs to the legislature, Commission on Higher Education, and Budget and Control Board. In this regard, one of the university's chroniclers, Wright Bryan, observed: "The

---

[89]Bryan, 141.
[90]Ibid.
[91]Workman, 277.

presidential automobile was on the road between Clemson and Columbia as much as it was on the campus itself."[92]

Possibly because he was an alumnus of Clemson, Edwards shared a special bond with students. The relationship was not always amicable, but students seemed to appreciate, albeit grudgingly, that when Edwards refused their demands he would at least listen.[93] In contrast, his association with the faculty was more distant and at times even strained. To some professors Edwards's "iron-fisted decision-making style" seemed antithetical to the liberal nature normally associated with institutions of higher learning. Others expressed concern about the president's lack of advanced academic training and what they perceived as his uneasiness with faculty involvement in administrative affairs. On the other hand, Edwards generally entrusted the academic operation of the university to the deans of the colleges and avoided telling the professors how to do their jobs.[94]

During the 1976-1977 academic year, the president announced that he was looking forward to his retirement in three years, when he turned sixty-five. He was soon showered with awards, plaques, and other honors celebrating his service to Clemson. By the time of his retirement, Edwards had personally awarded 28,750 diplomas. These represented at the time more than seventy percent of undergraduate degrees and all the doctorates conferred in Clemson's history. In his twenty-one years at the helm, almost $100 million had been spent in the construction of new buildings on campus and the expansion and renovation of old ones.[95] Clemson had become a university with a vastly larger and more diversified student body, faculty, and curriculum. Edwards, despite charges by his critics that he possessed neither a scholarly background nor image and that he placed too much emphasis on athletics, had made a vital imprint on both Clemson's human and physical resources. By 1979 the school had come of age.

---

[92]Bryan, 143.
[93]*Columbia Record*, 11 May 1979.
[94]*Charlotte Observer*, 17 Mar. 1979.
[95]*Anderson Daily Mail*, 11 May 1979.

• *President Bill Lee Atchley, 1979–1985* •

• 12 •

THE OUTSIDER BILL LEE ATCHLEY, 1979–1985

William F. Steirer, Jr.

Strife and controversy, particularly between the president and board of trustees, marked the administration of Bill L. Atchley, the ninth president of Clemson University. Conflict with the board had affected several previous Clemson presidents, but it lasted longer and was sustained with greater intensity during Atchley's presidency. In addition, much of it was played out in public before a national audience eager to watch a modern-day morality play unfold. Aware of the attention focused on him and the university, Atchley told a friend in May 1983, "Yes, it seems I am not able to even clear my throat these days without being in the paper, but I guess that goes with the territory."[1] Although Atchley's administration encompassed more than disputes over athletics at Clemson, most of what occurred during it reflected the controversy caused by that single divisive issue.

Atchley's resignation from the presidency on 1 March 1985, after he challenged the trustees either to support him fully or to let him go,[2] came six years almost to the day after the board had tapped him for the position on 24 February 1979. On that happier occasion, Atchley told the crowd waiting in the university's Alumni Center to meet the board's choice for

---

[1] See Bill L. Atchley to D. Wellsman Johnson (president, Abney Mills), 17 May 1983, Atchley papers, folder 14, Special Collections, R. M. Cooper Library/Clemson University (hereafter cited as RMCL/CU). The author is grateful to former President Atchley for permission to use his personal and presidential papers; access to both collections in RMCL/CU is restricted.

[2] *Greenville News*, 2 Mar. 1985.

president, "I think this marriage will be a good one."³ At the time, the wedding of an ex-professional athlete to a university committed to success in athletics looked like a good one. How ironic, therefore, that athletics would prove to be the principal reason for the divorce six years later.

Background, Personality, and Philosophy

Atchley was born in Cape Girardeau, Missouri, on 16 February 1932 and, like many young men, proved more interested in sports, school politics, and girls than in schoolwork. He graduated from Central High School as president of the student body and captain of the football team. He later reflected that such early experiences seemed atypical of a college president, particularly since he had believed that a baseball career would be his future and doubted that he would ever attend college. Atchley enjoyed his year as a pitcher in the New York Giants' farm system, but after a two year tour in the army he reassessed his future and went into engineering.⁴ He earned bachelor and master of science degrees (1957, 1959) in civil engineering at the University of Missouri at Rolla and a doctorate from Texas A&M in 1965.

Moving up the academic ladder at Rolla, Atchley became acting chairman of the department of engineering mechanics in 1965, assistant dean of engineering in 1968, and associate dean two years later. Developing an expertise in the study of energy, he served as chair of the Missouri Energy Council, as a member of the Southern Interstate Nuclear Board, and as a liaison between the academic community and the Missouri legislature on energy matters. Atchley acted as the science and technology adviser to the Missouri governor, Christopher S. Bond. He also gave an indication of the easy rapport he later enjoyed with Clemson students by coordinating the joint student-faculty inner-city projects operated by the school of engineers at Rolla.

In 1975 Atchley moved to the University of West Virginia as dean of engineering. There he encouraged the school's faculty to double the amount of research money raised and pushed the university into playing a leading role in energy matters. He advised the state legislature on energy proposals, initiated the proposal that produced the West Virginia Energy

---

³Ibid., 25 Feb. 1979.

⁴Bill L. Atchley interview with William F. Steirer, Jr., 13 June 1985; and Atchley to Gary F. Crooks (a writer compiling profiles of university presidents), 30 Mar. 1983, Atchley papers, folder 13. Written notes by the author from the Atchley/Steirer interviews have been placed in RMCL/CU. The author agreed to Atchley's request not to release certain names mentioned by Atchley in interviews for five years.

Research and Development Center, and chaired the governor's Commission on Energy, Economy, and Environment. By serving as the science and technology adviser to both the conservative Republican governor, Arch A. Moore, Jr., and the liberal Democrat, John D. Rockefeller IV, Atchley gained a reputation as an adroit political operator.[5]

His application materials for the presidency of Clemson in 1978 showed that he possessed administrative skills, that he had worked successfully with two state legislatures, and that he was deemed to be fair and open with faculty and students. But that record did not reveal what was most impressive about Atchley. He was a big, rough-hewn, and hearty man, genuinely likeable, and one who made a fine first impression on people. A person of simple tastes, Atchley was in columnist Randy Laney's words in the Columbia newspaper, *The State*, a man called "Bill" who was as "uncomplicated as black coffee and as direct as sunlight" and whose name "fits the personality like a tailored suit." Laney, like most others who met Atchley, found him to be "consistently candid, caring, and equally at ease" with everyone he contacted.[6]

Atchley appealed to a Clemson board of trustees looking for a new leader of the university who would be physically impressive, yet possess a "down-home" quality. P. W. McAlister, then board chairman, observed about Atchley: "Everything you see on paper just glowed through all the lines in every way. A real scholar, but did not give you an egghead impression. He was so natural. He didn't try to undersell or oversell himself." The lone faculty member involved throughout the board's six-month search for a president was equally pleased with Atchley, calling him "a very dynamic individual, a take-charge guy" who concerned himself "not with whether you know every answer to every hard question, but how you handle the question."[7]

Those who knew Atchley really praised him. He possessed "common horse sense," said Gene Budig, the president of West Virginia University. "He's shooting for the ideal, but he's practical, too." Budig also emphasized Atchley's unwillingness to be Machiavellian: "He's straightforward

---

[5]This information is from the deliberations of the university's committee that screened the candidates for president during Sept. and Oct. 1978. The author was president of the university faculty senate during 1978-79 and served on the presidential screening committee; he was, in addition, the sole faculty member on the presidential search committee that interviewed the finalists.

[6]*The State*, 19 Oct. 1980; and the Clemson University student newspaper, *The Tiger*, 2 Mar. 1979

[7]The quotations are from the *Charlotte Observer*, 16 July 1979.

and sincere; there's not a devious bone in his body. . . . He won't tolerate hanky panky."⁸ Years later a friend of Atchley's related a story about the fate of a graduate student who had lied to Atchley about research the student had supposedly done. The response was immediate, direct, vigorous, and unforgettable.⁹ The incident revealed a facet of Atchley's personality that often went unnoticed or was disregarded by his associates. He meant what he said when, shortly after receiving the appointment as Clemson's president, he told the student newspaper, *The Tiger*, "I believe in an open-door policy. I make sure I return my calls."¹⁰

Other features of Atchley's character included his keen sense of loyalty to associates (perhaps too much so) and to the institutions he served. He expected a similar level of loyalty in return; disloyalty was, in his mind, a cardinal sin.¹¹ Moreover, he faced problems aggressively, choosing to approach them by shaking them to pieces. The second faculty senate president at Clemson to work with him, Stassen Thompson, observed that it was Atchley's style to confront an issue by developing prompt solutions rather than appointing a committee to study the matter.¹²

Atchley showed his personal touch in administrative affairs when, during 1983 and the middle of the controversy involving the National Collegiate Athletic Association's (NCAA) placing of Clemson's football team on probation, the Clemson president encountered an unfortunate and sad event that resulted in serious legal charges of embezzlement and malfeasance against a university employee. His kindness to the defendant and family while still pushing the charges prompted the defendant's attorney to write thanking Atchley for his recommendation of leniency. It "is most encouraging to know that [in] your position of responsibility for all University affairs," said the lawyer, "you endeavor to maintain contact and interest in such a situation no matter how distasteful it may be, to see it to a conclusion and contribute as you have to ensure that the best interests of all parties are served."¹³

Certainly this personal approach had its downside. Critics claimed that Atchley's most serious problems stemmed from his readiness to act too

---

⁸*The Tiger*, 2 Mar. 1979.

⁹Atchley picked up the student and hung him by his clothes on a hook on the wall. Information on this incident was told to the author on 17 Jan. 1984 by a longtime acquaintance and friend of Atchley.

¹⁰*The Tiger*, 2 Mar. 1979.

¹¹Atchley/Steirer interview, 13 June 1985.

¹²*The State*, 19 Oct. 1980.

¹³William F. Derrick to Atchley, 2 Feb. 1983, Clemson University (hereafter cited as CU) President's papers, Atchley, folder 38, RMCL/CU.

quickly and impulsively, usually without careful cultivation of the ground beforehand. This occurred, they argued, in some of his firings of top academic administrators in 1980, in his attacks on legislators and governor alike for their approach to state budgetary matters, and even in the crisis over athletics. Opponents also maintained that Atchley's "ego" constantly blocked efficient management of the university[14] and that his emphasis on personal relations in administration meant that on crucial points he regarded himself as indispensable. Others believed that he personalized political and business affairs too much and that such a tendency led him to interpret opposition to his policies as personal attacks on himself rather than as differences of opinion or philosophy.

Underneath Atchley's exterior that projected a "what you see is what you get" image, hidden depths existed. One member of the board of trustees, Paul W. McAlister, following Atchley's formal interview in January 1979 with the university's presidential search committee, called the candidate "a diamond in the rough, who could come to dazzle us all."[15] Atchley exuded confidence and a strong ego, but he generally accepted criticism and learned from it. For example, shortly after he had assumed the presidency, he met faculty senators at a picnic. However, he apparently behaved toward two female senators, in their words, like "a typical male chauvinist." The senators, not amused by his behavior, pointedly informed him of their feelings. Taken aback by their reaction, Atchley proceeded thereafter to treat the university's women as professionals.[16]

Although he communicated well with small groups, Atchley did less well in speaking to large audiences. He finally realized the weakness, finding in March 1984 a tough-minded critic who advanced fifty-nine observations designed to help him improve. During the latter part of his presidency, he performed more effectively before mass groups.[17] When he first arrived as Clemson's new president, Atchley appeared to possess a knack for saying the things that people liked to hear. When he said, for example, that his wife, Pat, and himself were "just common people, and we just like to be people," the words fell on ears waiting for confirmation of his willingness to be part of the much-discussed "Clemson family." Similarly, he pleased engineers and non-engineers alike when he boasted

---

[14]See, for example, Joseph D. Swann to Buck Mickel, 8 Apr. 1983, Atchley papers, folder 13.

[15]The comment was made to the author on 21 Jan. 1979.

[16]The author heard about this incident that occurred on 4 Sept. 1979 and later interviewed the senators and others involved in it.

[17]Memorandum, 3 Mar. 1984, Atchley papers, folder 15.

in an interview with *The Tiger* on 2 March 1979: "I've had more people tell me, and it's a compliment to me, that I don't act like an engineer. I'm different and I'm glad to be different."

In retrospect, however, readers of Atchley's comments in the press months before he officially assumed the presidency should not have been surprised at his attitudes during the controversies that emerged later. *The Tiger* added about Atchley that he would not "put improper emphasis on engineering or athletics" because he was "concerned about the total university."[18] Simultaneously, the *Greenville News* quoted him as saying: "Athletics have to be put in proper balance. We're here for the main purpose of educating young people. Athletics can set a spotlight on an institution like Clemson, so that the president of the school can stand in that spotlight and tell about the fine students and faculty of the university."[19] He emphasized to the alumni magazine, *Clemson World,* that "Clemson must become a people's university for the entire state." His declaration in a press release that "I don't think we'll take a back seat to anyone, in anything, anywhere" would be repeated often. He intended to make the university's followers "proud of us and proud of Clemson and the education of young people in South Carolina."[20] Even before he moved into the president's office in Sikes Hall, Atchley had publicized the basic principles of his educational philosophy. He followed them consistently during his presidency.

Great Expectations, Broken Commitments, and Failure

An air of excitement at Clemson greeted Atchley as he assumed his duties on 1 July 1979. He seemed to be everything that Clemson people wanted. Faculty members believed that he would push the university toward academic excellence, open channels of communication between the faculty and administration, include the professors in university government, and fight for salary increases. Students hoped that the new president would listen thoughtfully to their concerns and respect their input into university affairs. Although Atchley subsequently met many of the expectations of such groups, the most important body he would have to satisfy was the board of trustees.

---

[18]See the quotes in *The Tiger,* 2 Mar. 1979.

[19]*Greenville News,* 25 Feb. 1979. Atchley also told *The Tiger,* 2 Mar. 1979, that he would not tolerate improper behavior in athletics or any other area of the university.

[20]See the CU press release, 26 Feb. 1979; and *Clemson World,* Fall 1979, 4.

As the long administration of Atchley's predecessor, R. C. Edwards, had ended, the trustees recognized that authority in governing the university had shifted significantly from the board to the president's office. The trustees intended to change the situation, which they revealed already during Atchley's interview with the presidential search committee on 21 January 1979. The trustees informed Atchley that they were hiring a president for no more than seven to ten years. When he inquired about what the board would expect of him, he was told that it anticipated he would increase the level of private fund-raising for the university and provide persons at the institution capable of assuming responsibilities up to, and including, the presidency. With regard to the latter expectation, however, Atchley later maintained that the board never allowed him to do that because it constantly prevented him from appointing his own "management team."[21] While he interpreted the board's injunction to mean hiring new people from outside the campus, the board intended for him to train and prepare persons already there.

The board also wished for Atchley to deal effectively with South Carolina's legislators and build a network of political associations and connections in the state's general assembly that would benefit Clemson financially and otherwise. The university had not possessed such influence, according to trustees like T. Kenneth Cribb, since State Senator Edgar A. Brown had chaired the board.[22] In addition, the board expected Atchley to improve the academic quality of the faculty and address what the board viewed as frustration among the professors at their lack of communication with the administration. The new president was also to establish a greater degree of "openness" at the university, which would include making the president's home an integral part of campus life by using it for receptions and meetings. Not only did the board anticipate that Atchley would communicate Clemson's purpose and mission more effectively to the public, but it wanted him to implement improvements on the campus without disturbing what its members proudly called "the Clemson family spirit." In this regard, the trustees looked for the university's en-

---

[21]Atchley/Steirer interview, 13 June 1985; and *The State,* 30 June 1985. On 21 Jan. 1979 the author heard Atchley told to expect the board to exercise the authority to veto any personnel decisions down to and including the level of dean. For an example of the sense of anticipation that greeted Atchley's arrival at Clemson, see Wright Bryan, *Clemson: An Informal History of the University 1889-1979* (Columbia SC: R. L. Bryan, 1979) 260-63.

[22]From the author's discussion with Cribb on 11 Dec. 1978, while both served on the presidential search committee.

rollment to remain at 10,000 students and for the friendly personal atmosphere that characterized faculty-student relations not to change.[23]

It was on campus that Atchley had the most success and came closest to fulfilling the expectations of him. His performance, however, produced no consensus among the faculty. While some praised his including of faculty in university governance and his improving lines of communication between the faculty and administration, others criticized him for allegedly opening his mouth too often at the wrong times, failing to acquire financial and other resources the university needed, and relying too heavily on poor advisers. Debates at faculty senate meetings over proposed resolutions of support for Atchley during 1983 and 1985 revealed the ambivalence felt toward him. Senators found themselves in the uncomfortable position of disapproving many of his policies and actions, but having to support him in controversy over athletics.[24]

Atchley believed that his greatest accomplishments were freeing the channels of communication within the university and integrating faculty and students more fully into decision making at the school. His "Proposals for Improved University Governance," issued soon after he took office, provided the basis for the new system that went into effect in January 1981.[25] During his first year on the job, Atchley defended the changes by insisting that they would build a spirit of mutual trust and sense of community on the campus.[26]

His reforms resulted not only from a desire to meet the objectives of the board of trustees, but they reflected Atchley's educational philosophy. At the first meeting of the new president's council on 30 January, he observed that "the buck still stops here," meaning that he was ultimately responsible for the decisions he made. Nevertheless, he urged the council to advise him without fear or restraint, declaring that "a university should be a place where ideas flow freely and are examined and challenged con-

---

[23]From the author's notes recorded during the deliberations of the presidential search committee, 1, 11 Dec. 1978; and 20-21 Jan. 1979.

[24]See "Minutes of Faculty Senate Meetings," 5 Apr. 1983, RMCL/CU; and Holly Ulbrich, memorandum, May 1985, in Atchley papers, speeches.

[25]Note the memorandum, "Proposals for University Governance," undated, in CU Clippings file, RMCL/CU.

[26]Atchley's address to general faculty meeting, 8 Aug. 1980, CU President's papers, Atchley, folder 26; and his address to general faculty meeting, 8 May 1980, President's papers, Atchley, speeches.

stantly."[27] Two years later Clemson's academic deans endorsed his style of administration.[28]

Atchley also claimed that the quality of the faculty had improved during his presidency. From the beginning he had demonstrated an interest in the faculty by meeting with departments and listening to their concerns. He promised to work toward raising salaries and providing faculty with greater research opportunities. When he resigned in 1985, faculty research and publications had increased substantially and, based on information from the National Science Foundation, Clemson's research program ranked for the first time in the top one hundred among America's major universities.[29]

Making that "transition . . . from the college atmosphere to the university atmosphere," as he told *The State* in June 1985, had not been easy. "All of us [at Clemson] did not always have the same philosophy and such about the way we should go. Change always comes about with some controversy." Although Atchley refused to be specific, he questioned the commitment that he had received at the university: "I don't think in some instances I got the loyalty. I don't know what the reason for that was. I guess they had a difference of opinion, or whatever. . . . But when I make the decision in this chair, and the person has had his say and we go out that door, whether they like the decision or not, they should march to the same drum. . . . And I don't think that I always had that here."

Such problems began before the athletic scandals. Atchley admitted, however, that the troubles with athletics had interrupted his attempts at restructuring the university to achieve the loyalty he demanded. He told *The State* in 1985 that upon his arrival at Clemson six years earlier, he would have preferred for all top administrators to present him with their resignations, thus permitting him to evaluate each one.[30] That had not happened. Instead, faced with the need to meet the directive of the board of trustees to develop leaders within seven to ten years, but lacking the board's mandate to implement the personnel changes he deemed necessary, Atchley moved quickly to make the ones he could. Regarding the

---

[27]Atchley to president's council, 30 Jan. 1981, CU President's papers, Atchley, speeches.

[28]See the petition from the deans, 5 Apr. 1983, CU President's papers, Atchley, folder 13.

[29]Note "Sources of University Research Funds," *The Chronicle of Higher Education*, 10 Dec. 1986, 8; *Clemson World*, Feb. 1987, 25; Atchley/Steirer interview, 13 June 1985; and *The State*, 30 June 1985.

[30]*The State*, 30 June 1985; and *Greenville News*, 30 June 1985.

changes he had made during 1979-1980, he later observed that several of the administrators he removed had been in their positions for ten years and that he needed to "put some different life, different thoughts, different ideas and innovativeness into the future of Clemson University."[31]

That first year he ousted deans H. Morris Cox (Liberal Arts), Geraldine Labecki (Nursing), and Wallace D. Trevillian (Industrial Management and Textile Science). Others forced to leave the university included Samuel Willis (Director of Agricultural Extension), Gordon Gourlay (Director of the Library), George Coakley (Associate Dean of Students), and Darryl Hickman (Assistant Vice President for Business). Atchley reassigned the vice presidents for executive affairs and development, Joseph McDevitt and Stanley Nicholas, to posts as Assistant to the President and Director of University Research, respectively. Although Atchley denied it, the changes resulted in political costs for him with the board and university community. Criticism of him eventually subsided, but what had occurred was never forgotten and, particularly in the case of Cox, continued to undermine Atchley's effort to establish his much-desired open communications. Rumors, which have since been shown to be unfounded, spread that Cox's removal had been handled so poorly that he threatened to sue the university, forcing it to grant him a large cash settlement.[32]

Although Cox's firing unleashed a wave of sympathy among the liberal arts faculty for its former dean, the professors' threats to boycott or picket classes never materialized.[33] Atchley, characteristic of his personality and style of administration, confronted the liberal arts faculty, challenging it to develop new programs and break with what he alleged were traditions of stodginess and conventionality. "I don't have a hit list," he explained. "But when I walked into the university, it was almost like walking into a forest for the first time. If you don't make decisions as they come along, everything begins to look alike." Atchley suggested that the College of Liberal Arts needed leadership that could make tough and honest decisions; he asked for its faculty not to look like everyone else, but to be unique.[34]

---

[31]Quoted in *The State*, 30 June 1985.

[32]According to the author's telephone interview with H. Morris Cox, 29 Mar. 1987, he received a year's sabbatical (faculty leave with pay), which was not unusual. See, moreover, *The State*, 30 June 1985.

[33]*Greenville News*, 21 Mar. 1980.

[34]*Anderson Independent*, 26 Mar. 1980; observation made by the author; and the cartoon in the *Greenville News*, 24 Mar. 1980.

Despite his wish for change at Clemson, Atchley's own administrative policies did not always provide a good model. For example, his record of recruiting minority students, even though their numbers increased at Clemson by 300 percent during his presidency and he established a special university office for minority affairs, fell far short of the projections made by the school and accepted by the federal government in 1978. Atchley indicated his wish to make all the people of South Carolina welcome at Clemson, but he told the Legislative Black Caucus in 1981 that the school would not enroll black students under false pretenses. He refused to support remedial programs or special curricula for Clemson such as those at the University of South Carolina (USC). Instead, he told the black legislators, Clemson would continue to attract black students "in the nontraditional areas" of engineering and the sciences. "If we are to close the gap between the haves and have-nots," he asserted, "we must educate our students in areas where jobs are available." But this approach also undermined attempts to enroll blacks by closing Clemson's doors to the larger numbers of them who pursued business administration, education, and the liberal arts.[35]

For many of the things that he wished to do at Clemson, Atchley lacked money. Because of declining revenues for state government that resulted from the state's weakened economy in agriculture and textiles, significant cuts were made in the university's budget five times during his six-year presidency. This severely curtailed planning for construction and new programs. Atchley failed to acquire public funds for badly needed building projects like the continuing education and performing arts centers. In 1979 the university requested $15,545,000 for a continuing education building. When the state refused to finance the project, Atchley hoped to build it with private monies as part of the Strom Thurmond Center for Excellence in Government and Public Service. The Thurmond Center was also to include a performing arts building, which the state refused to fund in 1984.[36] Nevertheless, Atchley found enough money to renovate Tillman Hall, upgrade computer facilities, establish twenty-five Provost research awards, create the Calhoun honors college, and return forty-three percent of indirect costs to the colleges to promote research (no such costs had been returned in 1979).

---

[35]See his speech to the caucus, 4 Sept. 1981, CU President's papers, Atchley, speeches, vol. II.

[36]Note the memo signed by James L. Strom showing capital funds requests from 1979-84, in CU President's papers, Atchley, folder 53; and Atchley's discussion of the continuing education and performing arts buildings as part of the Thurmond complex, in *Greenville News and Piedmont*, 13 Nov. 1983.

The lack of money also undermined Atchley's efforts to establish research institutes at Clemson, another mark of maturity for a university. These included the Thurmond Center, the South Carolina Energy Research and Development Center, and the million-dollar center for the study of large-scale integrated circuits for semiconductor companies. Atchley especially involved himself in "Project Leapfrog," the proposed venture with the semiconductor businesses. The Clemson president also played a role in the state's unsuccessful effort to establish the South Carolina Research Authority. Robert Henderson, the director of the Research Authority, credited Atchley with "being the initiator of the state's campaign" until it was indefinitely postponed in December 1984.[37]

Atchley's lack of success as a fund-raiser in both public and private arenas looms as his most significant failure at Clemson. He neither attracted large sums for the university endowment nor built a development office that could do so. Much of the disappointment of Clemson partisans with Atchley's inability to attract money centered on his relations with state political leaders. That association, despite Atchley's insistence that he possessed "a super working relationship" with Governor Richard Riley and that he had no difficulties in working with the legislature, was at best rocky and, at worst, disastrous.[38]

Clearly he had not met Kenneth Cribb's challenge to establish productive lobbying efforts on Clemson's behalf in Columbia. Atchley's frustration in this regard and the success of his counterpart at USC, James Holderman, in winning the battle for the state's resources, led the Clemson chief executive to criticize state leaders publicly. In 1980 he attacked Riley and the state Budget and Control Board for not supporting the provision of funds for a continuing education building and the Energy Research and Development Center at Clemson.[39] Four years later during the budget hearings of the Commission on Higher Education, he denounced as irrational and unfair the state's budgetary process and administration of higher education.[40]

This approach won him few friends in Columbia where, in November 1984, forty-five newspaper editors and publishers left him off their list of

---

[37]*Greenville News*, 3 Mar. 1985.

[38]During the author's telephone conversation with Atchley on 20 Nov. 1986 and interview with him on 18 Dec. 1986, Atchley acknowledged that Riley never understood Clemson's situation or had any affinity for higher education in general. The legislature, he maintained, was not much better.

[39]See the university press release, 17 June 1980, CU Clippings file.

[40]*The State*, 2 Sept. 1984.

the forty most influential South Carolinians (while including Holderman). People in Clemson also criticized this tactic.[41] Atchley later defended himself by arguing that he could rely neither on the politicians who were Clemson's friends in Columbia nor on other state leaders who possessed little sympathy for higher education or Clemson. "I had to do something to gain people's attention," he declared.[42] Atchley's proneness toward personalizing relationships also led him to view the alleged "unfair" treatment of Clemson by state officials as an attack on himself.

This tendency toward personalizing matters and always expecting loyalty and openness from others, moreover, affected Atchley's relationship to the board of trustees. Not only did he demand that others treat him with fairness, but he insisted that they adhere to the commitments he thought they had made to him. In this regard, problems between him and the board arose immediately upon his assumption of the presidency. Atchley believed that the trustees had promised to allow him to serve on the board of directors of three corporations or other large business enterprises, a standard practice of university presidents in raising money for their schools. During his first months at Clemson, however, the trustees prohibited him from accepting a place on the board of the South Carolina National Bank. Subsequently he was permitted to serve on only one board of directors, that of the American Federal Savings and Loan Association.[43]

Apparently even during the first months of Atchley's administration, several trustees had second thoughts about having hired him. Already on 10 January 1980, a trustee responded to the question, "How is Bill Atchley doing?" by declaring: "We've had to whip him into shape but we're there. He just doesn't know how we do things down here." Unfortunately, that sense of his being an "outsider" who lacked Clemson "family ties" remained with Atchley throughout his presidency. In February 1985, for example, a trustee informed John Norton, a writer for *The State,* that Atchley "was an outsider who didn't really care about Clemson."[44]

That was untrue, however. Once Atchley had assumed the presidency at Clemson, he loved both the job and the school. From the beginning, when the board of trustees placed restraints on him and, in his mind, re-

---

[41] See the Associated Press story, 20 Nov. 1984, Atchley papers, folder 17.

[42] Atchley/Steirer interview, 13 June 1985.

[43] Atchley/Steirer interview, 18 Dec. 1986; and P. W. McAlister to board members, 8 Nov. 1979, Atchley papers, folder 10.

[44] From *The State,* 3 Mar. 1985; and the author's conversation with a trustee on 10 Jan. 1980.

neged on promises he believed it had made to him, the board's action appeared to him to be an infraction of the rules that bound them all together and to Clemson. McAlister, the board chairman, recognized the depth of Atchley's emotion, although McAlister mistook its source. In August 1980 the chairman wrote to another board member, James C. Self, that the trouble between Atchley and the board over the Energy Research and Development Center was "a delicate situation and may be compounded by [Atchley's] pride and temperament." McAlister reminded Self that since Atchley had made the center one of his priorities when the board hired him, it had tactily agreed to the project.[45]

Tension between the board and the president mounted steadily. Some trustees accused Atchley of mismanaging the university, but his supporters fervently argued that such charges represented a smokescreen behind which lay other reasons for disgruntlement.[46] Board members with business experience attempted to persuade the others to stop meddling in Atchley's affairs and let him be president.[47] Atchley complained in the spring of 1983 that he continually had to deal with requests by trustees to give special treatment to student applicants and to find jobs for favored parties.[48] He finally told one board member, "Leave me alone."[49]

Moreover, *The State* reported that by the time the board had chosen State Senator James M. Waddell, Jr., as its chairman in the summer of 1983, he and Atchley already disliked each other intensely. It is unclear how many trustees knew of their animosity at the time of Waddell's election. However, *The State* declared that the choice of the senator to head the board did not improve Atchley's relations with it. In 1984 the president selected the university's board of visitors without consulting Waddell. In addition, Clemson sought approval for its budget requests from the state Budget and Control Board, of which Waddell was a member, without discussing the items with the senator.[50]

Despite the troubles, the board's official evaluations of Atchley's performance remained high. For example, the board recommended in 1984

---

[45]McAlister to Self, 14 Aug. 1980, Atchley papers, folder 10.

[46]For the two different views, see as examples, Self to Atchley, 25 Mar. 1985; and Billy Amick to Atchley, 25 Mar. 1985, Atchley papers, folder 19.

[47]*The State*, 3 Mar. 1985.

[48]Atchley to Robert R. Coker, 21 Mar. 1983, Atchley papers, folder 13.

[49]Atchley/Steirer interviews, 13 June 1985; and 18 Dec. 1986.

[50]*The State*, 3 Mar. 1985, claimed that Waddell had been elected chairman of the board with the agreement that he would stop trying to remove Atchley and seek to get along with the president. Atchley, for his part, confirmed the reports of animosity between them in Atchley/Steirer interviews, 13 June 1985 and 18 Dec. 1986.

Bill Lee Atchley 1979-1985 Kate Salley Palmer

that he receive a twenty percent raise, rating "his overall performance as excellent." It identified his strengths as "openness, candor, willingness to accept new ideas, sincerity, ability to communicate effectively with diverse groups (perhaps due to a background in education, industry, and agriculture), lack of an 'ego' problem (willingness to admit and correct errors), ability to identify and empathize with the problems of others, humanness."[51] Such words hardly seemed to describe a poor administrator.

The Conflict with the Trustees over Athletics

A continuing struggle over athletics highlighted the strained relations between Atchley and the trustees. In November 1982 the NCAA placed Clemson's football program on probation for two years because of seventy recruiting and other violations; the university later received a three-year probation from the Atlantic Coast Conference. Bitter controversy arose

---

[51]See the evaluation in Waddell's memo to the board ("Subject: President's Performance Appraisal"), 5 Oct. 1984, CU President's papers, Atchley, folder 55.

quickly because of the different responses of Atchley and the board to the scandal.

In retrospect the incident seemed predictable. On the one hand, Clemson had a board of trustees reasserting its authority after years of quiesence; a powerful athletic program which, through money and status, enjoyed vast influence in the state; a group of loyalists who sincerely believed that the way to "greatness" lay in visible achievement like football championships; and a sense that was more myth than fact that the university represented an all-embracing and all-enveloping "Clemson family." On the other hand, the university had a president who insisted on loyalty and openness in his administration; who dedicated himself to attempting to protect its reputation; and who rallied a large number of faculty, students, alumni, and business leaders to his side. To Atchley, as he told the press in June 1985, the issues at stake in the 1982-1983 controversy had involved "differences in philosophies, and maybe strong leadership, but I think when I was interviewed and came to this job, there was nothing false. They saw and got what they saw."[52]

It is doubtful that Atchley could say the same about what he saw during the interview. He had not asked then about potential problems with athletics, and so when news of the violations in the football program surfaced he was greatly surprised. During 1981 he learned that a slush fund had been established the previous decade by alumni who sought success in intercollegiate athletics. He also discovered that those involved believed they could purchase anyone's loyalty, including that of Atchley, to whom they offered a Mercedes automobile.[53]

Like many others associated with the university, Atchley had basked in the glory of Clemson's 1981 national championship in football. Quickly, however, his attention had turned to dealing with the NCAA investigation of the football program, which began in March 1982. The inquiry persuaded Atchley that the national title had done "nothing" for Clemson; while the investigation dragged on for nine months, he received letters from alumni supporting him and the school. One begged him "to somehow restore credibility and honesty to our athletic department. . . . But long-term I eagerly look forward to the day when I don't have to constantly defend the integrity of my university to everyone I meet. My thoughts are with you as you strive to correct the problems you face in the

---

[52]*Anderson Independent*, 30 June 1985.
[53]Atchley/Steirer interview, 13 June 1985.

situation, but I feel your integrity and honesty will allow you to be as tough as you need to be."[54]

Atchley and Thomas B. McTeer, Jr., who had succeeded McAlister as chairman of the board of trustees, met at the end of October in Chicago with the NCAA committee on infractions. Before they arrived, McTeer sent a note to the board of trustees that gave Atchley the support he thought he needed to present Clemson's case to the committee. "I regard this as a matter to be handled by the President," McTeer told his colleagues, "and therefore the role of the Board will be to make recommendations to him."[55] Atchley took charge of Clemson's defense and met privately with the committee on 29 October to outline his plan to reform the university's athletic department.

To tighten controls on recruiting and record keeping in the department, he proposed reorganizing its administration by dividing the responsibilities for its day-to-day supervision between the director of athletics, H. C. ("Bill") McLellan, and the associate athletic director. Eventually, he told the NCAA committee, he planned to establish a new position, which would report to his office, to coordinate athletic matters. It is uncertain whether, as Atchley has since insisted, his plan and personal appeal presented to the committee so impressed its members that they cut at least one year off the period of probation eventually given Clemson.[56]

Despite McTeer's memorandum, some board members began to criticize Atchley. They disliked the publicity he had received from his July article in *The New York Times* and his appearance in September on the national television program, "Today." His critics on the board disapproved of Atchley's dominating the limelight and implying that only he desired reform at Clemson. He had written in the *Times:* "I will personally oversee a complete and public airing of the findings to insure that no one involved in recruiting our athletes ever again breaks N.C.A.A. recruiting rules."

---

[54]Mark S. Stokes to Atchley, 15 Oct. 1982, CU President's papers, Atchley, folder 25; and Atchley's statement to the author on 24 Aug. 1982 regarding the meaning of the national title to Clemson. Stokes' letter is among 112 in folder 25: 71 supported Atchley's position; 23 demanded a stronger policy; 5 defended the status quo; 8 were generally negative toward Atchley; and 5 were solely concerned with Clemson's relationship to the Atlantic Coast Conference.

[55]McTeer to the board, 27 Oct. 1982, CU President's papers, Atchley, folder 20.

[56]See Atchley's "Statement to the NCAA Board," outlining the plan made public later on 23 Nov. 1982, in CU President's papers, Atchley, folder 41; also Atchley/Steirer interview, 13 June 1985.

Armed with McTeer's memorandum, yet aware of the opposition building in the board against him, Atchley announced publicly on 23 November 1982 the plan he had proposed to the NCAA committee. Possibly because Atchley would not be specific about changes in athletic department personnel and because he emphasized that many details of the new administrative structure still had to be worked out, the press described the plan as "vague."[57] He purposely decided to leave decisions regarding personnel obscure and approach matters cautiously, however, because of his realization of the power possessed by McLellan, Clemson's longtime athletic director. Atchley had no intention of firing McLellan, recognizing that the latter had served the university capably, if not always wisely (the NCAA had placed Clemson's basketball program on probation in 1975), and deserved to be treated with dignity.[58] He decided to save McLellan's job, but also planned to clean up the "mess" in football and keep it clean.[59]

But the trustees disagreed that the athletic crisis called for an administrative solution. Atchley later maintained that the board adopted a defensive attitude toward the affair and wished for it to be "swept under the rug."[60] The president informed the board that he would announce sanctions against football coach Danny Ford and other guilty parties at a faculty meeting on 20 December. Some trustees claimed that Atchley had agreed to clear all sanctions with the board first, and when McTeer and Atchley met in Columbia on 17 December, McTeer charged that the president had violated the agreement. Atchley angrily denied that such an arrangement had been concluded. He would, he said, brief the board at a weekend meeting. When no meeting was held, however, he announced the sanctions. His action triggered cries of "insubordination" from board members.[61] On 30 December the board met with Atchley and ordered him to stop commenting in public on athletic reform.

Meanwhile, illness had distracted McTeer from the crisis. At the point when a strong hand was needed to direct the board's actions, he was unable to provide such leadership. Matters drifted along, therefore, until the

---

[57]*The State*, 14 Jan. 1983; *Greenville Piedmont*, 18 Jan. 1983; Atchley's essay in *New York Times*, 4 July 1982; and "Clemson University News," 24 Nov. 1982 (special edition), 1.

[58]Atchley/Steirer interview, 13 June 1985.

[59]See his charge to the task force on Clemson athletic affairs (headed by Victor Hurst, former Clemson vice president for academic affairs), 1982, President's papers, Atchley, folder 16; and his memorandum, 6 Dec. 1982, President's papers, Atchley, folder 9.

[60]Atchley/Steirer interview, 13 June 1985.

[61]Ibid.; and *The State*, 3 Mar. 1985.

tumultuous board meeting of 14 January 1983. By then the faculty senate had voted overwhelmingly to support Atchley's plan, prompting an angry response from various trustees.[62] The board met with the president for four hours and then asked him to leave the room while the group deliberated further. Reporters waiting outside described angry voices and shouting coming from the room, both with Atchley present and absent. When the meeting ended, McTeer announced that the board had agreed to implement the president's plan.[63]

Although at least one trustee believed that Atchley had won the struggle and that the crisis would soon subside, subsequent events proved otherwise. Atchley later maintained that his opponents on the board campaigned to change the verdict and keep the issue alive until a different decision could be obtained.[64] While continuing to act as the university's spokesman on the affair, Atchley called together the persons involved at the school for a unity conference on 24 January. There he made his wishes clear and gained at least outward acquiescence.[65]

However, problems persisted, as shown by one board member, Self, who expressed puzzlement in a letter to McTeer about what was occurring. Self did not understand, he said, why trustees "chose to disregard" their "agreement" that Atchley would speak for the administration and McTeer for the board. Shortly after the 30 December meeting, Self continued, he had received telephone calls from newsmen who knew more about what had happened there than Self. Self complained that an orchestrated campaign was underway against Atchley and, in the face of such behavior, he declared to McTeer, he could not understand who would want to be a trustee "at this type of place."[66]

The faculty senate's vote of confidence in Atchley on 5 April 1983 apparently pushed matters to a head at the meeting of the board three days later. By then the public had bombarded both Atchley and the board with letters. The president's mail registered sixty-three percent in support of his position, twenty percent for a stronger policy, and seventeen percent op-

---

[62]*The State*, 14 Jan. 1983.

[63]*Greenville News*, 15, 16 Jan. 1983.

[64]Atchley/Steirer interview, 13 June 1985, during which Atchley named the non-board members whom he claimed were responsible for the campaign. On the evening of the board meeting of 14 Jan., one trustee volunteered to the author at a reception at the president's house that "our man" had won the battle "hands down."

[65]See Joseph B. McDevitt memorandum, 25 Jan. 1983, CU President's papers, Atchley, folder 9.

[66]Self to McTeer, 21 Feb. 1983, CU President's papers, Atchley, folder 25.

posed his plans.⁶⁷ Some of the letters favoring him contained strong words of encouragement. One from Donald F. Bolt, the chairman of the American Federal Savings and Loan Association, declared: "Don't let the BASTARDS get you down! They have finally shown their colors. There are a lot more of us behind you than you might think."⁶⁸

One writer urged the board, "Let us not be so *stupid* to let this thing get out of hand and permanently damage our entire school." Still another said, "I do not believe that it was the intention of Thomas Green Clemson to have the land that he gave used for a school that appears to be putting athletics ahead of academics." W. L. Carpenter, chairman of the J. E. Sirrine company, challenged the board to get its "priorities straight. Bill Atchley's approach to excellence in academics and athletics is a step in the right direction. . . . Don't let overemphasis in one area of college life injure the development of its real mission."⁶⁹

The board reacted variously. It held meetings to attempt to hammer out a unified position, once on 23 March with all members present and twice during the next week with only a few attending.⁷⁰ One trustee denied to Carpenter that a problem existed. The media speculation, he said, was not based on fact; no internal battle existed in the university and priorities were well established.⁷¹ However, another trustee, Buck Mickel, argued that the board must admit that it had disagreements and work to solve them. "Unfortunately," he advised McTeer, "the Board of Trustees is now on trial and it is my considered opinion that we must follow through with the plan that President Atchley has outlined—and we must, as a Board, support his efforts."⁷²

By the time the board met on 8 April, Atchley had suspended his plans to appoint an athletic coordinator responsible to the president who would monitor all athletic department activity. This presented the impression that the board had reversed its decision of three months earlier and now had won the conflict with the president. The perception lingered despite the board's official statement in January that it unanimously supported Atchley's actions and that academics would continue as the first priority

---

⁶⁷The 200 letters are in CU President's papers, Atchley, folder 25.

⁶⁸Bolt to Atchley, 4 Apr. 1983, Atchley papers, folder 13. The emphasis was Bolt's.

⁶⁹Carpenter to the board, 1 Mar. 1983; Robert S. Campbell (a former trustee) to McTeer, 5 Apr. 1983; and John L. Stelle to McTeer, 5 Apr. 1983, all in Atchley papers, folder 13.

⁷⁰*The State*, 5 Apr. 1983.

⁷¹Fletcher C. Derrick, Jr. to Carpenter, 14 Mar. 1983, Atchley papers, folder 13.

⁷²Mickel to McTeer, 23 Feb. 1983, Atchley papers, folder 12.

of Clemson. That the board had made Atchley wait outside the meeting room on 14 January also fostered the view that the president had lost.[73]

Atchley prepared himself thoroughly for the meeting on 8 April. According to a carefully constructed memorandum in his private papers, he promised to make no major changes in the athletic program without consulting the board, but in return he asked for its "clear public endorsement" of him. He discussed his administration's achievements, including the value of his fund-raising activities. Above all, however, he stressed the adverse effect his being fired would have on the university, particularly since most observers would assume that it was over athletics.[74] As it turned out, he had ample cause for concern. Apparently a four-man committee had been appointed to inform him that he had been fired,[75] but leaks that suggested the athletic department had been responsible for his removal prompted the board to change.[76]

Why, many of Atchley's supporters asked, did the president not proceed with his plans? Why did he not fire the athletic director, McLellan, present the board with a *fait accompli,* and appear as a martyr or hero if the board disagreed and removed Atchley? Although the president later responded that, in retrospect, such a course would have been the correct one, he maintained that in April 1983 it seemed important to him to remain on the scene and to work with the board for changes. He wished to accomplish other goals at Clemson. He admitted, however, that he had not realized the depth of the feelings among the trustees for athletics.[77] Nor, it should be added, did he realize how committed he had become to his view of what Clemson was.

Following the April meeting, the controversy slowly receded into the background. Although it never disappeared, it was no longer foremost in everyone's mind. Atchley, whose future now became the subject of numerous rumors, continued to develop ideas about the reform of collegiate athletics nationwide, hoping the situation at Clemson would help give

---

[73]*Greenville News,* 5, 9 Apr. 1983. Such treatment had angered Atchley and apparently his wife, Pat, even more. She observed that if that was the way university presidents were treated, she did not want her husband to accept another presidency. This was told to the author by Atchley during an informal conversation on 30 June 1985.

[74]See his "Suggested Comments for March 30, 1983," CU President's papers, Atchley, folder 13.

[75]*The State,* 3 Mar. 1985.

[76]*Greenville News,* 2 Apr. 1983.

[77]Atchley/Steirer interview, 18 Dec. 1986. In *The State,* 10 Mar. 1985, Herman Helms pointedly asked such questions in his daily column.

them credibility. In the fall of 1984 he sent a five-point proposal to the NCAA, which included recommendations for a national certification process for athletic programs (similar to academic programs) and punishments for coaches who violated rules.[78]

On 26 October 1984, the death of Stijn Jaspers, a Dutch cross-country star and Clemson athlete, stunned the university. An autopsy did not uncover a cause of death, but it was soon revealed that Jaspers had taken a pain drug illegally supplied by Clemson coaches. The tragedy rekindled the old antagonisms. Atchley was so completely excluded from the administrative handling of the Jaspers affair that he did not learn of the problem until 3 December, when Walter T. Cox, the vice president for student affairs at Clemson, informed him of the investigation and evidence of the involvement of illegal drugs.[79] Atchley felt himself the victim of mismanagement, lack of communications, and disloyalty, qualities he most abhorred. Based on information he received from William L. Traxler, the solicitor of the 13th circuit, the president initiated an investigation by SLED, the State Law Enforcement Agency. Atchley also announced the probe to the press, despite opposition from some of the trustees to him being the one to do so.[80]

Matters now moved swiftly. A retreat of trustees and university officials at Hickory Knob State Park on 24 January 1985 ended with a majority of the board deciding that Atchley had to be removed. His opponents on the board, without providing evidence, claimed that the president had responded by organizing a campaign to make them appear hostile to academics.[81] Two weeks later the faculty senate voted "no confidence" in McLellan, and on 15 February the athletic director asked for and received an indefinite leave of absence.[82]

The board had been wary of proceeding with a strong minority favoring retaining Atchley and had sought to achieve a consensus position.

---

[78]See the "College Football Association Newsletter," 24 Sept. 1984, Atchley papers, folder 20. In the months following the 8 Apr. meeting, Atchley was reportedly nominated for the president's post at his old alma mater, the University of Missouri-Rolla; he was reported in the running for the president's job at the University of Florida; and his name was mentioned in connection with positions at the U. S. Department of Energy and the Department of Education. Note *Anderson Independent-Mail*, 2 Mar. 1985.

[79]Atchley/Steirer interview, 18 Dec. 1985; the author's conversation with William L. Traxler, 18 Dec. 1985; and report of Traxler's on the investigation, 4 Jan. 1985, CU President's papers, Atchley, folder 37.

[80]*The State*, 3 Mar. 1985.

[81]Ibid.

[82]*Greenville News*, 8, 16 Feb. 1985.

Atchley later confirmed press speculation that those supporting him were realizing how difficult it was to move the other side and were weakening. McAlister, Mickel, Self, and more recently James Bostic, had fought tenaciously and steadfastly for Atchley, but made no converts.[83] At the marathon meeting of the board on 1 March, which lasted over seven hours, six of them without Atchley being present, the president resigned, effective 1 July.[84]

His resignation resulted from the ultimatum he delivered to the board at the meeting. Many reputations, he told the trustees, were at stake. "Whatever happens here today," he declared, "I intend to maintain and protect my reputation." If the board failed to give him a clear vote of confidence and permission to deal with McLellan, he continued, Clemson's honor would be damaged severely. He indicated that he continued to be a strong backer of athletics, but the academic program must receive first priority. In addition, he warned that the public would view his removal from the presidency as a sign that athletics had triumphed at Clemson. "No matter what your intentions and reasons may be," he said, "what you decide today, as far as almost everybody is concerned is athletics versus academics."[85]

Atchley's friends on the board finally decided that for the sake of unity, they would have to make concessions. Later Atchley agreed that harmony became possible only with the resignation of himself and McLellan (who was reassigned to a lesser post in the athletic department and eventually resigned) and the willingness of the pro-Atchley faction on the board to yield. He had understood such realities on 1 March. In addition, he had tired of the tension and anxiety and wanted the crisis ended one way or the other.[86]

Sympathy spread quickly for Atchley. Clemson students rallied in his support, 3,000 signing petitions on 6 March. The faculty senate met and voted 28-5 to condemn the trustees' "unwarranted intrusion" into the university's administration; asked for a commission to study the board's action; and voted 32-1 to thank Atchley for six years as president.[87] Busi-

---

[83]Ibid., 2 Mar. 1985, called McAlister and Bostic "two of his [Atchley's] strongest supporters on the board." The press disagreed on the amount of support Atchley had among the trustees; see, for example, ibid., 3 Mar. 1985. Atchley expressed his views during Atchley/Steirer interview, 18 Dec. 1985.

[84]News accounts are in *Greenville News*, 2 Mar. 1985; and *Anderson Independent-Mail*, 2 Mar. 1985.

[85]*The State*, 6 Mar. 1985; and *Greenville News*, 3 Mar. 1985.

[86]Atchley/Steirer interview, 18 Dec. 1985.

[87]*The State*, 7 Mar. 1985.

ness leaders also reacted to his removal, some with protests. For example, Siegfried W. Poser, the president of Greenville Machinery, a subsidiary of the German Kleinewefers Group, informed Judith Melton, a professor of German at Clemson, that the Jan Kleinewefers award for excellence for students studying German would be dropped for 1986.[88]

The board waited until two days before Atchley left the presidency on 1 July to elect Walter T. Cox Clemson's interim chief executive while it searched for Atchley's successor. Although the turmoil surrounding Atchley had dwindled by the time he left Clemson, two events marred his departure. State auditors objected to $3,350 spent by his administration to improve the flight skills of his administrative assistant, Ed Byars. Moreover, criticism descended on the trustees for granting Atchley $100,000 in severance pay, which was illegal in South Carolina. However, the board quickly changed the payment to compensation for a sabbatical leave, and the opposition disappeared.[89] After leaving Clemson, Atchley served as president of the National Science Center for Communications and Electronics Education Foundation, raising money for a national training and educational center in Georgia. On 1 July 1987 he assumed the presidency of the University of the Pacific in California.

Despite the overwhelming attention focused by the press and public on the problems caused by athletics at Clemson during Atchley's presidency, the differences between him and the trustees extended beyond that one issue. For some on the board, Atchley remained an "outsider" whom they viewed as being uninterested in Clemson's welfare. Misunderstandings on both sides appeared almost immediately on his arrival at the university; his ineffectiveness in increasing its share of state monies for important construction and other projects weakened his support both on and off campus. Nevertheless, Atchley succeeded in several important areas. Not only did he open the processes of communication and governance at Clemson, thereby enhancing the role of both students and faculty in decision making, but he moved the school toward greater maturity as a university by encouraging its missions of research and scholarship.

---

[88]Poser to Melton, 15 Mar. 1985, Atchley papers, folder 19. The award has still not been re-established.

[89]*Anderson Independent-Mail*, 4 June, 19, 23 Oct. 1985.

• *President Walter Thompson Cox, 1985–1986* •

· 13 ·
A GOOD SPORT WALTER THOMPSON COX, 1985–1986

John R. Wunder

During the fall of 1983, when Walter T. Cox was asked by a reporter for Clemson University's weekly student newspaper whether he would ever move to another college, even for a promotion, then vice president for student affairs Cox responded: "My career has been spent here, and when you recognize that I have been here since 1940 as an employee, you can possibly understand my dedication." He continued, " . . . it's really exciting to sit and talk to students and tell them how much I love Clemson and how proud I am of Clemson. So far as money or a higher position, *I would never go anywhere else.*"[1]

Dedication to Clemson clearly characterized the career of Cox, the tenth president of the school and third to have graduated from it. He was appointed interim president by the university's board of trustees after Bill L. Atchley resigned amid controversy in the spring of 1985. Cox served in that role from July 1985 to March 1986, when Max Lennon took over as Clemson's eleventh president. Despite the brief term of Cox's presidency, significant personnel changes occurred, and an effort was made to move beyond the public disputes over the role of academics and athletics at the university. Not only did he bring to his position a deep loyalty to the school, but vast administrative experience he had accumulated during his long career at Clemson. Much of this essay, therefore, is devoted to the years before he became president—to his rise from student, athlete, and graduate at Clemson through its administration to its highest office.

---

[1] See *The Tiger* (Clemson University [hereafter cited as CU], Clemson SC), 20 Oct. 1983. The emphasis is the author's.

The Young Walter Cox

Cox was born in Belton, South Carolina, on 19 September 1918, the son of Walter T. and Grace Campbell Cox. He was born while his father was in Europe fighting in World War I. The senior Cox returned to Belton after the war, where he made a living for his family as a funeral director and furniture store merchant. Young Walter's mother was a homemaker and a musician. Cox also had a younger brother.[2] Together they grew up in Belton, a small Anderson county mill town located a few miles from the Saluda river, one of the major drainage systems of Carolina's upcountry.[3] In 1935, after graduating from high school, Cox journeyed up the road to Clemson Agricultural College, a military, all-male, all-white land-grant institution. However, he did not enroll to study agriculture or engineering. Instead he wished to pursue medicine and football.[4]

During his undergraduate years, Cox concentrated on athletics and the military. He played offensive guard on the Clemson team and was redshirted in 1936. A member of the Block "C" Club, he also served as company commander in the cadet corps.[5] Later reflecting on his undergraduate days, he declared, "Being a student at Clemson was a great experience. In the military days, the training was excellent."[6] When asked about athletics, Cox fondly quoted former Clemson president, Enoch W. Sikes, who had said, "Football is a common denominator in the student body. It brings everyone together."[7]

Cox graduated from Clemson in 1939 with a bachelor of science degree in general science, with an emphasis on mathematics and economics. He received an offer to coach and teach at Boys' High School in nearby Anderson, but turned it down when Clemson's football coach, Jess Neely, asked him to play guard one more year.[8] Cox did graduate work in teacher education during the fall of 1939 and participated in what turned out to be one of Clemson's most glorious moments in athletics. The football team finished with an 8-1 record, its only loss to Tulane, and it played in the

---

[2]Interview, Walter T. Cox with John R. Wunder, 30 Dec. 1986.

[3]Lewis P. Jones, *South Carolina: One of the Fifty States* (Orangeburg SC: Sandlapper Publishing Co., 1985) 5.

[4]See "Vita," Faculty files, Walter T. Cox, in Special Collections, R. M. Cooper Library/Clemson University (hereafter cited as RMCL/CU), 1.

[5]Ibid., 1-2.

[6]*The Tiger*, 21 Feb. 1986.

[7]*Anderson Independent Mail*, 3 July 1985.

[8]*The Tiger*, 21 Feb. 1986; and Cox/Wunder interview, 30 Dec. 1986.

college's first postseason game, the Cotton Bowl, defeating Boston College, 6-3. Cox earned three varsity letters, and while he played the Clemson team compiled a 20-6-2 record.[9]

Athletic Careers

Neely departed from Clemson for Rice Institute in 1940, leaving primarily over salary differences. The loss upset J. C. Littlejohn, the college's business manager, who had backed Neely's request for a salary of $6,000. Neely had coached at Clemson from 1931 to 1940, during which Clemson athletics became profit making, and Littlejohn credited Neely with the success. Littlejohn had once written the head of the Alumni Association, "Another thing about Neely is the fact that he does not sit down and wait for old Clemson men to provide him with funds needed to supplement gate receipts and the athletic fees.... He makes every dollar do full duty."[10]

But not everyone shared these feelings. Christie Benet, a Columbia lawyer and member of the board of trustees, answered Littlejohn's pleas and strongly objected to paying the Clemson coach $6,000. "It seems to me," he declared, "that no coach under any circumstances should get more than the President of the institution and in fact I am not at all certain he should get that much."[11] The board refused to budge, Neely left, and his assistant, Frank Howard, took over as football coach.

This shake-up and dispute involving the direction of Clemson athletics had a significant impact on Cox. At first he thought of accompanying Neely to Rice, but instead Howard offered him a position at Clemson. Cox began his lengthy Clemson tenure on 1 February 1940, as football line coach, baseball coach, and ticket manager.[12] The latter duty would propel him into athletic department administrative affairs and further university responsibilities.

---

[9]The sources in RMCL/CU include "Narrative—WALTER THOMPSON COX," Faculty files, Cox; and Littlejohn papers, XD, folder 183. See, moreover, Cox/Wunder interview, 30 Dec. 1986.

[10]Littlejohn to W. D. Barnett, 9 Dec. 1934, Littlejohn papers.

[11]Benet to Littlejohn, 5 Jan. 1938, in ibid., XD (athletic department organization and functions), folder 177. Benet died in Mar. 1951. He had served as chairman of the board of trustees and United States senator. A native of Abbeville, he coached football at the University of South Carolina. See the information about him in microfilm, "Robert Franklin Poole Scrapbooks, 1940-1959," reel 2, scrapbook no. 1, 88 (hereafter cited as Poole scrapbook), in Poole papers, RMCL/CU.

[12]"Vita," 1, Faculty files, Cox.

The concept of an athletic department public relations and business manager had been controversial. At first, Clemson used part-time employees, who were found wanting. Moreover, the position became politicized when those who handled it did their job poorly. The president of the Alumni Association, W. D. Barnett, chastized Littlejohn for his hiring policies, asserting bluntly, "There is no question but what you had the right to employ Mr. [William] Elliot, but I did not contemplate your employing an advertising member of your staff. The fact that Mr. [E.C.] Parker's plans did not work out is no reason, in my opinion, for his employment as publicity agent, when, as Dr. Sikes stated, he has made such a miserable failure of it for a number of years." Barnett concluded his lashing by observing, "Probably other members of the Board had this kind of employment in mind when you were authorized to employ help, but I did not."[13]

In 1937 the board's athletic committee authorized President Sikes to hire a full-time public relations and business manager. The person would be paid half by the college and half by the athletic booster organization, IPTAY (then called "I Pay Ten a Year"). Split pay, however, meant split duties and, inevitably, allegiances. For the college the individual collected a list of alumni, contacted high school prospects, and publicized college events. The person acted as an all-purpose goodwill ambassador to the public. For the athletic association he was to obtain new members and collect dues, sell tickets, and help the head coach when so directed.[14]

J. H. Woodward first held the position, and his salary was fixed at $2,850.[15] Thus, the board of trustees considered the post to be so important that it paid almost one-half of what it would not give a president or head football coach. When Woodward moved to the Alumni Association, Howard tapped Cox at the beginning of 1940 for the job of coach and manager.

Cox held his first Clemson position for ten years, although it was interrupted briefly by his service in World War II. During 1942 and 1943, duty in the 147th Infantry Regiment of the 37th Division of the United States army took him to the Fiji Islands, New Caledonia, New Zealand, and Guadalcanal. He returned to Clemson at the end of 1943, working

---

[13]Barnette to Littlejohn, 16 Sept. 1931, and Littlejohn to E. W. Sikes, 15 Sept. 1931, Littlejohn papers, XD, folder 177.

[14]Athletic committee (H. L. Fulmer, G. R. Sherrill, D. J. Watson, R. R. Ritchie, and G. E. Metz), to Sikes, 9 June 1937, in Littlejohn papers, XD3 (IPTAY).

[15]See "Memo Regarding Employment of Mr. J. H. Woodward," in Littlejohn papers, XD, folder 177.

first in the Air Force Reserve Officers' Training Corps preflight program, in part to regain his physical condition that had deteriorated in the Pacific from his contraction of dysentery.[16]

This was a time of change for Clemson, which Cox recognized. He was not alone in returning to his alma mater, as many other veterans came, too. Visitors included such later notables as Charlton Heston and Henry Kissinger. "The veterans were coming back to Clemson from the war (thanks to the G. I. Bill)," Cox recalled later, "and living with their families in prefab houses on campus." The college administration needed someone, he noted, who could relate to this new student, a student who would not be in the corps. "These students were excelling in academics at a faster pace than the cadets," Cox analyzed. "I think this was a major move in an interest toward academics."[17]

Cox, with his newly obtained experience as a veteran, quickly reestablished himself in his old position as football ticket manager and baseball coach.[18] He served there until 1951, when President R. F. Poole decided to tap him for a new position, assistant to the president and director of alumni affairs. Like Cox, Poole had played football. "Sarge" Poole, however, had taken the field during the so-called "dark ages," 1914-1916.[19] Poole had accepted the recommendation to appoint Cox from a committee chaired by Woodward.[20] To the new post that involved dual responsibilities, Cox would bring ten years of similar experience.

Poole's administration was not dull. Problems with senior night, the book exchange, parking, and political candidates' speeches required Cox's attention.[21] Sports scandals were also sweeping national intercollegiate athletics, affecting particularly the College of William & Mary and West Point. The Charleston newspaper, the *News and Courier,* asked South Carolina college presidents to comment. Marshall W. Brown of Presbyterian College observed that the cause was alumni and fans "who became obsessed with the urge for victory." The president of the College of Charleston, George D. Grice, called for the elimination of professional football because, in his view, it was corrupting amateur athletics. Poole,

---

[16]"Vita," 1, Faculty files, Cox; and Cox/Wunder interview, 30 Dec. 1986.
[17]*The Tiger,* 21 Feb. 1986; and Cox/Wunder interview, 30 Dec. 1986.
[18]"Staff Biographical Information, 1968," 1, Faculty files, Cox.
[19]Assorted information is in the Littlejohn papers, XD, folder 183.
[20]See in RMCL/CU: *The State* (Columbia SC), 2 Sept. 1951, CU Clippings file; and Poole scrapbook, 126, Poole papers.
[21]See "The Past Presidents of Clemson College," 2, read before the Forum Club of Clemson, 25 May 1948, by Gaston Gage, in Gage papers, folder 28, RMCL/CU.

however, cautioned against overreaction. He urged continuation of strong athletic programs. Clemson, he noted, had not yet been touched by such problems, and he hoped the public would offer praise for good, clean programs.[22]

An even greater problem during Poole's presidency, however, was administrative confusion. Over thirty administrators of varying importance reported directly to him. To bring greater efficiency to Clemson, the trustees commissioned an outside review, and a five-volume report was presented during the summer of 1955. The board's acceptance of this report profoundly changed Clemson and provided the structure by which Cox would later reach the school's presidency.

Dean of Students

The 1955 report recommended restructuring the administration of Clemson into four divisions: academic, business and finance, development, and student affairs. A dean, who would report to the president, headed the office of student affairs. Subordinate to the dean were persons responsible for the university union, student life, the bookstore, student health services, student financial aid, career services, university canteen services, the department of bands, admissions, and the athletic department. For this multipurpose post, Poole choose Cox, his trusted assistant.[23]

Cox remained dean of student affairs until he was named interim president in 1985. When further administrative reorganization occurred in 1966, he was named vice president for student affairs, but that did not alter his basic responsibilities. During those thirty years, significant changes occurred at Clemson. Enrollment increased from 2,700 students in 1955 to nearly 13,000 in 1985, and the college became a university. Moreover, during the first year of Cox's deanship the corps of cadets was terminated and Clemson admitted women students. Cox's office only had three months to prepare the school for a nonmilitary, coeducational student body. The student body was officially integrated in 1963.[24] Wright Bryan wrote in his 1979 history of Clemson, "The administrator closest to the scene of over twenty-five years of changing student life at Clemson has been Walter T. Cox. . . . He has, in large part, guided the transition in

---

[22]See the clipping from *Charleston News and Courier*, 4 Sept. 1951, in Poole scrapbook, 118, Poole papers.

[23]"Vita," 2, Faculty files, Cox. Cox believes the report ushered in the modern era of qualitative growth for Clemson; Cox/Wunder interview, 30 Dec. 1986.

[24]"Vita," 3-4, Faculty files, Cox; and Cox/Wunder interview, 30 Dec. 1986.

campus life since Clemson became a civilian, coeducational institution."[25]

Such changes, which challenged Clemson's institutions, produced stress and crisis on the campus. Two critical events that particularly involved Cox were integration and athletic probation. Harvey B. Gantt, a black student from Charleston, applied for admission to the college's school of architecture. Gantt had been attending Iowa State University under the state of South Carolina's policy of maintaining separate but equal higher education by subsidizing black South Carolinians' education outside the state. Gantt chose to transfer during his sophomore year. After he applied at Clemson, architecture faculty, in consultation with the admissions office, requested examples of his work. On that basis, they rejected the application. White students, however, had not been required to submit drawing samples.[26] Gantt, thereupon, went to court.

At the 1962 United States district court in Anderson, Clemson officials were required to explain their actions. Trustee and State Senator Edgar Brown was asked if the board of trustees had attempted to implement new policies after the 1954 *Brown v. Board of Education* decision in which the Supreme Court ordered the end of segregated schools in America. "No," he replied, "Custom was custom."[27] Clemson officials had hoped to avoid integration and controversy. Nevertheless, they apparently realized, as President Robert C. Edwards had told the Spartanburg Rotary Club earlier that year, that "those of us who have administrative responsibilities in higher education are responsible for what happens on our campuses."[28] Edwards, Brown, Cox, and many others eventually met those responsibilities.[29]

On appeal to the United States court of appeals of the fourth circuit, Clemson lost. In *Gantt v. Clemson College et al.*, the court not only ruled that Gantt should be admitted, but it declared: "To require a Negro in all respects eligible for admission to a college maintained by the state to forego attendance there and to attend an out-of-state college, even with a state

---

[25]Wright Bryan, *Clemson: An Informal History of the University, 1889-1979* (Columbia SC: R. L. Bryan, 1979) 184.

[26]Ibid., 157.

[27]See the transcript in the United States District Court, Western District of South Carolina, Gantt papers, vols. I and II, 75, RMCL/CU.

[28]Edwards's remarks to the club, 16 Jan. 1962, are in CU President's papers, Edwards, RMCL/CU.

[29]George McMillan, "Integration with Dignity: The Inside Story of How South Carolina Kept the Peace," *Saturday Evening Post*, 16 Mar. 1963, 20-21.

subvention, is not a satisfaction of his constitutional right to equal treatment without regard to race."[30] Clemson, having already spent $32,697.21 on litigation costs fighting integration, decided against a further appeal and instead chose to desegregate and devote its energies toward a peaceful resolution of the controversy.[31] Above all else, its officials hoped to avoid the violence, bloodshed, and bad publicity that had surrounded James Meredith's efforts during the fall of 1962 to attend the Unversity of Mississippi.

The dean of students was required to prepare the student body for integration. Cox moved with care and deliberation. A confidential plan was proposed, entitled "Outline of the Advanced Plan of Law Enforcement, Maintenance of Student Discipline, and Arrangement for the Press," which was approved by Governor Ernest F. Hollings on 12 January 1963. It gave Dean Cox numerous responsibilities, including "maintenance of order and discipline of students," keeping the students informed, and taking whatever disciplinary action was necessary to provide for a calm transition from segregation to integration.[32]

The school carefully implemented the plan. On 28 January Cox announced to the students that Gantt would be admitted to the college. He did so through a stern memorandum that assumed an air of confidence in student reaction. "The sole purpose justifying the existence of Clemson College is a program of education," he declared. That meant students were not to participate in any disorder and were to carry their identification cards at all times. "Clemson College," Cox concluded in the memo, "enjoys an enviable reputation as an education institution, and none of us want anything to occur which could reflect unfavorably on the college, the Clemson Student Body and the citizens of South Carolina. . . . I know from experience I can count on your help."[33]

---

[30] Appeal from U. S. District Court for the Western District of South Carolina, 16 Jan. 1963, Gantt papers, vols. I and II, 4.

[31] Memorandum, Edwards to attorney general of South Carolina, 26 June 1963, Gantt papers, expenses file.

[32] "Outline of the Advanced Plan of Law Enforcement, Maintenance of Student Discipline, and Arrangements for the Press: Section Two," 12 Jan. 1963, Gantt papers, implementation files. In the fall of 1962 riots broke out in Oxford, Mississippi, when James Meredith, a black man, attempted to enroll at the University of Mississippi after a federal district court ordered the school to admit him. Mississippi Governor Ross R. Barnett and other state officials obstructed the enrollment, and President John F. Kennedy sent federal troops to the city to enforce compliance with the court order.

[33] See Cox to all Clemson students, 28 Jan. 1963, in Gantt papers, application for admission and admission to Clemson, file no. 1.

The students, despite agitation against Gantt from outside the college, responded positively to Cox. Chapters of "Concerned Clemson Alumni" sent petitions signed by Clemson graduates criticizing school officials and faculty for urging compliance. They called Cox's actions coercive and threatening to Clemson's traditions and termed his leadership communistic and promoting the mongrelization of civilization.[34]

Then an undergraduate newspaper appeared on campus. Cox, using the power mandated to him, tried to suppress it. President Edwards alerted President Thomas F. Jones of the University of South Carolina about the appearance of the virulent racist rag, *Rebel Underground*. It had previously been influential in promoting violence at the University of Mississippi. Edwards had reason to believe money financing the paper came from Mississippi and the White Citizens' Council.[35] The third issue of the *Rebel Underground* directly attacked Cox:

> Although we got good coverage with our last issue of RU, we heard of several cases where little do-good students gathered up some of our issues and carried them to the master gestapo agent, Dean Cox. What is the matter little boys? Are you afraid to let the other students read what we have to say? It is your kind that encourages us to work all the harder![36]

After a few paragraphs calling Harvey Gantt a "partially domesticated, semiliterate member of a cannibalistic race" bent on "[Negro political domination]" and "[racial amalgamation]," Cox again was the subject of racial wrath. "Congratulations to Dean Cox!" wrote the *Rebel Underground*. "In recognition for services rendered, the RU has proclaimed him to be an 'Honorary Nigger.' "[37]

Every rumor needed careful checking. State Senator Earle B. Morris received a letter from a Rock Hill minister who had heard of a student plot to kill Gantt.[38] Morris informed Edwards, who wrote to the minister, "I am forwarding you[r] letter and a copy of my reply to Dean Walter Cox

---

[34]For example, concerned Clemson alumni of Sumter SC to Clemson students, 24 Jan. 1963; concerned Clemson alumni of Greenville SC to Clemson students, 20 Nov. 1962, in Gantt papers, application for admission and admission to Clemson, file no. 1; and Bryan, 157.

[35]Edwards to Thomas F. Jones, 15 Mar. 1963, in Gantt papers, application for admission and admission to Clemson, file no. 1.

[36]A copy of the *Rebel Underground* (Clemson College, Clemson SC) Apr. 1963, in ibid.

[37]Ibid.

[38]Hawley Linn to Morris, 9 Jan. 196[3], in Gantt papers, letters file.

and I assure you and Senator Morris that we will be very alert to the situation you have described."[39]

Monitoring the integration of Clemson was a demanding task. It was especially important to the board of trustees and Edwards to avoid the embarrassment incurred by the University of Mississippi resulting from its refusal to desegregrate. Edwards wrote near the end of the ordeal to the editor of the *Greenville News* that he was weary: "I, too, am thoroughly fed up but I cannot allow myself to become complacent, apathetic, or to give up or quit."[40] Neither he nor his dean of students did.[41] Gantt entered Clemson peacefully, thereby integrating the college, and he graduated, later becoming a highly successfully architect in Charlotte, North Carolina, where he was elected that city's first black mayor. George McMillan, in March 1963 in the *Saturday Evening Post*, wrote that "[Clemson's] plan is probably the most complete and carefully thought-out one ever drawn up in the United States to meet the threat of racial violence."[42] Clemson continued to carry out the plan successfully. McMillan praised Governor Hollings, Edwards, Brown, businessmen Charles E. Daniel, John Cauthen, and A. L. M. Wiggins, and Clemson administrators, faculty, and students for recognizing the correct path to follow at a time of great unrest, to reach "integration with dignity."[43]

Handled less admirably, however, were Clemson's difficulties with big-time athletics. In 1975 the university's basketball program had been cited by the National Collegiate Athletic Association (NCAA) for violations in recruiting players and placed on probation, but an even greater problem involving Clemson's football program became public in 1982. On 29 March 1982 the NCAA notified the university that its football activities were a part of an official inquiry. It marked the second major investigation of Clemson's athletic programs in seven years. Many blamed the director of athletics, H. C. ("Bill") McLellan, for allowing another embarrassing situation to occur. Throughout the investigation the trustees and administration refused to comment or reveal information. The new president, Bill L. Atchley, was accused of stalling.[44]

---

[39]Edwards to Linn, 11 Jan. 1963, in ibid.

[40]Edwards to Wayne Freeman, 18 Mar. 1963, in ibid.

[41]According to "Vita," 3, Faculty files, Cox: "The Office of Student Affairs played a vital role in the smooth matriculation, registration and assignment of Gantt to his new environment."

[42]McMillan, 20.

[43]Ibid., 20-21.

[44]See, e.g., the accusations in *The Tiger*, 1, 12 Apr., 23 Sept. 1982.

Finally at the end of November 1982, the facts began to appear. *The Tiger* reported that the NCAA had found Clemson guilty of giving two Knoxville, Tennessee players money, free trips, and promises of employment for a family member. The NCAA placed Clemson on probation, restricting television appearances, bowl invitations, and athletic scholarships for two years. Atchley chose not to appeal the decision. Seventy violations were recorded, including the awarding of a scholarship to the girlfriend of a prospective athlete.[45] The infractions came within the administrative jurisdiction of the office of student affairs. *The Tiger*, in a special probation issue, declared that McLellan and head football coach Danny Ford were directly implicated by the NCAA.[46]

Atchley responded with plans to restructure the athletic department, and he sought to appoint a presidential representative who would monitor the department's activity. Atchley, a former professional baseball player, promised that "Clemson is one university where athletics will play a proper role."[47] The faculty agreed with the president. Their representatives voted to censure all individuals responsible for the football program. The trustees, however, refused to allow the administrative changes and nearly fired Atchley over the issue.[48] The incident provided the basis for two years of bureaucratic warfare between McLellan and Atchley. Most persons in the administration were forced to choose sides, which was to prove most difficult for Walter Cox.

Cox and the Atchley Presidency

Cox, when asked by a student reporter in 1983 what his relations with Atchley were like, responded positively, "I have a very fine relationship with him. He expects to be advised on what's going on at all times, and he expects me to carry out my responsibilities as I see fit." Cox concluded with a statement revealing his respect for authority and, in particular, the Clemson presidency. "I am responsible to the president for everything I do," he observed, "but everyone is."[49]

Reporting to Cox, the vice president for student affairs, was McLellan. The latter, director of the athletic department since 1971 and a

---

[45]Ibid., 11 Nov. 1982.

[46]Ibid., special probation issue, 2 Dec. 1982. The official NCAA report still is not available to the public. Access to the document is restricted. A copy is in RMCL/CU.

[47]*The Tiger*, special probation issue, 2 Dec. 1982.

[48]Several articles are in ibid., 20 Jan. 1983. See, moreover, *Greenville News*, 28 Feb. 1985.

[49]*Greenville News*, 20 Oct. 1983.

Walter Thompson Cox 1985-1986 — Kate Salley Palmer

member of its staff since 1958, had become a fixture in Clemson athletics.[50] Cox and McLellan were personal friends whose careers spanned nearly three-fourths of a century of Clemson history. Again, Cox found himself with dual responsibilities and dual loyalties. A choice between Atchley and McLellan was an easy one for Cox as was a choice between the president and the athletic director. However, deciding between loyalty to the presidency versus his friend, McLellan, would perhaps be his toughest decision.

The beginning of the end of Atchley's regime was marked by tragedy. On 26 October 1984 Augustinus "Stijn" Jaspers was found dead in his dormitory room. Jaspers, a cross-country runner, had represented his native country, The Netherlands, in the 1984 Olympics.[51] Clemson track coach, Stanley Narewski, praised Jaspers at the beginning of the 1985 season by observing, "Stijn is one of the best in the conference, the region, and perhaps even in the nation."[52]

[50]Ibid., 16 Feb. 1985.
[51]*The Tiger*, 16 Sept. 1984.
[52]Ibid., 13 Sept. 1984.

On 1 November 1984, only a few days after Jaspers's death, *The Tiger* carried two major articles. On the front page Cox was honored for his induction into the Clemson Athletic Hall of Fame.[53] Page two noted the death of a track star. A preliminary autopsy did not reveal a cause. Narewski and the track team were stunned. It was later learned that Jaspers had taken phenylbutazone, an antiarthritic, anti-inflammatory drug used for pain that had been illegally supplied by Clemson coaches. The prescription drug, which requires a physician's permission for use, had been obtained without prescription from a Nashville, Tennessee, druggist.[54]

On 30 October three coaches—Narewski; Samuel Colson, the strength coach; and Jack Harkness, the assistant strength coach— admitted they had distributed illegal drugs and steroids to athletes. Narewski had given Jaspers the phenylbutazone. James Brummitt, acting director of public safety, informed his superior, vice president of business and finance, Melvin Barnette, who had been employed at the university for twenty-seven years. By then three administrators knew the serious nature of the situation: Brummitt, Barnette, and McLellan.[55]

At the beginning of November McLellan telephoned Solicitor William Traxler at the latter's home. He told Traxler that the coaches had admitted supplying drugs to the dead athlete. Traxler informed the athletic director that the incident might be a matter for the grand jury. Meanwhile, a physician in Seneca, James Pruitt, wrote an autopsy report listing the cause of the young Dutchman's death as congestive heart failure, which had resulted from a congenital heart defect. Running had aggravated Jasper's condition.[56]

No indictments had been made by the end of November, and few persons on the Clemson campus knew what was occurring within the Atchley administration. Then Paul Jaspers, Stijn's brother, arrived determined to discover what had happened. He received little help from the athletic department. It refused to show him the autopsy report. The brother then found another athlete willing to tell his story about receiving illegal drugs. Together they went to the Clemson police. Paul Jaspers persuaded Pruitt to amend his brother's autopsy report, allowing for possible drug causes of death, and Jaspers encouraged Traxler to call a grand jury to investigate the affair.[57]

---

[53] Ibid., 1 Nov. 1984.
[54] See the articles on the death in ibid., 11 Jan. 1985.
[55] Ibid.; and *Greenville News*, 17, 20 Mar. 1985.
[56] *Greenville News*, 5 Mar. 1985.
[57] Ibid., 26, 31 Mar. 1985. The final autopsy report found the cause of death to be heart failure; the drugs were incidental.

On 3 December Cox informed Atchley of the problems in the athletic department. Cox said he briefed Atchley as soon as he found out there was an illegal drug involved.[58] Four days later Atchley called a meeting attended by McLellan, Cox, and Bobby Robinson, the assistant athletic director. The president told them that the situation was serious and that SLED, the State Law Enforcement Agency, would investigate. According to the *Greenville News*, McLellan begged for an internal investigation, but Atchley refused. Traxler had already called Atchley to tell him of the SLED investigation, but McLellan led many to believe the inquiry was Atchley's choice. The latter suspended the coaches, and they resigned on 11 December.[59]

Public reaction was swift. An editorial in *The Tiger* suggested that more housecleaning was necessary in the athletic department.[60] The faculty senate again voted no confidence in McLellan as athletic director, and the Clemson chapter of the American Association of University Professors echoed the sentiment.[61] The *Greenville News*, which began extensive coverage of the affair, noted, "The extent of the problem at Clemson isn't clear, but it certainly isn't limited to the resigned coaches and members of the men's track team who first brought it to light."[62]

Throughout January and February 1985 pressure continued to build. Rumors among the faculty and students told of administrative infighting, the Atchley versus McLellan camps, and attempts to involve the trustees. Some suggested Atchley might be fired. However, he was not the first to leave. On 16 February Atchley announced he had approved McLellan's request for an indefinite leave with pay pending the SLED investigation. Robinson became acting athletic director.[63] McLellan asked Cox for the leave as the two drove home from Columbia after attending a meeting of the trustees. Cox approved of the idea, took it to Atchley, and then called W. G. DesChamps, a trustee and chairman of the board's subcommittee on athletics. DesChamps told *The State* reporter that McLellan's leave had resulted from the latter's exhaustion caused by upstate newspapers and Clemson's faculty.[64] Cox publicly announced that McLellan's leave "was not a prelude to termination, and I hope that is clear . . . If I thought that

---

[58]Ibid., 5 Mar. 1985.
[59]Ibid.; and *The Tiger*, 11 Jan. 1985.
[60]*The Tiger*, 11 Jan. 1985.
[61]*The State*, 9, 10 Feb. 1985; and *Greenville News*, 10 Feb. 1985.
[62]*Greenville News*, 10 Feb. 1985.
[63]Ibid., 16 Feb. 1985.
[64]*The State*, 16 Feb. 1985.

this would jeopardize his position, I would have never recommended it."⁶⁵ Faculty Senate President David Senn said the decision was good for the university.⁶⁶

Amid the athletic crisis, Vice President Cox had another potential problem to solve. The Clemson Players, a group of students who had gained national reputations for their quality drama productions, planned to present the award winning play, *Equus*. One scene, however, called for a topless actress. After a complaint by a student who did not receive the part, Cox believed he had to act. He ordered the director to rewrite the scene so as not to include nudity. Although the Clemson Players complied and the play was produced, many students and faculty were concerned about the compromises in artistic integrity and freedom of speech they saw ocurring within the university.⁶⁷

This controversy quickly faded, however, with the revelation that the trustees would meet on 1 March to decide whether to fire President Atchley. The board's chairman, state Senator James Waddell, said there was no movement to oust Atchley, but South Carolina's newspapers carried statements to the contrary.⁶⁸ The *Greenville News* reported the board was split over the matter, but the fact a meeting was called, concluded the paper, suggested that the "trustees evidently favor nurture, promotion, and protection of athletics over the school's chartered purposes of teaching, research, and public service."⁶⁹

On 1 March, following a seven-hour closed-door session, Waddell announced that Atchley had resigned after the president had failed to receive a favorable vote of confidence, and that McLellan wished to be reassigned elsewhere within the university. Cox told Waddell that McLellan had in effect resigned the athletic directorship.⁷⁰ These events shocked the campus and state. Several hundred students rallied urging Atchley to reconsider, but he refused. The *Hartsville Messenger* editorialized, "The faded jocks have been allowed to use a fine academic institution as their playpen."⁷¹ A paper in Greenwood, the *Index-Journal*, assailed

---

⁶⁵*Greenville News*, 16 Feb. 1985.
⁶⁶Ibid.
⁶⁷Ibid., 20 Feb. 1985.
⁶⁸See the series of articles in ibid., 25, 26, 28 Feb. 1985; and *The State*, 24 Feb. 1985.
⁶⁹*Greenville News*, 1 Mar. 1985.
⁷⁰Note ibid., 2, 3, Mar. 1985; *The State*, 2 Mar. 1985; and "[Minutes] Meeting of the Board of Trustees of Clemson University," 1985, 1 Mar. 1985, 9, RMCL/CU.
⁷¹Quoted from *Greenville News*, 17 Mar. 1985.

the arrogance of the trustees and Waddell.⁷² The *Greenville News* hinted at even more revolutionary actions—changing the composition of the board of trustees. "If Chairman Waddell does not rein the impulses by which he and others are running roughshod over Clemson's reputation and mission," declared the paper, "the General Assembly needs to review the school's charter and take steps to reform its leadership."⁷³

An interim leader was needed, and a search for a new president had to begin. On 24 March the trustees met again in Columbia. They agreed on a process for a search, hoping to conclude it by October. They also passed a resolution affirming the priority of academics over athletics. In addition, some trustees wanted more information about a possible coverup of Stijn Jaspers's death, but Waddell insisted the situation was strictly an administrative matter.⁷⁴

Although many thought its own trustees had dealt Clemson an irreparable blow, Walter Cox did not. He saw no problem in finding a new president. "I've been on this campus fifty years," he assured the media, "and I've never seen it so good except for things you read about in the paper recently. This is a great institution, and it would be a great honor for anyone with the qualifications to provide the leadership as chief executive officer."⁷⁵

He moved rapidly to appoint a new athletic director, announcing on 3 March that a search would begin the next week for McLellan's successor. Shortly after he indicated that Bobby Robinson was the frontrunner, the search was concluded on 9 March with Robinson's appointment as director of athletics. Two others had withdrawn their names from consideration. Atchley immediately ratified Cox's choice.⁷⁶

The Cox Presidency

As Atchley's term approached its end, speculation increased about who would be named interim president. The press suggested Harry Lightsey, dean of the college of law at the University of South Carolina; Earle G. Morris, Clemson alumnus and state comptroller; Philip Lader, Winthrop College president and a possible candidate for governor in 1986; and Cox.⁷⁷

---

⁷²Ibid.

⁷³Ibid., 19 Mar. 1985.

⁷⁴Ibid., 25 Mar. 1985; and "[Minutes] . . . Trustees of Clemson University," 24 Mar. 1985, 10-11.

⁷⁵*Greenville News*, 3 Mar. 1985.

⁷⁶Ibid., 3, 9 Mar. 1985.

⁷⁷Ibid., 19 Mar. 1985.

When the board met on 29 June 1985, it unanimously chose Cox as interim president, and in a surprise move selected the first nonlife-term trustee, Louis Batson, Jr., as chairman replacing Waddell.[78]

"I'm humbled," Cox explained to the media, "because I've been so close to the President's office for so long, I know how hard I'm going to have to work." He added that he did not see himself as a "caretaker." "I don't like the word caretaker," he said, "that's a status quo. You either go back or forward . . . and we're going forward." Anxious to portray an activist presidency, Cox sounded eager for his new position, declaring that "I hope I can get right off the ground immediately."[79]

Cox served as interim president from 1 July 1985 to 6 March 1986. Those 249 days were significant in the growth and development of Clemson as a university. Cox not only realized that much damage had been done to the school's reputation, but he sought to clean up the loose ends in the Jaspers affair. Personnel matters would need immediate attention, and perhaps no other person except Cox within the Clemson hierarchy had the ability to make what many perceived to be necessary changes. In the process of ending the administrative upheavals, the trustees gave Cox what Atchley and so many other presidents had wanted—the sole power to hire and fire administrative staff, including vice presidents, deans, athletic directors, and coaches. Clemson's interim president possessed the authority to govern.[80]

On 29 July Cox placed Barnette, the vice president of business and finance, on medical leave. Within three months he fired Barnette. Before Barnette was removed, however, campus security had been taken from his responsibility and a new safety director was chosen.[81] Cox also supported the awarding of a year-long sabbatical to Atchley at a cost of $100,000. Moreover, the interim president took full responsibility for making an oral contract of three years with McLellan at $68,000 per year. McLellan accepted a forced retirement.[82] Gone by the end of October were Atchley,

---

[78]"[Minutes] . . . Trustees of Clemson University," 29 June 1985, 29.
[79]*Anderson Independent Mail,* 30 June 1985.
[80]*Greenville News,* 21, 24 Sept. 1985.
[81]Ibid., 9 Oct. 1985.
[82]See Statement By Clemson University President Walter T. Cox, 31 Oct. 1985, South Carolina Biography file, Cox, RMCL/CU. So much criticism was generated by the Atchley-McLellan settlements that the board of trustees opened its meeting of 14 Oct. 1985 to the press for questions and answers. See "[Minutes] . . . Trustees of Clemson University," attachment 2, AZ-1 to AZ-11 and attachment 3, A3-1 to A3-11. Atchley eventually accepted a position as president of a national science center for a communications and elec-

McLellan, Waddell, Barnette, Brummitt, Narewski, Colson, Harkness, and Stijn Jaspers. Of the primary players in Clemson's ordeal, only Robinson and Cox remained. Criticism of what some called payoffs to Atchley and McLellan were met head-on by Cox, who replied, "I have taken this course of action in the best interest of Clemson University—to bring to an end a rocky period in our history so that we can get on with the business of education and meeting the needs of the society we serve."[83]

Other highlights of the Cox presidency would have long-range consequences. The groundbreaking for the Strom Thurmond Institute occurred on 8 November 1985, which the vice president of the United States, George Bush, attended as an honored guest. A resolution adopted by the trustees placed a ceiling of $5.5 million on the cost for the new building. Moreover, a policy on the university's granting of honorary degrees was approved, and one of the first to receive a degree under the new policy was Harvey Gantt. Also the athletic department announced that it would give ten percent of its basketball and football revenues and ten percent of all net revenues from postseason play to the university's endowment fund for academic scholarships. Cox credited his newly appointed athletic director, Robinson, with developing the plan.[84]

Cox's greatest responsibility, however, was to prepare Clemson for its new president. True to his word, he had not been a caretaker. He had made decisions. Yet he recognized the short-term nature of his presidency. "All we need to continue this forward momentum is leadership," he told the press. "The selection of this president is so important, because on this person's shoulders rest the leadership. Without that leadership, we're going to plateau."[85] On 14 October 1985 the trustees announced the name of Clemson's eleventh president: a North Carolina native and then vice president for agriculture administration at The Ohio State University.[86]

Although the Cox presidency had been brief, it was punctuated with action and resolution. "It was a time of polarization," Cox later reflected. "I sought to restore confidence in the university administration, and my

---

tronics foundation, and McLellan was named athletic director at the University of Southern Mississippi. In Apr. 1987 Atchley was named president of The University of Pacific in California.

[83]Statement by Cox, S. C. Biography file, Cox.

[84]*Greenville News*, 19 Sept. 1985; "[Minutes] . . . Trustees of Clemson University," 27 July 1985, 30-31; and Oct. 1985, 2, 5.

[85]*Greenville News*, 13 Oct. 1985.

[86]Max Lennon was the new president. See "[Minutes] . . . Trustees of Clemson University," 14 Oct. 1985, 46.

top priority was quality education for Clemson's students."[87] A path had been cleared for a new kind of university administration. Gone would be many vestiges of Clemson's past. Even a new vice president for student affairs would be named. However, not every issue concerning the proper place of academics and athletics had been resolved. The athletic department remained in control of most of the funds generated by university-sponsored athletic events, and the office of academic affairs still did not supervise the admissions and scholarship divisions. Nevertheless, a new spirit of cooperation seemed more possible than before, and the person whose first job at Clemson required him to mesh the two competing interests was very much responsible for it.

On 5 April 1986 the trustees met to confer the title of president emeritus on Cox. In a certificate of appreciation, board chairman Batson wrote,

> During his eight months as Clemson's tenth president, Walter Thompson Cox moved swiftly and decisively and with patient firmness of purpose to restore the confidence of the faculty, staff and student body, to boost the morale of alumni and friends, and to reestablish with the people and leaders of South Carolina Clemson's reputation for high standards and sound management.[88]

Fred Richey, the president of the student senate, echoed these sentiments. He presented to Cox a resolution passed by the student body's representatives, extending to the new president emeritus "a formal commendation for the decorous servitude exemplified in his life at Clemson University."[89]

Upon receipt of such an honor at the age of sixty-eight, most persons would have retired. But not Walter Cox. He continued to serve as a special assistant to the president and as acting vice president for development in the new Lennon administration until his official retirement from the university during the spring of 1987.

---

[87]Cox/Wunder interview, 30 Dec. 1986.

[88]"[Minutes] Meeting of the Board of Trustees of Clemson University," 1986, 5 Apr. 1986, 8, RMCL/CU.

[89]Ibid.

• *President Max Lennon, 1986–* •

AFTERWORD

Max Lennon,
President of Clemson University

The tradition of Clemson presidents—the tradition of Clemson University—is one of vision. From those moments more than one hundred years ago when what is now Clemson University was but a glimmer of inspiration and hope in the mind of Thomas Green Clemson, the development of this institution has been shaped by individuals with the foresight to analyze how the present is evolving into the future and the wisdom to prepare the institution for dealing with those changes. As Clemson enters its second century, that tradition of vision must be continued for the university to position itself to respond effectively to the challenges of a changing world.

It is indeed a global vision that Clemson University must assume in preparing for the future. Because of advances in technology and communications, geography no longer determines the boundaries of relevance and interaction among the peoples of the earth. Developments anywhere around the globe can have significant and immediate impact on the lives and livelihoods of South Carolinians and all Americans. Just as Thomas Clemson realized, as he stated in his will, "that there can be no permanent improvement in agriculture without a knowledge of those sciences which pertain particularly thereto," success in today's global society and economy requires knowledge from many disciplines and a perspective that crosses international borders, whether one is a farmer or an engineer, an architect or a manufacturer, and especially if one is an educator.

Clemson University's tradition of excellence in undergraduate education must be continued, and it must continue to reflect an understanding of the demands Clemson students will face as graduates. The curricula must keep pace with the times and must be broad enough to prepare students for living, as well as for making a living. Beyond the classroom, the intellectual and social environment of the campus should itself spur students to exercise their imaginations and to develop their own visions of the future. These are the measures of quality for modern undergraduate education. The Clemson tradition dictates that these be the hallmarks of a Clemson education.

The future also must find Clemson University at the forefront of the search for new knowledge and new applications of knowledge. Research, graduate education, and public service are areas in which Clemson has significant opportunities for enhancing its stature, productivity, and impact as a major land-grant institution. The march into the future will be led by those with a clear vision of their strengths, needs, mission, and priorities and a blueprint for achieving excellence in selected areas of emphasis. Clemson, in concert with South Carolina's other two research universities, has begun to bring focus to its vision for the future and has charted the course to excellence. "Clemson University: The Second Century," a plan developed by the faculty and reviewed and supported by key leaders of business, industry, and government, lists five major areas of emphasis for research and public service in the years ahead: agriculture, engineering and basic science, marketing and management, quality of life, and textiles. The "Second Century" plan is but an outline, an academic agenda. The dialogue among Clemson faculty and with those whom Clemson serves has only just begun. As the discussion continues and advancements come, the details of the agenda will be adjusted to keep the focus on excellence with relevance.

The degree to which Clemson University will be able to follow its course to excellence will be determined largely by the degree to which the state and the private sector can be motivated to invest as partners in that effort. State funding is the umbilical cord supplying the basic resources essential to the university's existence. Beyond that fundamental support, however, there must be a long-term, consistent, and significant investment in higher education in South Carolina if the state and its universities are to mature into competitive forces in today's world and the world of tomorrow. South Carolina cannot afford to be without excellence in higher education. In keeping with its mission of service and tradition of leadership in the state, Clemson University must be a proactive agent in helping the state achieve that excellence by exploring the frontiers of developing technologies, new products, and new jobs. The cost will not be small, but the payoff could be the difference between success and failure for South Carolina and its citizens in the twenty-first century, only a few short years away.

Clemson's tenth president, Walter T. Cox, once listed what he called the three most significant points in Clemson's history. The first was the founding of the school by Thomas Green Clemson, which set in motion

Afterword • 263 •

the chain of events that has brought the institution to its one-hundredth anniversary. The second was the Cresap, McCormick, and Paget management study of the mid-1950s, which caused the institution to shift its gears and to begin the move from being a small, all-male, military college to being a major, coeducational, civilian university. The third key point in Clemson history that President Emeritus Cox cited was the development of the "Second Century" plan as Clemson's road map for preparing for the next one hundred years. Each of those events was a product of vision and of determination to be ready for the future. Thomas Clemson envisioned the benefits of scientific and technological education to coming generations of South Carolinians. Clemson's trustees envisioned the changing role of the institution in the 1960s and beyond. Clemson's faculty and administrators today are busy envisioning how the university can be of greatest service in the years ahead.

It is an exciting time to be the president of Clemson University. It is a humbling honor and a stimulating responsibility to serve an institution so distinguished by its tradition of vision, legacy of commitment to high quality, and uniqueness of spirit and sense of place. Clemson enters its future as it has lived its past: with a mission to serve, the determination to succeed, and the potential to excel.

APPENDIX

The Will of Thomas Green Clemson*

State of South Carolina,
County of Oconee.

Whereas I, Thos. G. Clemson, of the county and State aforesaid, did, on the 14th day of August, 1883, execute my last will and testament wherein I sought to provide for the establishment of a scientific institution upon the Fort Hill place, and therein provided what sciences should be taught in said institution; and, whereas, I am now satisfied that my intention and purpose therein may be misunderstood as intending that no other studies or sciences should be taught in said institution than those mentioned in said will, which was not my purpose or intention. Now, desiring to make my purpose plain as well as to make some other changes in the distribution of my property, than made in said will, I do now make, publish and declare this instrument as and for my last will and testament, hereby revoking all previous wills and codicils by me made, especially the will above referred to, dated August 14th, 1883.

Feeling a great sympathy for the farmers of this State, and the difficulties with which they have had to contend in their efforts to establish the business of agriculture upon a prosperous basis, and believing that there can be no permanent improvement in agriculture without a knowledge of those sciences which pertain particularly thereto, I have determined to devote the bulk of my property to the establishment of an agricultural college upon the Fort Hill place.

This institution, I desire, to be under the control and management of a board of trustees, a part of whom are hereinafter appointed, and to be modeled after the Agricultural College of Mississippi as far as practicable.

My purpose is to establish an agricultural college which will afford useful information to the farmers and mechanics, therefore it should afford thorough instruction in agriculture and the natural sciences connected therewith—it should combine, if practicable, physical and intellectual education, and should be a high seminary of learning in which the graduate of the common schools can commence, pursue and finish the course of studies terminating in thorough theoretic

---

*Reprinted from Alester G. Holmes and George R. Sherrill, *Thomas Green Clemson: His Life and Work* (Richmond: Garrett and Massie, 1937) 193-201.

and practical instruction in those sciences and arts which bear directly upon agriculture, but I desire to state plainly that I wish the trustees of said institution to have full authority and power to regulate all matters pertaining to said institution—to fix the course of studies, to make rules for the government of the same, and to change them, as in their judgment, experience may prove necessary, but to always bear in mind that the benefits herein sought to be bestowed are intended to benefit agricultural and mechanical industries. I trust that I do not exaggerate the importance of such an institution for developing the material resources of the State by affording to its youth the advantages of scientific culture, and that I do not overrate the intelligence of the legislature of South Carolina, ever distinguished for liberality, in assuming that such appropriation will be made as will be necessary to supplement the fund resulting from the bequest herein made.

Item 1. I therefore give and devise to my executor, hereinafter named, the aforesaid Fort Hill place, where I now reside, formerly the home of my father-in-law, John C. Calhoun, consisting of eight hundred and fourteen acres, more or less, in trust, that whenever the State of South Carolina may accept said property as a donation from me, for the purpose of thereupon founding an agricultural college in accordance with the views I have hereinbefore expressed, (of which the Chief Justice of South Carolina shall be the judge), then my executor shall execute a deed of the said property to the said State, and turn over to the same all property hereinafter given as an endowment of said institution to be held as such by the said State so long as it, in good faith, devotes said property to the purposes of the donation; provided, however, that this acceptance by the State shall be signified, and a practical carrying-out be commenced within three years from the date of the probate of this my will. During this term of three years, or as much thereof as may elapse before the acceptance or refusal of this donation, my executor shall invest the net produce of the land and other property; such invested fund awaiting the action of the legislature, and to form a part of the endowment of said institution if accepted, or to form a part of the endowment of the college or school hereinafter provided for, should the donation not be accepted by the State.

Item 2. The following named gentlemen, seven in number, shall be seven of the Board of Trustees, to wit:

R. W. Simpson, D. K. Norris, M. L. Donaldson, R. E. Bowen, B. R. Tillman, J. E. Wannamaker and J. E. Bradley, and the State, if it accepts the donation, shall never increase the board of trustees to a number greater than thirteen in all, nor shall the duties of said board be taken away or conferred upon any other man or body of men. The seven trustees appointed by me shall always have the right, and the power is hereby given them and their successors, which right the legislature shall never take away or abridge, to fill all vacancies which may occur in their number by death, resignation, refusal to act, or otherwise. But the legislature may provide, as it sees proper, for the appointment or election of the other six trustees, if it accepts the donation. And I do hereby request the seven trustees above named, or such of them as may be living, or may be willing to act, to meet as soon after my death as practicable, and organize, and at once to fill all vacancies that may have occurred, and to exert themselves to effectuate my purposes as herein set forth, and I hereby instruct my executor to notify them of their appointment herein as soon after my death as practicable. The name of this institution shall be the "Clemson Agricultural College of South Carolina."

Item 3. Should the three years expire without the State accepting the donation, in manner as hereinbefore provided, and if accepted, at the expiration of three years from my death no practical beginning has been made to carry into effect the purposes of the donation, or, if before the three years expire the legislature shall refuse to accept said donation, then the donation to the State is hereby revoked, and my executor shall execute his trust by conveying the said Fort Hill place, and the accumulated fund arising therefrom, together with all other property, real or personal, hereinafter disposed of and intended to be given to the said agricultural college, as an endowment, to the seven trustees named above, or their successors, who shall erect upon the Fort Hill place such a school or college for the youth of South Carolina as, in their judgment will be for their best interest; provided, that said school or college shall be for the benefit of the agricultural and mechanical classes principally, and shall be free of costs to the pupils, as far as the means derived from the endowment hereinafter provided and the use of the land may permit. The trustees shall securely invest the funds hereinafter provided and given to said institution and hold them as a perpetual endowment, and shall only use the interest derived therefrom and the income of the land to support and maintain said school or college, except that the accumulated fund derived from the land, and the interest derived from the fund hereinafter given said institution, from the time of my death, and as much as five thousand dollars of the principal fund may be used if, in the judgment of the trustees, it may be necessary to erect suitable buildings for said school or college. The name of this institution shall be the "Clemson Scientific School" or "College."

Item 4. It is my desire that the dwelling house on Fort Hill shall never be torn down or altered, but shall be kept in repair, with all the articles of furniture and vesture which I hereinafter give for that purpose, and shall always be open for the inspection of visitors, but a part of the house may be used by such of the professors as the trustees may direct.

Item 5. I give and bequeath to my granddaughter, Floride Isabella Lee, all of my silver plate and table silver, also all of the family pictures, except the large picture of John C. Calhoun, now hanging in my sitting room, also any one article in my present residence which she may select as a memento of me, also my decorations, and also the sum of fifteen thousand dollars ($15,000), to be paid to her on the day of her marriage, or when she becomes twenty-one years of age, if unmarried; provided, that if my said granddaughter should die unmarried, and before she is twenty-one years of age, then all of said property mentioned in this item shall revert to and become a part of the residue of my estate, and become subject to the trusts and conditions of Items 1, 2, and 3 of this my will.

Item 6. I give and bequeath to my faithful housekeeper, Mrs. Jane Prince, one year's provisions for her and daughter, and furniture and bedding, suitable to her condition, sufficient to furnish two rooms, and the sum of three thousand ($3,000), to be paid to her at the expiration of one year after the probate of this my will, and I also desire my executor to permit her to live at Fort Hill until he disposes of the property as herein directed.

Item 7. I give and bequeath to Hester Prince, the daughter of my faithful housekeeper, as aforesaid, the sum of three thousand dollars ($3,000), to be paid to her, or such person as may be selected by her and appointed her guardian, at the expiration of one year from the probate of this my will.

Item 8. I give to my executor, James H. Rion, as a memento of my friendship, the antique entaglio Marcus Aurelius Antonius sealing which I habitually wear, and also such one of my pictures as he may select, if the same is not selected by myself.

Item 9. I give and bequeath to my executor, or to be held by him subject to the trusts and conditions of Items 1, 2, and 3 of this my will, and for the purpose of adorning the Fort Hill residence as provided in Item 4 of this my will all of my permanent furniture, relics and articles of vesture, pictures and paintings, including the large painting or picture of John C. Calhoun, now hanging in my sitting room, and not otherwise disposed of herein, and all of my books.

Item 10. I direct my executor to sell, at public or private sale, as he may deem best, all the balance of my personal property upon my Fort Hill place, not herin disposed of, and to sell and convey all of my real estate lying and situate outside of the State of South Carolina, either at private or public sale, as he may deem best, and to hold the proceeds derived therefrom, together with the proceeds of the personal property, herein directed to be sold, subject to the trusts and conditions of Items 1, 2 and 3 of this my will.

Item 11. All the residue and remainder of my property of every kind and description whatsoever, after paying off the legacies above provided for, together with the property which may revert to my estate, should it revert thereto, and the proceeds of all my real and personal property herein directed to be sold, and all accumulated funds derived from the Fort Hill place and interest on my investments, I give and bequeath to my executor, to be held by him subject to the trusts and conditions of Items 1, 2 and 3 of this my will.

Item 12. I nominate, constitute and appoint my friend, James H. Rion, the executor of this will.

In witness whereof I have hereunto subscribed my name and affixed my seal before the witnesses below subscribing, the 6th day of November, A. D. 1886.

Thomas G. Clemson, L. S.

The above written instrument was subscribed by the said Thos. G. Clemson in our presence and acknowledged by him to each one of us, and he, at the same time, published and declared the same to be his last will and testament, and we, at his request, and in his presence, and in the presence of each other, have signed our names as witnesses hereto.

James Hunter
T. O. Jenkins
E. L. C. Terrie

Codicil to the will of Thomas G. Clemson

State of South Carolina,
County of Oconee.

I, Thos. G. Clemson, of Fort Hill, in the State and county aforesaid do make this my codicil to my last will and testament, dated the 6th day of November 1886, hereby confirming my said last will and testament, so far as the same is not inconsistent with the, my codicil.

Item 1. I will and direct my executor to pay my debts and funeral expenses as soon after my death as practicable out of the proceeds of any part of my estate that is the most available.

Item 2. I hereby revoke the 12th item of my last will and testament as aforesaid, in which I appointed James H. Rion as executor of my will, he having recently departed this life, and I now do nominate and appoint my trusted friend, Richard W. Simpson, of Pendleton, South Carolina, my executor of my said last will and testament and of this my codicil thereto, and in my said last will and testament the name of James H. Rion, wherever it appears, shall be stricken out, and Richard W. Simpson shall be inserted in place thereof.

Item 3. I revoke the 8th item of my said last will and testament, in which I gave to James H. Rion my sealing ring and one of my pictures, which he may select, and I do now give and bequeath to R. W. Simpson my sealing ring, which I habitually wear, and such one of my pictures as he may select.

Item 4. I do hereby revoke Item 6 of my said last will and testament, which contains a bequest to my faithful housekeeper, Mrs. Jane Prince, she having been otherwise provided for.

Item 5. It is my will and I do direct that neither the legacy to my granddaughter in the fifth item of my said last will and testament, or the legacy to Hester Prince in the seventh item of my said will, shall bear any interest until the same are due and payable, as provided in said items of my said will.

Item 6. I authorize my executor to purchase that portion of the original Fort Hill tract of land which set off to Gideon Lee, guardian of Floride Isabella Lee, and the same if so purchased shall become a part of the Fort Hill tract of land, and shall go with and be disposed of as I have in my said will disposed of the Fort Hill tract.

Item 7. I will and direct my executor to sell either at private or public sale, and for cash or upon a credit, both as he may think best, all the real estate of which I may die seized and possessed, except the Fort Hill tract of land, whether the same be situate in the State of South Carolina or outside of it.

Item 8. Should the Chief Justice of South Carolina decline to decide when the State of South Carolina has or has not accepted the donation given to it in the first item of my said will, then I give to my executor the same power as I in the said first item of my will gave to the said Chief Justice, and his decision shall be final.

Item 9. I hereby authorize and direct my executor to employ such persons as he may deem necessary to take charge of the Fort Hill dwelling house and the articles therein donated, and to manage the farm and to pay the said persons such a sum of money for their service as he may deem right and proper.

Item 10. In the view of the great responsibility and labor which my executor will encounter in managing the affairs of my estate, as directed in my said will, and in consideration of the great kindness he has shown to me, and of the assistance in taking care of my business when I have no other friend to help me, I will and bequeath that he, my said executor, shall have, take and receive in addition to the usual commissions allowed by law to executors as commissions for receiving and paying out money, five percent of the appraised value of my entire estate, both real and personal.

Item 11. I desire to state here that my granddaughter, Floride Isabella Lee, has received the one-fourth part in value of the original Fort Hill tract of land, the part which her mother, under the will of Mrs. John C. Calhoun, was entitled to, the same having been appraised and set off to her by commissioners appointed by Mrs. Clemson, and by Gideon Lee, her father and guardian, and she has also received through Gideon Lee, her said guardian, her mother's share of the estate of my son, John C. Clemson. Notwithstanding this fact, from a letter received by me some time ago from Gideon Lee, I am led to believe that as guardian of my said granddaughter, he will make claim to my estate a large balance alleged by him to be due my said granddaughter by me. I therefore desire and direct my executor to examine closely into such claim if so made, and if he, my said executor, is satisfied that the claim so made is justly due by me, to my said granddaughter to pay the same; but on the other hand, if he is not satisfied that the said claim or claims are justly due by me, then he shall not pay it or them unless compelled by law to do so, in which case I hereby revoke so much of the bequest of fifteen thousand dollars given in the fifth item of my said last will and testament to my said granddaughter as will be equal to the amount which my said granddaughter may recover against my estate.

Item 12. The desire to establish such a school or college as I have provided for in my said last will and testament, has existed with me for many years past, and many years ago I determined to devote the bulk of my property to the establishment of an agricultural school or college. To accomplish this purpose is now the one great desire of my life. I have not been unmindful of the interest of my said granddaughter, nor have I acted in this matter through any prejudice to anyone. It may be possible that the disposition of my property as herein made may not give satisfaction to my said granddaughter or to Gideon Lee, her father and guardian, but I trust that neither the one nor the other, or any other person lawfully authorized by law to represent my said granddaughter, will ever attempt to frustrate or defeat the purpose which I have herein sought to accomplish, but will respect the settled desire of my life as contained in this my will, but should my desire and request as herein expressed be ignored, and should Gideon Lee, as guardian of my said granddaughter, or should my said granddaughter herself, or any other person lawfully authorized by law to represent her, or any person as heir, legatee or distributee of my said granddaughter in their right as such, attempt to contest my will or attempt to invalidate it, or attempt to change or alter it in any particular whatever, then it is my will and I do direct that such attempt or attempts to contest, alter, change or invalidate my said last will and testament, or codicil hereof, shall as soon as commenced work an absolute revocation of my entire and of all my bequests to my said granddaughter, Floride Isabella Lee, as made in fifth item of my said last will and testament, and then and in that case, my said granddaughter, Floride Isabella Lee, shall receive no part of my estate whatever, and the money and articles mentioned in the fifth item of my said will shall go to my executor and be held by him subject to the trusts and conditions contained in Items 1, 2, and 3 of my said last will and testament; provided, that my executor shall sell in manner as to him may seem proper any of the articles mentioned in the said fifth item of my said last will and testament, except the family pictures. These shall be held by my executor subject to the trusts and conditions of Items 1, 2, and 3 of my said last will, and kept with the other articles mentioned in the eighth item of my said last will and testament, to adorn the Fort Hill house.

Item 13. It is my will and I direct that my executor shall not be held liable for, or responsible for any loses to my estate by reason of my errors of judgment or mistakes, as I am fully aware of the varied and responsible duties I herein have required of him. This codicil is written in part on the fourth page of my last will and testament to which this sheet is attached, and which is dated November 6th, 1886.

Item 14. I authorize and empower my executor to expend such sums of money as he may deem necessary to keep the Fort Hill dwelling house and premises in repair, and the Fort Hill farm in good condition.

In witness whereof I have hereunto subscribed my name and affixed my seal before the witnesses below subscribing, this the twenty-sixth day of March, in the year of our Lord one thousand eight hundred and eighty-seven (1887).

Thos. G. Clemson, (L. S.)

The above written instrument was subscribed by the said Thos. G. Clemson in our presence and acknowledged by him to each one of us and he at the same time published and declared the same to be his codicil to his last will and testament, and we, at his request and in his presence, and in the presence of each other, have signed our names as witnesses hereunto.

R. M. Jenkins
C. W. Young
J. H. Mounce

The foregoing paper bears this endorsement:
"This will was admitted to probate in common form on the 20th day of April A.D. 1888, and recorded in 'Will Book,' pages 234-244."

Richard Lewis,
"Judge of Probate"

INDEX

Abbeville, 6, 165
Abbeville Mills, 188
ACC. See Atlantic Coast Conference
Adger family, 22
Air Force Reserve Officers' Training Corps, 245
Alabama, 81
Alabama Agricultural and Mechanical College (Alabama Polytechnic College; Auburn University), 28, 63, 80, 81, 85, 96, 100, 118, 156
Alabama, University of, 63, 157
Allendale, 54, 55
American Association for the Advancement of Science, 181
American Association of University Professors, 254
American Chemical Society, 71
The American Farmer, 10
American Federal Savings and Loan Association, 227, 234
Anderson, 46, 144, 147, 170, 177, 242, 247
Anderson, Alexander P., 61-62
Anderson Daily Mail, 86, 165, 167, 169, 172
Anderson Independent, 110, 196
Anderson Tribune, 136
Arkansas, 199, 201
Army Air Corps, 170
Army Corps of Engineers, 179, 180, 188, 190-94
Army Signal Corps, 170
Army Specialized Training Program (ASTP), 170
Arthur, Dugan, 112-13
Association of Agricultural Colleges and Experiment Stations, 89
Association of Land-Grant Colleges and Universities, 181

Association of Secondary Schools and Colleges of the Southern States, xv, 142, 154, 170
ASTP. See Army Specialized Training Program
Atchley, Bill L. (president of Clemson, 1979-85), 215-38; achievements of, 222, 223, 238; and alumni, 230-31; appointed president, 215, 220; and athletics, xviii, 216, 219, 220, 229-37, 250-52, 254-56; background of, 216-17; controversy surrounding, 215, 229-30, 235, 238, 241; criticism of, 218-19, 222, 224, 227, 231; description of, 217-19; expectations of, 220-22; and faculty, 220, 222, 223, 233, 237, 251, 255; feels betrayed, 236; and fund-raising, 225-26; and love of Clemson, 227; and minority recruiting, 225; and National Science Center, 238; as "outsider," 227, 238; philosophy of, 218, 220, 222-23, 230; public view of, 233-34, 237-38; removes administrators, 223-24; resignation of, xvii, 215, 237, 241, 255, 257, 258; and state leaders, 226-27; and stress on research, xvi, 223, 238; and students, 220, 222, 237; and trustees, 215, 217, 220-21, 224, 227-38, 251, 255; and University of Pacific, 238
Atchley, Pat, 219, 235 n. 73
Atlanta, 96, 97, 145
Atlantic Coast Conference (ACC), 208-209, 229
Aull, George, 128, 133, 153-54
The Autocrat of the Breakfast Table, 47

Bamberg, 54, 55
Bamberg Herald, 55
Baptist Home Mission Board, 97
Barnett, Ross R., 248 n. 32
Barnett, W. D., 244

Barnette, Melvin, 253, 257-58
Barnwell Ring, 182, 183 n. 77
Barre Hall, 171
Barre, H. W., 155
Baruch, Bernard, 137
Baton Rouge, 50
Batson, Louis, Jr., 257
Beckwith, C. L., 88
Belton, 242
Beltsville, 13
Benet, Christie, Jr., xiii, 83, 243
Bethea, A. W. ("Red"), 205
Bladensburg, 9, 11, 12, 13
Blatt, Solomon, 182
Blease, Coleman Livingston, 115-16
Block "C" Club, 242
Blue Ridge Railroad, 14
Bolsheviks, 120, 122
Bolt, Donald F., 234
Bond, Christopher S., 216
Bostic, James, 237
Boston College, 243
Bowen, R. E., 266
Bowman field, 63
Bowman, R. T. V., 63
Boykin family, 22
Bracey, Edward, 174-75
Bracey, Spencer M., 174-75, 197 n. 41
Brackett Hall, 172
Brackett, R. N., 65, 66, 74, 155
Bradley, J. E., 266
Bradley, Mark E. ("Prep"), 165
Bradley, W. W., 95 n. 43, 165
Breazeale, Harold D., 204
Brown, Edgar A., xiii, 179, 180 n. 71, 183 n. 77, 189, 191, 192, 195, 196, 202, 205, 211, 221, 247, 250
Brown, Marshall W., 245
Brown v. Board of Education (1954), 197, 247
Brummitt, James, 253, 258
Brussels, 8
Bryan, Wright, 167, 173, 211, 246
Budget and Control Board, 211, 226, 228
Budig, Gene, 217
Burley, Robert, 141
Burns, J. F., 155 n. 39
Burns, S. A., 155
Burt, Armistead, 14, 15, 16

Bush, George, 258
Byars, Ed, 238
Byrnes, James F., xiii, 169, 178, 189, 193, 211

"The Calhoun" (literary society), 39
Calhoun, 26
Calhoun, Andrew, 3, 7, 15
Calhoun, Creighton Lee, 204
Calhoun, F. H. H., 96 n. 46, 148, 156, 157, 166
Calhoun, Floride Colhoun, 3, 11, 12, 13, 15, 270
Calhoun honors college, 225
Calhoun, James, 7-8
Calhoun, James Edward, 6, 7, 14
Calhoun, John Caldwell, 3, 6, 7, 8, 16, 266, 267, 268
Calhoun mansion, 145
Calhoun, Patrick, 10
California, University of, 206
Cambodia, 206
Carmel, 15, 17
Carnegie Foundation, 50, 85 n. 16, 95
Carnegie unit, 85
Carpenter, W. L., 234
Cauthen, Henry F., 182
Cauthen, John K., 199, 201, 250
Central, 147
Central College, 35-36, 50
Chamberlain, Daniel H., 54
Charleston News and Courier, 107, 110-11, 245
Charlotte, 250
Chester county, 49
Chicago, 232
Citadel, The. *See* South Carolina Military Academy
Civil War, xi, 3, 9, 11-14, 54, 70
Clarksville, 6, 7
Clay, Charles D., 90-91
Clemson, 145-46, 212
Clemson Agricultural College (since 1964 Clemson University), 55; accreditation of, 142, 154; administration reorganized, 177-78, 187, 189, 203, 246; as all-male and military, xiv, 23, 29-30, 45, 47, 61, 75, 84, 87-93, 112, 119, 135, 147, 176, 242; alumni of, 122, 136-37, 156, 157, 165, 166, 168, 169, 179, 181, 190,

Index

195, 203; and athletics, xvii-xviii, 47, 53, 62-64, 79, 82-84, 100, 109, 136, 156-57, 168-69, 175-76, 188, 207; becomes civilian, 161, 176, 177-79; becomes coeducational, 161, 178-79, 187, 246; becomes university, xi, 187, 189, 203-205, 246; board of visitors of, 41, 47, 131, 133; bylaws of, 95, 103; campus facilities of, 26-28, 39, 56-57, 95, 96, 101, 109, 117, 129, 134, 142, 145, 153-54, 155, 166-67, 171, 187, 191; Cemetery Hill of, 123; and The Citadel, 23, 47; curriculum of, xvii, 29-30, 35, 38, 46, 53, 57, 72, 134, 142, 149, 187, 196, 203; departments of, 42, 53, 57, 109-10, 111, 115, 119, 123, 127, 129, 133-34, 149, 155, 190; enrollment of, xv, 26, 38, 40, 46, 53, 57, 59, 95, 109, 118, 142, 144, 150-51, 166, 171, 176, 187, 203, 246; and epidemics, 56, 131; experiment station of, 26, 28, 30, 36, 42, 46, 48, 96, 155, 166, 193; extension program of, 110, 115, 116, 155; faculty of, 28-29, 45, 46, 60-61, 64-66, 72, 96, 111, 118, 130, 132, 142, 144-45, 152, 154, 164, 166, 170, 187, 247; financing of, 24-25, 42-43, 49, 62, 71, 84, 86-87, 93, 117-18, 138, 144, 150-54, 158; fires at, 40-41, 129, 137, 155; fraternities at, 148; graduating classes of, 47, 58, 118, 123, 138, 142, 149; and Great Depression, 150-54; and Hartwell project, 179-80, 190-94; integration of, 188, 196-202, 246-50; as land-grant school, xiv, xvi, 25, 71, 103, 123, 142, 167, 184, 242; library of, 39, 40, 42, 71-72, 96, 129, 137, 154, 155, 166, 187, literary societies of, 39; mission of, xvii, 24, 35, 39, 46-49, 58, 82, 84, 86-87, 88, 106, 203; and New Deal, 153-54; new retirement policy of, 181-82, 195; origin of, xi, 17, 18, 21, 24-25, 265-67; presidents of, xi-xviii; public view of, 23, 46-49, 65-66, 75, 79, 86-87, 93, 102, 105-106, 110-11, 114, 117, 136-37, 144, 158, 184; research at, xvi, 61-62, 95, 151, 166; and SATC, 118-19; scandal at, 108-109; schools of, 150; segregation of, 161, 174-76, 187, 197, 242; student unrest at, 41, 44, 53-54, 64-66, 73-75, 87,
90-92, 100, 102, 117, 119-22, 130-31, 135-37, 142, 144, 145, 163-64, 172-74; and teaching, 151; trustees of, xii-xiii, xiv, xv; and USC, xvii, 23, 47, 63, 79, 82-84, 156, 249; and World War I, 99, 117-19, 131; and World War II, 169-71, 184, 245

The Clemson Alumnus, 157
Clemson, Anna Marie Calhoun, 3, 4, 5-6, 10, 12, 13, 15
Clemson, Calhoun, 6, 11, 12, 13, 15
"Clemson Catechism," 106
Clemson, Cornelia ("Nina"), 9, 10
Clemson, Elizabeth Baker, 4
Clemson, Floride, 6, 11, 12, 13, 15
Clemson Hotel (Clemson House), 145, 153 n. 31, 155, 192, 200
Clemson, John Baker, 16
Clemson Players, 255
Clemson, Thomas Green, as agricultural scientist, 3, 9-10, 14; and Anna, 3, 4, 5-6, 10, 12, 13, 15; and Calhouns, 5-8; childhood of, 4; and College trustees, xii, xiii; as Confederate, 3, 11-14; and criticism of South, 14, 15, 16; death of, 18; as diplomat, 3, 8-9; education of, 4; foreign travels of, 4, 6, 8-9, 10, 11; and Fort Hill property, xi, 3, 6, 7, 9, 15-18, 265-71; and founding a college, xi-xii, 3, 14-15, 17, 18, 24, 25, 262, 263, 265-67; and "The Home," 9, 13, 14; and interest in arts, 5, 10, 11, 13; as land-grant benefactor, xi; marriage of, 3, 5; as mining engineer, 4, 12-13; personality of, 5, 10, 13, 16, 17; philosophy of, xiii, xvi, 3; as plantation owner, 3, 7, 8, 9; publications of, 9-10; as Superintendent of Agricultural Affairs, 10, 11; and USC, 14; will of, xi, xvi, 3, 17, 18, 21, 24, 86, 204, 261, 265-71
Clemson, Thomas Green, Sr., 4
Clemson University (until 1964 Clemson Agricultural College), and ACC probation, 229; administrative changes at, 177-79, 203, 224, 257-58, 259; and alumni, 243, 244; and athletics, xvii-xviii, 207-10, 229-37, 242-46, 250-56; becomes university, xi, 203-205, 246; board of visitors of, 228; and Calhoun home, 18;

campus facilities of, 212, 225; curriculum of, 203, 205, 212, 225; and emphasis on research, xvi, 223, 225, 262; enrollment of, 205; faculty of, 212, 220, 222, 236, 254, 255; financing of, 225-26, 262; and Fort Hill property, 18; founding of, xi; future of, 261-63; graduates of, 212; as land-grant school, xi, xvi; minority recruitment at, 225; mission of, 203, 262, 263; and NCAA probation, 209-10, 218, 229, 232, 247, 250; presidents of, xi-xviii; public view of, 254; scandals at, 209-10, 223; students of, 206, 212, 220, 222, 255; and USC, 207

Clemson World, 220
Clinkscales stable, 145
CMP. *See* Cresap, McCormick, and Paget
Coakley, George, 224
Cody, Josh, 157
Coker College, 143
Cole, Otis R., 135-36
College Avenue, 145
College of Charleston, 245
Colleges and Universities, xii, xiii, xiv, xvi, 146, 203
Colson, Samuel, 253, 258
Columbia, 26, 41, 63, 71, 182, 212, 226, 227, 232, 254
"The Columbian" (literary society), 39, 162
Columbia Record, 86
Commission on Higher Education, 211, 226
Confederacy, 11-14, 70
Cooper Library, 187
Cooper, Robert M., xiii, 134, 182, 195
Corcoran, J. J., 100 n. 1
Corcoran, W. W., 5
Cornell, Ezra, xi
Cornell University, 128, 132 n. 16
Cotton Bowl, 157, 243
Cox, Grace Campbell, 242
Cox, H. Morris, 224
Cox, Walter T. (president of Clemson, 1985-86), xi, 241-59, 262-63; as alumni director, 178, 245; appointed president emeritus, 259; as assistant to president, 245-46; and Atchley, 251, 254, 256, 257; and athletics, xviii, 242-46, 250-56; authority of, 257; background of, xiii, 242-43; as dean of students, 178, 246-50; dedication to Clemson, 241, 242, 256, 258-59; and faculty, 255; honored by students, 259; and integration of Clemson, 247-50; as interim president, 238, 257-59; and McLellan, 252; retirement of, 259; and trustees, 241, 257, 259; as vice president for student affairs, 236, 241, 246, 251, 255; in World War II, 244-45
Cox, Walter T., 242
Craighead, Edwin B. (president of Clemson, 1893-97), xvii, 31, 35-51, 56, 72, 82, 85; accepts presidency, 36; background of, 35-36; and campus facilities, 39, 42; controversy surrounding, 35, 40, 41, 44-45, 50; and curriculum, 38-39; death of, 51; and first graduates, 47; and fitting (remedial) school, 38; personality of, 35, 50, 51; philosophy of, 36-37, 39, 42, 43, 51; resignation of, 50, 73; and Tillman, 37, 41, 44, 46, 47 n. 38; and trustees, 36-37, 40, 41, 43, 44-45; at Tulane, 50, 85; at University of Montana, 51; welcomes students, 38
Crawford, Leonard, 173
Cresap, McCormick, and Paget report (CMP), 177-78, 179, 181, 182, 183, 189, 194, 195, 203, 211, 246, 263
Cribb, T. Kenneth, 221, 226
Crosman, R. S., 122 n. 57
Cummins, J. M., 112, 119

Dahlonega, 6, 7
Daniel, Charles E., xiii, 177, 178, 180, 181, 183, 188, 189, 193, 195, 201, 211, 250
Daniel Classroom Building, 187
Daniel, David W., 133, 155, 166, 182, 184
Darlington, 26, 46
Davidson, 63
Davis, Jeff, 67
Dawson, Francis W., 14
Deering-Milliken, 188
Delta Democrat, 201
Department of Agriculture (United States), 10, 110
DesChamps, W. G., 254
Dick, B. F., 113 n. 31
Dillon, 205
Dixiecrats, 183
Donahue, Edward, 130

Index

Donaldson, M. L., 44, 55, 56, 95 n. 43, 266
Donaldson, T. Q., Jr., 38, 45
Dorn, William Jennings Bryan, 202
Earle, Baylis, 127
Earle, Elias, 130
Earle, Eliza Jane Kennedy, 128
Earle Hall, 138
Earle, John, 127
Earle, Samuel B. (acting president of Clemson, 1919, 1924-25), xi, 127-38; as acting president, 114, 119, 127, 129-37; background of, 127-29; death of, 138; description of, 127, 128, 129, 133, 134; and engineering department, 127, 129, 132, 133, 137-38, 144, 166; and campus facilities, 129; and faculty, 130, 132; family of, 129; and long service, 127; philosophy of, xvii, 127, 129, 131, 138; retirement of, 138; and Riggs, 127, 129-33; and rivalry with agriculture, 127, 133-34; and students, 127, 131, 135-37; and walkout of 1924, 127, 135-37, 144; and trustees, 128, 132-33, 134-35, 137, 138
Earle Street, 145
Earle, Susan Hall Sloan, 129
Earle, Thomas John, 128
Edgefield, 7, 55
Edmonds, R. H., 84
Edwards, Effie Cook, 188
Edwards, John T., 188
Edwards, Louise Odom, 188
Edwards, Nancy Louise, 188
Edwards, Robert C. (president of Clemson, 1958-79), 187-212; accomplishments of, 187; as acting president, 187, 195-96, and alumni, 190; appointed president, 187, 196; and athletics, xviii, 206-10, 212; background of, xiii, 188-89; 205-206; and campus facilities, 187, 212; and Clemson's mission, 203-204, 206; and CMP, 190; description of, 210; and enrollment, 205-206; and faculty, 212; family of, 188; and Hartwell project, 180, 188, 190-94, 195, 211; and integration, xiv, 187, 196-202, 211, 247, 249-50; and IPTAY, 188, 207; legacy of, 210-12; public view of, 196; receives honors, 212; retirement of, 212; and state leaders, 211-12; and students, 212; and trustees, xv, 187, 192, 194, 195-96, 211, 221; and university status, xiv, 187, 203-205; as vice president, 188, 189, 190, 191
Edwards, Robert C., Jr., 188
Eisenhower, Dwight D., 194
Elberton, 177
Elliot, William, 244
Ellis, Mildred, 22
Emory and Henry College, 36
Engineering and Mining Journal, 80
Equus, 255
Evans, John Gary, 48
Evans, Mary, 132 n. 16
Evans, S. W., 166
Faculty Committee on Student Discipline, xiv
Fairview, 46, 49
Farmer's Association, 23
Farmer's Resettlement Administration, 167
Faulwetter, R. C., 130
Federal Emergency Relief Administration, 153
Ferrier, Wallace T., 170
Fiji Islands, 244
Florence, 175
Florida, 81, 156, 236 n. 78
Ford, Danny, 232, 251
Fort Hill Depository, 145
Fort Hill Presbyterian Church, 113
Fountain Inn, 188
France, 116, 163
Fredericksburg, 97
Freeman, Wayne, 201
Furman, Charles M., 28, 71
Furman University, 128, 138, 156
Gage, Gaston, xii n. 3, xiv n. 9
Gantt, Harvey, 188, 196-201, 203, 247-50, 258
Gantt v. Clemson College et al., 247
General Electric Company, 128
Gentry, John B., 183
Georges Creek, 54
Georgia, University of, 63, 80
Germany, 59, 163
Glenn, H. E. ("Pop"), 180
Godfrey Hall, 59, 145, 155
Godfrey, W. E., 155
Goodale, B. E. ("Big Ben"), 173
Gould, Jay, 11

Gourlay, Gordon, 224
Gowansville, 128
Grady, Henry W., 14
Gray Court, 162
Great Bridge, 164
Great Depression, xv, 142, 150-54, 155, 157, 158, 190
Greenville, 45, 144, 145, 162 n. 3, 177, 188
Greenville News, 110, 201, 220, 250, 254, 255, 256
Greenwood Index-Journal, 255
Greer, 49
Gressette, Marion, 197, 202
Grice, George D., 245
Guadalcanal, 244

Hall, Sidney B., 164
Hampton family, 22
Hampton, Wade, 54
Harcombe, J. D., 136, 155
Hardin Hall, 69, 145
Hardin, Lauriston B., 70
Hardin, Mark B. (acting president of Clemson, 1897, 1899, 1902), xi, xiii, 69-77; as acting president, 69, 72, 73, 75; assists Newman, 72; background of, 69-71; as Confederate, xiii, 69, 70; and curriculum, 72, 73; death of, 77; dedication to Clemson, 77; description of, 69; and faculty, 72-73, 74, 75, 76; family of, 71, 73, 76; as professor, 28, 42, 46, 65, 69, 71, 76, 96 n. 46; retirement of, 69; and Riggs, 76, 77; and student discipline, 74, 75-76, 77; and trustees, 69, 71-72, 73, 74, 76; and walkout of 1902, 73-74
Hardin, Mary M. Payne, 71, 73
Harkness, Jack, 253, 258
Harper, J. N., 115
Harris, J. W., 91-92
Hartsville Messenger, 255
Hartwell, 190
Hartwell Project, 161, 179-80, 188, 190-94, 195
Hartzog, Cornelia Harley, 55
Hartzog, Henry S. (president of Clemson, 1897-1902), xiii, 53-67, 69, 73, 82, 83; accepts presidency, 53, 55; and athletics, xviii, 62-64; background of, 53, 54-55; and campus construction, 59, 60; as clergyman, xiii, 53, 55, 56; death of, 67; and epidemic of 1897, 56-57; and faculty, 60, 64; marriage of, 55; personality of, 53; reforms fitting (remedial) school, 57-58; resignation of, 66, 74; and textile department, 58-59; and Tillman, 55-56; and trustees, 56-57, 58, 59, 60, 63; at University of Arkansas, 54, 66-67; and walkout of 1902, 53, 64-66, 83
Harvard University, 164
Hatch Act (1887), 25
Heisman, John, xviii, 53, 63, 82, 100, 156
Henderson, Robert, 226
Henry, D. H., 123
Herron, W. C., 120
Heston, Charlton, 245
Hickman, Darryl, 224
Hickory Knob State Park, 236
Ho Chi Minh, 203
Holahan, R. F. ("Butch"), 135-36
Holderman, James, 226, 227
Hollings, Ernest, 199, 202, 248, 250
Holmes, Oliver Wendell, 47
Holtzendorff Center, 129
Howard, Frank, 157, 243
Howe, Rice, 70
Hughes, E. T., 107, 112, 115
Huguenots, 69
Hunnicut Creek, 129
Hunter, James, 268
Hurst, Victor, 232 n. 59

I'll Take My Stand, 181
Iowa State College (University), 119, 197, 247
IPTAY, 157, 244

Jackson, Thomas J. ("Stonewall"), 70
Jaspers, Paul, 253
Jaspers, Stijn, 236, 252, 256, 257, 258
Jenkins, T. O., 268, 271
Johns Hopkins University, 143
Johnson's Island (Lake Erie), 13, 70
Johnston Institute, 55
Johnston, Olin D., 171
Johnstone, Alan, xii, 93, 95 n. 43, 103, 106 n. 15, 115, 121, 135, 155
Jones, Thomas F., 249
J. P. Stevens, 188

Keller's store, 145
Kenmore University High School, 22, 32

Kennedy, John F., 202, 203, 248 n. 32
Kennedy, Robert, 202
Kent State University, 206
Kentucky, University of, 156, 169
Kinard, Francis M., 178
Kissinger, Henry, 245
Kiwanis International, 143
Kleinewefers award, 238
Knapp, Bradford, 110 n. 23
Knoxville, 251
Labecki, Geraldine, 224
Lader, Philip, 256
Lander, Ernst M., Jr. ("Whitey"), 180 n. 71, 204
Laurens, 46, 162
Lee, D. W., 13 n. 27
Lee, Floride Isabella, 15, 17-18, 267, 269-71
Lee, Gideon, 15, 17-18, 269-70
Lee, Robert E., 13, 71
Lee, Rudolph E., 129, 155
Lee, Stephen D., xiii, 22, 23
Legislative Black Caucas, 225
Lehotsky Hall, 171
Leitner, Henry D., 169
Lennon, Max (president of Clemson, 1986–), xiii, xvi, 241, 258, 259, 261
Leppard, Ben T., 175
Leupp, Charles M., 10-11, 14
Lever, A. Frank, 110, 115, 155
Lewis, Richard, 271
Lightsey, Harry, 256
Lincoln, Abraham, 11, 70
Littlejohn Coliscum, 171, 187
Littlejohn, James C., 100 n. 3, 154, 155, 163-64, 166, 170, 171, 178, 180 n. 71, 180, 243, 244
Littlejohn, Robert M., 171
Little Rock crisis, 199
Locke, Tates, 208-10
Lockwood-Greene Engineering Firm, 191
Long Hall, 153, 155, 166
Long, W. W., 115, 152, 155
Louisiana, 38, 49
Lyceum of Natural History, 71
Lynah, James, 64, 75-76 n. 16
McAlister, Paul W., 217, 219, 228, 231, 237
MacArthur, Douglas, 169

McBryde, J. M., 23 n. 3, 55
McClure, Harlan, 197, 200
McCollum, Pickens S. ("Doc"), 173
McDevitt, Joseph, 224
McFeely, H. F., 131
McGee, William L., 46
McLaurin, D. L., 121 n. 54
McLellan, H. C. ("Bill"), xvii, 209, 210, 231-32, 235, 236, 237, 250-55, 257-58
McLeod, Daniel, 202
McMahan, John J., 87
McMaster, Fritz, 44
McMillan, George, 250
McTeer, Thomas B., Jr., 231-34
Malone, Moses, 209
Mann, C. D., 93
Manning, 46
Manning family, 22
Manning, Richard I., xii-xiii, 95 n. 43, 114, 115-16, 143, 155
Manufacturers' Record, 84
Martin, Samuel M., xiv n. 9, 60, 155, 166
Martin's drugstore, 145, 173
Maryland, 3, 9, 12, 13
Maryland Agricultural College (University of Maryland), 9-10
Matheson, K. G., 81
Maybank, Burnet R., 171
Mechanics Hall, 145
Mell, Lurene Howard (Cooper), 80
Mell, Patrick Hues (president of Clemson, 1902-10), 69, 75, 79-97, 101, 102, 103, 105, 106; accepts presidency, 79, 81; and athletics, 79, 83-84; background of, xvi, 80-81; contributions of, 95-96; controversy surrounding, 79, 93-95, 105; and curriculum, 85; death of, 97; debates Craighead, 85, defends Clemson, 84, 86-87; description of, 96-97; encourages research, 96; and faculty, 96; and military discipline, 79, 83-84, 87-93; national reputation of, xvi, 79, 81; philosophy of, xvii, 79, 84-85; publications of, 80; resignation of, xiv, 76, 79, 87, 94, 106, 112; and Tillman, 81, 93; and trustees, xiv, 79, 85, 87, 93-95; and walkout of 1908, 91-92
Mell, Patrick Hues, 80
Melton, Judith, 238

Memminger family, 22
Memorial Stadium (Death Valley), 169, 175, 179, 191, 207
Mercer University, 80, 81
Meredith, James, 197, 248
Methodist Church, 35
Metz, G. E., 153
Miami University of Ohio, 208
Mickel, Buck, 234, 237
Mid-American Conference, 208
Middleton, Mrs., 115
Milliken, Roger, 188
Mills, W. H., 113 n. 32
Minus, J. C., 91, 92
Mississippi, 201
Mississippi Agricultural and Mechanical College (Mississippi State University), xiii, 22, 265
Mississippi, University of, 22, 24, 197, 199, 248, 249
Missouri, 6, 35, 38, 49, 50
Missouri Energy Council, 216
Missouri-Rolla, University of, 216, 236 n. 78
Missouri State Normal (Central Missouri State University), 50
Montana, 38, 49, 51
Montana, University of, 51
Moore, Arch A., Jr., 217
Morrill Act (1862, 1890), 25, 26, 86, 88
Morris, Earle B., 249-50
Morris, Earle G., 256
Morrison, William S., 28, 38, 45, 64, 75-76 n. 16, 96 n. 46, 115
Mounce, J. H., 271
Munich, University of, 61

Narewski, Stanley, 252, 253, 258
Nashville, 253
National Association of State Universities and Land-Grant Colleges, 206
National Collegiate Athletic Association (NCAA), 208-10, 218, 229-32, 236, 250-51
National Conference of Christians and Jews, 157
National Invitation Tournament (NIT), 208, 209
National Science Center for Communications and Electronics Education Foundation, 238
National Science Foundation, 223
National Youth Administration, 153
NCAA. *See* National Collegiate Athletic Association
Neely, Jess, 157, 242, 243
Neosha Collegiate Institute, 36
Netherlands, The, 252
Newberry County, 49
New Caledonia, 244
New Deal, 153, 166
Newman, Charles Carter, 32
Newman, Grace Strode, 32
Newman, J. S., 28, 38, 44, 72
Newman, Q. B., 124
The New Northwest, 51
New Orleans, 50
New York Academy of Sciences, 71
New York Botanical Gardens, 61
New York Giants, 216
The New York Times, 231
New Zealand, 244
Nicholas, Stanley, 224
NIT. *See* National Invitation Tournament
Nitre and Mining Bureau, 12-13
Norris, D. K., 17, 58, 266
North Carolina, 142-43, 258
North Carolina State College (University), 163, 164, 175-76
North Dakota, 51
North Georgia Agricultural College, 81
Norton, John, 227
Norwich Academy (Norwich University), 4
New York, 10-11

Ohio State University, 258
Olar, 54
Old Capitol Prison, 70
Old Stone Church, 77
Olin foundation, 138
Olympics (1984), The, 252
Orangeburg, 46, 116
Orr, J. L., 23, 30, 31
Ouachita Baptist College, 67

Pacific, University of the, 238
"The Palmetto" (literary society), 39
Parker, E. C., 244
Paris exposition, 81
Partridge, Alden, 4
Patent Office, 10, 11
Peabody College for Teachers, 164

Index · 281 ·

Pearl Harbor, 168, 169
Pearson, R. A., 119
Pendleton, xi, 3, 11, 12, 13, 26, 91, 147, 269
Pendleton Farmer's Society, 14
"Pendleton guards," 91
Perry, Matthew, 197
Phi Beta Kappa, 164
Philadelphia, 4
Philippines, 169
Pickens, 144
Pickens, Francis W., 7, 9
Poole, Lila Yeargin, 162
Poole, Robert F. (president of Clemson, 1940-58), 161-84, 206, 245, 246; and alumni, 181, 245; appointment as president, 161, 163-66; and athletics, xviii, 168-69; background of, 162-63; and civilian education, 161, 176, 177, 178-79; and CMP, 178-79, 181, 182, 183, 189; and coeducation, xiv, 161, 178-79; and curriculum, 171-73; death of, 183, 195; description of, 161, 163, 183; and faculty, 166, 172, 181; family of, 161, 165; and Hartwell project, 161, 180; management style of, 161, 167-68, 171, 172, 180-81, 183-84, 189, 246; objectives of, 167; philosophy of, 181; prestige of, 181; publications of, 164; and segregation, 174-76; and students, 172-74, 181; and trustees, xv, 161, 164, 165, 169, 171, 172, 173, 175, 178, 179, 181-83, 191, 194-95, 211; and World War II, 169-71, 184
Poole, Sarah Margaret Bradley, 165
Poole's Chapel, 162
Poole, Ula Barto, 162
Poser, Siegfried W., 238
Powers, H. A., 39
Presbyterian College, 156, 245
Prince, Hester, 268
Prince, Jane, 267-68, 269
"Project Leapfrog," 226
Pruitt, James, 253

Quaker Oats Company, 61
"Questions and Answers Relating to Clemson College 1910," 106

Raffanel, 46
Raleigh, 176

Rawl, B. H., 103, 104, 115
Rebel Underground, 249
Reckling, W. A., 75
Redfern, Alexander, 39, 90
Redfern Student Health Center, 187
Reserve Officer Training Corps (ROTC), 176
Rhodes Engineering Center, 187
Rhodes, S. R., 155
Rice Institute, 243
Rice, L. C., 54
Richards, John G., 116
Richey, Fred, 259
Riggs, Emma Gowan, 100
Riggs, Eula, 100 n. 3
Riggs Hall, 155, 166
Riggs, Harpin, 100
Riggs, Walter Merritt (president of Clemson, 1910-24), 76, 92, 93, 99-124, 127; abolishes preparatory (remedial) class, 109-10; accepts presidency, 99, 107, 129; as acting president, 76, 99, 101-106; and alumni, 122; and athletics, xviii, 63, 76, 100-101, 114; austerity of, 114; authority and ability of, 103, 104, 107, 111-12, 119; background of, 99, 100-101; and campus facilities, 101, 109; and curriculum, 109-110, 119; death of, 123-24, 132; dedication to Clemson, 99, 100 n. 1, 106, 107-108, 111, 114, 115, 121; description of, 99, 101, 107, 114; and Earle, 119, 127, 129-33; and faculty, 103, 111, 115, 122; and glee club, 100, 114; legacy of, 124; philosophy of, 101, 102-103, 105, 106, 111; and politics, 115-16; and public relations, 105-106, 107, 110-11, 114, 115; and race relations, 115, 116-17; and religion, 113; and SATC, 118-19; and Schilletter affair, 108-109, 115; and students, 100, 103, 112, 119-22, 123; and Tillman, 102, 103-104, 105, 114; and trustees, xv, 93-94, 99, 101, 102, 103-106, 107, 111, 112, 118, 121-22, 129, 130; walkout of 1920, 117, 119-22; and World War I, 99, 116, 117-19
Riley, Richard, 226
Rion family, 22
Rion, James H., 17, 268, 269
Rion, Mary, 17

Robinson, Bobby, 254, 258
Rockefeller funds, 109, 114, 117
Rockefeller, John D., IV, 217
ROTC. *See* Reserve Officer Training Corps
Royal School of Mines (France), 4
Russell, Donald, 203
Rutgers University, 163, 165

St. Paul's Episcopal Church, 3, 18
Saluda, 7
Saluda River, 242
Sanders, Paul, 192
San Francisco, 8
SATC. *See* Student Army Training Corps
Saturday Evening Post, 250
Saunders, Bud, 156
Savannah River, 190
Schilletter, August ("Shorty"), 90, 108-109, 115
Scott, Winfield, 11
"Second Century" plan, 262, 263
Secretary of the Army, 193
Self, James C., 228, 233, 237
Seneca, 147, 253
Seneca highway, 145
Seneca River, 192, 193
Senn, David, 255
Shanklin, Virginia, 152, 210
Shaughnessey, Frank, 92
Sherman, Joe, 192
Sherman, William Tecumseh, 13, 54
Sikes, Enoch Walter (president of Clemson, 1925-40), xv, 141-58, 244; accomplishments of, 142, 158; appointment as president, 137, 141, 143, 144, 148; and athletics, xviii, 156-57, 242; background of, 142-43; and campus facilities, 153-54, 155; and curriculum, 149; death of, 158; description of, 141; and faculty, 149, 152, 154-55; and fraternities, 148; and funding for Clemson, 150-54, 158; as orator, 141, 142, 143, 144; philosophy of, 158; and religion, 141, 143, 157-58; retirement of, 158, 163, 182; and students, 147, 148-49, 152-53, 155, 157; and trustees, 143, 148, 152, 154; and view of education, 148, 149
Sikes Hall, 129, 145, 155, 220
Sikes, Ruth Wingate, 143

Simpson Agricultural Experiment Station, 193
Simpson, Richard W., xii, 17, 23 n. 3, 30, 38, 44, 45, 58, 65, 66, 93, 95 n. 43, 106 n. 15, 266, 269
Sims, Clough W., 45, 46
Sims, William Gilmore, 54
Sirmyer, E. A., 83, 88, 90, 93
Sirrine Company, 234
Sirrine Hall, 153, 166, 170
Skardon, Beverly ("Ben") N., 169
SLED. *See* State Law Enforcement Division
Sloan's store, 145
Smith-Lever Act, 110
Snyder, H. M., 101
Snyder, J. L., 89
Society for the Promotion of Engineering Education, 138
Southard, L. G., 120 n. 51
South Carolina, 3, 4, 14-15, 17, 35, 84, 87, 128, 143, 162, 183, 220, 238; business leaders in, 177; and campaign of 1890, 23; and Civil War, 11, 12; cotton manufacturing in, 58; desolation of, xi, 48; distinguished families of, 22; economy of, 146-47, 150; general assembly (legislature) of, xi, 18, 23, 24, 25, 27, 46, 85, 94-95, 103, 105, 115, 117-18, 137, 153, 192-93, 204-205, 221; secondary schools in, 38, 39, 48, 49, 58, 85, 109, 146-47; segregation in, 146, 202, 247
South Carolina College (University of South Carolina, USC), xiii n. 7, xvi n. 12, 14, 23, 29, 47, 48, 55, 119, 225; and Clemson College (University), 23, 47, 63, 79, 82-84, 156, 207, 226, 249, 256
South Carolina Council of Farm Women, 172
South Carolina Employment Security Commission, 178
South Carolina Energy Research and Development Center, 226, 228
South Carolina Intercollegiate Athletic Association, 100-101
South Carolina Medical College, 40, 134-35
South Carolina Military Academy (The Citadel), xvii, 23, 47, 54, 91
South Carolina National Bank, 227

South Carolina Research Authority, 226
South Carolina State College, 116, 174-75
South Carolina Textile Manufacturers' Association, 199
South Carolina, University of (USC). *See* South Carolina College
Southern Association of Agricultural Workers, 181
Southern Association of Colleges. *See* Association of Secondary Schools and Colleges of the Southern States
Southern Association of Science and Industry, 171
Southern Baptist Theological Seminary, 55
Southern Intercollegiate Athletic Association (SIAA), 101
Southern Interstate Nuclear Board, 216
Soviet Union, 203
Sparkman bill, 171
Spartanburg, 26, 41 n. 20, 91, 128, 144, 191, 247
Sputnik satellite, 203
Starke, William Pinkney, 16, 17
The State (Columbia), 40, 41, 44, 47, 50, 66, 82, 83, 84, 95, 111, 121, 168, 217, 223, 227, 228, 254
State Law Enforcement Division (SLED), 199, 236, 254
Stehle, Mabel, 132 n. 16
Stepp, James M., 170, 180 n. 71
Strode, Henry A. (president of Clemson, 1890-92), xiii, 21-32, 35, 36; accepts presidency, 21, 22, 23; background of, 21-23; and campus construction, 25-28, 31, as Confederate, xiii, 21, and curriculum, 25, 29-30, 31; death of, 32; family of, 22, 24; and fitting (remedial) school, 29; hires faculty, 25, 28-29; philosophy of, 29; as professor, 28, 31-32, 72; resignation of, xvii, 21, 30-32, 72; and trustees, xvii, 21, 22-23, 25, 27-32
Strode Tower, 187
Strom Thurmond Center for Excellence in Government and Public Service, 225, 258
Student Army Training Corps (SATC), 118-19

Taps, 162, 167, 168, 188
Tenhet, Joseph, 120

Tennessee, University of, 169
Terrie, E. L. C., 268
Texas A & M University, 169, 216
Thach, C. C., 85
Thompson, Benjamin, xi
Thompson, Jacob, 10
Thompson, Stassen, 218
Thornhill, T. Wilbur, 178, 179, 180, 191, 192, 193, 211
Thornwell, E. Allison, 65, 74
Thornwell, J. H., 66
The Tiger, 109, 123, 132, 169, 210, 218, 220, 251, 253, 254
Tillman, Benjamin R., xvi, 41 n. 20, 46, 116; as Clemson trustee, xii, 37-38, 44, 66, 95 n. 43, 115, 266; and Craighead, 37-38, 41, 44, 45, 46; declining health of, 104; defends liberal arts, 49; as governor, 23, 25, 27, 30, 37-38; and Hartzog, 55-56; and Mell, 81, 93, 94; and origins of Clemson College, 23, 104; philosophy of, 103-104; and Riggs, 102, 103-104, 105; and Strode, 30, 31; and T. G. Clemson, 17; as U. S. senator, 23, 44, 45, 55, 95 n. 43, 103
Tillman, Benjamin R., Jr., 47, 93-94
Tillman, George, 39, 46, 47-48
Tillman Hall, 38, 200, 145, 161, 225
Tillman, Henry, 93, 94, 106
Timmerman, George Bell, 175, 197
Tompkins, D. A., 59
Trans-Mississippi Department, 12
Traxler, William L., 236, 253-54
Trenton, 55
Trescott, Katherine, 115
Trevillian, Wallace D., 224
Truman, Harry S., 194
Trustee House, 145
Trustees, Board of (Clemson Agricultural College; Clemson University), and administrative reorganization, 177-79, 203, 257-58, and Atchley, 215, 217, 220-21, 227-38, 251, 255; and athletics, 229-37, 244; and campus, xiv, 26-28, 134-35, 171; composition of, xii-xiii, 24, 155; and Cox, 241, 257, 259; and Craighead, 36-37, 40, 41, 43, 44-45; and curriculum, xiv, 25, 29, 134-35; and Earle, 128, 132-33, 134, 137, 138; and Edwards, 187,

192, 194, 195-96, 211, 221; executive committee of, 25, 31; and faculty, xiv, 28, 65, 74-75; and Hardin, 69, 71-72, 73, 74, 75, 76; and Hartwell project, 179-80, 191; and Hartzog, 55, 56-57, 58, 59, 60, 63, 66; and integration, 250; meetings of, 165, 177, 179, 194, 211; and Mell, 79, 87, 93-95; nepotism of, 95, 105, 106; and new retirement policy, 181-82, 195; origin of, xi-xii, 21, 24; and Poole, 161, 165, 171, 172, 173, 175, 178, 179, 181-83, 191, 194-95, 211; and presidents, xiv-xv, 163; public view of, xii, 86, 87, 136, 177, 233-34, 238, 255-56; and Riggs, 76, 99, 101, 102, 103, 104-106, 107, 111, 118, 121-22, 129, 130; and segregation, 110, 175, 247; and Sikes, 143, 148, 152, 154, 244; and Strode, 21, 22, 23-25, 27-32; and student discipline, xiv, 41, 65, 74-75, 79, 83, 121-22, 206; and T. G. Clemson, xii, xiii; and Thurmond Institute, 258; and Trustee House, 145

Tulane University, 50-51, 169, 242

Tyler, John, 8

United States Department of Education, 236 n. 78

United States Department of Energy, 236 n. 78

United States Military Academy (West Point), 208, 245

USC. *See* South Carolina State College

Vanderbilt University, 36, 157

Venable, Charles Scott, 23 n. 3

Vickery, Kenneth N., 197

Vietnam War, 202, 205

Virginia Military Institute, 28, 70, 88

Virginia Polytechnic Institute, 63

Virginia, University of, 21-22, 164

Waddell, James M., Jr., xiii, 228, 255-56, 257, 258

Wade, John Donald, 181

Wake Forest College, 142-43, 156

Walhalla, 46

Wannamaker, J. E., 30, 95 n. 43, 106 n. 15, 266

War Department, 88, 90, 91

Washington College (Washington & Lee), 71

Washington, D.C., 5, 6, 8, 10, 14, 70, 123, 153, 154, 170, 181

Washington Post, 209

Watkins, William L., 192, 202, 204

Welch, C. W., 71, 72

Welch, Williams, 45, 46

Westinghouse, 128

West Point, 88, 89, 91

West Virginia Research and Development Center, 217

West Virginia, University of, 216, 217

White Citizens' Council, 249

Wiggins, A. L. M., 250

Wilkinson, R. S., 116

William and Mary College, 164, 245

Willis Samuel, 224

Wilson, Melford A., 178

Wilson, Woodrow, 115, 118, 143, 154

Winthrop College, 46, 162, 256

Wisconsin, University of, 204

Wofford College, 36, 63, 101, 156

Wolcott, Rosamond, 118, 132

Woodward, J. H., 244, 245

Works Progress Administration, 153

World War I, 116, 117-19, 163

World War II, 135, 161, 168, 169-71, 184, 203

Wounded Knee, 38

Wyche, Cecil, 198, 199

Yeargin, Mary, 162

Young, C. W., 271

Young Men's Christian Association (YMCA), 42, 96, 109, 114, 117, 122, 129, 145, 147, 155, 157, 158 n. 47, 179